THE BATTLE OF THE BRIDGES

THE
BATTLE
OF THE
BRIDGES

The 504th Parachute
Infantry Regiment in
OPERATION MARKET GARDEN

FRANK VAN LUNTEREN

CASEMATE
Philadelphia & Oxford

Published in the United States of America and Great Britain in 2014 by
CASEMATE PUBLISHERS
908 Darby Road, Havertown, PA 19083
and
10 Hythe Bridge Street, Oxford, OX1 2EW

ISBN 978-1-61200-232-3
Digital Edition: ISBN 978-1-61200-233-0

Cataloging-in-publication data is available from the Library of Congress and
the British Library.

For a complete list of Casemate titles please contact:

CASEMATE PUBLISHERS (US)
Telephone (610) 853-9131, Fax (610) 853-9146
E-mail: casemate@casematepublishing.com

CASEMATE PUBLISHERS (UK)
Telephone (01865) 241249, Fax (01865) 794449
E-mail: casemate-uk@casematepublishing.co.uk

MIX
Paper from
responsible sources
FSC® C011935

CONTENTS

MAPS

Dedicated to all the officers and men who served in the 504th Regimental Combat Team in World War II. Their sacrifices will *not* be forgotten.

"As the stars that shall be bright when we are dust,
Moving in marches upon the heavenly plain;
As the stars that are starry in the time of our darkness,
To the end, to the end, they remain."
—Laurence Binyon, *For the Fallen* (1914)

"It seems to me that these young boys who paid with their lives are forgotten very soon. But I have not forgotten and never will."
—Katherina Bachenheimer (Mother of PFC Theodore H. Bachenheimer), Letter to the Quartermaster General of the Memorial Division, March 12, 1947

"Leading a small group of men at night into enemy territory is the most frightening aspect of combat."
—1st Lt. Roy M. Hanna, Interview with the author, May 3, 2008

"The guy with all the ribbons isn't always the guy that has seen the most action."
—1st Lt. Robert C. Blankenship, Letter to Cpl. Francis W. McLane, July 28, 1944

FOREWORD

When the 504th Parachute Infantry Regiment [PIR] conducted a daylight river crossing over the Waal River in Nijmegen, Holland, they secured a major objective of Operation Market Garden, and achieved what few other units could accomplish. The date was September 20, 1944, and the actions of the 504th were some of the most courageous and daring of WWII, firmly etching their place in a history that will never be forgotten. The regiment's lead was 3rd Battalion commander Major Julian Cook, who had the strength and swagger expected of a young leader. Cook was a 26-year-old officer, just four years past his graduation at West Point and still full of the vigor of immortality such an age affords, but with a maturity critical for effective military leadership. This leadership style was a success with both the battalion and the army, and Cook's gallantry in action would result in the award of the Distinguished Service Cross—the nation's second highest medal for valor. The attributes of Major Cook were prevalent throughout the regiment, comprised of very young, but very dedicated and brave officers and men who had grown in strength, maturity and combat skill since their first combat jump a mere 14 months earlier in Sicily. Most of the leaders and soldiers of the battalion and the regiment had only recently joined the army, and in some cases just a few months prior to heading into the rigors of combat. Their courage and fierce determination in the battles of Sicily, Italy, Holland, Belgium and Germany would make them renowned as one of the most decorated units of the war.

The origins of this esteemed group of sky warriors began May 1, 1942, at Fort Benning, Georgia, just two years after the Airborne Test Platoon began testing the airborne concept (June 1940). When the 504th initially formed, its ranks were brimming with young soldiers having just completed parachute training. The innovative concept heralded huge innovations in warfare and strategically prepared the US Army's first airborne units for a new dawn of combat operations for an American fighting force on the precipice of war. Leading this newly created unit was Col. Theodore L. Dunn, a seasoned, senior officer with more than 17 years of service under his belt. Even before they left the States or breached an enemy line, the 504th endured numerous challenges during exhaustive training in airborne and infantry tactics. In 1942, they integrated into the 82nd ABD and transitioned to Fort Bragg, NC, to join their sister regiments, the 505th and 325th (the division's glider-borne regiment).

As part of its integration into the 82nd, the regiment completed a rigorous evaluation by AGF HQ. Most of its battalions failed, resulting in significant leadership changes for this new unit. In December 1942, Dunn was relieved of command and the leadership shifted to a young lieutenant colonel who had been doffing the silver oak leaf rank for a mere three months and had been a soldier for just under eight years. A 1935 graduate of West Point, Lt. Col. Reuben H. Tucker III was serving as the 504th executive officer when he was unexpectedly tapped to fill the shoes of Dunn, making Tucker, at age 31, one of the youngest regimental commanders in the army. He had, however, a leadership edge: he had been with unit since the beginning and had formed a tight bond with his fellow soldiers and leaders. He had lived and breathed the training alongside them and possessed a unique command style that would launch the young team into a stratosphere of success. Once he took the reins of the battalion, he spared no time in ensuring the unit was on time and on target, then moved forth and built a formidable fighting force unlike anything combatants of wars past had ever seen.

That force saw combat in Sicily, successfully conducting their first combat mission in July 1943, despite suffering significant casualties from friendly fire the night of their first combat jump. The regiment was called on just two months later to turn the tide for Fifth Army on the Beaches of Salerno. Late on the night of September 13, the first paratroopers were on the ground just eight hours after receiving the order from the 82nd Division Commander, Maj. Gen. Matthew Ridgeway. The regiment formed and moved into the battle lines just before daylight. Lt. Gen. Mark Clark, Commander of Fifth Army, called the 504th one of the best units he had seen during the war. Clark was so impressed, in fact, that he requested that the 504th remain attached to Fifth Army when the 82nd moved to England to prepare for the Normandy landings.

It is the beaches of Anzio that most people associate with the 504, and it is here that the fear the regiment struck in the heart of their enemies earned them the hallmark description "Devils in Baggy Pants," coined by German defenders. Bravery, courage, and determination melded with their strong leadership, making them one of the most notable regiments of the war. In *On to Berlin*, Lt. Gen. James M. Gavin, former commander of both the 82nd ABD and 505th PIR, stated that Tucker was "probably the best regimental combat commander of the war."

The pages of this book reflect in significant detail who these young men were, how they came together and how they fought together successfully from North Africa to Berlin. It is also a testament to the more than 500 men of the regiment who sacrificed their lives in combat from July 1943 until May 1945, and serves as an indelible tribute to the bravery and courage that were the very core of the 504th PIR during WWII. It is the cornerstone and foundation for the beloved call of every soldier who wears the wings of US Army warriors of the sky: Airborne!

Christopher Tucker
Brigadier General (USA, Ret.)
Son of Maj. Gen. Reuben H. Tucker III (USA, Ret.)

ACKNOWLEDGMENTS

The authors of the first regimental history, 1st Lt. William D. Mandle and PFC David H. Whittier, were faced with a huge challenge. Only limited and incomplete documentation was available as they compiled their manuscript from December 1944 through May 1945. In retrospect, it is unfortunate that Cpl. George B. Graves, Jr., a clerk in Regimental Headquarters who was discharged as a private, was not a regular part of the writers' team back in 1944. Graves had envisioned writing a book on the history of the 504th Regimental Combat Team [RCT] when the unit was still in action during the Holland Campaign. During the many months he was overseas, he kept a private diary and continually sent retyped reports, photos and medal citations to his wife to keep for his book. Although he finished a beautifully composed scrapbook for his own collection, the book remained unwritten. In a way, I feel as if I am finishing what George Graves had planned to do back in 1944.

I was very fortunate to have received much cooperation from multiple sources: the three children of Lt. William Mandle—Steve, Shannon and Kim—kindly supported me in every possible way, not least by supplying dozens of photos from their late father's archives. Lieutenant Mandle wanted to write another regimental history in serial form, but was diagnosed with cancer and died in 1962 before he could finish his manuscript. Steve transcribed dozens of his father's wartime letters and sent them to me. Thank you all three for your continual support, which bettered my research and gave me a rare, privileged view of the life and work of a young lieutenant during WWII.

Mike Bigalke not only shared photos, letters and reports from the late

Cpl. George Graves's scrapbook, but also sent photocopies of regimental reports on the Italian campaigns he had located in the Donovan Research Library at Fort Benning and a much-treasured original *Propblast* regimental newspaper from April 1945, now a valued piece in my collection. Robert Wolfe did the same with the reports and lists of decorated troopers we had seen during our August 2007 visit to the United States Army History Military Institute in Carlisle, Pennsylvania.

Fellow historian John C. McManus (author of the excellent *September Hope*) and Fred Baldino, James McNamara, Jr., and Timothy Rose generously provided photocopies from the Cornelius Ryan Archives, including questionnaires by Baldino, McManus and Rose that I had selected from the list on the archive's website. Steve Mrozek, official 82nd Airborne Division Historian for many years and the author of two great books, supplied invaluable copies of the August 1944 regimental roster, which enabled me to trace down veterans I would otherwise have never found.

Raymond and Kathleen Buttke I first met in September 2004 when we visited the Liberation Museum in Groesbeek along with Phil and Judy Rosenkrantz, veterans Albert Clark (A Company), Francis Keefe (I Company), and Francis's nephew, Jack Barry. It was Francis who first asked me to write this regimental history in August 2007 when I was guest speaker at the 504th PIR dinner. Raymond and Kathleen shared their research on troopers killed in the Waal Crossing, and Phil gave permission to use the letters and wartime photographs of his uncle, Sgt. David Rosenkrantz.

In the Netherlands, help was received from Jan Bos, unit historian of the 376th Parachute Field Artillery Battalion, who graciously provided a copy of his 376th PFAB history and scans of unique wartime photographs by Capt. Louis Hauptfleisch. Dennis and Gerda Hermsen supplied me with information on the late Richard Gentzel and William Sandoval, and also supplied numerous personal photographs from the American Cemetery in Henri-Chapelle. Egbert van de Schootbrugge contributed Ted Bachenheimer's Individual Deceased Personnel File, which gave me rich insight into the post-war correspondence of the army and understanding of the relatives of a deceased paratrooper. The epigraph from Katherina Bachenheimer's letter to the Memorial Division comes from this source.

I also owe hearty thanks to two great friends, Johan van Asten and Jos Bex. Jos put me in contact with the family of the late Peter Colishion and contributed maps based on the Waal River Crossing. In August 2007, Johan accompanied me to the 61st Annual Convention of the 82nd Airborne Division in Harrisburg, Pennsylvania. An unsung hero, he has spent years battling the Nijmegen municipal bureaucracy in the effort to increase official awareness of the importance of properly maintaining and preserving the Waal Crossing monument erected by Dutch civilians in September 1984.

Jan Timmermans at the Graafs Museum in Grave and Anne-Marie Jansen at the Van 't Lindenhout Museum in Neerbosch supplied photographs and background on local events in September 1944. Ben Overhand shared his knowledge of the Den Heuvel battle and photographs and documentation concerning Lieutenants Kennedy and Preston and Staff Sergeant Baldwin. Brig. Gen. Ben Bouman (Ret.) kindly provided written recollections and answered many questions regarding his short time with B Company in Holland. Arjen Kuiken provided five unique and formerly unpublished photographs of the Provinciale Geldersche Electriciteits Maatsshappij power station on the south bank of the Waal River. I relied on my father Wim to enhance the digital quality of several photographs, a talent my publisher (and I!) greatly appreciated.

Valuable information also came from the United Kingdom. Roy Hamlyn, a longtime friend, shared his recollection of bringing the canvas boats up to Nijmegen, thus supplying the very first testimony by a participant in this part of Operation Market Garden. Sadly, he passed away in 2013. Jan Bos put me in contact with Roy Tuck, a participant as a 19-year-old sapper in the Waal Crossing, who answered all my pointed questions and contributed an excerpt of his memoir.

Carl Mauro II not only provided his late father's war memoirs, but also proofread chapters, supplied several unique photographs and drew the excellent, detailed maps in this book. Thank you, Carl, for your full support!

My excellent literary agent, Gayle Wurst of Princeton International Agency for the Arts, presented my voluminous manuscript of the complete regimental history (800-plus pages!) to Casemate Publishing. Together she and I divided the plethora of material into several volumes, each focused on one or two campaigns. *Battle of the Bridges* is the first to be culled from the rich history of the 504 RCT. Thank you, Gayle—without you, it would never have made it into print.

The hardest part of the writing process was deciding what to include or leave out. I decided early on to write as complete a history as possible, but whenever a regiment is researched in detail, new information always crops up. Some stories were forcibly briefly told, like that of PFC. Ted Bachenheimer; although his wartime exploits could easily fill a whole chapter, it would be unjustified in regards to the many gallant actions of other members of the 504th RCT. Considerations of length also caused me to focus on the 504th PIR, although I interviewed some veterans (mostly officers) of the 307th Airborne Engineer and 376th Parachute Field Artillery Battalions.

Unlike most accounts of Operation Market Garden, *Battle for the Bridges* essentially includes rear-area activities, the invaluable work of the chaplains and medics, contributions by the Dutch Resistance, friendships with the Dutch and English populations and friendly-fire incidents. Accounts of medical detachments within American airborne troops during WWII are rare, so I was privileged to locate former Maj. Ivan J. Roggen and Capt. Charles R. Zirkle, Jr., whose eye-witness testimonies contribute greatly to this book. Both have now passed on. Char Baldridge, historian of the 359th Fighter Group, kindly provided the memoirs of the late Capt. Paul D. Bruns, another battalion surgeon. Their help, various wartime newspaper articles, and discussions with Chaplain Delbert Kuehl enabled me to include the essential contributions of medics and chaplains.

Researching the morning reports for eight months of combat for every company, I was able to fill in numerous omissions in the *Roll of Honor of the 82nd Airborne Division*, published by the Liberation Museum in Groesbeek, and make this book a more accurate account. Wherever possible, I have complemented eye-witness testimonies and official reports from the 504th RCT with German reports, Dutch eye-witness accounts, and British war diaries and regimental histories in the attmpt to create as balanced a view as possible. It was a great joy to discover the Distinguished Service Cross Citations of some members of the regiment that have never before appeared in print. On a personal level, I was equally delighted to discover that 2nd Platoon, A Company, 504th PIR liberated a cousin and four nieces of my late grandfather, who were amongst the first of my family to be liberated on September 18, 1944.

These acknowledgements would not be complete without sincerely thanking the hundreds of American citizens who graciously opened their family archives and shared material (newspaper articles, letters, medal citations, photographs and personal recollections) about their husbands, brothers, fathers, uncles, grandfathers and great uncles who once served in the 504th RCT. Their contributions, although sometimes seemingly small in their own eyes, were invaluable. Many of their names can be found in the footnotes and photo credits.

The sons of the late Maj. Gen. Reuben H. Tucker—Jeff, Scott, Glenn and Christopher—were very helpful in answering questions about their father and, in Jeff's case, providing unique photographs from the family collection. Christopher generously agreed to write the foreword for this book, which he has done in a splendid manner! I deeply regret that Glenn passed away far too early, and before I had the pleasure of presenting him with a copy of this book.

A final word of thanks must go to Mike St. George of the Colonel Reuben Tucker Chapter of the 82nd Airborne Division Association. Mike, a post-war 82nd ABD trooper who conducted research on Ross Carter's *Those Devils in Baggy Pants*, first proposed me as an Honorary Member of the Colonel Reuben Tucker Chapter. Truly my cup runeth over to be so-associated with the 82nd Airborne Division. Thank you, Mike, for your friendship and enthusiastic support!

Based on calculations stemming from the morning reports of A Company, I estimate that over 6,000 Americans served in the 504th in WWII. Between the invasion of Sicily and the surrender of Germany, 644 were killed or died of sustained wounds. May they never be forgotten!

Frank van Lunteren
Arnhem, April 2014

Practice jump of the 504th Parachute Infantry Regiment. *Courtesy: Mandle family*

CHAPTER 1

REPLACEMENTS: LEICESTER, ENGLAND, JULY 1–SEPTEMBER 10, 1944

After spending over 60 exceedingly hard days on the Anzio Beachhead, Colonel Reuben Tucker's 504th Parachute Infantry Regiment sailed from Italy to England in April 1944 on the British ship *Capetown Castle*. They were to rejoin their parent unit, the 82nd Airborne Division, near Leicester. Due to heavy losses sustained in Italy, the 504th PIR was not included in the Normandy invasion in June 1944. A few dozen of Tucker's troopers all the same volunteered to serve in Normandy, where they acted as pathfinders or bodyguards for the division staff.

"Back in Naples the rumours became abundant," recalled the recently promoted PFC David K. Finney of Headquarters and Headquarters Company. "Each day a new one would make its rounds, growing as it was passed from man to man. The most absurd one was that our division was to be sent back to the States. I don't think anyone believed this, but we were wishing it were true. The one good thing, we were all packed and ready to go anywhere. Then it happened. On April 10, with rumours still flying, we marched down the Via Umberto to the Docks of Naples. We were halted just below a sleek-looking English ship, code-named the *Capetown Castle*. We were marched up the gang plank and shown to the deck we would be living in for this voyage to England. […]

"Later, as I lay on my bunk listening to and feeling the throb of the ship's engines, I kept thinking of the places we had been—not of where we were going. I felt sad to be leaving Italy with all the deaths I had seen and so few pleasant times. I also thought about some of my friends that had died too young and the great sadness their families would suffer."[1] S.Sgt. Ernest W. Parks, D Company, boarded the *Capetown Castle* with his regiment: "Anzio became extinct from human eyes. Many experienced the fellowship of dearest friends gone forever and it seemed as though ten thousand memories would last forever."[2]

The summer months of 1944 were spent shaping the regiment back into a combat-ready outfit. Rifle platoons, enlarged with an additional rifle squad, now consisted of three rifle squads and a 60mm mortar squad. Acquiring enlisted replacements took time, but it was even more difficult to find officers, and especially surgeons, to replace those who had been killed or wounded. By mid-July 1944, it became clear that the need for replacement surgeons in the 82nd and 101st Airborne Divisions was particularly crucial, due to the heavy losses sustained in Normandy.

Typical of the new surgeons who responded to the call was 29-year-old Capt. Paul D. Bruns from Iowa. Stationed since October 1943 on a small airfield in East Wretham, England, Bruns had a job as a surgeon with the 369th Fighter Squadron of the 359th Fighter Group that kept him far away from the battlefield. Feeling the need to be more active, he "attended a meeting where personnel were being recruited for the depleted Airborne Divisions." He recalls: "Volunteers were asked to stand up. I recall a fellow officer saying, 'My God, sit down.' In retrospect, I can agree that was good advice, but of course I wasn't one to take advice, even when I knew it was good."[3]

The next stop was jump training near Leicester: "Those weeks of training I would just as soon forget. It consisted of one hour of running every morning, followed by two hours of calisthenics and one hour of instruction. This routine was repeated each afternoon. The raison d'être of all these exercises occurred aboard a C-47 when the order 'Stand up and hook up!' was given. I understood the psychology of such rigorous training when I looked out of the plane door. Jumping was easy compared to the harshness of running and exercising ten hours a day.

"Physicians in the parachute troops are there for three main reasons: psychological purposes, first aid and triage. If a paratrooper knows the physician will jump with him in combat and be there to care for him if he is hit or hurt, this gives him the courage and confidence to jump. In return, the physician enjoys a special privilege for parachuting with the troops; namely, he is not always expected to perform routine formal activities such as parades, drills, and reviews.

"My first parachute jump was a riot. The chute opened with such a jerk that the helmet covered my face. By the time I got it back in place I was sitting on the ground wondering where in hell I could possibly be. Now, at a time in my life when I really believed I had accomplished the greatest feat known to mankind, a little urchin walked up to me and said: 'Got any gum, chum?' We learn humiliation at such odd times."[4]

Bruns graduated from Parachute School on August 5, 1944, and was shortly assigned to the 1st Battalion of the 504th, stationed in Evington near Leicester. He soon realized it would not be easy to blend in as a replacement surgeon: "Joining a unit of combat veterans was a new and strange experience. I interpreted their standoffishness to mean they would reserve an opinion of me until after they saw how I acted under fire. Well, fine with me. They were pretty battered from previous campaigns in Sicily and Italy. Many had an attitude that one more combat mission would be their last. The law of averages would catch up. During early September 1944, we had many 'dry runs.' Missions were scheduled then cancelled. I remember General 'Ike' gesturing with his arms, saying: 'Gather 'round. I know all you men would rather go home. So would I, but we've got a job to do first.' Briefings indicated the forthcoming mission would be far from easy."[5]

In the afternoon of August 10, after visiting the 101st Airborne Division in the morning, Gen. Dwight D. Eisenhower reviewed a parade of the entire 82nd Airborne Division, almost brought back to strength by some 6,000 paratroop and glider infantry replacements. General Eisenhower gave a complementary speech about the division's performance in the Normandy Campaign and decorated those officers and men who had earned the Distinguished Service Cross. Among recipients were Lt. Col. Charles Billingslea, Maj. Willard E. Harrison and PFC Thomas L. Rodgers (honored posthumously).

Capt. Adam A. Komosa, the Headquarters and Headquarters Company commander, believed Eisenhower's presence meant another mission was rapidly approaching: "When the top brass suddenly starts appearing on the scene and taking particular interest in you, you know you are getting 'hot.' After the parade in Leicester, General Eisenhower gave us a pep talk. 'I'm just as much in a hurry as you are to get this war over with and go back to the States and go fishing,' he said. His closing words were: 'I've owed you [paratroopers] a lot in the past, and I suspect that I will owe you a lot more before this is all over with.' That indeed proved to be a prophetic statement."[6]

Even after the review, replacements kept arriving. Some arrived during the night, like 21-year-old Cpl. Edwin M. Clements, whose account vividly evokes the perplexity of the green replacements and the condition of the still-depleted regiment: "We docked in Liverpool in the dead of night. It was raining and foggy and it took us over two hours to unload, collect our two huge duffel bags and get on the trucks that would take us to our assigned units. Except that my two bags could not be found, and the trucks couldn't wait. Even though the bags were heavily labeled and marked with my name, rank, and serial number, I never saw them again, including the beautiful monogrammed Dopp kit and a number of other personal items that my parents had thoughtfully sent with me. So off I go to win the war with a small musette bag containing shaving stuff, a bunch of dirty underwear, and a few pair of socks.

"We unloaded while it was still dark. I was told to find a cot in a 12-man tent. All I knew was that I was in the 82nd Airborne Division, in a camp near the city of Leicester. It was pitch dark and I was cursed loudly since I woke two men by stepping on them. Finally I found an empty cot, and without undressing except for my boots, fell on the cot and slept.

"I awoke to the usual sound of reveille and found I was now a part of the 1st Platoon, B Company, 1st Battalion, 504th PIR, which had seen action in Sicily and most recently Italy, including a long and hazardous period on the Anzio beachhead.

"My squad leader, a young man whose name was Jerry Murphy, put me in touch with the company supply sergeant, one of the more memorable characters in B Company. Sgt. Charles J. Hyde heard my sad story and very quickly supplied me with almost everything I needed in terms of clothing and equipment. But the true measure of Hyde's efficiency was his ability to beg, borrow, scrounge, and even steal if necessary when the usual sources of supply had dried up.

"Murphy, although acting as squad leader, was still a private, though his job called for sergeant's stripes. I had come over with the two stripes of a corporal on my sleeve, which apparently created a bit of a problem. Later that day it was resolved when I was told to report to the Company Commander.

"Captain [Thomas C.] Helgeson could have served as a perfect role model for a WWII parachute officer. Not tall, but wide-shouldered, thin-waisted, and flat-bellied, he was also blond and blue-eyed. His uniform was spotless, his boots glistened and he came to the point quickly. 'Corporal Clements, your rank and training entitle you to fill the job of an assistant squad leader of a rifle squad even though you have never been in combat. I am sure you would not feel comfortable leading a squad of combat veterans who have been in combat in Sicily, Salerno, and on the Anzio beachhead.' He didn't wait for my response. 'Therefore, I am demoting you to private immediately. You are dismissed.'

"This was the unit—or what was left of it—that I joined in Leicester. In fact not a large number of troopers who had jumped into Sicily lasted through all the campaigns that followed. Attrition was supposed to be offset by replacements, although the numbers always fell below full strength. Some of the men in B Company had seen little or no action, arriving when the unit was in a reserve position, but I was fortunate in that my platoon sergeant, [S.Sgt.] William J. Walsh ('Knobby'), had been with the regiment since it was activated. He had come over with the regiment prior to Sicily, fought through all the major campaigns and had achieved relatively high rank as first sergeant, which he kept for only a short time."[7]

Another young replacement was 18-year-old PFC Walter E. Hughes from Brooklyn, New York. Hughes had worked on his stepfather's tugboat since the age of 12, and had quit school at age 15: "War was already on in Europe in 1940 and I knew it would not be long before our country would be in it. I joined the War Shipping Administration and started working on several Government tugs, DPC 21, Port Clinton, Port Vincent, wherever they needed an able-bodied seaman. As a seaman I was deferred from Military Service. I never liked that idea, but accepted it even after Pearl Harbor right into 1943. That's when I rejected my deferment and enlisted in the army."[8]

Opting for the US Army, Hughes believed he would receive an assignment similar to that of several of his friends, who had ended up on tugboats or smaller ships used by the army. This was not to be. Assigned basic training in the field artillery at Fort Bragg, he learned he could earn $50 more in the paratroops: "I volunteered for the paratroopers, made my five qualifying jumps and two night jumps and was headed overseas. It was August of 1944. We left New York Harbor alone on a New Zealand cargo ship, which had seen better days, probably during World War I. But for a steamer she was quite fast, and off the coast of Newfoundland joined several other cargo ships and several small Canadian patrol boats. By the fourth day out we were pretty much on our own and I kept thinking, 'If we are torpedoed what should I look for to hang on to?' By the ninth day we were joined by what looked like a destroyer. I could not make out the flag, but it wasn't either American or British. I never did find out, but they were on our side and that's all that counted.

"On the 11th day we arrived in Liverpool and were herded aboard a train amid a welcome band and a lot of ladies serving tea and cakes. Had to give them credit: already fighting a war for over five years, and they still showed spirit and perseverance. We also noticed the lack of young men. I fell asleep aboard the train and am not sure if it was ten or 12 hours to where we off-loaded onto a platform with our two bags.

"By that time our number (originally 32 troopers) had dwindled down to 12 men. A sergeant called us to attention and this young lieutenant with a clip-board came out of the station and started reading off the names. He then asked if anyone had basic in wire and radio communications. I acknowledged that I took my basic training in the field artillery wireman's and radio school. He advised me to pick up my bags and report to one of the trucks standing by.

"When I reached the truck, a corporal was leaning against the fender smoking. I asked him what artillery unit we were going to. He said, 'This truck is from the 504th PIR.' I told him, 'The lieutenant must have made a mistake. I'm not an infantry man.' Knowing I was a green replacement, he said, 'Why don't you go tell him?' So like a dunce, I did. He gave me a hard look and said, 'Welcome to the infantry, son. Now get your ass and those bags aboard that truck!' That's how I volunteered for the infantry.

"I was now a 'Strike and Hold' trooper in the 504th PIR. Little did I know I would see some of the fiercest fighting in the European Theater, and serve side by side with some of the finest soldiers to ever wear the uniform of the US Army, every one a legend in his own way. I was one of the 'Devils in Baggy Pants' and I promised myself I would never let anyone down. I would do what I trained to do, I would make my family proud of me, even if I had to die for it."[9]

In the small suburb of Evington, a corporal was waiting to direct the new arrivals to their respective companies: "I was told the town's name was Leicester, but as a replacement don't expect to see it for a while. The camp itself was busy. I felt good. I was finally with an outfit. A corporal told me to report to the sergeant in the first tent in the second line of tents. He was a thin guy and I would get to know him later as Sergeant [George S.] Davis. He pointed out one of the tents and told me to take the second bunk.

"As I had missed chow, he sent me up to the mess hall for something to eat. My first meal with the Devils consisted of several glasses of milk and some pie that was supposed to be apple. That's all the guy cleaning up could find. I returned to the tent and several troopers appeared and introduced themselves. I believe they were Bill Hicks, Bill Martin and Ed Hahn. I guess I was home."[10]

Hughes learned he had been assigned to Captain T. Moffatt Burriss's I Company. "I had arrived in England without a weapon, so Sergeant Davis told me to take one from the supply. I asked Lieutenant [Robert] Blankenship, 'What weapon should I take?'

"'Anything you can,' he replied, so I chose a Thompson submachine gun."

New in the outfit, knowing that another combat mission couldn't be far ahead, Hughes was anxious to find out how to survive in a battle. He presented this question to Pvt. William E. "Ed" Hahn, a veteran of several campaigns. "Stick to Captain Burriss," Hahn replied. "He is bullet-proof."[11]

Another thing Hughes soon learned was that it took a long time for anyone to remember his name. The veterans were just not interested; experience had taught them that most replacements were hit in their first battle. He could well be no exception to this unwritten law. Because of his accent and youthful appearance, they dubbed him "the kid from Brooklyn," a name that would stick for quite a while.

Hughes started in Sergeant Davis's wire section as a wireman along with Private Hahn. He would later sometimes serve in the 1st Platoon. His uncertain time as a replacement was now over—he was among seasoned veterans he looked up to. He summarizes his time in Evington: "Most of my memories of the camp at Leicester were of pulling guard duty, training, rain and the local farmers who emptied the buckets that comprised our latrines. The pubs, especially the Swan with the double necks, fighting a losing battle with the English over the money exchange, and the strong, warm beer. Almost forgot the Donut Dugout, run by a Red Cross lady, whose name I think was Louise.

"Rumors were we would be going into combat very soon. It would be the mission to end the war. I began to think I would not get to see much action, if the war was almost over. Of course for the guys who fought in Sicily, Italy and Normandy this was good news, the sooner the better."[12]

In preparation for the upcoming mission, Lieutenant Colonel Billingslea was promoted to colonel on August 21, and transferred to the 325th Glider Infantry Regiment [GIR] to take command. His predecessor, Col. Harry L. Lewis, was sent to the States for cancer surgery. Billingslea's reassignment made the lack of field-grade officers within the 504th apparent. Lt. Col. Warren R. Williams, Jr. was the logical choice for his successor, being the only remaining lieutenant colonel. Major Harrison of the 3rd Battalion had recently returned to England. Colonel Tucker elevated him to battalion commander, giving him the 1st Battalion. Capt. Arthur W. Ferguson was transferred to the 3rd Battalion as executive battalion commander, having previously served in the 2nd Battalion.

Seven days after Billingslea left the regiment, a change took place in the top command of the 82nd Airborne. Major General Ridgway was appointed corps commander of XVIII Airborne Corps and succeeded by his 37-year-old assistant division commander, Brig. Gen. James M. Gavin. Although promoting Colonel Tucker to brigadier general and assistant division commander may have seemed a logical choice, no such action was taken. Long after Tucker's death, Gavin revealed in an interview that he had favored the 504th RCT commander as his assistant, but Ridgway had refused because Tucker "didn't give a damn about administration and paperwork. In fact, he was famous for screwing up everything having to do with administration. One story going around was that when Tucker left Italy he had an orange crate full of official charges against his soldiers and he just threw the whole crate into the ocean. Ridgway and I talked about it and we decided we just couldn't promote Tucker."[13]

Maj. Julian A. Cook, the 3rd Battalion commander, didn't believe the reason was Tucker's limited administrational skills: "Billingslea got along well with both Tucker and Gavin, but the latter two were never really friends. As a 504 man I felt, and so did the regiment, that Gavin was jealous of Tucker."[14]

In early September a new staff officer of XVIII Airborne Corps, 28-year-old Maj. John T. Berry, was sent to Colonel Tucker. A veteran of the 509th Parachute Infantry Battalion and 508th PIR, Berry had served in North Africa and Normandy. At that time the senior command spots in the three battalions were held by Maj. Willard E. Harrison and Maj. Abdallah K. Zakby in the 1st Battalion; Maj. Edward N. Wellems and Capt. William Colville, Jr., in the 2nd; and Maj. Julian A. Cook and Capt. Arthur W. Ferguson in the 3rd. Colville and Ferguson had served together as executive officers in the 2nd Battalion at Anzio, one being in charge of the administration and command post, the other as tactical executive officer. Tucker applied the same solution in the 1st Battalion: Berry, the stronger administrative executive, received the first assignment; Major Zakby became the tactical executive officer.

Not long after Major Berry's assignment, another training jump was staged on September 5. It was not a complete success, as there was a strong wind and several men landed in trees or hedgerows. First Sergeant George A. Siegmann, A Company, landed in a hedgerow and broke his left leg and hip, and was eventually evacuated to the States. First Lieutenant Payton F. Elliott, the 3rd Platoon leader of I Company, was severely injured when a supply bundle broke his back during the jump. He would spend almost nine months in various hospitals in England and the United States. Elliott was succeeded by 1st Lt. Edward W. Kennedy.

Among the last replacements to join the 504th in September 1944 were two recent graduates of the Parachute School in Ashwell near Leicester: 2nd Lieutenants Frank J. McKay and Harry W. Rollins. Both had volunteered for the paratroops in England and graduated on August 26, 1944. McKay was assigned to the reconstituted Regimental Reconnaissance Platoon and Rollins became assistant platoon leader of the 1st Platoon, D Company. Although these new officers completed the required number for the regiment, they lacked combat experience. Furthermore, they not only had to learn to adapt themselves to their new capacity, but they also had to acquaint themselves with the men under their command.

Lieutenant McKay, for instance, learned there was already another officer in the Recon Platoon, 1st Lt. Donald M. Crooks. S.Sgt. Myrl D. Olrogge, Jr., of Niagara Falls, New York, was made platoon sergeant. Colonel Tucker believed that the presence of two officers would maximise Recon Platoon's ability to obtain information. First, it would be possible to send out two simultaneous regimental patrols without affecting the strength of the rifle companies. Second, if McKay got hit, Crooks could assume command. McKay learned a lot from Crooks and Olrogge.

While all the changes in command took place, the men of the 504th continued to prepare themselves both physically and psychologically for the "mission to end the war." Again, PFC Walter Hughes captures their activities and state of mind: "It was now September and the training intensified. My seventh jump was a training jump, they said, somewhere in the moors. I didn't even know what a moor was. Some of the veterans were busy trying to get papers filled out to get married and change their beneficiaries on insurance policies. I spent a lot of time writing home to my mother, brothers and a girl I knew."[15]

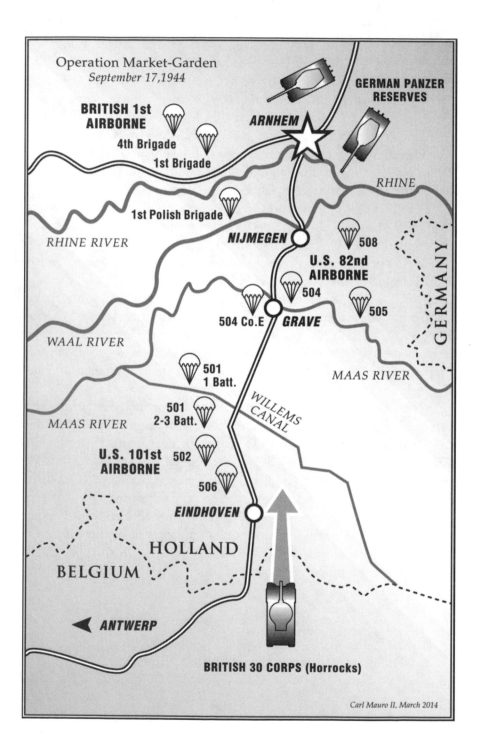

Operation Market-Garden
September 17,1944

GERMAN PANZER RESERVES

BRITISH 1st AIRBORNE
4th Brigade
1st Brigade

ARNHEM

RHINE

1st Polish Brigade

RHINE RIVER

NIJMEGEN

508

U.S. 82nd AIRBORNE
504

505

504 Co.E   *GRAVE*

GERMANY

WAAL RIVER

501 1 Batt.

MAAS RIVER

501 2-3 Batt.

WILLEMS CANAL

MAAS RIVER

U.S. 101st AIRBORNE   502

506

EINDHOVEN

HOLLAND

BELGIUM

◄ *ANTWERP*

BRITISH 30 CORPS (Horrocks)

Carl Mauro II, March 2014

CHAPTER 2

THE SEVENTEENTH MISSION
LEICESTER, ENGLAND,
SEPTEMBER 11–16, 1944

Replacements arriving in early September were just in time for the seventeenth mission that had been planned since D-Day. Word about this assignment, code-named Operation Market Garden, first got to Tucker in the evening of September 10 when Gavin assembled his regimental commanders. Gavin had been briefed about the operation at the headquarters of Lt. Gen. Frederick A. M. Browning of the British I Airborne Corps in Moorpark. By midnight a draft order had been prepared for the regimental commanders and Gavin instructed them to work out the details of the areas and tasks to which they had been assigned.

Meanwhile, no other member of the 504th RCT was yet aware of the preparations at higher headquarters. Life repeated the same pattern it had followed earlier that summer. Some of the newcomers wondered if they would ever get a chance to jump and fight, while some veterans slowly began to imagine their trip home, once the war was over. It seemed like time stood still as the Glenn Miller Orchestra, conducted by Glenn Miller himself, gave an exclusive performance to the division on September 11. Overjoyed when he read the announcement on the bulletin board, Sgt. Mitchell E. Rech of A Company snatched one of the 8 x 11-inch posters and mailed it home as a souvenir.

On September 12 the battalion commanders were instructed on the operation, followed by the company commanders two days later. Colonel Tucker informed his officers about the origin of the operation. On September 4, the Allied Commander-in-Chief of the Allied Forces in Europe, Gen. Dwight D. Eisenhower, placed the newly established First Allied Airborne Army of

Lt. Gen. Lewis H. Brereton under the command of Field Marshal Sir Bernard Law Montgomery, commander of the British 21st Army Group. Brereton's army comprised all the American Troop Carrier Groups, the British 38th and 46th Wings of the Royal Air Force, the XVIII US Airborne Corps commanded by Maj. Gen. Matthew B. Ridgway (the former 82nd ABD commander) and the British I Airborne Corps. The XVIII Airborne Corps comprised the 82nd and 101st Airborne Divisions.

Field Marshal Montgomery wanted to break through the weak German defensive positions in the Netherlands before the Germans had the opportunity to reorganize. His plan for Market Garden, designed on September 9, called for the 82nd and 101st Airborne Divisions, the British 1st Airborne Division and the 1st Independent Polish Parachute Brigade of the First Allied Airborne Army to be dropped in the Netherlands. The paratroopers would seize vital bridges to enable ground forces, the British Second Army of Lt. Gen. Miles C. Dempsey, to make a strong push into Holland from Belgium towards the Zuider Zee, cutting off all the German forces in west Holland. Upon reaching the Zuider Zee, ground forces would swing to the right, enter Germany and capture the Ruhr area east of the Rhine River. Germany would thus lose its most important industrial area and be forced to surrender. Numerous V-2 launch sites could also be destroyed, and the Siegfried Line could be outflanked without sustaining too many casualties.

The 82nd ABD was to jump near the city of Nijmegen in the central part of the planned "corridor" of airborne troops. Gavin ordered the 508th PIR to occupy the towns of Berg en Dal and Wyler east of Nijmegen and the high ground around Berg en Dal. One battalion of this regiment was to capture the Waal Bridge across the broad Waal River north of Nijmegen. The 505th PIR was to capture the towns of Groesbeek, Mook and Riethorst. Both regiments would land east of Nijmegen.

Colonel Tucker's regiment would land southwest of Nijmegen on the far side of the Maas-Waal Canal. The mission of the 504th PIR was to capture four bridges, numbered seven through ten across the Maas-Waal Canal west of Nijmegen, and the Maas Bridge across the Maas River at Grave, southwest of Nijmegen. Captain Helgeson's B Company was to capture Bridge Number 7 near the village of Heumen; Captain [Charles W.] Duncan's A Company would capture Bridge Number 8 and 9 north of B Company; and Capt. Albert E. Milloy's C Company would capture the Honinghutje Bridge—a double-span road and railroad bridge code-named Bridge Number 10.

One 2nd Battalion rifle company would be selected by Colonel Wellems to jump on a small drop zone [DZ] south of Grave to capture the long bridge over the River Maas, while the rest of the battalion simultaneously attacked the bridge from the north. The 3rd Battalion would patrol to the west to guard the flank of the regiment once they had landed, and act as regimental reserve.

Since the Normandy invasion, 16 airborne operations had been cancelled at the last moment. Many junior officers and enlisted men believed that the combat alert in the morning of September 15, when all passes were cancelled, would be more of the same. Tucker's troopers were trucked to two airfields: 2nd and 3rd Battalions were sealed in at Spanhoe at 2130 hours; 1st Battalion, Regimental Headquarters and Service Company were sealed in at Cottesmore. Many still thought the operation would be cancelled before take-off, causing mounting tension.

First Lt. Chester A. Garrison recalled the atmosphere in the hangar where the 504th bedded down on the night of September 15: "The cots were set up close together in neat lines with barely an aisle to denote where one company or battalion separated from another. Since the disposition of the 2nd Battalion and its four companies constituted a personnel matter, I stood by should there be any confusion.

"There was. Noise and activity drew my attention to where the 2nd Battalion ended and the 3rd began. Someone was violently upsetting the cots in the last line of F Company. Personal equipment was being scattered over the floor as the cots were removed. Enlisted men from both F (2nd Battalion) and Headquarters (3rd Battalion) were standing silently by without interrupting the mayhem. I understood the situation as I got closer to it.

"The ravager was Maj. Julian Cook, the commander of the 3rd Battalion; with no reason, no enlisted man dared to interfere. I was stunned for the moment, but I quickly realized I was the only officer present to take any action. I saluted Major Cook and asked if I could help in any way since 2nd Battalion personnel were involved. He dumped another cot and raged that men from the 2nd Battalion had stolen 3rd Battalion cots and he was retrieving them. I replied that we would have to discipline such men, but did he know if the cots he was taking were the ones stolen? That gave him pause. With flashing eyes he said that his men must have their cots back. I agreed, but also stated I must know which cots and which men were involved. Beginning to deflate, he muttered something like 'Damn thieves' as he strode off.

"I told the F Company men to retrieve their cots, and I would consult with their company commander, Captain [Beverly T.] Richardson. The men started to put things in order. Of course, some of the cots could have been stolen by F Company jumpers, but proving who did what was complicated."[16]

T/4 Albert A. Tarbell, H Company, who had joined the 504th at Anzio, was taken to Spanhoe Airfield: "I was looking forward to my first combat jump. We all knew that we were to make a combat jump sooner or later and in a way were glad to get it over with."[17] Sgt. Albert B. Clark, A Company, went "over maps and sand tables" for "several days" at Cottesmore Airfield. "We found out that we were going into Holland. We knew where we were going and what our objectives were."[18]

Pvt. Edwin M. Clements, 1st Platoon, B Company, worried about making a combat jump with full equipment: "My squad leader, [Sgt.] Jerry Murphy, noticed my astonishment, laughed, and quickly assured me that I not only could get all this equipment stowed, but I could jump and land safely with it. A fairly complete list included: main parachute, reserve parachute, M-1 rifle with three bandoleers of ammunition, two hand grenades, a boot knife, a three-day supply of C- and K-rations in small cans and boxes. I also packed a tent half, a woolen blanket, a gas mask and a musette bag containing underwear, socks, an extra shirt, toilet paper, shaving supplies and two full canteens of water, and whatever else I thought I might need.

"The atmosphere in camp changed almost overnight. Tension began to build. This was quickly followed by the general announcement that we were now in an alert stage. Invasion currency was issued. All leaves and passes were canceled and those who were already on leave were recalled immediately. Afterwards, no one could leave or enter the base without a special pass.

"In an incredibly short length of time, we moved to a stage-one alert, which meant that we had to be prepared to load up and jump within 24 hours. Again, in a matter of a few hours, we were assembled by platoons and given our first mission briefing. We were going to jump about 55 miles behind the German lines, seize and hold three bridges so that armored columns could move over these bridges, and ultimately turn east to get into the German Ruhr Valley, bypassing the Siegfried line. [...] That was our 'big picture' briefing. More detailed mission briefings would be scheduled later.

"The risks were substantial. First, the drop was scheduled from 1300 to 1330 on Sunday, September 17, 1944, the first major daylight combat parachute operation of the war. Daylight posed a different set of problems, including the need to have air supremacy all of the way to the drop zone. The C-47 could only fly low and slow. This was dangerous since it did not have self-sealing gas tanks and would be very vulnerable to routine ground fire.

Weather was important. Storms and other forms of heavy weather at take-off or over the drop zone would be hazardous. Excess winds at any of the multiple drop zones could scatter the jumpers all over occupied Holland.

"Obviously, surprise was terribly important. If the Germans were waiting for us, or even close to the drop zones, we were in deep trouble, since we were at our most vulnerable position on the drop zone and for several hours afterwards.

"By the time the mission objective briefing got down to the 1st Platoon, [S.Sgt. William] 'Knobby' Walsh put it this way: 'Sometime in the next 12 hours, we are going to load up on trucks and go to an airfield near Nottingham. We will draw rations, ammunition and our chutes there. We will also be responsible for rigging and loading two bundles, which we will drop in the middle of the stick. We will be going to Holland and we won't be picking tulips. We think it's going to be Sunday (September 17) but we will have to be ready at least 12 hours before H-Hour, and I guarantee we will be.

"'Our first job after we land is to pick up our bundles and drag ass off the drop zone to the northeast corner. We are jumping on a huge sugar beet field so it will be flat. There will be a windmill in the northeast corner and that's where we will assemble. From there we will go about two miles to a small canal, where we will take and hold both ends of the bridge for as long as it takes. We will be about 55 miles behind the enemy lines, so don't expect any help until about two or three days later.

"'I am going on the plane with the first two squads (about 18 jumpers in those days), but I am not going to jump first. Instead I am going to wait until all you guys are out, and I hope I don't have to kick anyone out of the plane.' (Actually, by jumping last, Walsh was putting himself in real jeopardy. Once we had crossed the water, we would be in German-occupied Europe and at risk of being shot down and/or disabled. Where you were seated in the plane had a great deal to do with your chance of getting out of the plane successfully, and Walsh knew this better than most.)

"He continued, 'Remember, we are going to be by ourselves for two or three days and you are going to have to carry enough food, water, and ammo to support yourselves at least that long. Each platoon will draw down a bazooka and five rounds of ammo.' (The bazooka was a fairly crude anti-tank rocket, which could be fired by one man. It was our only defense against tanks, which could literally destroy an airborne operation if they were on, or in, the vicinity of the drop zone).

"The veterans, who knew exactly what we were getting into, quietly went about their business, checking their equipment and writing that oft-delayed note to mom and dad or the girl friend. But a few were still making a lot of noise abetted by the bad whiskey smuggled into camp. It was late and raining hard when I finally turned in, and I could not sleep."[19]

Second Lieutenant Hanz K. Druener, a replacement officer, had recently joined the 2nd Platoon of D Company as assistant platoon leader: "I was somewhat anxious, not having been in combat before. However, training with my platoon, which included many troopers and non-commissioned officers who had participated in combat jumps, made us look forward to the operation. Some of the combat-experienced personnel mentioned that previous combat had been conducted at night. However, they felt that our superior air cover would keep German fighters out of the sky."[20]

Some veterans, like Sgt. Charles L. Peers of C Company and S.Sgt. Ernest W. Parks of D Company, still recuperating from wounds received at Anzio, would rejoin the regiment too late to participate. Others, like 1st Lt. Louis A. Hauptfleisch, had "mixed feelings since a daylight operation presumably offered greater assurance of on-target delivery as opposed to a night-time operation, but it also meant we were more vulnerable targets for enemy ground fire and air attack. However, most of us felt that the 'powers that be' would always in their infinite wisdom select the best circumstances for our operations. A good army lives on rumors—mostly encouraging—and yes, we believed that with a successful effort on our part, the war conceivably could be over by the following Christmas."[21]

Even though a lot of officers questioned the credibility of the promise that the war would soon end, they were looking forward to a daylight jump. "After two night jumps, Sicily and Salerno, especially the foul-up in Sicily, I—and most of the old-timers—preferred a day jump," recalled Captain Ferguson of the 3rd Battalion. "By then, we didn't have too much confidence in the Air Corps dropping us at night in the right location. We heard some talk, or had been told, that if the Holland invasion was successful the war would be over by winter, but no one paid any attention to it. Our thoughts were of today, *NOW*, not tomorrow or next winter. The old veterans had learned long before not to think too much of the future, but to live each day, one at a time. Winter was an eternity away and our thoughts were on staying alive and doing our job, *now*."[22]

A few officers, like the captain of E Company, Walter S. Van Poyck, were not looking forward to another combat mission: "I had a strong premonition I wasn't going to make it back. My battalion was given the mission of dropping one rifle company south of the Maas to secure the south end of the Grave Bridge and to establish a roadblock on the road south of Grave leading to Eindhoven. The remainder of the regiment was to drop east of the Maas.

"Our battalion commander, Ed Wellems, called us three rifle company commanders together, and we drew lots for the mission. I lost, and my company, Easy, was tapped for the job. On the surface, it looked like a very sticky one.

"After the Sicily and Salerno night drops, I personally welcomed a daytime drop. I knew we would be more vulnerable to ground fire, but I felt the control and assembly advantages in daytime outweighed this. My basic fear was of jumping too late, landing in the Maas or too close to the bridge to allow mobility of deployment for our two-fold mission. My men hoped this would be our last mission. I personally felt that the war could end by winter."[23]

One of Van Poyck's junior officers, Lt. Carl Mauro, 1st Platoon, differently recalls how E Company got its mission: "The 2nd Battalion of the 504th had the necessary experience, outstanding reputation and war record, and it was selected to provide one of its companies to take what Tucker called the 'suicide' assignment: jumping alone south of the Maas River only several miles from the small city of Grave. It was decided that either Company E or Company F would be selected.

"Which would it be? Captain Van Poyck commanded E Company and Captain Richardson commanded F Company; both were courageous and experienced leaders. The choice would be decided by the flip of a coin. We officers and men were crowded about the two company commanders, eager to learn who would get the 'suicide' mission. Van Poyck flipped the coin and Richardson made the call: Richardson won the flip and could have the mission for his raucous company. Surprisingly, he said, 'You take it, Van!' Richardson didn't want the special mission. And without hesitation or another word, Van Poyck replied, 'I'll take it!' The guys in E Company, my company, sent up a thunderous howl. We had lost the flip but won what everyone was now calling the most difficult and dramatic assignment, or so it seemed, of Market Garden. Was this genuine bravado display or simple airborne braggadocio?

"I have often wondered why Captain Richardson could win the toss of the coin, that night of September 16, 1944, and then decline the special mission. That was not paratrooper style! Had he accepted the challenge, I am certain that men from F Company would have cheered as loudly and lustily as did the men from E Company. However, F Company would jump, the next day, on the north side of the Maas River with the 504th (less E Company) on one of the three 82nd drop zones and be responsible for taking the north side of the long Grave Bridge: the 505th and 508th regimental drop zones were a few miles further east and north, only a mile from the German border.

"As soon as word of the coin toss got around the airfield, many of our friends came over to shake hands, congratulate and wish us the best of luck. 'Hey!' I said, 'aren't we all going to the same place tomorrow?' 'Not exactly,' was the reply everyone had for us."[24]

Another E Company officer, 1st Lt. John S. Thompson, recalled that when several 2nd Battalion officers and men first got word of Operation Market Garden, they figured it "to be just another trip to the airport, with a good possibility of being called off at the last minute. The men were getting used to the delays and cancellations, but at the same time were getting itchy to go on another mission."

But the more he learned about the details, the more Thompson started to look forward to the mission: "This was to be an ideal airborne operation, and perfect for the 82nd Division. We were to jump 57 miles behind enemy lines in the vicinity of Grave, Holland, seize and hold the Grave Bridge, also seize and hold Bridges 7 and 8 [and 9 and 10] over the Maas-Waal Canal, and capture the longest span bridge in Europe over the Waal River, located at Nijmegen. The mission, when completed, would give the British tanks a clear path to the Zuyder Zee and provide Allied forces a left flank sweep around the Siegfried Line defences. What a wonderful mission, and this one was soon to become a reality. […]

"Now we really went to work—all gear was made in readiness, checked and double-checked. Maps were issued and gone over in detail, sand tables erected with scale models, and the terrain surrounding the area where we were to jump was gone over with every man. Of course the focal point was the Grave Bridge.

"E Company, which was the only part of the 82nd scheduled to jump south of the Maas River, was to drop about 1500 yards southwest of the river and bridge, move out under a prearranged plan, capture and hold the southern approaches to the Grave Bridge. The 3rd Platoon, of which I was platoon leader, was to be on the left flank, moving along the bank of the river and canals. We were to knock out any enemy resistance on the west side of the bridge entrance and hold what ground we could seize. There were flak towers on each side of the south entrance to the bridge and anti-aircraft emplacement spotted at strategic points along the banks of the road leading to the bridge.

"The little town of Grave was to be our beacon on staging our jump. This beautiful little town would be easy to spot because it was completely surrounded by an extremely high wall of fir trees. The men in my platoon were ready and eager to go, and I know they realized that this jump would be a little more personal in scope than any before. We had gone over each detail with the men many times."[25]

PFC Willard M. Strunk of the 2nd Platoon in A Company recalled that "we were told on September 15 but did not leave till September 17. It was getting awful boring sitting in one spot. So any change was welcome. Training every day and garrison life was getting awful monotonous. The first reaction to a daylight jump was—the Germans will have us as sitting targets, and to hold that many bridges and take them during daylight hours is going to be rough. I don't think we had thoughts of ending the war by winter, but that it was going to be a long, hard battle and edging closer to Berlin."[26]

September 16 was spent checking equipment, drawing ammunition and preparing for take-off the next morning. Chutes and equipment bundles were taken to the airplanes by Service Company and everyone went to bed early, since the next night could be spent in a muddy foxhole.

S.Sgt David Rosenkrantz from H Company in Evington,
1944. He was killed at the Heuvelhof Farm during
the German counterattack on September 28. His body
is still missing to this day *(Courtesy: Phil Rosenkrantz)*

CHAPTER 3

DROP ZONE "O"
OVERASSELT, SEPTEMBER 17, 1944

Two teams of pathfinders of 12 men each would precede the serials transporting the 504th PIR to drop zone "O" at Overasselt. First Lieutenant G. Wilfred Jaubert, the 2nd Battalion S-2 officer, was placed in overall command and led Team 1, while 1st Lt. Horace V. Carlock of C Company commanded Team 2. They received their final pathfinder briefing at 0830 hours on September 17 and were then transported to their assigned planes. Lieutenant Jaubert and his men had not participated in the Normandy invasion because they had been kept in reserve. Their mission now was to set up radar navigational aids and lay out panel markings to mark the drop zone with a large "T" and indicate the wind direction with smoke pots. At 1313 hours the first serial, carrying the 3rd Battalion, would reach the drop zone. The 1st and 2nd Battalion serials would follow in two-minute intervals, respectively, at 1315 and 1317 hours. Other regimental units were equally dispersed among the three serials.

At 1025 hours the pathfinder teams departed in two aircraft from Chalgrove Airfield. Coursing east to France, they then turned left and flew over the front lines in Belgium to their destination. The paratroopers received flak from a flak tower and a mobile 20mm flak wagon near the Grave Bridge as they leapt out of the door at 1245 hours. Accompanying P-47 fighter planes quickly dove down and neutralized the northern flak tower and the 20mm flak wagon. Lieutenant Carlock closely watched for the first man in Lieutenant Jaubert's stick to jump, and jumped simultaneously with his team. Both teams came down together—a far cry from the Normandy invasion—in farmer Lucassen's meadow between the De Hut and Gaasselt farms. Lieutenant Jaubert's team set up all their navigational elements and Lieutenant Carlock's men provided security.

At exactly 1300 hours the first serial of the 505th PIR came over on their way to DZ "N" near Groesbeek. Thirteen minutes later the first serial of Tucker's troopers came down. Lieutenant Colonel Williams found the flight a "very good trip. It was most comforting to see the size of the airborne armada and the fighter protection. As we passed over the Dutch countryside, I saw a number of German soldiers ducking into houses or frantically riding down the street on bicycles. Where there were no German soldiers, the civilians waved. A C-47 close behind us was hit by anti-aircraft fire and burning. We counted the troops as they jumped and were relieved to see two separate parachutes follow the string of jumpers."[27]

The C-47 he had spotted going down was carrying a stick of 1st Platoon, H Company. Their ordeal will be described in the following chapter. Pvt. James S. Wells, Headquarters Company, who also saw the plane going down, described the flight in a November 1944 letter to his parents: "When we boarded our transport planes, I felt like there were thousands of little butterflies in my stomach. I had what seemed like a thousand pounds strapped on here and there. Over the coast of Holland everything looked so peaceful and quiet down there that you wouldn't think a war was really going on. Then Jerry opened up with his ack-ack. We were lucky in our plane—didn't catch a bit of it. Finally those familiar words came to my ear, 'Stand up and hook up!'

"All sense of everything seemed to leave me. After checking our equipment, we heard another familiar word, 'Go!' We went. On the ground, I gathered my belongings and started for our objective, and in a hurry, too. Jerry has a habit of finding where you are. After meeting a few of the boys and quickly deciding which way to go, we headed for our objective, an important bridge.

"After ducking a few bullets and returning some, we took the bridge. We stayed there for a couple of days. My buddy and I were on an outpost, 300 or 400 yards in front of the lines. Our job was to let no one sneak up and try to run the company out of their position or blow up boats that might come up the canal. We spotted a house 200 yards away and decided to investigate. There were some very nice people there and a priest who spoke English. They invited us to have some fresh eggs and fresh milk, which we didn't refuse."[28]

Pvt. Nicholas W. Mansolillo, 1st Battalion Mortar Platoon, remembers: "because of our positions we stayed in our seats, so we carried on individual conversations, five- to six-man groups. There were 18 men in our plane, 17 enlisted and one officer. One conversation was that this was a British operation and we would be under their command, and they would be our source of resupply, excluding ammo. We would be eating their food, smoking their cigarettes and maybe wearing their uniforms if we needed them. We joked about this.

"As we talked on, time went by. The cockpit door opened. One of the plane crew said, 'We are now approaching the coast of Holland.' When we turned to look out the windows, all we could see were big patches of water as we flew onto the main land. Then someone said the Germans must have flooded all the canals when they found out we were on our way."[29]

Mansolillo became worried when "the pilot of our plane said just before take-off that our stick was going to land very close to the bank of the Maas, and if there was any delay going out the door, or a break in the flight formation, some of us might end up in the river. Being number 16 in the stick of 18, I was very much concerned. Remembering past experiences of the Sicily jump, I started to make plans to prevent myself from being a likely candidate to end up in the river. I thought of leaving some of my gear behind in the plane, but it seemed that I needed everything.

"Under the conditions and circumstances, I came to one conclusion: I would take off my reserve, leave it in the plane and mention it to no one, for if word got to our mortar officer, who was sitting by the jump door, he would order me to leave it on regardless of my plans. There was a standing order— we had been told from our first jumps at Fort Benning that the reserve would be worn at all times; disobeying would subject us to court-martial. And here I was, going against regulations on a combat mission. I made up my mind to take that risk.

"As I headed for Dutch soil, my reserve was headed back to England. Our entire stick landed on solid, dry land a good distance from the river. I was sure happy and relieved it happened this way, for I sure had my doubts about making it in a river landing."[30]

Cpl. Fred J. Baldino, 2nd Platoon, A Company, was impressed by the scenery: "I remember how neat the farms and buildings were and how most of the houses seemed to be neatly whitewashed. The Dutch Underground was immensely helpful when and after we landed. I was surprised at how many of the Dutch spoke some English. The Underground was in touch with our officers and gave them much information, from what I gathered."[31]

Private Fay T. Steger of the same platoon, who flew in a different C-47, wrote down his detailed memories of the last preparations at Cottesmore and the flight across the Channel: "Our plane into Holland was a split load, which I didn't like to start with. I was always partial to the 2nd Platoon of A Company and would have felt better had the plane been all 2nd Platoon men. This trip was for keeps and it was also a good distance over enemy territory. I just knew those enemy flak guns were going to get real busy when they spotted us. At a time like this, you seem to think of all the things that could go wrong. Maybe our plane would be shot down somewhere over Holland. Maybe somewhere in Holland our planeload of paratroopers would make a last-ditch stand, surrounded by Germans—cut off from any source of medical supplies.

"If that time came, I wanted to be with 2nd Platoon men, men I knew and trusted when the chips were down. Men like Baldino, Snead, Isom, Starling, Gibson, Clark, Sebastian and the others. You don't worry about men like them. No matter what the objective, when the smoke cleared away, they would be there. I had never known them to give the enemy one inch of ground.

"It was always move up—maybe only three yards or from boulder to boulder or one ditch to another—but always move up a little bit closer to Berlin. Today we were really going to move up; it was us or them. It was strike and hold, or die. There could be no retreat; there was no place to retreat to. Each and every man realized this and would fight like a demon.

"Each plane would carry six equipment bundles underneath the fuselage. Each contained about 300 pounds of extra ammunition or hand grenades, bazookas, mortar shells, TNT, etc. Each had its own colored chute to designate its contents. We rolled our equipment bundles, checked them good and hooked them up underneath the plane.

"There wasn't anything in these bundles that wouldn't explode if some German gunner happened to plant one lucky shot between them. Seventeen paratroopers, a C-47 crew and a C-47 were going to end up in one blinding flash and then come down in little pieces. It would be a hard way to die, and it didn't seem fair because we wouldn't be taking any Germans along. Besides that, the German gunner would probably get an Iron Cross from Hitler himself. The crew chief would trip these equipment bundles when the seventh man left the door.

"Equipment bundles are dangerous, especially for the seventh man, because he is close when they are released. There is no control over them and they can swing into your chute and foul it. If a man is hit with a swinging bundle, it's like being hit by a 300 lb. ramrod. It will snap his back like a matchstick and he will die in mid air. I have seen troopers get tangled with bundles and ride them to the ground without a scratch. It is all in your luck at the time.

"I can't remember which company the balance of our plane load was, but I think it was Headquarters Company. They had a lieutenant in charge and he had decided his men would jump behind the A Company men. Sgt. [Vannas C.] Smith was to be our lead man. We lined up in the order we were going to jump and I came up as number-six man and Clark drew number seven. I told him to quit bitching. He wasn't in the Girl Scouts, and if an equipment bundle didn't kill him the Germans probably would. Besides, that nice little English girl he had at Leicester could always find another GI—there would still be plenty of them in England after we were gone. By this time he had a personality about like a barracuda. He wasn't taking the rib very well, so I laid off.

"About this time the lieutenant must have started to think about the flak we were going to have over Holland. Instead of jumping with his own men, he decided to move up and jump behind Sergeant Smith as the number-two man. This moved everybody back one man and made me number seven. Right away I got mad and said to Clark, 'Sure, that damn lieutenant wants to be close to the door so he can get out real quick if we get hit and the plane gets on fire. Why in hell didn't some German shoot him at Anzio? That's the whole trouble with this army—we got too damn many lieutenants. Besides, we can win this war without him.' Clark thought it was real funny. He said, 'Quit your moaning. If the bundles don't get you, the Germans will. No use of you being so fussy.'

"About this time the crew chief came along. He had a flak vest with him and the guys said, 'What are you doing with that flak vest?' He said, 'I had my choice: parachute or flak suit.' Somebody said, 'Boy, you must have rocks in your head. You're not going to look very bright sitting up there with a flak suit on when the plane gets one wing shot off. That flak suit is not going to float very well. You had better go back and draw a chute.' But he wouldn't.

"About this time the pilot and co-pilot came along and I noticed they each wore a pistol belt with an army .45 on one hip and a canteen of water on the other. We were not used to seeing pilots wear side arms and I thought to myself, 'This ain't going to be a milk run.' Somebody said, 'Come on, you guys. What do you want to do? Die in bed?' And we climbed aboard.

"The engines coughed a little smoke and he had them running. We taxied out and took off. The sun was shining bright. It was a beautiful day and the green fields of England below were more beautiful than ever. Why would anyone want to leave such a wonderful place as this? Those damn stupid Germans! Why did they have to go and start a war for in the first place?

"Nobody spoke in the C-47. With the door off you have to yell at the top of your lungs to be heard above the engine's roar. I think each man was busy with his own thoughts and memories. Time was growing short. I looked down at England and wondered if I would ever return. I had many a good time in England. It seemed like living in the Waldorf Astoria after the mud of Anzio. I looked at the bright sun above and wondered if I would live to see it go down that night.

"My glance wondered over to the crew chief in his flak suit sitting by the door. I thought, 'How stupid can a man get?' Sergeant Smith sat right across from the door. Here was a soldier who knew his job well. He was always coolheaded in a firefight, always one trick ahead of the Germans. He had the respect of his men and he had earned it. It was good he came along. Next came the lieutenant. I cursed him again under my breath and wished the Germans had shot him at Anzio.

"The coast of England disappeared behind us and we were over the Channel. The fighter escorts joined our armada of slow-moving C-47s. I can't remember for sure, but I believe the P-47 fighters were below us and the P-51's above. We were sandwiched between them like a slice of cold meat between two pieces of bread. The noise was beyond imagination now. The fighter planes flew in a circle to keep pace with the slow-moving C-47s. A fighter would zoom under us and about the same time another would roar over us. The roar of their engines added to the roar of our own, and with no door on, made a noise I shall never forget.

"The Holland coast was beginning to appear and seemed to be coming up fast. I guessed it was because we were flying so low. Now we were straight above the Holland coast. Below I could see the barbwire entanglement held with those tall, sharp stakes. To be impaled on one of those was not a pleasant thought. We met the Holland coast and the German flak at the same time. Dead ahead a few hundred yards I could see the flak burst with those puffs of white smoke. The flak seemed to be just about on a line with us and I thought, 'Man, it didn't take the Germans long to get our altitude. Now all they have to do is keep firing.'

"At this point we were looking right down their gun barrels and every time they fired, they winked at you with a red flash of fire. I thought about the 1800 pounds of explosives just below our feet and the wing span of a C-47. How could they miss? To our left was a C-47 towing a glider. I saw the shell burst about halfway between them. It cut the tow rope. The C-47 went straight ahead, but the glider's nose dipped down. He banked toward us and disappeared toward the Channel.

"The house below us was a two-story with a dormer on our side. The Germans had two ack-ack guns in there and a steady stream of fire came out of both windows. One of our fighters spotted their guns. He peeled off and dove in with his guns blazing. I could see his tracer bullets tearing shingles off the dormer. We heard no more from the Germans in the bedroom.

"A little farther to our left the Germans had a tugboat in what happened to be a small harbor. They must have had eight guns on it, and they were throwing everything at us but their helmets. Another fighter peeled off and went after it like a hawk after a mouse. He made the dive and released a bomb that went through the air like a football. It took the tugboat dead center. There was a flash of fire and then black smoke. A few more Krauts had just died for the fatherland.

"We had a real seat for the show. It reminded me of sitting in the front row balcony of a theater. We were looking down with nothing to obstruct our view. 'Those flyboys are gonna earn their pay today,' I thought. We were getting inland now and the flak let up. I could see the Hollanders below us waving their hats and handkerchiefs. They seemed to be cheering us on. I thought about the nice new invasion currency we had been issued and wondered if a lone trooper could pay them to hide him and bring him food in case he was lost or separated from the main body. Or would they turn him over to the Germans, probably to be shot on the spot? I knew the German High Command didn't have much love for the 82nd— not after Sicily, Italy, Anzio, Normandy and now Holland. We had been a rock in the German black boot for quite a while now, and no doubt they were getting a little tired of us.

"Our Catholic chaplain, Captain [Edwin J.] Kozak, who was really a great guy, had given us Holy Communion that morning just before we took off from England. I thought about this and made my peace with the Lord. I didn't want to die, but if I must, I was as ready now as I would ever be. I said to the Lord, 'I put my life in your hands. Thy will be done.'

"We were getting near the DZ now and the red light went on. Sergeant Smith stood up and gave the order to stand up and hook up. His words were coated with ice or cold steel, I don't know which, but you could tell he meant what he said. We all hooked our static lines on the cable and Sergeant Smith stepped in the door. He was watching the ground real close and I knew he was looking for some object that would tell him we were over the DZ.

"I was watching the ground through the window from a standing position and could see this German ambulance (we always called them 'meat wagons') on the road just below us. I thought then, 'We won't have to go very far to find the Germans. Maybe we will land right in their position.'"[32]

At exactly 1315 hours the green lights flashed on in the C-47s in serial A-9 as they arrived above DZ "Oboe" northwest of the village of Overasselt. Another campaign was to start for A Company. Steger continues his story: "I watched Sergeant Smith real close now. He stood in the door, his left foot two or three inches outside the plane, his hand on the edges of the door to give himself that pull. His jaw was set, not a muscle in his face moved. He looked like a man carved out of stone. I thought to myself, 'he can whip ten Krauts.' By this time my nerves were as tight as the E string on a violin and I was anxious to go.

"I felt the plane slow as the pilot feathered the engines. The green light came on and Sergeant Smith was gone. The men moved out real fast, as they always did, and in less than two seconds I was in the door. I will never know for sure what happened. Maybe I slipped or lost my balance or maybe the pilot wiggled the tail of that C-47 just as I came to the door. But for some reason, I fell down in the door. We were trained to get out fast because at 95 or 100 miles an hour, the faster they jump the closer they will be together on the ground.

"My mind was working fast and clear. I thought, 'Why waste the time to stand up?' I dove out head first and I also thought about the crew chief tripping those equipment bundles. I was going for the ground head first and I knew what was going to happen when that chute opened. Me and all that equipment—rifle, helmet, pack, trench knife, .45 pistol, hand grenades, bayonet, reserve chute, first-aid kit, rifle ammunition, pistol ammunition, rations and canteen of water—were going to turn around in one split second. WHAP! She opened and now I was feet first. […]

"The sky was full of chutes, like leaves coming down in autumn. I could see the equipment bundles with their bright-colored chutes of blue, orange, green, and other colors. They were below me so I could forget about them. In the plane next to ours they lost one man on the way down. An equipment bundle broke his back in the air."[33]

The man who was hit by an equipment bundle was Pvt. Max D.

Edmondson, 1st Platoon, A Company. Shortly after Fay Steger saw Private Edmondson being fatally hit, he witnessed C-47 42-100517, which had just delivered B Company paratroopers, going down: "The planes flew straight for a little ways after we jumped and then banked into a right turn. The Krauts had zeroed in on this turn and I could see the flak bursts in the air. Two C-47s started the turn. One must have taken a direct hit. The whole left wing exploded and he headed for the ground. I wondered if it was the plane we had just left and thought about the crew chief with his flak suit on. I watched for chutes, but none blossomed in the air. We had just lost a crew of good soldiers. The price of freedom had always been high.

"I looked to the ground. It looked soft and level. I couldn't see any Krauts. There was a small house below and I was going to come in pretty close to it. If there were Krauts in it, I knew they were going to blast us before we could get out of our chutes. I didn't see any German panzers in the area and this was a great relief. I was floating down to earth, armed to the teeth—virtually a one-man army, a beautiful target for the Krauts, and I had the feeling of being as helpless as a day-old baby.

"I wanted to get on the ground, get out of that chute and get my finger on the trigger of that M-1 rifle. I started to curse the pilot: 'Those dumb pilots can't tell a foot from a yard. They must have come in at 5,000 feet instead of 500.' I knew better. I knew they were low when we stood to jump, but I cursed them anyhow. It seemed as if I had been up there all morning.

"I heard a couple of Kraut machine guns bark, a sound I knew all too well. I could tell they were quite a distance away. There was no reason to worry about them at this point. There were men and chutes on the ground below. The ground was coming up fast. There were no Krauts in that house, because if there were they would be firing by now.

"I came in real nice. My knees buckled and I was in Holland. I rolled over on my back and started to unfasten the chute harness. BROOM! A burst of automatic rifle fire came across the DZ. It crossed my mind that there *were* Krauts in that house, and we were gonna have it out right then. But it was one of our own boys, who had hit the ground with a BAR [Browning Automatic Rifle] in his hands and the safety off. He sent one good burst across the DZ but never hit anybody."[34]

Sgt. Albert Clark remembered: "It was a nice day and we got a beautiful view of England as we flew over. The English Channel was quite calm and things were really nice until we came on a flak barge that started shooting at us. It seemed like out of nowhere two P-47s appeared and dropped two bombs. The first one hit and the barge seemed to jump out of the water. The second just disintegrated the barge and that was the end of it. This happened while we were flying over the Dutch Low Lands that the Germans had flooded. As we got closer to our destination, we could hear flak, but it didn't seem to be very close.

"This was our first daylight jump and things looked beautiful and peaceful. We soon enough got the green light and were out of the planes. Our DZ was a nice, sandy sugar beet field, and it was a very soft landing.

"I started to join the rest of the platoon. I had gone a short distance when it felt like something was crawling on my right cheek. I thought that I wiped it off, but a little later I felt it again and when I put my hand up, it was covered with blood.

"When I rejoined the rest everybody asked what had happened. Did I get hit with some shrapnel? I said no, that there wasn't any flak that close to us. When my cheek was finally cleaned off, a very tiny puncture was found in my cheek just below the eye. Since I had jumped with my Tommy gun in my hands, it had come up and the front sight had hit me in the cheek—the front sight being very small."[35]

Private Steger recalled that the paratroopers were not allowed to cut pieces out of their parachute after they had landed: "The day before in England when we had drawn our chutes, we had been given quite a speech. The troopers were known for cutting a chunk out of their chutes to save for a souvenir. The lieutenant said there was to be no more of this. Those chutes cost the taxpayers lots of money and they didn't want them cut up. Any man caught cutting a chute would sign a statement of charges for about $300 to be taken from his army pay. I wanted a piece of that chute real bad and I thought, 'To hell with the lieutenant and his speeches, to hell with the taxpayers and to hell with the $300.' I took out my jump knife and cut out a bottom panel and stuffed it in a side pocket alongside a grenade. (I still have this parachute panel and jump knife and also the invasion money, and have never regretted what it cost the taxpayers.)

"Somebody on the other side of the DZ was hollering, 'Move up, you guys! Over here! Don't you know there's a war going on?' A column was moving out in single file and I fell in line. I could hear rifle fire up ahead. I felt pretty good now. I was on the ground, rifle in hand, and things were going according to plan. I had that mischievous feeling of a boy in the neighbors' apple tree when the neighbors are on vacation."[36]

Pvt. Edwin M. Clements, 1st Platoon, B Company, awoke "from an uneasy sleep feeling queasy. Breakfast was out of the question, but I did gulp down a large GI coffee and a piece of bread."When the troopers finally began to enplane, he remembers loads so "heavy and cumbersome, almost all of us needed some help in boarding" by the crew chief. After "another interminable wait […] in a long line of C-47s […] take-off began with the familiar roar of the two engines. We began to move slowly down the runway, and I said a special 'Hail Mary,' because take-off in a fully loaded C-47 was always critical."

Private Clements also recalls the astounding noise level, which "increased 100 percent" when the jump door was finally opened after crossing the North Sea. "Since we could now be getting ground fire, including anti-aircraft, the doors were opened in case we got hit. At least there was a chance that if the plane was disabled, some or all the jumpers could get out.

"Every now and then I would peek out the tiny porthole windows. The first thing I saw were P-51 fighters—a lot of them—swerving in and out of the formation attacking anti-aircraft towers. We began taking evasive action, changing our heading slightly, in order to avoid the flak bursts, which appeared as pleasant little powder puffs. When they exploded nearby, the plane shook and vibrated badly. At one point, a plane near us, but not in the same formation, was hit, began smoking, and started down. It held a fairly steady course, enabling most of the jumpers to get out, but I only saw part of the jump. By that time, we were over the flooded lowlands of Holland, which guaranteed a much greater chance of survival than the ocean. Ironically, that plane carried the only paratrooper I knew whom I had trained with in Demolition School and had traveled overseas with, Cpl. Lawrence DeMont. I hadn't seen him since he was assigned to another battalion. He landed safely in shallow water, was quickly captured, and spent the rest of the war in a German prison camp."

As the familiar commands to stand up and hook up began, Private Clements's plane did not slow down and lose altitude as it normally would on approaching a drop zone, but instead "seemed to be increasing speed. The plane was pitching and yawing. It was becoming very difficult to keep from falling. The plane was taking evasive action, and was still searching for a heading that would take us to the proper drop zone. Finally, the last command but one was given, 'Stand in the door!'

"We shuffled forward, anxious as always to get out of the airplane. I was carrying my rifle at port arms and I wanted to make sure not to get it caught in the door. 'Go!' Stumbling, lurching, trying desperately to stay close to the jumper immediately ahead of me, I finally reached the door and dived out. I realized immediately on the opening shock that I had jumped at the highest speed and lowest altitude ever. I swung under the canopy maybe twice before I hit the ground. Fortunately, it was a plowed sugar beet field and it only took seconds for me to realize that all my limbs were intact."[37]

This was also the first combat jump for the 1st Battalion surgeon, Captain Bruns: "Although it was pretty dumb, I jumped with a bottle of bourbon strapped to my chest and happened to land in the DZ beside a radar pathfinder man in the 504th. I was scrambling to get out of my chute when I heard him say, 'Take it easy.' So I did. To my surprise I was close to a large farmhouse, where I later established an aid station."[38]

While many men remembered the time on the tarmac as a seemingly interminable wait, for Private First Class Finney, a radio operator in Headquarters and Headquarters Company, it passed swiftly, and almost as a dream. At Spanhoe Airport, "the tarmac was filled with C-47s lined up and ready to go. We put our packs on the ground and used them to lean against as we sat down, waiting to board our designated plane. I felt very good about this jump. Nothing seemed to bother me. We were told our DZ was to be at Grave, Holland, were briefed on what to do on landing, and told, 'Let's go!' Then we were on our feet, putting on our parachute and attaching the reserve chute to the harness. We slowly walked to the plane and were boosted up the ladder to the door. Time moved swiftly—it seemed only seconds when first one engine started then the other one coughed and came to life. The vibration from the speeding propellers gave me a sense of purpose. There was a smell of burning gasoline from the blue-white smoke filling the air outside the cabin. The pilot pushed the throttle slowly forward and the plane began rolling down the runway and came to a stop, waiting for the signal to take to the air.

"When we started rolling again the sound of the engine seemed more angry and ready. We bumped several times as we sped along the runway gaining speed. We felt the wheels leave the runway, the bumping stopped and we were on our way. The sunlight sparkled on the water as we crossed the English Channel. Time seemed to be fleeting by. The captain of the plane told us over the speaker that we were nearing the dikes of Holland. Many had been destroyed by the Germans in an attempt to delay any attempts of invasion. Miles of terrain were flooded as water rushed over the low land. A plane near us was hit and began smoking as it started to go down. We counted the parachutes as the men left the plane. All of the paratroopers made it out, but did they survive the watery landing?

"Our plane veered to another direction and then continued back to the same direction as before. We noticed several windmills sitting on little pieces of land. The flood from the broken dikes became less evident and then finally the higher land was beneath us." After Finney went out the door, land loomed up almost immediately. "I was coming down towards a group of trees and began climbing on my risers in hopes of avoiding this, but luck was not with me. I kept my legs crossed as the branches began rushing across my body and passed by my head. There was a sudden tug on one of my risers as it tangled on a limb and stopped my fall. Six more feet and I would have touched the ground. I hit the quick release on my harness and slid to the ground.

"With my rifle in hand, I was starting to leave when someone yelled for help. Looking around I noticed another trooper dangling from another tree. I told him to hit the quick release. It was obstructed by equipment attached to his body. He was lucky it did not release him during the jump. I tossed my knife up to him and told him to cut his risers. He cut himself loose and I grabbed his legs and lowered him to the ground. I noticed he was a 2nd lieutenant, as he had not removed the bars from his helmet. He asked me where I was headed because he wasn't sure which way to go. I told him I was to meet up with the men from my squad northeast of where we landed: 'You can go with me if you want to,' the lieutenant said. I left quickly to join up with the others from Headquarters Company."[39]

Lieutenant Colonel Williams recalled that "the Dutch civilians were delighted to see the Americans. They formed work parties to help us assemble and move equipment from our supply bundles and resupply drops. The house next door to the 504th Command Post was converted into a temporary hospital and Dutch women assembled voluntarily to help care for casualties.

"Approximately four hours after the drop, two Dutch women came into the CP [command post] with soup and boiled eggs for the staff. They said they did not have much to provide, but they were sure we didn't have time to cook lunch and they did not want us to go hungry."[40]

Lieutenant Hauptfleisch, the regimental adjutant, found the flight "basically uneventful except for scattered flak. [...] As the last man to drop from my plane, I unfortunately landed on top of a building in the village of Overasselt south of Nijmegen. I crashed through the tiled roof top and suffered leg injuries, but managed to carry out my assigned duties."[41] For Cpl. George D. Graves, Jr., Regimental S-1 section, "The flight in from the coast was 'interesting' but not too bad. I bailed out over a dense wood and made my first tree landing in over two years of parachuting. I was lucky enough to escape without a scratch."[42]

The daylight drop turned out to be successful for the 1st Battalion: out of 612 officers and men who jumped above DZ "O" at Overasselt, two men were killed and ten were injured or wounded during the drop. For the three planes of Headquarters and Headquarters Company that were part of this serial, three men out of 51 were injured or wounded.

CHAPTER 4

CAPTAIN BOHANNAN'S LAST
FLIGHT: HEIJNINGEN, OVERASSELT,
GRAVE BRIDGE, SEPTEMBER 17, 1944

M ajor Cook's 3rd Battalion would perform a supporting role within the 504th RCT, being responsible for patrolling to the west, north, east and south of Overasselt. Capt. Carl W. Kappel of H Company recalled that "the 3rd Battalion plan of attack was to drop east of Overasselt on Drop Zone "O," and organize and assemble in the nearby wooded area in SOP [Standard Operation Procedure] perimeter assembly: Battalion Command Post in the center; Headquarters Company 300 yards north; G Company 300 yards south; I Company 300 yards east, and H Company 300 yards west. G Company was to block all enemy movement on the Grave-Nijmegen highway with roadblocks at Lunen and Alverna. I Company was to clear the enemy from their portion of the battalion sector from [the small lake] East Wychensche Ven, establish roadblocks at Diervoort and contact 1st Battalion in the vicinity of Diervoort. H Company was to eliminate all enemy resistance in the drop zone, screen the assembly of the battalion, establish roadblocks at Mary's Hoeve and become the battalion reserve upon movement of G and I Companies to their assigned sector."[43]

The recollections of 2nd Lt. Ernest P. Murphy, assistant platoon leader of 3rd Platoon, H Company, resemble those of many other men in his battalion: in the C-47 heading to Holland, "some men laughed and joked, some smoked and some prayed silently—all to keep their courage up. The men who had been in combat before were quiet and reserved. They understood and knew what was going to happen in a very short time."[44]

Capt. Fred E. Thomas of G Company described a fairly uneventful flight in the company journal for September 17: "Up at 0630 and made prepara-

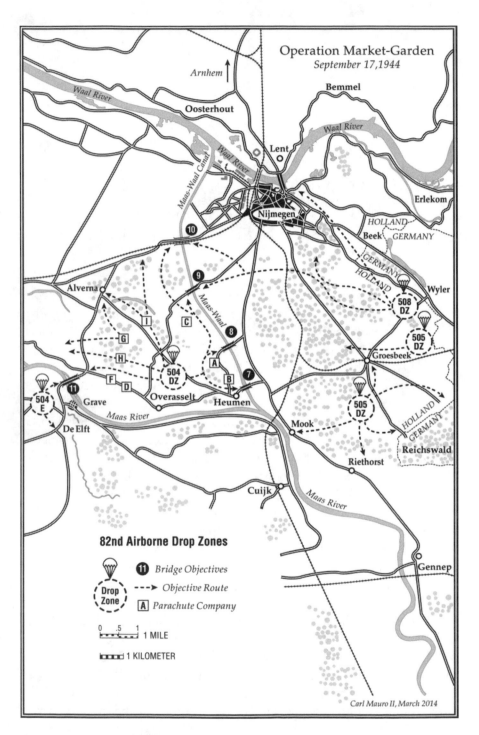

Operation Market-Garden
September 17, 1944

82nd Airborne Drop Zones

⑪ *Bridge Objectives*

Drop Zone   - - - → *Objective Route*

Ⓐ *Parachute Company*

0 .5 1   1 MILE

1 KILOMETER

Carl Mauro II, March 2014

tions to move out. Rumors have been going around that today is the day we take off to initiate the start of the fourth invasion that this unit has played an important part in since coming overseas about 15 months ago. Colonel Tucker assembled the men and officers and gave them a final talk regarding our mission. We secured all of our equipment and moved out to our planes by planeloads and emplaned at 0930 after short, last-minute briefings by the jumpmasters and pilots. At 1034 hours we took off and after circling the field several times in order to make up the formations we headed toward Holland.

"Our flight from Spanhoe airfield to the English Channel was uninterrupted, except as we neared the suburbs of London, several flights of other C-47s passed under us. We also noticed a large number of them towing gliders. We reached the coast of Holland about 1232 hours. The land below us was very flooded and only the higher level roads showed above the water. However, the impression that we had was that the water was not very deep."[45]

T/5 Seymour Flox, the senior medic in H Company, at first was almost jovial in a letter to his mother, although it turned a somber note in conclusion: "At the airport, after we were briefed, and we knew definitely it would be Holland, you would expect everyone to be on edge and sweating it out. But not this bunch of men. We were playing football and shooting crap for the invasion money we were given, and some of the fellows, after studying their maps, just went to sleep.

"We really got a number-one breakfast at the airport. It was pancakes, chicken, corn, potatoes, bread, cake and coffee. Then we got our chutes and got in the plane for a last-minute pep talk. On the way over we read magazines we had in our pockets and smoked and joked with each other. But it only took about nine seconds for all of us to get out once we got the go signal. Not one of the men got excited when the flak started, or vomited up the breakfast.

"We had a smooth ride over and encountered some flak over the flooded area in Holland. We were lucky and only had one plane shot down on the trip over, but one of my good friends was hurt pretty bad on that plane."[46]

Tragedy struck as the 3rd Battalion C-47 formation reached the coast of Holland. Black puffs from exploding German anti-aircraft fire appeared in the sky. Flying over the Dutch peninsula of Walcheren, the three bundles under the belly of *Bette*, the C-47 piloted by Capt. Richard E. Bohannan and 2nd Lt. Douglas H. Felber, 34th Troop Carrier Squadron, were hit by exploding flak fire. Captain Ferguson, 3rd Battalion executive officer, witnessed the event: "shortly afterwards, smoke was observed coming from equipment bundles attached beneath the C-47 flying to our rear. Yellow and red streamers of flame appeared in the inky black smoke."[47]

Besides the five-man crew, the plane carried 1st Lt. Isidore D. Rynkiewicz, assistant platoon leader; 12 of his men from H Company, 1st Platoon; and three men from the Regimental Demolition Platoon, Sgt. Earl V. Force, and PFCs Joseph A. Foley and John F. McAndrew. The demolitionists had been spread in pairs of two among the various sticks in order to have specialists at hand whenever needed. One of the equipment bundles thus contained Composition C, which required only a blasting cap to detonate. When an exploding flak grenade ignited the Composition C, 2nd Lt. Robert L. Cloen, co-piloting a C-47 on the right wing of the plane, broke radio silence and urged Captain Bohannan to release the bundles.

Bohannan had been awarded the Air Medal on July 16, 1943, for "his skill, courage and devotion to duty" during Operation Husky. He was an experienced pilot and graduate of the College of William and Mary in Williamsburg, Virginia, where he received his degree in 1941.[48] Most likely Bohannan and his co-pilot, 21-year-old Lieutenant Felber, finding it impossible to release the bundles, and realizing that the left engine and part of the fuselage were already on fire, noticed the flooded fields below and tried to dive down and extinguish the fire by landing in the water.

This was the first flight for one of the crew members, Sgt. Thomas N. Carter of Winston-Salem, North Carolina, who was sent to replace the usual crew chief when he had fallen ill. "Therefore I didn't know the crew," he testified. "I was standing back in the door and paratroopers were already hooked up as the airplane got on fire."[49] Meanwhile, another pilot took over Captain Bohannan's place as flight leader of the squadron's third element.

Wounded by shrapnel were jumpmaster 1st Lt. Rynkiewicz and PFCs Norman N. Handfield, Walter P. Leginski and Everett R. Ridout. Another trooper aboard, 18-year-old Pvt. George Willoughby, recalled: "After we got airborne and headed for the coast, I was so uncomfortable with all the equipment on that I got down on the floor of the plane and told a trooper next in a line, Ridout, I believe, to let me know when we crossed the Channel and reached land. I carried a land mine in my left leg jump suit pocket and a Gammon grenade in my left leg pocket; two fragmentation grenades in my jump jacket pockets, K-rations, a sniper rifle with ammo bag and 200-plus rounds of ammo, gas mask, pack and other items. I was awakened when we reached the coast across the Channel. I immediately got off the floor and sat in my seat across from the lieutenant and the door of the plane. I could see out. It was only a short time before I could hear the crack of small-arms fire and hear and see puffs of anti-aircraft gunfire.

"Shortly after, the plane started filling with smoke. As I looked across the plane I noticed that Lieutenant Rynkiewicz had been hit in the left knee and Handfield, the BAR man, was hit on the back of his hand. To my right, a trooper was on the floor of the plane. Again I think this was Ridout. I remember saying, 'Let's get the hell out of here!' and we started standing up."[50]

Private First Class Leginski sat on the left side of Lieutenant Rynkiewicz and Private First Class Ridout sat next to him. They were both hit by small shell fragments in the legs and buttocks, while Rynkiewicz was more seriously wounded. The plane began to fill with smoke and Leginski and Ridout asked Lieutenant Rynkiewicz if he didn't think it best for all to jump since the plane was on fire. Without replying, the lieutenant slumped forward in his seat, seemingly unconscious. Realizing their jumpmaster was no longer able to give the command to jump, they both hooked up and without further hesitation jumped out.[51] The crew chief, Sergeant Carter, stood near the door: "I jumped after two men had jumped out of the door," he later recalled. His task as crew chief had become redundant, and at first he could not believe that paratroopers were not exiting the plane as well.[52]

First Lieutenant Virgil F. Carmichael, the 3rd Battalion S-2 officer, watched as Bohannan's C-47 was hit and the three men jumped out: "As we were near Waalwijk [Heijningen] in Holland, I noticed a clump of trees just outside our plane and below it on the ground. We were flying at about four or five hundred feet elevation. This clump of trees contained a small area of high ground above the flood water. Just as our plane was opposite these trees, I saw a sudden burst of what appeared to be 20mm anti-aircraft fire that sprayed back to the rear. The fire was interspersed with tracers.

"Upon seeing this ground fire, I sprang to the door and watched the bullets strike a plane farther back in our formation. I counted the ships and estimated that it was in H Company, which later proved to be correct. Immediately after the gun fired, one of fighter planes covering our flight swooped down and placed him out of action. He only fired one burst. Our plane, hit in the equipment bundles underneath the ship, began trailing smoke and the equipment bundles burst into flames. I stood in the door and watched our men evacuate. Their parachutes were camouflage and the Air Corps chutes were white nylon. I counted the chutes as they left the plane and saw that after the camouflaged chutes, one white chute came out, which we figured to be the crew chief. Immediately after the white chute left the plane, the plane nosedived over and, apparently at full throttle, at about a 45 degree angle, plowed into the water, which flooded the land below. Upon impact, a white chute billowed out through the front of the plane."[53]

Private Willoughby recalled that after Sergeant Carter dove out the door "within seconds, the plane was so full of smoke you could not see anything. Some men near the cockpit started coughing and pushing for the door. [They may have been the navigator, 1st Lt. Bernard P. Martinson and the radio operator, S.Sgt. Arnold B. Epperson, which would explain the white chute that billowed out the front of the plane.] At that time, others and I fell through the floor of the plane. We were hooked up and when my chute opened, I could smell flesh and see the skin hanging from my face and hand. I had released my rifle when the flames burned my hands.

"I looked down and saw that only a small strip of land along the road was not flooded. I started working my chute to land near the road. When I landed, I rolled over and pulled my .45-caliber pistol from its holster and pointed it in the direction of a man near me. He put up his hands and shouted, 'Hollander!' I realized he was friendly, so I put my pistol back, got out of my chute and crossed the road to see if I could help any of the men who had landed in the water.

"I saw [Pvt.] Donald [F.] Woodstock had landed in water about waist deep. As he walked toward the bank where I was standing, he stepped off into a deep trench about four to six feet wide that was around the flooded area. He came up shouting a few choice words and I helped him to dry land. We took our packs off and placed them behind a small, empty house. We then started checking on the others. Everyone had done a good job landing on dry ground or near the edge of the flooded area."[54]

Floating beneath their blossomed parachutes, Leginski and Ridout came down from a higher altitude than the 13 paratroopers they saw fall through the floor of the plane. Trailing a lot of smoke, it suddenly went from a level flight into a deep dive and crashed some distance away. The crash killed the four remaining crew members: Captain Bohannan and Lieutenant Martinson and S.Sgt. Epperson. Martinson's body was found outside the plane, so he must have been blown out of the C-47 ready to jump—a chance he would never have. The sudden steep dive was most likely caused by the burnt control cables, which were located in the belly of the aircraft.

While Leginski and Ridout landed east of the town of Dintelloord, on the west side of the small Dintel River, the others came down in the flooded Heijningse Polder between the east bank of the river and the village of Heijningen. Both are in the west of the Province of Noord-Brabant, some 65 miles away from the drop zone at Overasselt. Ridout landed in a flooded field and Leginski came down some 50 yards away on dry ground. As they unsnapped their parachute harnesses, they could see the remainder of the stick coming down on the other side of the Dintel River.

The pair patched up each other's wounds as best as possible and hid their camouflage parachutes. Crawling along the irrigation ditches crisscrossing the field in an effort to move as far as possible away from their landing point, they spotted German staff cars and motorcycles racing up and down the road towards the next town, which they later learned was Heijningen. Approximately one mile farther on, they concealed themselves in the brush and decided to await nightfall.[55]

Back in Heijningen, Sergeant Carter "landed on top of a house and fell off the back."[56] He joined forces with Sergeant Force and Privates First Class Foley and McAndrew of the Regimental Demolition Platoon, Cpl's James C. Bailey and Lawrence J. DeMont, PFC William F. Stewart and Pvts. Roy M. Biggs (the platoon medic), Mark L. Kaplan, Richard C. Reardon, Willoughby and Woodstock. Willoughby continues: "We assembled in the small house. Lieutenant Rynkiewicz and Handfield were in the house next door. The Air Corps sergeant and others went upstairs to keep a lookout for the Germans while the Dutch people took care of our burns. Both of my hands and my face were wrapped with gauze and I looked like a mummy. I could only see out of my right eye. I held my hands up along my chest because it was painful when they were lowered to my side.

"It wasn't long before a truck came down the road with some German soldiers in it. They stopped between the house that Rynkiewicz and Handfield were in and the house we were in. They dismounted and came in the direction of our house. One of the Germans threw a potato-masher-type grenade at the window. It bounced and struck the one in charge on the leg. He jumped around like he had a broken foot. Someone waved a white piece of cloth out the window and we were taken out of the house. We were loaded on the truck and driven to a small town [Steenbergen, west of the Dintel River], where we were herded into a building and questioned by a German officer. I was hurting so bad I moved to the side of the room and lay down on the floor. I don't remember how long we were there. It was getting late in the afternoon by the time the questioning was over.

"We were loaded onto an old school-type bus and travelled all night, arriving in Utrecht the following day. Mark Kaplan and I were sent to a field hospital located in a big church in town. In the hospital, we met up with two troopers from 501 PIR, 101st ABD. There was [Pvt.] Stanley P. Hunt from Philadelphia, who had gotten a bad ankle sprain when he landed. The other young trooper had lost three fingers on his right hand. [...] There was also a British trooper blinded by a mortar round from German fire at Arnhem."[57]

Meanwhile, Leginski and Ridout were successfully evading the Germans. Shortly after dusk on September 17, they heard a man whistling and softly pronouncing the word "Oranje." It took them a few moments before they realized the man wasn't calling his dog, but trying to contact them. They recalled from their briefing in England that the Dutch Underground used the code word "Orange," or "Oranje" in Dutch. Venturing out of their hiding place, they shook hands with the Dutchman. Motioning them to follow him, he led them to the Dintel River, which they waded, and then walked for about half an hour until they reached a barn where they were provided with dry civilian clothes and bedded down for the night.

At 0600 hours, both men were awakened by another Dutchman who informed them in English that the Germans were aware of their location in the barn. He had arrived ahead of the Germans to take them to the nearby town of Fijnaart on bicycles from the farm, aided by another member of the local Underground.

As the four of them rode along the Fijnaart-Heijningen road, local civilians stared at them in disbelief: German officers had just confiscated all the civilian bicycles in Fijnaart. The Dutchmen took them to the house of a Hendrik Nijhoff, who hid them in the cellar of his carpentry shop. From Nijhoff and other Dutch Resistance members, Leginski and Ridout learned what had happened to the rest of the crew. All but Lieutenant Rynkiewicz and Private Biggs had fallen into German hands and had probably been taken to Breda. In the wreckage of the plane, the bodies of Captain Bohannan, Lieutenant Felber and Staff Sergeant Epperson had been found. The Dutch handed them the dog tags and other personal belongings of the deceased. Eventually these items were forwarded to the Dutch Red Cross, which relayed the information to the authorities who informed the next-of-kin.

Learning that Biggs and Rynkiewicz were treated in a hospital in Willemstad, some six miles away, Leginski and Ridout wrote a note to the lieutenant explaining their situation and asking for instructions. A Dutchman acted as messenger and later returned with a message from Rynkiewicz, who wrote that his left knee had been shattered beyond repair and that Private Biggs had been badly burned about the face and body. They were both well cared for and he wanted Leginski and Ridout to stay hidden until further developments. It was the last news they received from their officer; he and Biggs were captured by the Germans and eventually sent to POW [Prisoner of War] camps.[58] Rynkiewicz ended up in Stalag VI C Bathorn and Biggs in Stalag II A Neubrandenburg. The crew chief, Sgt. Thomas Carter, was taken to Stalag Luft IV Gross Tychow and then Stalag Luft I in Barth.

First Lieutenant Carmichael, who had seen Captain Bohannan's C-47 crash, soon received the news that the Dutch were protecting paratroopers. "On Monday evening, September 18, while we were at Nederasselt, a Dutchman came to our CP and substantially stated with a heavy accent that he had heard 'by the telefono' that four of our soldiers [Lieutenant Rynkiewicz, Private Biggs and Privates First Class Leginski and Ridout] were west of's Hertogenbosch, and he wanted instructions about their disposition. I assumed that they were part of our H Company planeload that had been shot down, and instructed him to have them rejoin our unit. They later did" [sic: two did not].[59]

Back in Fijnaart, Leginski and Ridout had little reason to expect they would have to remain for 48 days in Nijhoff's carpentry shop in Fijnaart. While the Americans hid in the cellar, soldiers from one of the training battalions of the Hermann Göring Panzer Division came to the shop to make wooden coffins and crosses almost every day. Every few days another weapon was recovered from the wreckages of the C-47 and a nearby British Hamilcar glider, whose occupants had all been killed in the crash. The weapons were mud-splattered and often needed cleaning and repair, which Leginski and Ridout carried out. They offered their services in the night raids the Dutch conduct on German soldiers, but the Resistance workers turned them down for fear of retaliation.

Escape was impossible: no civilians were allowed on the streets after 2000 hours and the area was full of German units and directly behind the German front line facing the British Second Army. Leginski and Ridout lived on apples, cheese, ersatz bread and small slices of pork once a day. On November 1, British artillery shells began raining down on Fijnaart, a barrage that continued uninterrupted for three days until the town was practically obliterated. During the shelling, Leginski and Ridout wore Red Cross brassards and aided the Dutch civilians who had crowded into the cellar as best they could.

On November 4 British soldiers entered the cellar, ending Leginski and Ridout's ordeal. Their status explained, they were taken to Antwerp, where they jumped off the British truck to hitchhike their way back to Holland.

Before long they were arrested by British Military Police for being out of uniform. Again matters were straightened out, but no one could tell where the 504th was positioned. The next morning Ridout and Leginski spotted a 505 PIR jeep, and got a ride to Nijmegen where they found the 504th Regimental CP. Both men reported in at 1900 hours, were debriefed and received new uniforms, and placed on active duty status in H Company.

Many other members of 3/504 had successful jumps after witnessing the tragedy that befell Captain Bohannan's last flight. Major Cook's description of his own flight is imbued with confidence: "We knew assembly after the drop would be easier in daylight and that the Air Corps would deliver us with some precision. Felt we had full control of all. You could see the whole aerial armada stretched out. Since it was daylight we could look over the countryside. I saw a plane (C-47) shot down, saw a fighter plane suppress an ack-ack position. I also saw many C-47s shot down after we jumped."[60]

Captain Ferguson, too, was considerably luckier than Captain Bohannan on that fateful September 17, as the C-47 carried him and his men toward the DZ at Overasselt. Passing over a Dutch village with only one main street, he observed its residents "in the rear of their homes waving white objects at our formation, and at the same time a German convoy was passing in front of the homes, heading in the general direction in which we were flying. I recall vividly a feeling of warmth, comradeship, and understanding for these people. They were letting us know that they welcomed us, and I am sure, as mine did, all our spirits rose, giving a more meaningful purpose to our mission."

When the red light flashed, signifying the plane was 20 minutes from the drop zone, the Maas River, Grave Bridge and Grave simultaneously came into view, "just like the aerial photos we had burned into our memory." The jump itself played out like a vivid dream: "The plane throttling down, the wind screeching and tingling against my face as I looked down and out, every nerve crying out for action. Passing over the river, the dike, purple smoke rising from the drop zone (a signal from the pathfinder group who had preceded us by 20 minutes); looking back into the plane and signaling the troopers, who were now hooked up and ready to go, that we were right on target. Large round black balls of smoke appearing with ear-splitting explosions around the plane. The green light flashing on. 'Go!' I yelled toward the men, at the same time turning and stepping into space. A feeling of relief coming over me—everything going according to plan."[61]

Captain Thomas and his men also had a successful jump, after watching in horror as Captain Bohannan's plane went down. "Nearly everyone was a little excited and the whole incident happened so fast, no one knew exactly how many men jumped from the plane. Quite a few of the chutes that opened after the men had jumped were scorched. [...] Utmost credit should go to the pilot and co-pilot of the C-47: it was through their unselfish devotion to duty, by holding the plane on a level flight with the tail raised, that the parachutists were able to get out of the doomed plane. [The pilot and co-pilots did this] in the hope that it would save lives, knowing that the delay in their own exit meant their own death.

"Our attention was now called to the fact that we had little time left in which to secure all of our equipment and adjust our chutes, so for the moment the incident some of us had just witnessed was forgotten. The flak fire from the ground, which had gotten the afore-mentioned plane, had practically ceased as we neared our DZ. We jumped while the red light was still on the door, at 1310 hours. The timing turned out to be just right because we all landed together and assembled in record time."[62]

First Lieutenant Allen F. McClain, leading the 3rd Battalion 81mm Mortar Platoon, also had a good jump after witnessing the fiasco of the downed plane, which had been flying directly behind him. "At the precise time the C-47 was hit, a P-47 fighter plane came from nowhere and knocked out the anti-aircraft gun emplacement. You saw it happen but didn't believe it could be true. We had a number of untried or new men in our plane. This was enough for Sgt. [Charlie G.] Cooper, who I think slept with his wad of tobacco in his mouth. He had a big one to liven up the trip. He sang airborne songs: 'He ain't gonna jump no more,' 'Worms crawl in,' 'We gonna all be dead and stacked like a load of wood,' etc. Needless to say, some wished they never heard of parachutes. Those of us who had seen action were for the most part quiet, thinking of many things apart from the war.

"My planeload landed exactly where we were supposed to, across the dike and north of the Grave Bridge. The Dutch Underground came out and assisted some to our rendezvous with the rest of our battalion. There was only one sprained ankle in my group. We did encounter some fire before and after we hit the ground. I landed knee-deep in a drainage ditch, which put a radio I had strapped to my right leg out of commission."[63]

When Pvt. James H. Legacie, Jr., a member of 1st Platoon, H Company, witnessed the plane next to him going down, he recalled that Corporal Leginski was one of the men in the plane. "I remember that Legacie and Leginski were always mixed up for guard duty. I would be coming off guard and be told to go back on it right away. Things like that. He escaped and joined us some weeks later."[64]

Legacie's platoon leader, 1st Lt. Edward J. Sims, details the action of "the remainder of Company H, which jumped at about 1305 hours on the designated area near Grave." This was Sims's second combat jump. Still recuperating from a leg wound sustained on the Anzio Beachhead, he "had no desire to remain in England while my unit went into combat.

"Initially we supported other units in securing the Grave Bridge over the Maas River and other bridges over the Maas-Waal Canal. Intelligence reports placed some 4,000 SS troops and a German tank park in the Grave and Nijmegen area, but resistance near Grave was light and all of our initial objectives were secured by 1800 hours the first day.

"Upon landing, I re-injured my back, but did not go for treatment because I felt nothing could be done. For the next several weeks, I carried on in less than top physical condition. We set up a company command post near a small cluster of homes, where I met my first Dutch family and their fifteen children. The mother made room for me to stay with them, and that evening she prepared a delicious stew using beef she had previously preserved. They wanted to celebrate our arrival and their liberation from the Nazis."[65]

"Pretty well loaded down with equipment," H Company T/5 Seymour Flox "made a pretty hard landing. I just skimmed over a house and landed just beside a haystack. There were three Dutchmen sitting there watching the big show and when they saw I was coming down near them, they ran like the devil himself was after them. You have to give the Air Corps a lot of credit on this mission because they did a marvelous job. They dropped us right on our drop zone and in no time we were assembled and ready."[66]

It was the first combat jump for Pvt. Hugh D. Wallis, who had joined the 3rd Platoon on the Anzio beachhead. After witnessing the crash, the men in his plane "stood up and hooked up for the rest of the way in to the jump zone." On landing, they "set up a defensive circle on the north end of the Maas Bridge to protect the troopers taking the bridge. I was a bazooka man, so I was on the roadblock. This was at the bridge at Grave. We had no contact with the Germans on the first day of the landing."[67]

Sgt. Leroy M. Richmond placed Cpl. John J. Foley, Jr., the assistant squad leader of Wallis's squad, at the back of the same C-47 to make sure everyone would jump: "My plane had Sergeant Richmond, myself and our squad. Lieutenant Murphy was in a different plane. I was to be the last man out. Sergeant Richmond said that if the man in front of me was afraid to jump, I had to kick him out. Once we had parachuted into Holland, one of my men ran up to me and asked, 'Who was it that fell?' I didn't know, but we did see one man fall down with a collapsed parachute."[68]

Captain Kappel's company was "to drop early, as close to the regimental objective as possible, destroy enemy on the ground, and protect the assembly of the rest of the battalion. As we neared the drop zone, we were exactly on course and on time. All my men were laughing and enjoying themselves. I was calling out landmarks from my door position to the remainder of the crew. As we neared the Maas River, my aircraft, which was the lead aircraft of the formation, applied flaps and abruptly slowed down. This delighted us despite the fact that we began to draw flak from the German positions in and around the Grave Bridge. Slowing down the aircraft to jump speed contrasted with our previous experiences, when the pilots increased speed to above safe jump speeds when they were fired on."[69]

Sitting next to Kappel in the C-47 was his radio operator, 21-year-old Albert A. Tarbell, of Mohawk origin. Tarbell thought his captain "was just about the bravest man that ever was. I wasn't the only one that thought that way about him. We would have gone any place with him. I was like a bodyguard to him. Wherever he went I was with him. We figured that the Germans would never expect us on a nice sunny afternoon. Also there was less chance of getting lost, and our chances of regrouping were a lot better. On the other hand, the Germans on the ground could zero in on our doors as the fellows jumped out. They could shoot at us and we could not return the fire until we hit the ground. I believe that everyone settled on the theory that, being the aggressor, we had the edge on them.

"Our plane ride across the English Channel was uneventful until we hit the coast of Holland and anti-aircraft guns opened up on us. Immediately a fighter plane swooped down on them like a hawk after a chicken and knocked them out. A short time later someone hollered and wanted to know if we were over the DZ. They had seen chutes from one of our other company planes. I was seated near Captain Kappel, next to the door. We looked out of the window behind us and saw flames and smoke under the plane next to us. We started counting the number of chutes opening and in a few seconds the plane was out of our view and down.

"Further inland, we were carrying on a conversation with 1st Sgt. Michael Kogut who was seated directly across from us. The next instant he was lying on his back in the middle of the aisle with a funny expression on his face, wondering how he got there. A bullet had come through the seat and into his chute. It missed him, but the impact threw him to the floor. A few seconds later we reached our DZ and he jumped with the chute."[70]

Capt. William A.B. Addison, the Regimental S-4, "enjoyed watching the British Spitfires that covered our trip dive into the anti-aircraft positions that fired on us. Capt. Mack Shelley passed around a pint of scotch. There were about twenty of us in the plane. Then he threw the empty bottle at an anti-aircraft position."[71]

The Protestant chaplain, Captain Delbert A. Kuehl, accompanied Capt. Moffatt Burriss and his stick to Holland. One of the paratroopers took two pictures of their stick before take-off. For some of the men on the photo, like PFC Walter J. Muszynski, it would be their last. "As our plane crossed the Channel into Holland," Kuehl recalled, "we saw that the Germans had flooded great areas—evidently to avoid our seaborne invasion. We soon saw many built-up areas with anti-aircraft gun emplacements. Soon they were firing furiously at us. [...] We saw a stream of tracers coming right at us, as if we were going to swallow them. Moffatt and I were standing at the door. The instinct to survive made us both jump away from the door and behind the paper-thin aluminum fuselage, which afforded us no more protection than the open door. The volley raked the back of the fuselage to the tail. Moffatt and I looked at each other and began to laugh."[72]

Capt. Henry B. Keep, the 3rd Battalion S-3 officer, wrote to his mother a few months later: "What a sight it was—this great herd of planes bearing men across the Channel, over the inundated lowlands, and on into the heart of enemy territory. We were the group that was dropped in and secured the Nijmegen area. All around these clumsy, vulnerable troop carriers swooped the small, quick fighters, sweeping out of the sky from nowhere only to disappear a moment later, zooming around us like a bunch of wasps. What superlative protection they provided. A flak tower would open up from the incongruously peaceful-looking Dutch countryside and hardly before the first burst had died away, out of the sky would sweep one of the fighters, spitting fire as it rushed at the Kraut gun.

"This operation must have been a breathtaking experience to those privileged to watch it from the ground—hour after hour, the constant drone of thousands upon thousands of planes, a never-ending stream of fighting men. I wonder what the Germans thought when they saw it. I was not bothered at all until after we crossed the Channel—until then it seemed just like any other routine jump. But when we hit Holland and began that long flight over enemy-occupied territory, expecting heavy flak, it was a little more uncomfortable. You feel so helpless in the lumbering, defenseless crates.

"Suddenly someone yelled, 'Look!' and we all craned out the windows and door. One of the planes in our flight was on fire and men were piling out of it, their chutes opening in the air. The pilot kept the plane level until all the jumpers had escaped, and then it plummeted to the flooded land below. [...] Fortunately, our plane was not hit despite the fact that as we neared the DZ, the flak became heavier. Luckily, at no time was it as severe as we expected.

"I was glad to jump when we reached the DZ. Those planes were definitely too hot for comfort. The Air Corps dropped us perfectly on the DZ, at the exact spot we wished—and all together. Of course, it was daylight and naturally that helped immeasurably. [...] We hit the ground and assembled in record time. The men had been well-briefed, the Air Corps had dropped us perfectly, it was daylight, and the DZ was free of the enemy. The Krauts had been taken by surprise and were totally unprepared for an airborne landing in this area. How different all these factors were from events of the past."[73]

The first contacts with the local Dutch population were almost uniformly excellent. PFC Walter E. Hughes of I Company, a replacement who joined the company in England, headed into combat for the first time. "I landed near a farmyard and could see people looking out the window, and to tell you the truth, I was scared shitless. I didn't know if I should shoot the window out or what, but a small child came out the door with an orange flag and gave it to me."[74]

Lieutenant Carmichael recalled that "the Dutch farmers came out with fresh milk and set about systematically rolling up and carrying off all of our parachutes. For the first two nights in Holland, we appropriated a Dutchman's house for our CP. This man was exceedingly gracious. He had a fine small cottage of about six or seven rooms with a story and a half, furnished in good taste. He assured us we were welcome to use it as our command post, and he and his wife moved elsewhere during our stay. Otherwise, the Dutch appeared to me to be rather haughty and not too well pleased that we had upset their routine of life. The man who had been so friendly to us was Baron Van Hövell tot Westerflier-Sanders. His home was 'De Knotwilg' at Nederasselt."[75]

According to Captain Kappel, "the Dutch civilians and members of the Dutch Underground [...] were a significant help, and were most anxious to help in every way imaginable, actively assisting from the moment of the drop, although the odds were in favor of the enemy. I still remember farmers showing up with horses and wagons picking up ammunition from the drop zone and bringing it to our firing positions."[76]

The 3rd Battalion suffered the most jump casualties of the battalions that dropped on DZ "O": out of 574 officers and men, 23 men were injured or wounded during the drop; and one officer and 12 paratroopers from H Company and two men from the Regimental Demolition Platoon were shot down in Captain Bohannan's plane. This left Cook with 540 officers and other ranks, excluding 3rd Battalion men like Pvts. Albert R. Essig of I Company and Dominic R. Moecia of H Company who were part of the pathfinder teams. For the three planes of Headquarters and Headquarters Company that were part of this serial, two men out of 50 were wounded.

Captain Addison had a close call after the drop. After checking on supplies and ensuring that the four jeeps assigned to his supply section were properly loaded, he procured a motorbike and rode off to watch the 2nd Battalion take the Maas Bridge. When a bullet whizzed by as he crossed over a viaduct, he suddenly realized that all the paratroopers were undercover below the dike.

The G Company Journal records that "upon landing Captain Thomas assembled most of the company and moved out toward our objective, the Grave Bridge. We moved through an orchard of apple trees and came to a house in which several very much surprised and scared Dutch people were all huddled in a corner. One of them was made to understand that we wanted the direction to the bridge. He led us a short distance of about 50 yards and pointed to the bridge. We then moved over to a grove of trees that was to be our battalion assembly area. The Battalion CO and his staff were already there and directing the various companies to their positions. We moved to our positions and checked our losses on the jump, opened our radio channel and reported to the Battalion CP.

"About 15 minutes later we stacked our musette bags and bed rolls in a pile and moved out toward our company objective. As we moved up the road toward a group of houses we passed the Regimental CP which was being set up. Further up the road, near the crossroads, we ran into one or two snipers. They evidently quickly withdrew because our troopers were seen moving over ground that they would have to be firing from. It turned to our right and proceeded down the highway for a distance of about 300 or 400 yards.

"At this point the captain had noted a house in which we had been directed to set up our CP as practically as the situation allowed. A sniper fired into the front room of our CP before he was silenced by our platoons, which were moving back up the road in the direction of the Grave Bridge. At dusk the positions were set up by the platoons that had been ordered to dig in and hold. During the night there were several large demolition explosions and several fires, but it was not learned until later just what caused them."[77]

Captain Kappel, H Company, remembers events differently: "H Company losses were the heaviest of the battalion; in fact, their one aircraft was the only one in the division shot down prior to jumping. To demonstrate the superior flexibility of an airborne operation, H Company was completely assembled and equipped. G Company, whose mission was a roadblock at Alverna, was not completely assembled. Accordingly, the battalion commander directed that H and G Companies change missions.

"As the company commanders left on the double, we found that G Company had completed their assembly under the executive officer and had formed on the road toward Alverna, while H Company under their executive officer was formed and waiting to move in the opposite direction. Rather than turn the companies, the G Company commander pointed to Alverna, I pointed to Grave, and the companies moved out on the double. [...]

"H Company moved into positions astride the road with the 2nd and 3rd Platoons across the road facing north, and the 1st Platoon facing south. Two mortars were faced north, one south, since the sweeping of the area indicated little or no threat from Grave. Civilians reported approximately 500 Germans in the town of Grave. At about this time the Battalion received word that the Grave Bridge, No. 11, was entirely in the hands of the 2nd Battalion."[78]

Meanwhile Captain Burriss's I Company had also assembled and the 1st Platoon of 1st Lt. Robert C. Blankenship moved out, heading north toward Diervoort to set up a roadblock. At 1630 hours Blankenship reported the presence of a flak wagon north of the Wychensche Ven (a small lake) and the report from Dutch civilians that 75 Germans defended Bridge Number 8 at Hatert. S.Sgt. William H. White would posthumously receive the Silver Star for his part in this patrol: "For gallantry in action September 17, 1944, about two miles from Nijmegen, Holland. Staff Sergeant White, platoon sergeant of Company I, was with the point of his platoon, whose mission was to contact the unit on the battalion's right flank. The platoon was proceeding towards the bridge crossing the Maas-Waal Canal when they encountered an enemy patrol mounted on bicycles at a bend in the road. They immediately deployed and took positions below the bend. The enemy patrol of four men began withdrawing under the protection of a terrace on the left of the road.

"Staff Sergeant White with utter disregard for his own life dashed across the open field towards the terrace. The enemy patrol saw that Staff Sergeant White was attempting to cut off their escape and immediately concentrated fire from their machine pistols on him. Firing his Thompson submachine gun [TSMG] from the hip as he ran through the hail of bullets, Staff Sergeant White continued until he had reached the ditch at the edge of the road to the rear of the enemy. He charged down the ditch at the four Germans, firing as he moved forward and wounding two enemy, but ran out of ammunition when he was still five yards away. Grabbing his TSMG by the barrel as a club, he rushed the two remaining Germans. They immediately threw down their weapons and surrendered.

"Staff Sergeant White's quick thinking and determined actions neutralized a patrol that would have been able to furnish the enemy with vital information concerning our whereabouts. His display of courage is a credit to the Armed Forces."[79]

At 1845 hours G Company reported two small trucks deposited some 40 Germans north of Alverna, some three miles northwest of the DZ. Two hours later this group plus two tanks attacked a G Company platoon just south of the village, forcing it to withdraw. An I Company patrol that went north of the Wychensche Ven reported no contact with enemy upon their return at 2140 hours.

Captain Ferguson recalled that on Sunday night "a German train going east passed through portions of the 82nd Airborne Division around 2100 hours at Nijmegen and on across the border into Germany. No one attempted to stop the train. I understand General James Gavin also saw the train. After England, it was hard to get used to the idea of combat again."[80]

CHAPTER 5

CAPTURE OF THE MAAS BRIDGE
GRAVE, SEPTEMBER 17, 1944

Lieutenant Carl Mauro, assistant platoon leader, 1st Platoon, E Company, was in one of the last "planes carrying E Company and had an excellent look at what was transpiring in front of me as the 'sky-trains,' as the C-47's were called, lumbered onward at 120-130 miles an hour. At the time to jump, the pilots tried their best to decelerate the engines to 90 miles an hour while keeping the tail high, as the jumpers left the plane. These were stressful moments for the courageous pilots."

Once the pilot activated the red light, Lieutenant Mauro gave the familiar commands. His men stood up and hooked up in good order, checked equipment and counted off from the back of the stick: 'Number sixteen, OK!' 'Number fifteen, OK!' and so on, until the count reached 'Number one, OK!' and the jumpmaster. In just a few minutes, the red light would go off and the green light flash on."

Only seconds away from the DZ, Mauro "had one last fleeting look at all I could see in an instant. I observed anything that would help me indicate the prevailing wind velocity and direction—in the air and on the ground—especially how the parachutes from the planes in front of me were drifting in relation to our flight path. Where were most of my E Company comrades falling? I wanted to jump as closely to them as possible. In what direction was our objective? I wanted to get as close as possible, and yet not too far away from my fellow troopers and equipment bundles. Within those few seconds, before going out the door, I had to determine the most strategic time to release the equipment bundles hanging on racks beneath the belly of the plane.

"I gave the command to stand in the door, and all the men quickly shuf-

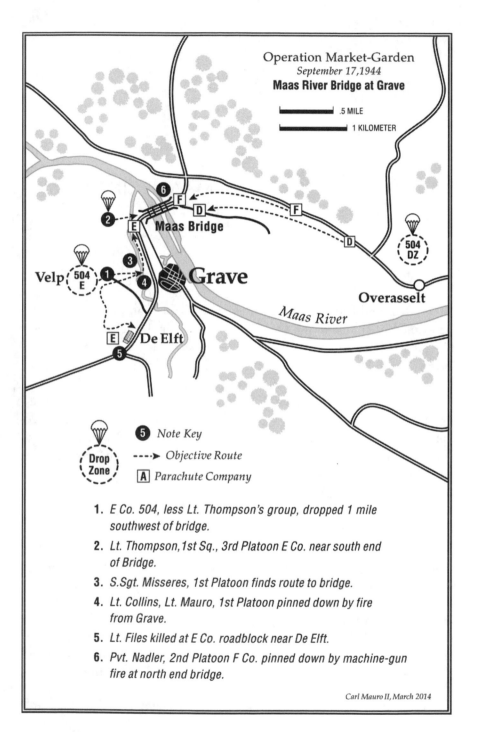

Operation Market-Garden
September 17, 1944
Maas River Bridge at Grave

.5 MILE
1 KILOMETER

Maas Bridge

Velp

Grave

Overasselt

Maas River

De Elft

Note Key

----> *Objective Route*

Drop Zone

A *Parachute Company*

1. *E Co. 504, less Lt. Thompson's group, dropped 1 mile southwest of bridge.*
2. *Lt. Thompson, 1st Sq., 3rd Platoon E Co. near south end of Bridge.*
3. *S.Sgt. Misseres, 1st Platoon finds route to bridge.*
4. *Lt. Collins, Lt. Mauro, 1st Platoon pinned down by fire from Grave.*
5. *Lt. Files killed at E Co. roadblock near De Elft.*
6. *Pvt. Nadler, 2nd Platoon F Co. pinned down by machine-gun fire at north end bridge.*

Carl Mauro II, March 2014

fled forward, pressing hard, pushing to be as close to each other as possible, to get out the door as rapidly as possible. Every fraction of a second delayed between jumpers meant hundreds of yards between individuals and away from the bundles when they reached the ground. I did not give the familiar interrogative, 'Is everybody happy?' that the jumpmaster yelled before the jumps at the Parachute School.

"The time had come. I had the green light; I had picked my spot on the DZ. I didn't have anything at my feet to kick out the door as some jump-masters had. After observing the drift of the chutes filling the sky in front of me, I pushed the button near the green light to release the supply bundles and yelled, 'Let's go!' and 16 young men followed me out the door.[81]

"As I remember, this jump in Holland was not much different from my previous 24. It would be my last. I had never jumped so low; I estimated it was no higher than 500 feet, because it seemed I hit the ground quicker than on other occasions. The average jumping altitude was 1,000 feet.

"As soon as I went out the door, I had a problem; my helmet fell over my eyes and while pushing it back on my head as I dropped through the air, it fell off! Embarrassed, I felt like a damn fool. I landed without my helmet and didn't have one for the next 24 hours."[82]

First Lieutenant John S. Thompson, 3rd Platoon leader, E Company, also vividly remembers standing in the door of his C-47, carefully studying the terrain below, "watching for any landmarks familiar on the maps. There was a slight haze, even though the sun was shining brightly. Soon, the green light was flashed on, and this was it. I was still looking for our company drop zone but could not make it out. I guess our plane was a little too far to the left to the formation. I could see up ahead the little walled town of Grave with the majestic bridge just 1,000 yards to the north of town. There was also a good-sized road running north and south leading to the entrance of the bridge.

"I could not recognize the actual drop zone from my vantage point. All I could see was a series of fairly wide crisscrossing canals. The land area in between was not very large. We were now fast approaching the bridge area and the feeling innermost in my mind was that the bridge was our one and only objective. The fastest way to get there was to jump as close as possible to it and use the surprise factor to overcome any possible superiority in numbers the enemy might have.

"The bridge was in clear view now and I could plainly see the flak towers straddling the southern approaches to the bridge, gun emplacements and many foxholes. Men were running around and there were several vehicles on the road. I picked out a plot of land just before the bridge and gave the signal to jump. We were only 900 to 1,000 yards from the ground, and the descent was uneventful.

"We were well separated when we landed, which worked out well. There was considerable enemy fire now coming from the vicinity of the bridge and along the road. Four of my men landed in the canals, which were quite deep. One man went in all the way, and the weight of his gear kept him under for a while. He was water-logged when he was pulled out and was in no condition to assist us for a while. This left us with 17 men, two wet walkie-talkies, and plenty of firepower, including two bazooka teams, which turned out to be a very decisive factor in our attack on the bridge.

"The remainder of Company E could not be seen, nor could we communicate with them because of water-logged radios. We were very close to the bridge, and to wait any time at all would destroy our surprise factor. Word was passed to each man on the proposed plan of attack. Two squads moved down the edges of the canals toward the road and bridge. One squad on the left flank was to skirt the bank of the Maas River, approach the bridge and come up underneath the road span. They were also to observe any enemy movement on the bridge itself that might indicate possible demolition attempts.

"We could tell that there was mass confusion around the bridge, of which we took advantage. We moved quickly toward the bridge as enemy fire from the left side of the bank, particularly from the flak tower, continually kept going over our heads. The road leading up to the bridge was highly banked on either side, and from our depressed elevation we could not actually tell how many enemy we were facing.

"Our left squad was making very fast time, and we had a hard time keeping up. They were to come up under the bridge and meet the two remaining squads swinging to the left. We felt quite naked out there, especially with the enemy on high ground, but we had good cover in spots because the canals had steep banks and depressions.

"We were now about 50 yards from the bridge and on a pre-arranged signal the two frontal squads were to take up positions and fire on the gun emplacements and foxholes to allow one bazooka team to edge close enough to effectively fire on the flak tower on the left flank. With this accomplished, the first shot from the bazooka went wild. The second shot hit at the base of the structure housing the flak guns and tore one side out. There was to be no more enemy fire from there. Two enemy were shot trying to climb the tower on the right bank. About six hand grenades and some Composition C did a good job on two machine-gun emplacements. Men were running all over the place.

"We were now moving as fast as we could up the steep bank to the road and the approach to the bridge. Our squad on the left was already there, and three of my men were chasing three enemy and a motorcycle across the bridge to the north. They caught up with them halfway across, and we gained an addition to our (just initiated) motor pool. Everything was happening very quickly. The enemy were in turmoil, and we definitely had the advantage. Some were taking off across the fields toward Grave. Others disappeared over the other side of the road and down the bank, where many foxholes were located.

"Two men were sent to inspect the bridge spans to look for possible demolition set-ups and, if possible, work their way to the north approach to the bridge. No enemy fire was now coming from the two flak towers, and for the time being we completely ignored them. We set up one machine-gun emplacement on the right side. The gun was in excellent condition and there was plenty of ammunition. We also acquired a good supply of their potato-masher grenades, which came in very handy.

"All of a sudden, down the road from the vicinity of Grave came a command car loaded with personnel followed by two truckloads of troops. We felt so good at this time that we didn't care what they sent at us. We had the bridge, we were well dug-in and had plenty of firepower. So far, our casualties were one waterlogged paratrooper and two men with slight flesh wounds.

"I sent one bazooka team to take up positions on the left bank of the road and the other took positions on the right. The vehicles were now only about 150 yards away from our positions. By the way they were proceeding toward the bridge, either they did not know what they were riding into or didn't care. I am of the opinion it was the former.

"Our bazooka team on the left was to pick off the command car and the bazooka team on the right was to get the first truck. They would be backed up by our two machine-gun emplacements and rifle and automatic fire. The two bazooka men on the left picked out a large foxhole on the upper half of the road bank, an excellent vantage ground vis-à-vis the approaching vehicles. Just as they were about to fire at the command car, the upper part of their bodies slowly rose out of the hole, until they seemed to be standing in a shallow depression up to their knees—a sudden elevation caused by two German soldiers hiding at the bottom of the hole who could no longer withstand being stepped on! This caused a quick change in plans, and our bazooka team on the right fired and hit the command car. The doors flew off and two men fell out. The car kept going with no driver.

"By this time, the left-flank bazooka team had regained its composure and fired on the first truck, knocking off the front left wheel. Men spilled out of the back as the truck went over the bank. The second truck had stopped and was trying to back down the road. Some of the men were jumping out and taking up positions along the banks.

"All this time the command car kept coming toward us. We were firing at it with rifles and machine guns. Although there was no driver, it still held two occupants in the back seat. As the vehicle approached, it veered sharply to the right and tipped over. Two bodies fell out, one rolling to a stop in front of me, which made a good shield against the fire now coming from the enemy along the road bank.

"All this time, which in reality was very short and sometimes a fierce skirmish, a good part of the men from the second truck had dashed over the left bank and were hidden from us by a slight curve in the road about 150 yards away. They followed the lower bank back toward Grave, and by the time we found out, they were out of range. The immediate area was now being cleaned up, and not knowing what else may be coming from Grave, we left the overturned command car right where it was. Small-arms fire was now heard in the vicinity of Grave, and we were still on the lookout for enemy tanks. They never came.

"We secured our positions and checked the flak towers for enemy hiding there. We did not realize as we approached the bridge that the large-calibre anti-aircraft guns mounted in the towers continually fired high because heavy armor plate and sand bags circled the gun emplacement and the long rifles could not be depressed low enough to be effective against our advance. It was indeed fortunate that we landed so close to the bridge. We also discovered that there had been no trouble from the flak tower on the right side of the road because our escort fighter planes had done their work well before we jumped."[83]

In another plane, the D Company captain, Victor W. Campana, was impressed by the "beautiful sight of the air armada as I looked out the open door. British Horsa gliders being towed as far as the eye could see, plus our own C-47s in formation. [...] With the air superiority we appeared to have at that time, I did not think much of being shot down by enemy aircraft. Flak was more than a possibility, since we would be going over 'Flak Alley,' as Air Force briefing officers had indicated."[84]

One of Campana's officers, 2nd Lt. Harry Rollins, 1st Platoon, was making his first combat jump, having just completed jump school in England. "The order was that the first officer to gather 15 troops at the near end of the bridge was to lead an assault to the other side to secure the bridge and keep the Germans from destroying it. I was the first officer to show up at the [D Company] rally point, and led this attack with the available troops. With soldiers dropping all around me, I got this horrible feeling that I might be the only one left. I looked behind and Colonel Tucker said, 'Keep going, Rollins. You're doing fine.'"[85]

Twenty-three-year-old 2nd Lt. Hanz K. Druener, assistant platoon leader of the 2nd Platoon, "landed in a field next to a cow which kept sniffing me while I was trying to get out of my chute. I looked skyward and saw a C-47 get hit by enemy anti-aircraft fire and burst into flames before the paratroopers could get out. I just wanted to get out of that exposed position, but later I thought it funny that a cow should greet me on my first day in combat. The Dutch civilians were very friendly. Since I spoke German I often talked to them and we were able to capture documents that had been abandoned by the Germans in houses they had used as command posts."[86]

Holland was the third combat jump for 2nd Lt. John E. Scheaffer, assistant 3rd Platoon leader, who had participated in all the regiment's previous campaigns. He felt "anxious due to rumors of SS troops and tanks at the drop zone. Daylight operations were far better than night operations. Most conversations were in regard to jumping that far behind enemy lines and would the British Second Army be able to get to us in time so that we would not be cut off." In all, he regarded it as a "very pleasant trip: sun shining, occasional view of fighter air cover. Dutch people walking home from church and waving at the planes. This was to be the mission that would end the war."[87]

Captain Richardson's F Company landed near D Company. "It took ages to untangle from my chute and check my rifle. I was trying to walk on a bad ankle when I looked up to see the rest of the men from my plane still several hundred feet in the air," recalled Pvt. Philip H. Nadler of the 2nd Platoon.[88] This was Nadler's first combat jump since joining the 504th in December 1943. Another soldier in his platoon, Pvt. Leo M. Hart, had previously served in B Company before being transferred to F Company in Italy, but had never before "experienced ack-ack. It bothered me more than I thought it would, and created a very strong desire to get out of that door. I expressed this verbally. I was fascinated by our combat fighter planes flying below. It was assuring."[89]

In terms of drop casualties, the 2nd Battalion fared worse than the 1/504 but was luckier than the 3/504. Out of 624 officers and men, Pvt. Curtis C. Morris of E Company fell to his death, and 15 other men were injured or wounded during the jump.[90] This left Major Wellems with 607 officers and other ranks, excluding 2nd Battalion men like 1st Lt. G. Wilfred Jaubert who were in the pathfinders. For the three planes of Headquarters and Headquarters Company that were part of this serial, one man out of 49 was wounded.

"The 2nd Battalion assembled most of its men at its assembly point and moved out towards its objective about 1430 hours," recalled Captain Campana. "There were at least two platoons of F Company, half of D Company and most of the 81mm Mortar and LMG [Light Machine Gun] Platoons of Headquarters Company. Order of march: F, D and Headquarters Companies. Remnants of F and D Companies had made straight for the bridge, orders having been given prior to the jump that in case men were scattered on the drop, they were to make their way immediately to the bridge, the primary objective.

"The battalion struck out west to the dike road and followed it in defilade for several hundred yards. We turned north on the main road and met the 3rd Battalion moving west towards its objective. As the 2nd Battalion came to the approaches from the bridge, it met remnants of D and F Companies, which had cleared the area of snipers and wiped out a flak tower on the northern approach to the bridge. A few prisoners were now being brought in by D Company men."[91]

Private Nadler of F Company recalled that his 2nd Platoon set out to cut telephone wires running parallel to the Grave-Nijmegen road. Crossing an open field, they reached an area between the dike and the riverbank not far from the bridge. Here the platoon was pinned down by two machine guns and a number of men were wounded, including Pvts. Clarence B. Corbin (medic) and Paul D. Vukmanic, whose wounds were severe: "We had to knock out a flak tower, several machine guns and riflemen between the dike and river (150 yards). The fight lasted two to three hours."[92]

During the F Company advance to the Maas Bridge, Pvt. Raymond S. Thomas, an assistant machine-gunner, noticed that Private Vukmanic had been wounded. Thomas would later be awarded the Bronze Star "for heroic conduct in action against the enemy, September 17, 1944, near Grave, Holland. During his company's attack on a strategic bridge at Grave, Private Thomas saw an assistant machine-gunner [Vukmanic] fall, seriously wounded, whereupon he left his position of cover and crawled approximately 50 yards across an exposed dyke under heavy enemy flak fire to the aid of the wounded man.

"Private Thomas took this unselfish action when he observed that no medical aid man was readily available to administer necessary medical treatment to the wounded soldier. After reaching his comrade, Private Thomas then picked the man up, and, using his own body as a protective shield against the enemy fire, carried him back to a position of cover, where treatment and evacuation were possible.

"His mission of mercy completed, Private Thomas then returned to his machine-gun position which the gunner had continued to operate during his absence. His heroic action at the risk of his own life greatly inspired those who witnessed it."[93]

Major Wellems remembered that "Company F reached the north side of the bridge under scattered sniper fire and 20mm fire coming from the northern approaches to the bridge. Only one 20mm gun was there. The strafing of our aircraft on the flak installation saved probably between 20 and 30 men. The Germans also were scared by the large number of dropping paratroops. They scattered and couldn't get back to their positions. Our airplanes had driven the gunners from this one flak tower and they couldn't get back because Company E was commanding the approach to the north end and the entrance to the flak tower. Lieutenants Stuart McCash and Richard Swenson, both from F Company, 2nd Platoon, occupied the flak tower.

"At 1530 Colonel Tucker arrived from the drop zone. There was an exchange of small-arms fire and our men fired mortar and small arms at the four flak positions and knocked out one with a bazooka. [...] A patrol comprising Lieutenant McCash and one enlisted man went across the bridge to contact Company E because they were not sure what was on the south end of the bridge and they could hear scattered small-arms fire there."[94]

Seeing his assistant platoon leader and another trooper set out across the bridge, PFC Henry D. Covello urged his comrades to move forward. Private Nadler recalled: "When the last shot had been fired, we expected to cross the bridge into Grave. We were ordered to hold our position. We had all fought hard and wanted to move in. Covello, smoking rifle in hand, stepped up onto the bridge and shouted, 'Let's go, men! Let's go!' He kept it up until the company commander told me to drag him back to safety. I stepped up and said, 'Come on, Horatio. We'll name the bridge after you.' He and the company commander asked me about the name. I told them about the Roman hero. This nickname seemed to give Henry recognition and, if anything, made a stronger fighter of him."[95]

Lieutenant Scheaffer of D Company is also credited for knocking out a 20mm gun position at the north end of the bridge. His Silver Star citation reads as follows: "Lieutenant Scheaffer took command of a patrol when his battalion was held by machine-gun, rifle and 20mm fire. With his patrol, he set out to flank well-entrenched enemy positions on the north approach to the Grave Bridge, dashed over open terrain in the face of heavy small-arms fire and charged a machine-gun position and two protecting riflemen, wounding several enemy soldiers and capturing six.

"As the Germans prepared to turn mortar fire upon the battalion, First Lieutenant Scheaffer personally led the assault on a 20mm gun position, killing one German and capturing two himself. He then turned the 20mm gun on the enemy mortarmen. The courage, leadership and decisive action of First Lieutenant Scheaffer cleared the bridge defenses, permitted capture of the bridge intact and enabled the unit to seize the town. Entered military service from New Cumberland, Pennsylvania."[96]

First Lieutenant Earnest H. Brown, the 1st Platoon leader in D Company, recalled that "the bridge was lightly defended but they did have a flak tower and a couple of machine guns. The firefight lasted about 30 minutes and the bridge was taken intact. Thus within two hours of our jump, we had accomplished our primary mission."[97]

Around 1600 hours Lieutenant McCash and the enlisted man returned from the south side of the bridge and informed Major Wellems that Lieutenant Thompson and one planeload were on the southern end. Radio contact was meanwhile established with Captain Van Poyck, who was advancing from his drop zone at the village of Velp, southwest of Grave, to link up with Thompson. Colonel Tucker, still present at the scene, had been manning a 20mm gun from one of the flak towers with Wellems and the Regimental S-2, Capt. Fordyce Gorham, which forced German gunners in another tower to abandon their position. He now ordered the entire 2nd Battalion to cross the Maas Bridge and take Grave.

As Captain Campana remembers the attack: "We heard that an enemy patrol had come over to the north side of the river, so the companies were organized and positions were being dug along the dike bank. A change of orders then sent D Company to move across the bridge, followed by F and Headquarters Companies. One platoon of D Company (1st Platoon under

Lieutenant Brown) was attached to E Company, while the remainder of the company was to establish a perimeter defense south and west of the bridge, tying in with F Company on its left flank. The battalion crossed the bridge at about 1730 hours, subject to enemy 20mm, machine-gun and rifle fire. The Battalion crossed safely with only one casualty, Lieutenant Middleton [of F Company], who was hit in the hand by a bullet."[98]

The 2nd Battalion S-1 officer, Lieutenant Garrison, was in a sweat by the time he reached the south end of the Maas Bridge: "From the north end [...] we slunk from girder to girder while bullets from scattered Germans on the south flank whistled around us and zinged off the steel superstructure. Not only were we dangerously exposed to the enemy, but we also felt certain that the bridge was wired and at any moment would blow up under us. Indeed, it was wired, but no German remembered to work the plunger or to note that wires were cut. By the time I reached the south end, I was asweat from energy and anxiety. The walk had been long and too much like our fearful stumbling through the black tunnel in the Italian mountains. My whole body recognized the feel of war again. The Germans were still the enemy; only the terrain and countries had changed."[99]

The 3rd Platoon of F Company, 1st Lt. William L. Watson commanding, remained at the northern approach to the bridge to prevent the Germans from retaking it, while the 15 prisoners who had already been taken were sent under guard to Overasselt for interrogation at the Regimental CP. Meanwhile 2nd Lt. John C. Barrows and six men from his 2nd Battalion demolition squad were delousing the bridge of explosives with the help of 2nd Lt. John A. Holabird and engineers from C Company, 307th Airborne Engineer Battalion. The switch mechanism in the flak tower to blow the bridge had already been destroyed by small-arms fire, but dynamite charges still present had to be removed with care. Major Wellems recalled "boxes of explosives in the girders fitted into them and painted like them.[...] When we got to the flak tower, we found that the Germans had installed phone communication across the river. The flak tower was hitched up to several such flak positions."[100]

Meanwhile the majority of E Company had assembled at their drop zone near Velp and was ready to set out when Cpl. Hugh H. Perry from Lieutenant Thompson's stick showed up. He reported that Thompson was already advancing to the Maas Bridge with his stick and that the SCR-536 radio had been waterlogged and was useless. Although Lt. Patrick C. Collins's 1st Platoon was already spearheading the company's advance to the bridge, Van Poyck decided to abandon the movement when heavy fire from Grave to their east pinned down the lead platoon. He radioed Lieutenant Collins, told him to bring his platoon back, and follow the 2nd Platoon and Company Headquarters to the De Elft crossroads south of Grave. Spotting it on the map, Van Poyck realized that whoever controlled this crossroads could control three major transportation arteries—the Elftweg leading north to Grave, the Bosschebaan running southwest to the city of 's Hertogenbosch and the Hoogeweg running south to Uden (and the 101st Airborne Division)—and thus cut off any German movement between the towns of Grave and Uden.

Part of the 1st Platoon never received word of the sudden change of plans. S.Sgt. Alek Misseres, the platoon sergeant, recalled that during the initial advance to the bridge "there was a lot of sniper fire coming from the right, probably from the outskirts of Grave. Lieutenant Collins saw a ditch leading from this point to a small canal. The ditch was partly filled with water and the 1st Squad waded right through it to the canal. The 2nd Squad went through some high weeds on the flat ground, where it got pinned down. Lieutenant Collins went over to the ditch to try to stop the 1st Squad until the rest of the company caught up, but it had gone too far for him to catch up with it. The 2nd Squad got into the ditch, and the 1st Squad, under Sgt. Arley Staley, sent back a runner, [Louis H.] Tuthill, who met Lieutenant Collins in the ditch."[101]

While Staff Sergeant Misseres moved forward with the 1st Squad and eventually linked up with Lieutenant Thompson at the Maas Bridge, Lieutenant Collins and his runner, Pvt. William A. Maney, got into serious trouble when they went into the ditch to call the 1st Squad back. They ran into Private Tuthill, who led them to a junction of the ditch and the canal and climbed over small canal bank. Just as Lieutenant Collins climbed over, three German soldiers cut loose with machine pistols and a machine gun. Collins headed about 20 yards to the left and was then joined by Private Maney and briefly by Cpl. Taylor Isaacs, who saw the Germans had them pinned down, and rapidly crawled back across the bank. Tuthill also decided to move back and Lieutenant Collins called out to his 2nd squad on the other side that they were to wait, as he wanted to make a reconnaissance. He quickly learned there were other active German machine-gunners: an advance along this route would clearly be suicidal. Worse, after managing to get out of the canal, Maney was now pinned down.

Assistant platoon leader Lieutenant Mauro moved forward to aid Lieutenant Collins, an action that led to the Bronze Star for bravery: "During the initial stages of the attack on Bridge No. 11 by Company E, the platoon leader of the foremost platoon was entrapped in a canal. After he had progressed halfway across, he was subjected to a hail of enemy machine-gun and sniper fire. However, he was unable to climb out of the water because of the high, steep banks of the canal. This necessitated his continually swimming about and dodging bullets until he became exhausted and numb from the cold water. Hearing his cry for help, Lieutenant Mauro, accompanied by a Staff Sergeant [Alton G. Machost], without hesitation voluntarily left his position of comparative safety in a ditch and crossed approximately 75 yards of open terrain exposed to the full concentration of the enemy fire.

"After reaching the canal, they pulled the then-helpless officer from the water and dragged him back under the full observation of the enemy situated in four flak towers and snipers, who immediately began to fire on them. Mauro, with skill and cool determination, successfully regained the safety of the ditch. These courageous and unselfish actions on the part of Mauro, voluntarily made in an effort to rescue a stricken comrade, with utter disregard of his life, typify the highest standards of conduct in action and were an inspiration to all who witnessed them. His exemplary heroism reflects the highest credit upon the military service."[102]

After this ordeal, Lieutenant Mauro led the 1st Platoon to the E Company CP in De Elft: "This location reminded me of a crossroads in rural America where one found a well-worn country store with two gas pumps out front. Some sort of a wooden building on the premises that I never entered became E Company's command post for the next six or eight hours. This was the spot Van Poyck was seeking; it was so-planned the day before when we were still in England.

"Captain Van Poyck ordered the roadblock to be set immediately, with one bazooka team on each side of the road. The demolition squad from Headquarters Platoon brought forth the mines they had jumped with—not trusting to put them in bundles that might get lost. The small mines were just for this specific purpose and this place. Sixteen mines were placed across the hard surface of the main highway with no intention of camouflaging or burying them. Lt. John Murphy was responsible for setting up small outposts on both sides of the road. The bazooka teams dug in and positioned themselves to repel any attacking vehicle or tank. Sharp's 2nd Platoon dug out an emplacement for his mortar squad and they zeroed in on the enemy outpost near Grave—specifically, on the base of a windmill there. Others manned light machine guns, Tommy guns, and rifles to cover the road in both directions and protect the bazooka teams.

"My men in the 1st Platoon were not particularly involved with the road-block protecting the main highway. Our main function was to cover the company's rear. Lieutenant Collins had not joined us and I hadn't seen him since he had been dragged into the drainage ditch; I knew he was now in the command post, recuperating. [...]

"Soon after the mines were placed on the road and all the outposts were manned [...] two tanks appeared from the south, moving towards Grave on the main highway; we were only about 40 yards from the mines we had placed on the road earlier. Our bazooka teams were taking aim on the approaching tanks when, very loudly, someone yelled: 'Don't shoot! It's the British!' But the British weren't due until the next morning, at the earliest. For only a few seconds there was much jubilation and running towards the tanks—then *Bang*! A shell burst in our midst, caroming off the branches and trunks of trees, causing shrapnel to fly in all directions. This was a big hello from the German tanks, followed immediately with bursts of their machine-gun fire. [...]

"When that first shell came crashing into the trees several men were hit: they were withering on the ground. Close by, a medic yelled, 'Help me, lieutenant!' And I saw that my friend Lt. John Murphy was on the ground on his back, grimacing as he wiggled, waggled, twisted and turned, groaning as he kicked the air while the medic tried to hold him still. I got on my knees and grabbed his legs, as the medic suggested, and tried to diminish his erratic movement. 'Merf' groaned a lot while the medic gave him a shot of morphine. After a moment or two, he was moaning but calm; others came to move him."[103]

PFC Lyman D. Brainard and Pvt. Paul A. Kunde, a bazooka team from the 2nd Platoon, tried to knock out the tank with two rounds. Kunde later recalled that "it was definitely a smaller tank like a Mark III and it produced small repeat fire. Brainard's first shot went over the top of the tank. The second shot landed within a few feet of the tank. It backed into a barn near our position, then re-emerged, turned and drove away down the road. The bazooka took over a minute to reload. We wanted to fire a third time, but by then the tank was already out of range. I wasn't close enough to see the effect of the tank fire or Lieutenant Files getting hit."[104]

Cpl. Louis E. Napier, a 21-year-old machine-gunner in Lieutenant Sharp's 2nd Platoon, recalled the German tank showing up at De Elft: "Lt. Hanford Files was on the other side of the road while I was manning a light machine gun on the top floor of a building. There was also a machine gun between a tree and the house. As the tank appeared, several American paratroopers ran up the road. Lieutenant Files was shot right in the throat. Shrapnel wounded two or three others."[105]

Lieutenant Files was mortally struck, and Lieutenant Murphy's arm and chest put him out of action for quite some time. There were two more incidents at 1930 hours, when two Germans on a motorcycle coming from Grave navigated their way through the mines lying across the top of the road. Although many paratroopers opened fire, they escaped unhurt. Some three hours later, a small German patrol crept up to the 2nd Platoon position but was discovered by Private Kunde when it was about 20 yards away. He quickly threw a Gammon grenade, driving the Germans off. The next morning blood was discovered in the area—evidence that one or more had been wounded.

According to the E Company After-Action Report, at 2300 on September 17, "Lieutenant Thompson was at the bridge with Sergeant Misseres and the 1st Squad, 1st Platoon and the 1st Squad of the 3rd Platoon. The remainder of the 3rd Platoon was along the dike on the west side of the road at 524613. The 1st Platoon continued along the dike southeast to connect with the rest of the platoon which started at 525613 and continued to Company Headquarters at De Elft. The 2nd Platoon was on the east side of the road along the dike, beginning at 526616 and continuing along the dike southeast to 519618.

"About 2330, there was much noise in Grave. It sounded like civilians singing 'Tipperary.' So Lieutenant Sharp, Sergeant [Augustine V.] Coppola and four men started toward Grave. They saw flashlights at 529620 and since the men were making noise with equipment, especially bazookas, Lieutenant Sharp and Sergeant Coppola went on alone. They went up the right road and saw German vehicles and German troops burning papers. Lieutenant Sharp and Sergeant Coppola walked down the street to see what was going on. Since the Germans were destroying their own stuff, they decided to let them alone and came back to report that the Germans were ready to pull out. The civilians were still singing 'Tipperary' and the national anthem."[106]

Postcard of Bridge Number 7 at Heumen, captured by
B Company on September 17, 1944. *Author's collection*

CHAPTER 6

THE MAAS-WAAL CANAL BRIDGES: HEUMEN, MALDEN AND HATERT, SEPTEMBER 17, 1944

Major Harrison's 1st Battalion had received the toughest mission of all that fell to the 504th PIR: to take four bridges spanning the Maas-Waal Canal west of Nijmegen. Capt. Thomas C. Helgeson's B Company had been ordered to take Bridge Number 7, a lockbridge across the Maas-Waal Canal at Heumen. This was the southernmost bridge, nearest to the 505th RCT, which had landed in the vicinity of Groesbeek. First Lieutenant William A. Meerman's 3rd Platoon was leading, followed by the 2nd Platoon and 1st Platoon, with Company Headquarters in the rear. PFCs Harris V. Duke and Herman C. Wagner were lead scouts, about 100 yards to the front. Flank guards were deployed on either side of the platoon to prevent a flanking German counterattack. Apple orchards on both sides of the paved road provided some cover to within 150 yards of the bridge, which rose about 20 feet above the surrounding area.

As they neared the lockbridge, the 3rd Platoon received sudden fire, sending the men diving into ditches on either side of the road. As Captain Helgeson recorded in his official report: "Sergeant Lawrence Blazina was killed on the road. Machine-gun fire was coming from a house on the Island [the unofficial name for the Betuwe area between the Rhine and Wall Rivers], cutting branches off trees on the road. T/5 [Raymond G.] Larabee and PFC Ralph W. Jetton fired four bazooka rounds at the house, but none went off. They fired four rifle grenades (two smoke, two HE). The HE exploded, but the smoke did not.

"Initially, Lt. William Meerman's 3rd Platoon were the closest to the bridge, positioned about 100 yards away on the left side of the road. Lieutenant Meerman, pinned down behind the elevated ground to the left side of the road, was protected against machine-gun and rifle fire coming from the bridge and the Island. A row of barbed wire ran from the road for about 500 yards along the elevated canal bank.

"The ground dips on the right side of the road. The 2nd Platoon, led by [2nd] Lieutenants [Maurice] Marcus and [James R.] Cummings, got into this depression. A group of eight men, led by Lieutenant Marcus and Corporal Nau with Lieutenant Cummings, met no opposition, went on the dike and placed a light machine gun at the point where the barbed wire began. The machine gun, manned by [Privates] Pritchard and [Charles] Piazza and [Sgt.] Shelton W. Dustin, covered the bridge. A second machine gun was set up midway between the barbed-wire juncture with the dike and the road along the dike, also covering the bridge.

"Lieutenant Marcus decided to get across the bridge. Marcus, Cummings and eight men did so at about 1500 hours. Lieutenant Marcus gave the signal to move, and the machine gun at the juncture of the dike and the barbed wire fence opened fire. The men crossed the dike, which was about five meters high, ran across the sloping ground in defilade, firing as they went at the house and the bridge.

"While Lieutenant Marcus and the others were going across the defilade, I ordered 26 men of the 1st Platoon to the top of the dike, where they occupied German-dug holes. The purpose was to build up a base of fire to cover the crossing. All men fired at the crossroads beyond the bridge and down the road. They had three BARs besides the machine guns already set up. [Second] Lieutenant Richard A. Smith was in charge of the 1st Platoon and had Cpl. Francis J. Cleary as runner.

"At the same time, I ordered one squad of the 3rd Platoon under Lieutenant Meerman on the other side of the road to move forward as far as possible and build up a base of fire. One machine gun was placed about ten yards from the road on the elevation, firing at the house on the Island. Lieutenant Meerman also put one BAR about 25 yards from the road around the curve of the elevation to fire the same mission. Another light machine gun was put at the edge of the orchard under PFC Clark M. Comin, Jr., to fire on the same mission. I ordered 1st Lt. Henry C. Dunavant, executive officer, to move his two mortars behind the houses on the right of the road and fire on the house on the Island."[107]

Corporal Robert Stern, an assistant squad leader in the 2nd Platoon, recalled the approach to the bridge: "we were drawing fire but we couldn't tell where it was coming from. There was a little warehouse or something over to our left, and the bridge had a building on top of it, so most of us laid down fire on that because we thought that's where it was coming from."[108]

Sgt. Lee W. Cox, a mortar squad leader, moved forward to the junction of the road and the dike to direct the mortar squad's fire. Twelve 60mm mortar rounds were fired upon the enemy, pinning them down. Lieutenant Marcus meanwhile led an eight-man group forward to a flight of concrete steps leading from their cover behind the dike onto the bridge, where one of Marcus's men, Cpl. Charles E. Nau from Tyrone, Pennsylvania, conducted a gallant frontal assault. In 1945, he received the Distinguished Service Cross "for extraordinary heroism in connection with military operations against an armed enemy on September 17, 1944 near Heumen, Holland. As a rifle-squad leader, Cpl. Nau was leading his squad in a daring frontal assault by his platoon on an important highway bridge five miles southwest of Nijmegen, Holland, when his platoon leader fell seriously wounded. Completely disregarding his own safety and exposing himself to withering small-arms fire which at times cut his clothing, Cpl. Nau immediately assumed control of the assault element and led it boldly across the bridge.

"During the course of the attack his squad killed or wounded six of the enemy. The impetus of the assault inspired by Cpl. Nau's heroic leadership swept the enemy from the bridge, prevented them from detonating the prepared demolitions laid to destroy the objective, and enabled follow-up troops to quickly mop up and consolidate the vital bridge objective. By his intrepid direction, heroic leadership, and aggressive attitude, Cpl. Nau set an inspiring example for his men, reflecting the highest traditions of the Armed Forces."[109]

Watching the attack on the lockbridge from a distance, Captain Helgeson saw Lieutenant Marcus get hit after Corporal Nau ran across the bridge: "When he got halfway over, Lieutenant Marcus started across. When Nau reached the end of the bridge, Lieutenant Cummings started across. There was fire on them all the time, but they didn't know the direction from which it came.

"T/4 Onie A. Burnett, radio operator, started across, and he and Lieutenant Cummings caught up with Marcus. Just as Burnett caught up he was hit in the neck. Burnett then handed the radio to Marcus and ran back across the bridge. He was hit at the other end of the bridge, this time fatally. Lieutenant Marcus turned left to get to a sand pile on the northeast side of the road and was seriously wounded, falling in front of the pile, pinned down.

The ground here again was in defilade. Nau was in a hole in this corner.

"Sgt. Jerry M. Murphy and two men attempted run across the bridge, but Murphy was killed at the far end. The other two were not wounded— [Private Ernest R.] Farmer and [Private First Class Joseph A.] Eggrie. The Germans seemed to be picking off officers and non-coms. [Second] Lieutenant [Charles R.] Hewette [of the 3rd Platoon] also ran across. [Staff] Sergeant James R. Lowe, with the 2nd Platoon, attempted to cross and was pinned down midway, but dashed on over after a while.

"In the meantime, six men from the 3rd Platoon, under Lieutenant Meerman and Sergeant Dustin, got across the dike and built up a base of fire along the road leading to the bridge and covering the Island enemy positions."[110]

Sergeant Murphy, a squad leader in the 1st Platoon, ran across the bridge and was killed just as he reached Lieutenant Marcus's group. "Murphy came over," recalled Corporal Stern, "and shouted out 'I made it!' *Boom!* He was down and already off the bridge. I don't know who got Burnett off, as I didn't see anyone. They were real good."[111]

From a distance, Private Edwin M. Clements saw his squad leader Murphy go down: "About 200 yards away I saw a small bridge. It proved to be Bridge 7. I noticed a ditch paralleling the road leading to the bridge. We had no difficulty working our way to the ditch using every bit of cover possible, and began heading for the bridge itself. Within about 15 minutes we were quite close to the canal and I quickly identified Murphy. Small-arms fire increased as the Germans saw that our objective was the bridge itself. Apparently, someone had made an effort to cross earlier, but had not made it and was lying on the bridge. At that moment, I saw a trooper rise up to lead a dash in force across the bridge. I don't think he knew he could be seen, but he was. It was Jerry Murphy, my squad leader. He turned slightly to motion the squad forward, paused momentarily, spun around and fell to the ground." [112]

Clements then recalled that S.Sgt. William J. Walsh appeared with part of another squad and lined Clements and his squad up along the dike. Walsh pointed out some buildings to their left and said, "Start firing at the windows and doors. After a few rounds, move a few feet away and wait for return fire. Then you'll have a real target." This fire enabled Lieutenant Hewette and S.Sgt. Lowe to run across the bridge.

Not long after Lieutenant Marcus went down, Corporal Stern crawled over to render first aid: "I went out on my hands and knees and asked Marcus, 'Where are you hit?' I don't know if he told me or not. Anyway he was hurting, so I took his first-aid kit off his helmet and gave him a shot of morphine. About that time [Private Fred] Grainger, our medic, came out. I told him to stay back but he came out anyway—I remember this very clearly. He kneeled down a little on one knee and with the same motion took his helmet off and said 'Where are you hit, Sir?' A shot rang out and he was shot right through the head, killing him instantly. He fell sort of on Marcus. I got down and lay on my stomach."[113]

A 3rd Platoon rifle-squad leader, Sgt. Robert E. Waldon saw Private Grainger moving forward to aid Lieutenant Marcus: "A medic, a heck of a nice guy, went out to help the guy that got shot, and they shot him right in the red cross on his helmet—a great Red Cross. No doubt that's what he was, and they just shot him. Killed him instantly."[114]

PFC Elmer C. Pankow and Pvt. Louis Costa, two members of the Regimental Demolition Platoon who had jumped with a B Company stick, believed the Germans in the control house might blow the bridge at any time. Crossing the bridge was too dangerous due to enemy fire, and they had seen Marcus, Burnett, Grainger and Murphy shot down. Spying a half-sunken rowboat on the western canalbank, they quickly got in and started paddling across under enemy fire. On reaching the east bank, they searched that end of the bridge for demolition wires, removing blasting caps and cutting wires. Both men were awarded a Bronze Star in February 1945 for their action.

Around the same time that Costa and Pankow reached the east end of the bridge, at 1700 hours, Lieutenant Meerman, Sergeant Dustin and "nine men moved across the road behind the powerhouse, intending to assault the positions." According to Captain Helgeson, after they got around the corner of the powerhouse, they "met heavy fire from enemy positions, so they retired behind the powerhouse again. There were three men across the bridge. At 1630 to 1700, Lieutenant Smith took across a boatload of six men and a medic [Pvt. Joseph A. Seemiller]. They were fired at during the crossing, but no casualties were suffered. There were then eleven men on the far side, pinned down at the crossroads beyond the bridge."[115]

Around 1800 hours Captain Helgeson sent Sgt. John W. Kellogg and seven of his men from the 2nd Platoon to the houses on the west side of the canal, just north of the bridge. Recalled Helgeson: "the patrol [...] occupied the houses and fired on the Island. Lieutenant Meerman and Sergeant Dustin with nine men waited until 1930 (dusk) for the attack. The German positions were fired on by rifle fire. The men were in defilade and in the darkness and weeds, so there was little return fire. They came out from behind the powerhouse on its right-hand side and moved into a skirmish line. They infiltrated west along the bank so they could throw grenades into the German positions. Pvt. Edward Schutt fired rifle grenades at German positions while other men moved to take a German machine gun position.

"Sergeant Dustin threw a Gammon grenade through a window into the house and another at a German who came up from a nearby dugout. He called on those in the dugout to surrender—there were two officers and ten or twelve noncoms, plus five civilians in the dugout. A young boy in civilian clothes came out and said the officers and noncoms were afraid to come out, lest they be shot. Sergeant Dustin went down after them and got one officer who could speak English to call on his men in the house and other positions further north to surrender. He did, and they came out with their hands up. They got between 35 and 40 prisoners. It was then about 2300. One man, [Private Edward J.] Schutt was killed. There were no wounded. Six killed and one wounded for the whole operation."[116]

Twenty-seven-year-old Sgt. Shelton W. Dustin from Farmington, Maine, was one of the acting rifle-squad leaders in the 3rd Platoon of B Company. Like Corporal Nau, he would later receive the Distinguished Service Cross "for extraordinary heroism in connection with military operations against an armed enemy on September 17, 1944, near Heumen, Holland.

"As an acting rifle-squad leader, Sergeant Dustin courageously led his eight-man squad in an assault on a strongly fortified control island which seriously menaced the security of a vital highway bridge which had been captured by other elements of his company.

"Unmindful of all personal dangers and cognizant of the necessity for clearing the Island of all enemy, Sergeant Dustin led his squad through intense small-arms fire to within 25 yards of the enemy's forward position. At this, the enemy, numbering approximately 45, retreated to a house and air-raid shelter in the center of the Island. Vigorously pressing the assault, Sergeant Dustin, spearheading his squad's attack, moved to within ten yards of the house into which he threw a Gammon grenade, killing three of the enemy that had taken refuge there. Almost immediately, a shot was fired at him from the air raid shelter. Sergeant Dustin whirled and threw a Gammon grenade into the air-raid shelter, killing three more Germans. Following the explosion, he rushed into the entrance of the shelter and forced the remaining 39 enemies to surrender.

"By his exemplary bravery and superior leadership Sergeant Dustin accounted for 45 of the enemy and insured the security of the vital bridge objective. His indomitable courage and aggressive leadership set an inspiring example for his men, thereby reflecting the highest traditions of the military service."[117]

Shortly before dark, Lieutenant Marcus was put in a rubber boat and paddled back across the Maas-Waal Canal. He was subsequently taken to a first-aid station. Marcus would receive the Silver Star for leading his platoon across the lock bridge. Second Lieutenant Cummings, the assistant platoon leader, assumed command of the 2nd Platoon. The capture of the Heumen lockbridge had cost B Company one wounded platoon leader and six men killed, including a medic. Among the dead was Sgt. Donald W. Forein, a squad leader in the 3rd Platoon, most likely killed around the same time as Private Schutt.

At 1900 hours that evening Major Harrison called regimental headquarters to report that Bridge Number 7 at Heumen had been taken. Unaware of the actions of Privates Costa and Pankow, he erroneously stated that the 1st Battalion had not been able to clear out the explosive charges on the bridge due to enemy fire.

Captain Milloy's C Company was tasked with the capture of Bridges Number 8 and 9. With 16 additional Headquarters Company men attached, Milloy's company departed from the DZ and picked up a misdropped B Company mortar squad along the way. "The company moved out in platoon columns northeast by north along a secondary road until it was within 1,000 yards of Bridge 8," recalled Milloy. "At this point, a platoon of Company A, which had landed east of the drop zone, cut across the company's line of march, drawing small-arms fire from the bridge.

"Germans on the road southwest of the bridge were firing. The company moved north 200 yards and set up mortars and a base of fire. While the 2nd Platoon, under Sgt. William L. Reed, built up a support position, the 1st Platoon was ordered to make a frontal assault on the bridge down the road to the dike. As the 2nd Platoon put down a base of fire, the 1st Platoon started up and ran into [Captain Roy E.] Anderson, Headquarters Company commander, and his BAR men pinned down by enemy fire.

"The 1st Platoon moved up faster than expected under fire. As Albert Milloy testifies: the base of fire was stopped when one of the noncoms reported that the 1st Platoon reached the woods. I moved forward with the 2nd and 3rd Platoons; as they swung right, the 3rd Platoon was pinned down by sniper and automatic fire. S.Sgt. Frank Dietrich, 3rd Platoon sergeant, then sent word for the 2nd Platoon to move up. At 1615 hours, just as S.Sgt.

Fred E. Gonzales, 2nd Platoon sergeant; 2nd Lt. Milton L. Baraff, 3rd Platoon leader; and the 2nd Platoon BAR team dashed toward the bridge, the bridge went up in smoke."[118]

Sgt. Thomas J. Leccese, an experienced rifle-squad leader in the 3rd Platoon, earned a Silver Star for his part in the battle for Bridge Number 8: "Sergeant Leccese, while leading his rifle squad in the forward elements of his platoon toward the platoon objective, observed an enemy force of approximately 20 men hurrying towards the positions designated for his platoon. Recognizing that if the enemy force reached these key positions first, his platoon would suffer heavily and find difficulty in accomplishing its objective, Sergeant Leccese immediately, and without orders of any kind, detached three of his men and engaged the enemy force. For four hours, under continual enemy machine-gun and mortar fire, Sergeant Leccese's small group kept the enemy from moving further, thereby enabling his platoon to advance and seize its designated objective. His prompt, courageous, and determined action accounted for ten enemy dead and forced the withdrawal of the remainder. Sergeant Leccese's gallantry reflects great credit upon himself and the Armed Forces."[119]

Second Lieutenant Reneau G. Breard commanded the A Company platoon that cut through the C Company formation: "My 1st Platoon's mission was to take the bridge on the Maas-Waal Canal, the second from the Maas River, north of B Company, at Malden. I got within less than 100 yards and we started crawling up a ditch to get close when it blew up. No one [in my platoon] was hurt. I got hold of Captain Duncan on the phone, and we stayed in position there for a couple of hours and sent a patrol up north to the next bridge [under Sgt. Mitchell E. Rech]. Half the platoon or a squad went there. I am not sure. The first bridge nearest the Maas River was taken intact by B Company."[120]

The Mortar Platoon leader, 1st Lieutenant Richard F. Mills, ran forward with five men from the 2nd Platoon, A Company, in an attempt to rush the bridge and be the first to cross the Maas-Waal Canal. They were still running as enemy small-arms fire from across the canal swept up and down the road. Just as Lieutenant Mills and his small group reached the bridge, the Germans blew it up. A tremendous explosion lifted the bridge high and large pieces scattered all over the area. Mills and Pvt. George S. Andoniades, Jr., from A Company were both badly wounded.

First Lieutenant Joseph G. Wheeler's 2nd Platoon of A Company was nearing the bridge area as the explosion took place. Pvt. Fay T. Steger remembered that "George [Andoniades] had come in with the last load of fresh meat (replacements) to replace the men we had lost at Anzio, and this was to be his first taste of fire. He was a nice-looking boy with black hair and brown eyes. We were in single file at about 30-foot intervals between men and moving up at a steady pace. This was too slow for George, who started to pass the men in line.

"When he got alongside me I said, 'George, don't get hoggish! I'll bet you two to one the boys will save some for you.' George didn't pay any attention. He kept passing the men in the column and I saw him disappear up ahead.

"We moved up maybe another 300 yards. George was lying alongside the trail. He had taken a bullet through the chest. It had entered about three inches below the collar bone and came out about two inches above his belt. It must have hit his lung because every time he would breath, a blood bubble would rise from his lips. I didn't say anything. I just looked in his eyes. Those brown eyes looked awfully sad, like he thought he was going to die. A medic was by him, so I kept my place in line.

"The angle of the bullet told me there was a Kraut sniper up there and he wasn't very far. We went another thirty yards and a bullet took the canteen cup off the trooper ahead of me. We all hit the dirt and I knew then we had found what we were looking for. The battle for Holland was about to begin and I wondered how long it would last. I didn't wonder about who the winner was going to be because I knew it wasn't going to be Hitler."[121]

Sergeant Clark was with Company A as they started for their objectives. "Just as the advance party got close to the bridge, it was blown. Somewhere along the way some came across a group of Germans in a concrete structure and someone threw a Gammon grenade in and one of them caught it and that was the end of all of them. The second bridge was blown before we even got close to it."[122]

Bridge Number 9 at Hatert, just north of A Company's objective, was also blown as C Company troopers neared the bridge. Only Bridge Number 10, a railroad bridge and a road bridge laid side-by-side, had not yet been captured. "During the next few hours after crossing the small bridge," recalled Private Clements, 1st Platoon, B Company, "we moved into several positions without a lot of opposition. Finally night fell and I found myself behind a large dike with orders to dig in. We all soon learned to hate that phrase, since it meant that at any time, if you stopped for any reason and intended to be there for as little as 15 minutes, you had to dig a hole for yourself.

The purpose, of course, was to protect against any kind of lofted shell like an artillery or mortar shell. This was good advice since a four-foot hole, wide enough to crouch in, was enough to protect yourself against almost anything except a direct hit. Unfortunately, the only thing we had to do this with was a small spade, almost always dull, that took a long time to dig a proper hole even under the best of circumstances.

"By the time night fell, I realized that I had dug four holes and I was exhausted. Finally I noted the seasoned vets were digging minimum holes, making up for the lack of depth with whatever was lying around. I was learning, but slowly. Then began what was the longest night of my life. The squad was told to dig in in front of the dike. Instead, following [Pvt. 'Ikey'] Iaquinto's lead, I dug in on top of the dike, which was about 12 feet tall. We dug a two-man hole so we could take turns sleeping during the night.

"We had just finished when our platoon leader showed up to check our positions. 'You don't have a flat field of fire,' he said. 'You'll have to re-dig that hole in front of the dike.' Of course he was right. If attacked, we would be firing down at our targets instead of straight across. It took us another hour to dig a new hole, my sixth of the day, and by this time it was quite dark. In front of us was a broad, flat field with many interlocking barbed wire fences. As we opened up a can of rations, I realized that I hadn't eaten since the day before.

"Since I was very tired but not sleepy, I took the first watch (two hours) so that Ikey could sleep. We would then alternate sleeping and watching all night long. So, with my rifle cocked, fully loaded, and the safety off, I waited for the attack, and waited and waited. I did this all night long, even when I was supposed to be sleeping. I much later realized that this was typical rookie behavior, and that the combat veterans took advantage of it to get more sleep, knowing the rookie would be awake all night."[123]

The bridges across the Maas-Waal Canal were defended by three companies of Landesschützen Battailon II/6, which formed part of the 406th Landesschützen Division. This division was made up of so-called "ersatz" troops: recovering wounded, WWI veterans and administrative troops. Very few NCOs had combat experience and the average age in the battalion was 59-years-old. The 5th Kompanie defended Bridge Number 8 and was reported "lost" on September 17. At the town of Hatert, the company of *Hauptmann* Ernst Sieger was situated. Sieger's company was responsible for defending Bridge Number 9 at Hatert, and the riverbank about 125 meters south of the railway bridge in Nijmegen, where his 3rd Platoon tied in with

Capt. Moffatt Burriss (with Thompson gun) and some of his I Company troopers were accompanied on the flight into Holland by the Protestant chaplain, Capt. Delbert Kuehl (standing with helmet on). Medic in the front row is Pvt. Robert Dority and standing second from the right is Pvt. Francis Keefe. The paratrooper seated second from the right in the front row may be Pvt. Jack Seitzinger, who was killed three days later. *Courtesy: Moffatt Burriss*

C-47s standing ready for take-off at Spanhoe airfield, September 17, 1944. *Courtesy: Mandle family*

Three I Company troopers in Evington, Summer 1944.
Note the sign on the tent. *Courtesy: Moffatt Burriss*

Lt. James Dunn, A Company, was
wounded within hours after crossing
the Waal River. His diary provides
valuable insights into Operation
Market Garden. *Courtesy: Mike Dunn*

Lt. Edward Kennedy, I Company,
died of wounds after walking into
a minefield during a night patrol.
Courtesy: Ben Overhand

3rd Battalion passing in review for Generals Dwight Eisenhower and Louis Brereton and other high ranking officers, August 1944. *Courtesy: Mandle family*

Group of I Company paratroopers in Evington, Summer 1944. Pvt. John Gallagher is standing in the back row on the far left. Second from the left in the front row is Lt. Harry Busby, who had a premonition that he would be killed in Holland. *Courtesy: Dain Blair*

View on Bridge Number 10 at the Maas Waal Canal from the Service Company jeep of Pvt. Irving Kidder. Photograph most likely taken on September 20, 1944. *Courtesy: Paul Kidder*

Teenagers from the Kinderdorp Neerbosch orphanage at the Maas Waal Canal, September 1944. Seated in the front with a walking stick is Wim van Lunteren, a cousin of the author's late grandfather. *Courtesy: Wim van Lunteren and Van't Lindenhout Museum*

American P-38 Lightning fighter bombers strafing the flak positions around the Maas Bridge, September 17, 1944. *Courtesy: Graafs Museum/Jan Timmermans*

E Company dropping near Velp, September 17, 1944. Note the C-47 on the right proceeding closer to the Maas Bridge. This is the plane of Lieutenant Thompson. *Courtesy: Graafs Museum/Jan Timmermans*

Flak tower on the north end of the Maas Bridge at Grave, September 1945.
Courtesy: Mandle family

North end of the Maas Bridge at Grave, September 1945. It was the longest
bridge in Europe that was captured by the 504th. *Courtesy: Mandle family*

British XXX Corps troops crossing the Maas Bridge at Grave, photographed on September 18, 1944 by Capt. Moffatt Burriss from the north end of the bridge. *Courtesy: Moffatt Burriss*

Colonel Tucker's troopers jumping above the Regimental DZ at Overasselt, September 17, 1944.

Maas River

Maas Bridge

Overasselt

De Gaasselt farm

Gaasseltsedam

347398

Lt. Col. Warren Williams (with radio) and Capt. Fordyce Gorham (right)
in the center of Overasselt, September 17, 1944. *Courtesy: Louis Hauptfleisch*

German prisoners are escorted past the provisional Regimental CP
in Overasselt, September 17, 1944. *Courtesy: Louis Hauptfleisch*

German prisoners are marched into Overasselt. *Courtesy: Louis Hauptfleisch*

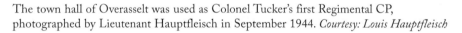

The town hall of Overasselt was used as Colonel Tucker's first Regimental CP, photographed by Lieutenant Hauptfleisch in September 1944. *Courtesy: Louis Hauptfleisch*

Left: Lt. Col. Julian Cook (front) and his 3rd Battalion staff photographed in May 1945. Back row: Lt. Thomas Pitt (S-1), Capt. William Kitchen (Battalion Surgeon), unknown, Capt. Henry Keep (S-3) and Lt. Virgil Carmichael (S-2). *Courtesy: Mandle family*

Below: An unidentified 504th lieutenant and two troopers in a captured German staff car in Overasselt, September 1944. *Courtesy: Louis Hauptfleisch*

Members of the regimental staff inspect a captured German staff
car in Overasselt. *Courtesy: Louis Hauptfleisch*

German prisoners lined up in Overasselt. *Courtesy: Louis Hauptfleisch*

The resupply mission of B-24 Liberators near Overasselt on September 18, 1944 again caused excitement of the local inhabitants. *Courtesy: Louis Hauptfleisch*

German prisoners are marched into the fields around Overasselt to collect dropped supplies, September 18, 1944. *Courtesy: Louis Hauptfleisch*

Capt. Fordyce Gorham interrogating German prisoners in Overasselt.
Courtesy: Louis Hauptfleisch

Dutch citizens and some of Col. Tucker's troopers at the post office in
Grave, September 18, 1944. *Courtesy: Graafs Museum/Jan Timmermans*

Windmill near Hatert. *Courtesy: Mandle family*

Willem "Willy" van Ee was a Dutch volunteer who joined E Company at Nijmegen and would remain with them until the war's end in May 1945. *Courtesy: Sari van Ee*

This man, Ben Bouman has worked with B Co. 504 in the past and is unquestion alright.

Henry C Dunavant
1st Lt Inf

Pass issued to Ben Bouman by Lt. Henry Dunavant, B Company, as proof of his reliability as a Dutch guide. *Courtesy: Ben Bouman*

Above: Lt. Henry Dunavant, company executive officer of B Company, photographed in front of his airplane on September 17, 1944. *Courtesy: Linda Clark*

Right: Maj. Abdallah K. Zakby (with mustache) and other 1st Battalion officers in England, Summer 1944. *Courtesy: Mandle family*

Sgt. Grady Robbins of the 3rd Battalion Machine-Gun Platoon was killed during the attack of I Company in the morning of September 21, 1944 near Lent. *Courtesy: Kathleen Buttke*

Sgt. Thomas Carter (seen as a POW) made his first combat flight as a crew chief on September 17, 1944. He was the only crewmember of Capt. Richard Bohannan's fated C-47 to survive the flight into Holland and was captured. *Courtesy: Thomas Carter*

Kompanie Runge of the Fallschirm-Panzergrenadier Division 2 Hermann Göring. This company was commanded by *Hauptmann* Max Runge.

The 1st Platoon was positioned south of Bridge Number 9 and defended the area until the hamlet of Droge, just north of Bridge Number 8, where Kompanie Rümmele was positioned. The 2nd Platoon was kept in reserve and would be used for reconnaissance. The 3rd Platoon was also to create a bridgehead across the river from Bridge Number 9, in case Allied armored forces came up from the Belgian-Dutch border. While the Hermann Göring Division and some old bridge guards and flak units were responsible for the defense of the Waal Bridges, Landesschützen Battailon II/6 was to defend the west side of Nijmegen: the Maas-Waal Canal was its main line of resistance. Sieger had set up his headquarters in the monastery school in Hatert, while the battalion command post was miles away to the east, in the German village of Kranenburg.

"When on September 17, 1944 the battle started with the landing of enemy paratroopers," recalled *Hauptmann* Sieger, "the company was on the east side of the Maas-Waal Canal, with the order to defend the MLR to the last man and the last round and destroy the enemy. Company strength was two officers and 164 NCOs and enlisted men. Combat experience and equipment were lacking. The average age of the recruits was 59-years-old; they were non-combatant veterans of the First World War and non-suitable cadre members who either had not fought in that war, or had been part of a branch other than the infantry. Very few non-commissioned officers and men had already been in combat.

"Apart from incomplete equipment, the company needed to acquire vehicles and horses to be mobile. Earlier passing German troops had confiscated almost all of these around Hatert, so the company had immense trouble to obtain them. Such was the company situation when enemy airborne forces and paratroopers came down in unknown strength in the Malden-Groesbeek area at 1430 hours on September 17. The landings were seen from the company command post. Our 1st Platoon was led by Feldwebel Ingendahl, who had been assigned from Battalion II/6 a few days earlier. The 2nd Platoon was led by *Feldwebel* Engelmann, since the actual platoon leader, *Oberfeldwebel* Möhle, had received leave on the afternoon of September 17, due to his father's death. The 3rd Platoon was commanded by *Stabsfeldwebel* Von der Heide. *Leutnant* Königsmann was with me.

"*Feldwebel* Ingendahl, whose platoon covered the left flank of the company sector, reported that his link-up with the nearby 5th Kompanie had been lost; the 5th Company guarded the bridge at Droge [Bridge Number 8], which had been blown; and he was in fire contact with the enemy. This report came to the company command post about two hours after the spotted parachute drop, and *Leutnant* Königsmann had already sent two squads of the reserve platoon to cover our left flank, south of the village of Hatert. These groups were reinforced by the light machine-gun crew of Pionier Kompanie 434. The east side of the village was defended by the remainder of the company. This created an all-round defense of Hatert with an opening to the north in the direction of neighboring Kompanie Runge.

"Around 1830 hours, Pionier Kompanie 434 received orders to move to Lent. The report was delivered by *Oberinspektor* Wieland, who arrived by motorcycle. He had received at the same time the order to pull back his Pionier Bau Kompanie from Malden. I asked Wieland to withdraw along my company command post, so that I could learn the latest on the situation in Malden. Forty minutes later, Wieland re-entered and reported that Malden was clear of enemy troops, but there was no sight of the Pionier Bau Kompanie or the 5th Kompanie. I then ordered the two committed squads of *Leutnant* Königsmann to merge with the 1st Platoon, because *Feldwebel* Ingendahl reported increasing exchanges of fire and enemy forces on the other side. The remainder of the company had meanwhile been relocated to the school in Hatert, about 300 meters from the CP. If the situation required, we would move the CP in that direction. Even with insufficient vehicles, we could still take all the material and equipment.

"Around 2000 hours I received orders from Kampfgruppe Runge through an *oberleutnant* to move via the Nijmegen-Malden-Mook road toward the southern edge of Nijmegen, on the left flank of Kampfgruppe Runge. Runge was defending the bridge on the southwest side of the city across the Maas-Waal Canal [Bridge Number 10] that leads toward Grave. Because of this order I gave the command to blow the Hatert-Overasselt Bridge in the center of the company's sector, after parts of the company on the other side had been withdrawn. The bridge was completely destroyed at 2015 hours.

"I sent couriers with orders to the platoon leaders to move and reassemble at the Hatert-Hees road. The collection point was precisely placed where the dam converges with the street. *Feldwebel* Ingendahl meanwhile received the exact order through the non-commissioned officer Gummersbach and then through the leader of the Company Group, *Feldwebel* Pursche. I stayed with *Leutnant* Königsmann at the collection point, and as it got dark the company marched off in sections toward Bridge Number 10, as the platoon leaders of the 2nd and 3rd Platoons later reported to me.

"After *Feldwebel* Pursche reported that the 1st Platoon was on its way, I left a guide at the collection point and went with *Leutnant* Königsmann to Kampfgruppe Runge to receive battle orders from *Oberleutnant* Böhme. It was now dark, just before 2200 hours. I gathered the company in *Oberleutnant* Böhme's CP, where I ascertained that only two squads from the 1st Platoon had arrived; the remainder, along with two squads of the 2nd Platoon were missing. I gave orders to find out whether the guide had reported in, and discovered he had not. I thus ordered non-commissioned officer Keller to drive to the company collection point and investigate the whereabouts of *Feldwebel* Ingendahl and his men.

"Keller reported around midnight that neither he nor the guide had been unable to locate them. Further inquiries were impossible because I had meanwhile received a repeated order from Kompanie Böhme to move into position on his left flank, and it was now pitch dark. It is possible that *Feldwebel* Ingendahl was surprised as he moved out and had to find another escape route [FVL, trans.]."[124]

The 504th Regimental S-3 Journal entry recorded at 0108 hours reads: "First Bn called: Have 30 prisoners, shall we send them in now or later? (Send them in now.)"[125] Eventually 32 prisoners of war were brought in and identified as members of the 5th Kompanie of Landesschützen Battailon II/6. These men were unaware of the tactical withdrawal of *Hauptmann* Sieger's company, nor could they predict that Sieger's men would cross swords with Tucker's troopers on more occasions during the following days.

City of Grave from the air, looking west in 1945. The city
was liberated by Major Edward Wellems' 2nd Battalion
on September 18, 1944. *Courtesy: Mandle family*

CHAPTER 7

CONSOLIDATING THE REGIMENTAL SECTOR: GRAVE, NEERBOSCH, NIJMEGEN, WYCHEN, SEPTEMBER 18–19, 1944

Although Tucker's troopers captured most of the regimental objectives, there were still two left to secure: Grave and Bridge Number 10 at the Maas-Waal Canal. Captain Campana, the D Company commander, recalled that "about 0230 hours on September 18, the battalion moved out to seize and occupy Grave. Order of attack—F, D and HQ Companies—no opposition was encountered. The battalion set up perimeter defense of the town and waited for junction with the British. Patrols were sent out day and night for several miles to learn the whereabouts of any enemy forces."[126]

Dutch civilians revealed that on the previous night, a Dutch SS-Battalion had withdrawn to the east and tracked vehicles had been heard around 0440 hours, but no counterattack developed. First Lieutenant Chester A. Garrison, the 2nd Battalion S-1 officer, described the streets as he entered the center of Grave: "As I rounded the corner of the town hall, I entered the town square, where a large crowd of Dutchmen had gathered. Several of them pointed to the center of the square. There I saw that citizens had formed a tight circle around three young women bunched together. Their clothes were torn, and their hair had been shaved off. Swastikas had been painted on the bald domes so recently that black paint still dripped down to their foreheads, ears, and necks. They were desolate Dutch girls who had lived with the occupying Germans, prostituting themselves for food, clothes, and money—and fun? The crowd was not unruly, only determined in its revenge."[127]

Major Wellems established the 2nd Battalion CP in the town hall, affixing "Cider White CP" above the entrance, in reference to the battalion's official call sign. Not long later he was cheered by a jubilant Dutch crowd gathered in front of the CP. Four-and-a-half years of occupation had ended for the citizens of Grave. Wellems recalled that the war went on as his troopers "established outposts and a perimeter defense, made roadblocks to the east (one already existed to the south, Company E) and sent patrols out south, southeast, east and west. No patrols were sent across the river to the north. Prisoners began to trickle in, roadblocks increased and were strengthened in mines."[128]

As the 504th nervously awaited the arrival of British tanks, Lieutenant Garrison reported in the battalion journal that "several American Air Corps men were brought out of local hiding and sent back to Division." They received a "tremendous resupply by parachute and glider in the afternoon." The "bundles were much dispersed" and some fell in the river, requiring the "organization of troops, townspeople, and vehicles to recover them." Thanks to captured automobiles and trucks, supply functioning was eased, and there was "no serious trouble from German troops," although there were "rumors concerning the possibility of scattered hidden troops a short way down the river. Division required immediate reports of landing from all jump commanders."[129]

Dutch civilians informed Major Wellems that a small Gestapo detachment had been in the city and a battalion of approximately 500 men of the Fallschirm-Panzergrenadier Division 2 "Hermann Göring" —and not an SS-Battalion—had fled east toward Nijmegen. At 0830 hours news came through that two tanks seen at De Elft the previous day had been spotted by local residents a few miles south of Grave. This report led to the attachment of two 57mm anti-tank guns commanded by 1st Lt. Russell G. Busdicker of B Battery, 80th Airborne Anti-Aircraft Battalion, in the late afternoon.

At 0630 hours Major Cook and Captain Keep left the 3rd Battalion CP to look over the battalion positions. Cook was satisfied with the set-up: more means of transportation were expected later that morning, but meanwhile, captured German vehicles, civilian cars, bicycles and horse carts had temporarily solved the problem. However, at 0915 hours, 1st Lt. Charles A. Drew of G Company reported by radio that civilians had stated that Germans were advancing south from Kasteel Wychen along the road toward the villages of Balgoij and Keent. Anticipating a German attack on the west side of the American perimeter near Nederasselt, Major Cook instructed 1st Lt. Robert C. Blankenship to take two squads from his 1st Platoon of I Company to deal with the situation.

That morning, Captain Thomas and his G Company men "looked around to see what we could find to eat and then dug in positions and foxholes. Several members had picked up bicycles and we had the use of a truck of ancient (BC) vintage and a car that was little better. About 1300 hours the Company CP moved up about one-and-a-half or two miles and set up in a very large, clean house about half a kilometer [about 550 yards] outside of Alverna. Platoons were set up along the road, some being in Alverna itself. Foxholes were dug around the Company CP and guards posted for the night."[130]

Captain Kappel "dispatched two squads of the 3rd Platoon to Wijchen. One tractor trailer of about fifteen-ton capacity, three motorcycles and one prisoner were captured. The enemy deserted the town, burning their vehicles. There were no casualties to H Company. Beginning at about 1430 hours, 450 gliders passed to our right, bringing in three battalions of artillery, one anti-tank battery, and the [307th Airborne] Medical Company, landing on LZ 'N.' Upon return to the H Company perimeter of the 3rd Platoon, two squads of the 2nd Platoon were assigned to penetrate the town of Hernen, capture transportation, and in general keep the enemy off balance. Two captured enemy motorcycles were attached for transporting machine guns, reconnaissance and communication. The patrol encountered no enemy and consequently no prisoners or vehicles were taken."[131]

The glider elements were late in arriving; their departure had been postponed for a few hours due to heavy fog in England. One trooper of Service Company, Pvt. Edward J. Miller, was killed in a vehicle accident. The jeeps and trailers were divided over two glider serials: one departed from Balderton Airfield and landed at 1518 hours at LZ "N" near Groesbeek, and the other serial departed from Cottesmore Airfield and came down at LZ "T" around 1445 hours. Capt. Adam A. Komosa, who had received a jump injury a few weeks earlier, could not jump with his own Headquarters and Headquarters Company and was scheduled to land in a glider. Komosa recalled that "our glider load consisted of Flight Officer Waldrip, the pilot; a jeep and my jeep driver; two Dutch commandos; and myself as co-pilot. My sole responsibility during the flight was to pull the parachute release handle located overhead, in order to break the landing roll of the glider just as we came into the landing. There was no mention of what I should do should the pilot become a flak casualty. Even though I had never been at the controls of a glider before, it was quite obvious to me what my responsibilities would be should such an incident occur.

"When the Dutch commandos reported to me, they immediately complained that they were not issued any invasion currency and expressed their grievances about the shabby treatment they were accorded by the British with whom they fought. After obtaining the necessary rations and money for my two Dutch passengers, we loaded into the glider, a Waco CG-4A.

"The glider elements took off between 1000 and 1100 hours with each C-47 power aircraft towing two gliders. As we rolled down the runway the horrible metallic noise of the glider wheels gave me the feeling of being pulled down the runway in a metal wheelbarrow. Just before becoming airborne, pilot Waldrip picked up the intercom speaker and attempted to contact the pilot in the tow plane. No dice! Apparently the wire in the towline between the plane and the glider had broken somewhere along the line. Too late! There was no turning back. From now we had to play it by sight.

"After we became airborne and assembled, we headed eastward across the English Channel in an endless flying wedge of C-47s and gliders. Over the Channel, the British glider elements flew below us in absolutely no formation. They looked just like a swarm of gnats flying over the water. Below these formations a number of British Horsa gliders were scattered in the drink along our flight path, surrounded with orange dye markers. Glidermen were either swarming over the plywood hulls or swimming in the water. The British prepared themselves well for this contingency, because for just about every glider I saw in the water, there was either a rescue craft picking up the survivors or one streaming on its way to do so. I saw none of the American canvas-covered gliders in the Channel. The reason for this was that we used a nylon tow line, while the British used hemp, which had very little play when the gliders hit bumpy air currents.

"As we passed over the Scheldt Estuary, a flak gun opened up on us. About that time a P-51 fighter plane flew along side of us and waggled his wings. I waved back, then he pealed down into the flak position like a falcon pouncing on his prey. After spewing his stream of angry machine-gun fire into the target, he soared back up to our level, wagged his wings again, and we received no more flak from then on. It was a comforting feeling, since none of us in the glider had any parachutes.

"The critical moment was soon upon us. We were now approaching our landing zone. But I noticed that Waldrip had already reached up to pull the tow-release lever in preparation for releasing the glider from its power craft. I shouted to him, 'Not yet, this is not our DZ!' He just looked straight ahead, and as the glider on his left released, so did he. I said, 'Oh hell! We've released too soon. We are not over our LZ.' Waldrip was completely oblivious to my conversation. He held a tight grip on his wheel, and as though in a trance, he maneuvered his glider through a swarm of other powerless gliders into what appeared to be the best available landing area.

"As we were just a few feet from the ground, the glider nicked the posterior of a cow, lunged over into a barbed wire fence fortunately running into the direction of the flight path, then finally approached the touchdown. But, lo and behold, a canal ran across our front. There was no zooming over it. We had no power. Waldrip yelled, 'Chute!' I pulled the landing parachute lever. Soon we felt a soft tug to our rear as it opened. Now we were rolling across Dutch terrain with that canal ominously looming before us. I pictured the glider plowing its nose into the opposite bank and the jeep behind us giving us a 'home ram.' But the glider slowed down enough so that it sort of lobbed itself over the canal and plowed through the opposite bank, tail up.

"When we came to a screeching halt, the floor of the cockpit was practically torn out. Waldrip immediately pulled out his jack knife, cut through the canvas, jumped out through the opening, and went into a crouching position with his Tommy gun. In the meantime, I pulled the lever to open the nose of the glider in order to get out and unload the jeep. In probably less than a minute, all five of us were loaded on the jeep and on our way to make contact with our parent unit.

"Along the way we saw many crazy sights. Among the hundreds of gliders in the most awkward positions, one was jammed into a windmill with its tail jutting into the air at an angle of about 65 degrees from the horizontal. On arrival at the CP, the Dutch commandos detached themselves to make contact with the Dutch Underground, while Flight Officer Waldrip joined his colleagues, who were pooled under Lt. Col. John P. Geiger, the Division Chemical Warfare Officer. The mission of this group was to guard the POWs and to assist in the recovery of aerial resupply. The glider pilots were extremely anxious for the British land tail to make contact with the paratroopers so that they could get back to their bases where they felt more at home."[132]

One of the Dutch commandos aboard Captain Komosa's WACO was 24-year-old Cpl. Valentijn G. Kokhuis, who had never flown in a glider before. He reported to Colonel Williams and was assigned to the 3rd Battalion as guide and interpreter. Kokhuis would receive a commendation from Tucker on October 10, 1944, for being "an efficient and versatile soldier of excellent character who displayed unusual ability in locating and dealing with Nazi collaborators and assisting the 504th Parachute Infantry as well as the Allied cause in numerous other ways."[133]

Captain Kappel sent radio operator Albert Tarbell out to the DZ to meet the H Company jeep and guide it to the company sector: "I was on the ground on D+1 to meet our jeep driver with his jeep and trailer. The landing master told me to be careful of the gliders when they came in. As luck would have it, his glider landed just a little way from where I was standing."[134]

According to Kappel, "B-24 bombers brought in resupply at DZ 'O' at 1620 hours. Drops were at a very low altitude but poorly concentrated. About 80-percent was recovered, the best record to date. Boxes of rations, detached from parachutes, struck company and platoon CPs, burst open and scattered rations all through the company area in true foxhole delivery.

"All available men of Company H, less patrols and skeleton defense crews, were immediately put to work stock-piling ammunition first, then rations, in convenient piles throughout the area. The Battalion S-4, with the assistance of Dutch civilians, farm wagons, and those animals the Germans had left to the Dutch, immediately began concentrating these small piles into larger ones. This was soon taken over by the Division G-4. Jeeps and trailers began to appear on the roads from the glider lift."[135]

Captain Komosa remembered the inspiring "roar of hundreds of aircraft motors reverberating over the flat Dutch countryside" as a "a flight of 135 B-24 bombers thundered in at an altitude of about 500 feet and dropped hundreds of equipment and supply bundles bearing multi-colored parachutes. In an attempt to dislodge a hung-up equipment bundle, a crew member lost his balance, slipped through the bomb bay and plunged to his death." Dutch civilians "eagerly assisted the less-than-enthusiastic glider pilots" in the recovery, and Komosa witnessed "one young Dutchman get painfully hit across the side of his head by an oscillating ammunition bundle as it fell to the ground. The Dutch people received us with much enthusiasm and insisted that we come into their houses for bread, milk and cheese. That awe-inspiring B-24 flight overhead gave us a feeling of invincibility. No longer did we feel our isolation over 50 miles behind the German lines."[136]

Thirty German prisoners were put to work packing parachutes on Hendrik Jansen's farm in Overasselt, while 1st Battalion patrols moved north to secure Bridge Number 10. It was captured by Lt. Lloyd Pollette and two platoons of the 508th PIR, while the 1st Platoon of A Company patrolled along the west side of the Maas-Waal Canal in the direction of the bridge, a movement which forced the surrender of the Germans at the bridge. Platoon leader Lieutenant Breard recalls patrolling "north into the outskirts of Nijmegen" where they "found a bicycle factory and started assembling them. Getting grease for the assembly line was a problem."[137]

Seventeen-year-old Wim van Lunteren and his five younger sisters were living at Kinderdorp Neerbosch, a Protestant orphanage in the small village of Neerbosch at Westkanaaldijk 301, located a few hundred yards northwest of Bridge Number 10.[138] Wim and about a dozen other teenage boys walked over to the bridge in the late afternoon of September 18, bringing handfuls of hay and apples to the American paratroopers at the Maas-Waal Canal. In return they received cigarettes and candy. One of Wim's friends, Jan van Deelen, was offered his first American cigarette by Private Steger of A Company.[139] They exchanged addresses and kept in touch for a few years after the war. Wim felt strange being liberated, knowing that his older brothers and sisters, grandparents, uncles, aunts and cousins were still under German occupation in central and northern Holland. Even so, he later remembered the liberation as the beginning of the best time he spent in the orphanage.

A Company platoons dug in on top of the dike parallel to the Maas-Waal Canal. Cpl. Fred Baldino, 2nd Platoon, remembered all went well until dusk, when "a trooper came down the canal, below where we were dug-in, and looked up. It being dusk, I presume he thought we were Germans from the outline of the helmets. He fired up at John and shot him through the head. I was only about 30 feet from him when he got shot.

"We all yelled at him and a few guys ran after him, but he took off under the underpass of the dike and nobody ever caught or identified him. One of my buddies said he was from the 307th Airborne Engineer Battalion. How very sad it was." Private Burnett died in the arms of his assistant gunner, Pvt. Daren Broadhead. On the spot, Broadhead became the new 2nd Platoon BAR gunner.

"We all felt very bad over this incident because Burnett was such a well-liked buddy of ours," Baldino later wrote. "It is sad enough to be killed by the Germans—but to be killed by your own troops is disastrous. The sad thing is I did not know any of his family. I tried to find them, but the name is very common, and I never had any luck."[140]

At the time Operation Market Garden took place, 21-year-old Benjamin Bouman was hiding in the village of Mook. "Ben" had seen 505th paratroopers descending near Groesbeek and later encountered a patrol from the 82nd ABD Reconnaissance Platoon. On September 18, he bicycled to the lockbridge across the Maas-Waal Canal on a visit to his girlfriend Truus, who lived in nearby Heumen. Bouman talked to members of 1st Platoon, B Company, dug in on the east side of the lockbridge. He then went into the lockkeeper's house, where he had seen German guards before the airborne landings. Checking out the premises, he discovered five German soldiers hiding in the loft, and persuaded them to give up. Bouman handed over his prisoners to 2nd Lt. Richard A. Smith, then proceeded to his girlfriend's and cycled back to Mook late that afternoon.

Throughout the day, Dutch civilians transmitted messages that German tanks were approaching, but most appeared to be false. German defensive forces were in a state of chaos until early morning, September 18. The previous day, *Hauptmann* Hagemeister, the Ortskommandant (local garrison commander) of Nijmegen, had fled across the Waal toward Elst. *Oberst* Fritz Hencke of the Luftwaffe managed to gather 750 men and organize a defensive position around the Waal bridges. This force, known as Kampfgruppe Hencke, was composed of several smaller forces: Kampfgruppe Runge, Kampfgruppe Reinhold and Kampfgruppe Euling.

As previously mentioned, Kampfgruppe Runge was a company of the Panzergrenadier Division 2 "Hermann Göring," commanded by *Hauptmann* Max Runge. The other two units were part of *SS-Brigadeführer* Heinz Harmel's 10th SS-Panzer Division "Frundsberg." These three battle groups were augmented by 20mm and 88mm flak gunners near the Waal bridges, police reservists, railway guards and Hencke's Ersatz Fallschirmjäger Regiment. *SS-Sturmbannführer*. Leo Reinhold, commander of Kampfgruppe Reinhold, led a combined force of his own SS-Panzer Regiment 10 and SS-Panzer Pionier Bataillon 10, which reinforced German troops in Nijmegen by supervising the Rhine ferry at Pannerden and defending the road bridge. Just southwest of the road bridge, *SS-Hauptsturmführer* Karl-Heinz Euling and his I. Batallion of SS-Panzergrenadier Regiment 21 were dug-in at Hunner Park. His men had been pulled from their positions at the Arnhem road bridge in the wee hours of the morning and quickly transferred through Nijmegen via the Pannerden ferry. Later that day, Euling's men and other elements denied the 508th PIR access to the south end of the road bridge.

Still in the area as well, the three companies of Landesschützen Battailon II/6 had withdrawn then regrouped during the night. "In the early morning of September 18, 1944," recalled *Hauptmann* Sieger, "contact was achieved with the left flank of Kompanie Böhme and the company secured almost one kilometer extending south beyond the Nijmegen-Grave road. Pionier Kompanie 434 was attached to the company on the left. Strong enemy pressure on the Gravsche Brücke [Bridge Number 10] and in the city of Nijmegen required several dispositions, as ordered by Kampfgruppe Runge. The bridge itself remained under heavy fire, causing Runge to be drawn into the battle, and the wires for blowing the bridge were damaged. About midday communication with Kampfgruppe Runge ceased, as they had given up their bridgehead and moved towards Nijmegen in the direction of the Nijmegen-Arnhem railway bridge. They had failed to notify us. Pionier Kompanie 434 did receive the order to retreat and also moved off. I decided to join them, due to the danger of capture. The march followed the canal and the Waal until reaching the Nijmegen-Arnhem railway bridge.

"Kampfgruppe Runge absorbed us and confirmed that the company was to withdraw to the newly created bridgehead. The heavy equipment was moved on the ammunition wagon across the railway bridge to Lent. Only the drivers could cross; all others had to remain at the bridgehead. The company's first assignment was to secure and hold the railway dike as far as the railway station. On the west side of the railway dike some stragglers joined up. The Company CP came under enemy fire in late afternoon, causing some wounded.

"Around 2000 hours the company received the order to occupy the northwest side of the city and to secure and hold the railway dike at the new harbor. For fire support, two 20mm flak guns and a Russian 45mm anti-tank gun were employed. The Company CP was at the new harbor.

"The night of September 18–19 was quiet. In the morning, the company started consolidating its position on the northwest side of the city. Shortly before noon we learned the enemy had moved about 15 tanks and armored vehicles to reinforce his forces in Nijmegen. Kampfgruppe Runge confirmed the destruction of a [British] armored reconnaissance vehicle. The military action took place at the bridge in the northeastern parts of the city and at the railway bridge.

"Moving west from within the city towards the railway bridge, the enemy attacked with tanks, armored reconnaissance cars and infantry. Heavy fire rained down on the Company CP and harbor. I received the order to secure the entrance to the bridge and formed a group for this purpose. I ordered *Leutnant* Königsmann to fight his way to the company and take charge. Our line received extraordinarily heavy, relentless fire from a Sherman tank, killing or wounding several men in our group. The fire lasted for about an hour, before the tank was put out of action by members of the Einheit Runge. The Company CP had been completely demolished and encircled by the accompanying enemy infantry. Having disposed of the enemy tank, *Hauptmann* Runge then launched a counterattack that relieved our Company CP.

"As the enemy approached, parts of Pionier Kompanie 434 on the west side of the city headed toward the Waal, intending to cross. There *Leutnant* Königsmann gathered part of the Pionier-Einheit and both 20mm flak guns, and immediately sent them into action while *Hauptmann* Runge launched a counterattack from the Company CP area. Because of strong enemy fire, increasing casualties and the fall of darkness, the counterattack did not achieve its goal, which meant enemy fire from the houses, and a breakthrough to the southeast was impossible. In view of the situation, we could also expect an enemy attack from the west, so *Leutnant* Königsmann gathered the remnants of the company, about 80 men, at the electricity works approximately two kilometers northwest of the railway bridge.

"*Leutnant* Königsmann then formed a reconnaissance patrol consisting of one *Feldwebel*, one *Unteruffizier* and one *Gefreiter* and proceeded to the Company CP to clarify the situation. The Company CP was dismantled and the company withdrew to the bridgehead at the railway bridge. Except for a few men who had crossed with Pionier Einheit, every man save the wounded were brought back.

"The company took up quarters in the *Luftschutzraum-Verpflegungslager* [the air-raid shelter at the field hospital] in the immediate vicinity of the bridge. During the counterattack an entire flak-gun crew was killed or wounded. The remaining battle groups were then merged under the command of *Oberst* [Günther] Hartung (Training staff, Fallschirmjäger Armee, Oberkommando Ausbildungsstelle in Nijmegen). *Hauptmann* Zyrus (Fallschirmjäger) led the defense of the railroad bridge, *Major* [Engelbert] Melitz (Luftwaffe) was in charge of the area between the railroad and road bridges, and a *Hauptmann* from the Hermann Göring Division was in charge of the road bridge. The headquarters of *Oberst* Hartung were in Lent."[141]

Hauptmann Sieger's report does not disclose that a single 504th paratrooper, PFC Theodore H. "Ted" Bachenheimer, from the 1st Battalion S-2 section, rode a Dutch bicycle into Nijmegen and frightened the German defenders (including Sieger's unit) at the Central Station in Nijmegen facing D Company, 2/505. At 0600, Bachenheimer's immediate superior, 1st Lt. James H. Goethe, reported to Captain Gorham at 0600 hours that it had been quiet all night, which may have encouraged Bachneheimer to make his way into Nijmegen. At 0650 they received a radio report from the 1st Battalion commander, Major Harrison, at the Regimental CP in Overasselt: "Bachenheimer led patrol into Nijmegen. Found about 300 Hollanders armed and ready to fight. Reported Bridge north of 10 blown (not confirmed)."[142]

When Bachenheimer returned that afternoon, he requested two volunteers to accompany him by bicycle back to Nijmegen to join the Dutch Resistance group in the town. PFC Willard Strunk from A Company and a German-speaking Pennsylvanian, Pvt. William "Bill" Zeller from Headquarters Company, 1st Battalion, accepted. As Strunk recalled, "There weren't two bike riders in the platoon. So, being a farm boy from Kansas who had never ridden before, I volunteered, and Bill Zeller and I went with Ted by bicycle to Nijmegen.

"After the first sniper shot, I was the best damn bike rider in the country. Ted took us to the Underground headquarters in a transformer factory, where he took charge at their request. We later moved the headquarters into a school house [the Agnes Reiniera School on the Groenestraat], where one wall was full of souvenirs. Ted organized patrols to clean out Germans in the city. The town was being continually bombed [by German artillery].

"It was a big job keeping up the Dutch people's morale. It was raining every day. Seeing that people got food and shelter was a big morale-builder, as was seeing that the wounded were being cared for. Ted was one of the finest soldiers any country would ever want. He was a very calm in all circumstances. At night he would organize patrols and go behind German lines to get information on German positions. He could speak German fluently. While on patrol, he often talked to the Germans, who the combat patrol then took prisoner. He was very serious about his work. He would sit and discuss ideas about how to get information from the Germans. We used anything we could. Once we thought of using a boat to go up the river. The night we were going to use it, the current was too strong for the boat to move upstream. We abandoned that idea."[143]

Verlee, the local Resistance leader, transferred the leadership of the Resistance group to Bachenheimer. On September 19, he and a member of the railway company Nederlandsche Spoorwegen moved to chase the Germans out of the central station in Nijmegen. In 1952, he posthumously received the Bronze Lion, the Dutch equivalent of the Distinguished Service Cross, for having "Distinguished himself by brave conduct against the enemy when, after having been dropped on September 17, 1944 near Grave, he proceeded alone and in a daring manner during the afternoon of the 19th toward the railway station at Nijmegen. In particular, he met a foreman in charge of the tracks for Netherlands railways, and the two moved from the viaduct near the Graafseweg across the railway yard and entered the station.

Both entered unseen, and in an exceedingly bold move, the foreman took a carbine, ammunition and hand grenades from a train, while Bachenheimer covered him with his weapon. They proceeded with extreme caution to the public address system on the second platform, which the foreman then activated.

Bachenheimer menacingly ordered the occupying enemy, who had just gathered for a meal, to surrender, firing his automatic weapon directly in front of the microphone, causing the entire enemy group of about 40 men to flee the station in panic.

Finally, Bachenheimer and the foreman moved to the west end of the station, expulsing enemies by firing on them, and held the station until well-directed enemy artillery fire from across the Waal forced them to withdraw, after which the station was once more occupied by a strong enemy party."[144]

That morning, initial British forces finally arrived at the Maas Bridge at Grave, establishing the first link-up with the southern part of the so-called "airborne corridor." Lt. Gen. Frederick Browning, commander of I Airborne Corps, headquartered at Groesbeek, drove to Overasselt to confer with Brig. Gen. James M. Gavin. First Lieutenant John S. Thompson of E Company recalled: "on the morning of the 19th, the Irish Guards spearheading the British Second Army were contacted south of Grave, and it was a welcome sight to watch them from our positions all that day with their array of tanks and trucks."[145]

Many young Dutchmen offered their services to the 504th as scouts, interpreters or riflemen. One, Willem van Ee, a 22-year-old from Arnhem, had been hiding in Nijmegen when Operation Market Garden began. With the Waal bridges and the southern shore of the Rhine River at Arnhem still under German occupation, it was impossible for him to rejoin his parents, and he was accepted as a rifleman in E Company, 2nd Platoon. Private Kunde recalled that one of the squad leaders, Sgt. Dwayne J. Ahrendt, took Willem under his wing and paid for all his expenses, since their Dutch friend could not be placed on the pay roll. Another platoon member, Sgt. Willis D. Sisson, remembered that he nicknamed the tall Dutchman "Willy." The name stuck, and Willy became close friends with his platoon members, who arranged to provide him with a uniform, helmet and other equipment.[146]

But not all 82nd officers were happy about the issue of weapons and uniforms to Dutch volunteers. Colonel Williams, the regimental executive officer, recalled that "on the third day after the drop, General Gavin arrived very upset at the 504th CP. The day before he had directed that we cease giving the rifles, jackets and helmets of wounded paratroopers to young Dutchmen and stop using them to augment our forces. He asked why this was still being done, to which we replied that maybe someone had not gotten the word. He stated, 'I'll say they haven't, because that guard on the first crossroad was dressed in an American uniform and armed with an M-1 rifle and he could not speak English.' In spite of instructions to the contrary, our troopers continued to equip and utilize a number of young Dutchmen to augment their ranks. These Dutch were most anxious to fight the Germans and proved very capable soldiers."[147]

The Dutch volunteers were not only helpful as guides and riflemen, but also as translators during the interrogation of German prisoners. Living next to Germany and having experienced four-and-a-half years of occupation, many civilians had become familiar with the German language. Captain Komosa recalled that "the original group of prisoners was mostly a rear-echelon hodgepodge, a mixture of old men and wounded veterans. I saw one cocky young Afrika Korps German among the group. When asked what a youngster such as himself was doing back in the rear area, he arrogantly replied that he was wounded in Africa and could never again fight in a combat unit.[...] There was also a corpulent sailor. It was indeed a motley bunch, but these Germans nevertheless maintained their arrogant Prussian-type discipline."[148]

On the afternoon of the 19th, the 3rd Battalion was placed in division reserve and moved across Bridge Number 7 into the southern suburbs of Nijmegen. Captain Thomas's G Company Journal for the day read: "The Dutch family living in the house prepared a breakfast for the CP group who were staying in the house. While we were eating, 16 prisoners captured during the night by the platoons came into the CP under guard. They were immediately sent back to the Battalion CP. The company's musette bags had been brought forward to a central dump where the men could get them. However most of the bags and bedrolls were missing and the few that were there had all been thoroughly searched. Everything of any value to us had been removed by the Dutch when we left our bags at the battalion assembly area.

"About 0930 hours word was received from battalion that the first British armoured car preceding General Dempsey's tanks had crossed the Grave Bridge. A little later they passed our Company CP, followed by tanks. The British went only a short distance past the Company CP before discovering that the next bridge up the road had been demolished. They then turned around, returned to the crossroad and went by a different route. Early in the afternoon, another prisoner was returned to the CP and then went back to the Battalion CP.

"Captain Thomas was in Alverna looking for a likely place to set up our Company CP. The only likely place turned out to be a bar. The possible psychological effect that this might have on the men must have been considered, because a schoolhouse was substituted later. When the CO and several of the men who were with him entered the schoolhouse, it was discovered to contain some new Jerry radios and about five or six large boxes of Jerry S-3 equipment. Word was sent back to Battalion Headquarters to the S-2 and S-3 officers who came by and looked the equipment over. A few of the lesser articles of this equipment are still at present in the company. By this time the whole company was assembled in an area just at the outskirts of Alverna and word had been received that Company G would be the reserve and that the regiment was moving up.

"About 1830 word was received that Company I would take our place as reserve company and that we should prepare to move out. Company G moved out about 1900 up both sides of the road, with the British armed forces moving up the center. We crossed a canal whose bridge had been partially blown up but had been repaired by the Engineers. Almost immediately after crossing, we turned to the right along the canal. We walked past many Jerry trenches that had been dug-in. Some distance over to our left were many large fires which we were told was the city of Nijmegen."[149]

CHAPTER 8

SUICIDE MISSION
NIJMEGEN, SEPTEMBER 20, 1944

hen Major Cook and Captain Keep went forward on the evening of September 19, Captain Ferguson was tasked to lead the 3rd Battalion to its new location at Jonkerbosch, a forest on the southwest edge of Nijmegen. He had a difficult time reading the map in the dark as they crossed the bridge at Heumen and moved north via the village of Hatert. By 2115 hours they had closed in the woods and reported ready as division reserve.

About 15 minutes later Cook and Keep reported in at the Hotel Sionshof to receive word of their next assignment. General Gavin informed Cook that his battalion was in division reserve and that he needed to search for boats. He replied that both these pieces of information were news to him. Gavin replied that "it was an oversight that they hadn't told me [...] He said I was going to make the assault, that we had to make a river crossing and that I should go looking for boats.

"I was dumbfounded. That's it. I had to say I didn't have any boats and he said, 'Well, you should have been looking around.' Then I was told that the bank on the north side of the river where I was going to make the crossing was over 20 feet above the water level. Straight up, like a wall or something. I was wondering what kind of mountain-climbing instrument I would be able to get a hold of. It was very disturbing.

"He told us that we had to get the bridge to relieve the troops at Arnhem and they were hurting. I don't know if we actually knew how bad it was. I thought that we were going to do it the next morning, so I said, 'Well, my troops are coming up here.' The idea ran in my mind, why the hell are we marching in the wrong direction? He said, 'Let them go in there and we will get some trucks in to them in the morning.'

"Gavin was probably also asking the British for boats, [saying that otherwise] the troops couldn't cross, but he was also working the other way to try and make me get them, [instilling] a great sense of 'My God, how am I going to do this? I can't swim across.' We decided to let the troops go into position, and I think I went back to regiment and reported what I was going to do. I talked to other people, and I am not sure where he called Tucker in on all this."[150]

In fact, Tucker also received word of the planned river crossing that night: "On the night of September 19, I was informed by Division Headquarters that the 504th was to make an assault crossing of the Waal River and to establish a bridgehead on the north end of the road and railroad bridges. I was directed to contact British XXX Corps at General Horrocks's headquarters, where I would meet a British armored commander who would support the 504th crossing with tank fire.

"The division directive to me said to make the crossing September 20, establish the bridgehead and to contact the British armored [unit]. This was not a written order but was given to me by [Lt. Col.] Jack Norton, Division G-3."[151]

First Lieutenant Virgil F. Carmichael, the 3rd Battalion S-2 officer, recalled Major Cook's return to his new CP at Jonkerbosch: "Julian returned to the CP about midnight, and said that General Gavin had told him the battalion was to cross the Waal River in boats the next day. Cook, a courageous and loyal soldier, had asked Gavin about the boats to be used on the assault crossing, and Gavin told him that he would have to collect small boats from the natives along the riverbank. It was all very uncertain. At that time, Gavin either did not know, or had no assurance, that the British would supply collapsible canvas boats for the crossing. We were all frustrated. The Krauts were still along our side of the river at places, so we didn't know if we could even get to the bank where we had been told to cross."[152]

Contrary Cornelius Ryan's *A Bridge Too Far*, Tucker was not present at the meeting where Gavin suggested crossing the river to Browning and Horrocks. As oft-quoted, Ryan stated that the boats were late in arriving and that "all through the night General Horrocks and his staff had been trying to speed their arrival."[153] But in reality Brigadier Charles P. Jones, commanding officer of the Royal Engineer units of the Guards Armoured Division, received the request for boats by phone, early on September 20. He arranged for them to be brought up as soon as possible by 282nd Company, Royal Army Service Corps [RASC] from a depot in Belgium, where his boats were still being stored, and drove to Gavin's headquarters to offer him the use of rafts and two companies of Royal Engineers [RE] to ferry anti-tank guns across.[154] In short, Gavin, Browning and Horrocks failed to arrange boats on time for the crossing to take place during the night.

Captain Keep wrote two months later to his mother: "Division gave the mission of taking the Nijmegen Bridge to the 504th as well as seizing a railroad bridge contiguous to it, which also spanned the broad Waal River. Needless to say, it necessitated a river crossing. In our 18 months of almost steady combat we have seen and done many things—from parachute jumps to establishing bridgeheads, to acting as mountain troops, to say nothing of being used plenty as regular infantry. But a river crossing was something new."[155]

While Major Cook briefed the 3rd Battalion staff officers and company commanders, Colonel Tucker left his Regimental CP to visit XXX Corps Headquarters: "Early in the morning I went to XXX Corps and met General Horrocks and was introduced to Lieutenant Colonel [Giles A.M.] Vandeleur, who would support us. He and I took off with one of his armored cars and a small security group. Suffice it to say we travelled in Nijmegen mostly on foot trying to locate a house, roof or any raised point from which we could see the crossing area. We never found one until we came up to the crossing site about noon."[156]

It was decided to search for a high building in west Nijmegen from which to observe the crossing. The 2nd Battalion was meanwhile alerted to sweep the area to the riverbank clear of Germans. As 1st Lt. Chester A. Garrison, 2nd Battalion adjutant, wrote in the battalion journal that day: "Good sleep, though cold without blankets in foxholes. Up by 0700, ate, and prepared for march. Major Wellems and Captain Norman [2nd Battalion S-3] went to Regiment to get the situation. Captain Colville moved out the battalion (Headquarters and D Companies) by 0800 in column of twos, well separated. Morning somewhat hazy. Sixteen [sic: eight] German planes suddenly appeared along the line of march, flying very low; however, the men were well dispersed and able to take cover under the high trees and in house doorways. Progress was very slow and had numerous halts while the advance elements of D Company probed the way along the streets of the Nijmegen suburbs. Passed through Hees, where there was a temporary halt called for Headquarters Company while D Company went into position under cover along the banks of the Waal River.

"This was accomplished without accident, whereupon Headquarters Company moved into position behind them and on the reserve side of the dikes and into prepared German foxholes, etc. F Company was relieved by a British unit and moved out towards the battalion sector. Headquarters and D Companies were set by 1200. The plan was for them to cover (by intensive small-arms, machine-gun and mortar fire) the 3rd Battalion assault-boat river crossing. The 1st Battalion was to follow the 3rd, and finally the 2nd. The purpose was to get troops to the other side to seize that end of the very important Nijmegen Bridge, which was being firmly held by Germans. D Company got into a firefight with the Germans on the opposite bank, but Regiment ordered them to cease fire so as not to divulge positions, strength and the scheme of events."[157]

Garrison's battalion commander, Major Wellems, recalled that "at this time Company F was guarding the Grave Bridge. Company E was outposting the main highway between the Grave Bridge and the bridge over the Maas-Waal Canal. Company D and Headquarters Company were engaged in sweeping between the Maas-Waal Canal and Nijmegen and in taking up positions for a river crossing. They had only one company of 120 men to do the job (the cleaning up) for the river crossing. They had orders to get this sweeping up done by 1200 and at that time were in position along the dike all the way from the factory to the end of the small peninsula where the river and the canal meet."[158]

First Lieutenant Earnest H. Brown, 1st Platoon leader of D Company, remembered that "we walked from the area of Grave to Nijmegen, about eight miles, and on arrival there, my platoon was ordered to proceed to the power plant and to make sure the riverbank area was clear of any German troops. We were to remain there to give fire support to our 3rd Battalion as it made a river crossing."[159]

In the power station of the Provinciale Geldersche Electriciteits Maatschappij (the regional electricity company), or PGEM, several employees were still present on the morning of September 20. Among them were assistant chief manager Willem Kuiken and the chief manager, Jaap van Gent. The power station was a relatively modern building that had been opened in June 1936. Partisans in Eindhoven called via the PGEM phone line on behalf of British officers to ask Van Gent to report on the condition of the Honinghutje Bridge across the Maas-Waal Canal. "The question was whether it could hold 40-ton tanks," Van Gent recalled. "Unfortunately I had to report that the bridge could only carefully—and just by a few tanks at a time—

be crossed. An emergency repair in short time would be impossible."[160]

Van Gent and the employees at the factory were not the only ones who were glad to see the Allies. A number of young male partisans who went under the name of *De Pandoeren* (The Pandurs) were also at the power station.[161] According to their leader, 22-year-old Jacques G. Brouwer, the group was born in 1941, with the intent to contribute their fair share to the liberation of their country. The uncle of another member, Theo Rietbergen, former Sgt. Maj. J. de Blécourt of the Royal Dutch Indian Army, trained them in the use of weapons and acted as their military commander.[162] By July 1944, the Pandurs had been recognized as a real resistance group by the national OD (Orde Dienst, a group founded by Reserve officers of the Royal Dutch Army who kept track of German troop locations and gathered information about valuable objects such as airfields, bridges and power stations) and De Blécourt was instructed by the local OD leader to guard the PGEM power station in Nijmegen, where they officially acted as Luchtbeschermingsdienst (air wardens).

On September 20, Pandur members present at the power plant included Jacques Bouman, Brouwer, Jan Engels, Nicolaas Hoekman, Kempen, Van Leeuwe and Van der Sande. Brouwer recalled that as the 508th PIR entered Nijmegen from the east, "the German guards in the power station became nervous" and suffered from low morale. Describing the battles in the city center and at the bridges, he recorded his distress at the destruction of his beloved city: "For the second time [since the 446th US Bomb Group had bombed Nijmegen on February 22, 1944] we watched with bitterness as our city burned."

When "a mauled SS-company came in from the Maas-Waal Canal and wanted to set up a defensive position," Mr. Van Gent, the director of the electric company, and some of the Pandurs persuaded the German commander of the futility of the plan and made him believe that his men still had a chance to escape via the railroad bridge with Van Leeuwe acting as guide. The Pandurs knew "that the Americans were there already and we therefore wrote Van Leeuwe off. Near the harbor [at the railroad bridge] he escaped in the darkness, whereupon the locally unknown unit walked right into the American fire and was scattered. [Van Leeuwe then returned to the power station.]

"During the night the German guards [stationed at the bridge] were told that *der Krieg* was over for them. We surprised them one by one, disarming them quickly, and locked them in one of the cellars by order of the sergeant major.

"Monday and Tuesday we were unaware of the situation in the city. We heard firing back and forth. The food supply became a problem as many wives and children of power station personnel had come to the power company to take shelter. A volunteer from the company, Henk Geurts, joined us, and that evening we scrounged a nearby farm for food. Under fire from the other side of the Waal as he approached the river, Jan Engels drove the cows from the floodplains and then showed his astonishing milking skills, all to the benefit of the children.

"Sgt. Maj. De Blécourt immediately began a training session in the use of the rifles and bayonets. We had our OD cuffs and received our sentry posts. Tuesday evening three SS types wearing 'Herman Göring' cuffs walked into the power station, and were disarmed under heavy protest and added to our collection. The total number of prisoners was 13 men. The situation became a bit difficult and Wednesday morning the sergeant major sent two scouts out to make contact with the allies."[163]

Jacques Brouwer and Albert van de Sande, selected for this task, encountered "the leading part of the Allied column" in the Bredestraat in Hees. "A unit [this must have been D Company] accompanied us to the power station," Brouwer recalled. "First we turned our prisoners over to them. In the afternoon larger groups arrived. In the small harbor of the power station they worked on boats and assembled them there. With these began the heroic crossing over the Waal to seize the opposite end of the road bridge.

"We were not allowed to participate in the crossing. We tried to make ourselves useful by dragging the wounded out of the floodplains and bringing them safely behind the dike. An aid station had been set up in the hall of the power station, and it was soon filled with about 30 wounded."[164]

Upon entering the power station, Colonel Tucker was greeted by Jaap van Gent and Jacques Brouwer. They turned over their prisoners and told him that from the ninth floor he would have a splendid view across the Waal River. Van Gent warned Tucker and Vandeleur that there were still 150 to 200 Germans positioned in the nearby silk spinning factory, NV Kunstzijdespinnerij NYMA. To his surprise, Tucker sent only 15 men to deal with them.[165]

Chosen to clear out the NYMA factory was 2nd Platoon, D Company, commanded by 1st Lt. Edward T. Wisniewski, whose assistant platoon leader, 2nd Lt. Hanz K. Druener, could speak German: "Our job initially was to go up there and set up our weapons so that we could protect the crossing of the other battalion. We went up before the 3rd Battalion got up there. It was early in the morning of the 20th and I was with the lead platoon for the simple reason that I was the only one in the unit that could speak German. I got up on the riverbank. There was a little jetty by the factory building with an enclosure open to the top. I got out on the jetty to look the situation over. It was pretty quiet.

"Suddenly, across the river I saw some people moving, and we were told there were a lot of partisans. We all carried these orange cloths with us. So I stood up there and waved the orange cloth I had, expecting they would wave back from across the river. Unfortunately, they weren't partisans; they were Germans. They fired back across the river and pinned me and one of my radio people down on the jetty for about two hours.

"In the process of pinning us down, they killed my immediate superior officer, Lt. Edward Wisniewski. We put the Red Cross flag up to get him, but the Germans wouldn't let us. H Company moved through us to get to the riverbank. Wisniewski was lying about 40 to 50 yards from me. After he was hit, I could hear him moan. We tried to get some medics out there, but every time they moved, they either hit one of them, or they couldn't make it out of there. Wisniewski lay out there for about the same length of time I would say that I was pinned down."[166]

Also severely wounded were Pvts. Norris B. Case and James W. Helffrich. Case, the platoon's radio operator, tried twice to run forward to aid his platoon leader but heavy enemy machine-gun fire drove him back. The third time he managed to reach him, but was mortally wounded by shrapnel as he applied first aid to Wisniewski, who had been wounded in the head. Case died later that day of his sustained wounds. His mother later received his posthumously awarded Bronze Star.[167]

Lieutenant Carmichael, 3rd Battalion S-2, remembered that "we approached the south bank of the river near the west edge of the factory complex, and along the top of the dike at that place was a high woven wire fence into which had become intertwined a heavy growth of thorny rose bushes. One platoon of D Company had moved into the area earlier that day and a Lieutenant Wisniewski of D Company had gotten shot by the Germans who were occupying a factory to our north[east]. Wisniewski was out in the open several yards from cover and was unable to move from his wounds. He cried for help for some hour or two, but we were unable to help him because when our medics started to his assistance, the Germans would shoot. Some of his good friends were almost frantic with despair that they could not help him, but shortly before we crossed the river his cries ceased. […]

"We assembled on the side of the dike away from the river, with the wire-covered fence between us and the river. We sat around on the grass for some 30 or 40 minutes waiting for the bombers which were supposed to come and bomb the fort on the other side and bomb out and strafe the many anti-aircraft-guns emplacements protecting the two bridges."[168]

Captain Campana recalled: "During the day of crossing, after checking with the battalion commander we evacuated wounded of the 2nd Platoon, which was on the point of land nearest to the enemy. Lieutenant Wisniewski was badly wounded in the head (died two-three days later in hospital). We utilized a white flag and had medics with identifying Red Cross bands on helmets and on sleeves. Some days later elsewhere, we honored this informal truce to allow Germans to do the same thing."[169]

With the 2nd Platoon of D Company pinned down, Campana dispatched Lieutenant Brown's 1st Platoon to capture the NYMA factory. Pvt. Virgil W. Widger, a 24-year-old rifleman in the platoon, recalled that after the building was captured, his squad came across a safe. Using a British Gammon grenade, they blew it up and found it full of French Franc banknotes. Everyone filled their "baggy pants" with money, but did not know if it was any good. Over the next days it was used as toilet paper, fuel to cook with, etc. One day late in September one of the platoon members was sent into a town on an errand. "Stop wasting money!" he shouted on return. "It's as good as gold!" Unfortunately, a lot had already been used up. [...]

Meanwhile Colonel Tucker, accompanied by his staff officers, Major Cook and 3rd Battalion company commanders climbed the stairs to the ninth floor to have a look at the river. In the words of Captain Burriss, I Company commander: "We had a panoramic view of the countryside. It was awesome! The river at this point was about 300 yards wide, the length of three football fields, and we could tell by the swirling, foaming waters that the current was strong. This was no ancient, meandering river. It flowed straight and deep and swiftly. On the opposite (north) side, we saw green, grassy flatlands that ran for about 900 yards, then rose to form a dike with a two-lane road on it. This was the route we would follow to the railroad and highway bridges.

"As we viewed the area through binoculars, we could see enemy machine-gun positions along the dike and also on the flat terrain. We observed mortar and artillery units behind the dike and 20mm guns on the railroad bridge. An old fort bound by a moat towered above the dike, a perfect observation post from which to direct artillery fire at our crossing site.

"The railroad bridge was upstream to our right, a mile above our crossing, and huge Nijmegen Bridge was two miles beyond it. The dike road between the railroad and highway bridges was lined with houses and buildings, which we assumed contained enemy troops.

"What we saw that morning appeared to be an impregnable defense—a textbook example. The river itself was a dangerous obstacle. The terrain between the river and the dikes provided the Germans with a natural shooting gallery. They occupied the high ground and would be firing down on us all the way. Also, they commanded superior firepower. It looked like a suicide mission."[170]

Captain Kappel recalled they "had a good look at the river. Frankly, I wasn't too happy about a daylight crossing. Even then I seem to recall there was quite a bit of firing going on. I remember we were told we had the southern bank, which I don't think was entirely true."[171] Major Cook, however, thought later that they "were readily relieved to finally see that the other bank wasn't a sheer cliff or wall 20-foot high above the water. The water looked pretty swift and it looked pretty damn far but [...] by that time we also knew that we were going to get boats from the British."[172]

For the Battalion S-3, Captain Keep, the scene from the top of the tower was "indelibly imprinted in my mind forever, I felt rather funny inside. I think everyone else did too, although no one said a word—we just looked. The bank of the river on our side was a high plateau absolutely open with a flat top of between 200 to 300 yards. Suddenly the cliff dropped off, a sheer fall of about 100 feet to the beach and then the Waal River itself, a seemingly placid 200 yard-wide waterway with a strong current sweeping everything towards the bridge, discernible against the haze in the distance. Once across the river, the situation appeared little better.

"What greeted our eyes was a broad flat plain void of all cover or concealment; the first terrain feature which would offer us assistance was a built-up highway [the dike road] approximately 800 yards from the shore, against the bank of which we would have our first opportunity to get some protection and be able to reorganize. It would be every man for himself until that embankment was reached.

"We could see all along the Kraut side of the river strong defensive positions, a formidable line both in length as well as in depth—pillboxes, machine-gun emplacements and what was really wicked-looking, one or two [one] big Dutch forts between the place where we were landing and the two bridges. One lone little battalion was to overcome all that. A 20mm [antiaircraft gun] was firing at us as we took all this in from the tower."[173]

Lieutenant General Horrocks turned to Colonel Tucker and asked if his regimental combat team would be able to cross the river and take the objectives. "If we take the bridge," Tucker asked in return, "what assurance do we have that your troops will get to Arnhem immediately?" General Horrocks replied that tanks of 1st Grenadier Guards would be held ready to drive across the Waal Bridge at the earliest possibility. "Nothing will stop them," he added. [174]

"While there, the plan of attack was formed," Captain Keep continues. "We were to cross the Waal and land at a point about two miles up the river (west) from the bridge, fight our way across the broad expanse of field on the other side and make for the road embankment, where we would momentarily reorganize before pushing on. After regrouping there, we would turn to the right (or east) and attack parallel to the river, overcoming all resistance and mopping up strong points in the two-mile area we had to take before reaching the bridge, which obviously we would capture by coming from the rear.

"While all this was going on, another part of the division would wrest from the Kraut what remained in enemy hands of Nijmegen on the friendly side of the river. We were to shoot a flare as soon as both bridges were taken and the British armor would cross, for as you know from the papers, this was supposedly a British sector. That was the plan in a nutshell.

"As we wound our way down the twisting stairs of the tower no one said a word, but from ensuing conversations I have learned that all our thoughts were identical. How could this operation succeed? At least three-fourths of our battalion would be killed and the rest would drift downstream. It was a humanly impossible mission. However, it had to be done and quickly."[175]

Major Cook learned that the attack would be postponed once more, to 1500 hours: "They told us that we couldn't make the assault until Nijmegen was cleared. They had to clear a certain amount in order for the boats to be brought up and the tanks to be brought in and they wanted to secure the southern side. So that kept on delaying it."[176]

The positive side of the delay was that it allowed time to form a sketchy assault plan. Tucker decided the 3rd Battalion "would make the crossing and fan out to the west wall in front of [the] road bridge. First Battalion was to follow 3rd Battalion to complete the arc of the bridgehead and 2nd Battalion, when available, would support the crossing by fire. C Company, 307th Engineers, would assist with assault boats, which would be delivered at [the] crossing site."[177]

In detail it meant that I Company would cross on the left and H Company on the right in the first assault wave, followed in the second wave by Headquarters Company on the left and G Company on the right. Major Zakby, executive officer of the 1st Battalion, would then come up with C Company of the 1st Battalion and act as "beach master." Captain Duncan's A Company and Captain Anderson's Headquarters Company, 1st Battalion, would follow swiftly along with Major Harrison. B Company was scheduled to cross as the final unit.

Captain Ferguson, 3rd Battalion executive officer, would cross in the second wave of the assault. Captain Burriss's I Company would set up a basic perimeter and clear out the dike and the area immediately west of the landing site, so no German counterattack could cut off the 3rd Battalion or threaten their advance to the bridge.

Tucker gave Cook the 3rd Battalion Section of the Regimental Demolition Platoon, commanded by 1st Lt. William D. Mandle, and a forward artillery observer team from the 376th PFAB, commanded by 1st Lt. Whitney S. Russell of Headquarters Battery. Capt. Frank D. Boyd, forward artillery observer of the 376th PFAB, sat "in a house from where I could observe the river crossing. Across from 'my' house was a very tall chimney that had German observers on top of it. I remember that Lieutenant Hutton fired many rounds at it, but our little 75s did not have enough penetration or explosive power to knock the chimney down. The 376th was to send over forward observer teams with the infantry. One team consisted of Lt. Whitney S. Russell, [Pvt.] Robert M. Scott, Richard Barr and Rick Martin.

"The German observers at the other side of the river must have noticed that something was going on. Soon German artillery fire fell on this bank. Lieutenant Russell and his section were crossing an open field when shell fragments killed Private Scott. The team came to the house and I told Lieutenant Russell that I would take my section and go over in his place, but he said that they would rather go ahead and keep busy than to sit around and think about Private Scott. He also declined my offer to give him one of my men."[178]

Lieutenant Russell's team was attached to II Company while 1st Lt. Samuel Romanchak and his assistants were attached to I Company. Romanchak would eventually receive a certificate of merit for directing artillery fire on the north bank for six-and-a-half hours. Second Lieutenant Robert S. Hutton of B Battery, 376th PFA, would act as forward observer from the ninth floor of the power station. Hutton had jumped with a small camera and took photographs of the crossing, but he destroyed them after they had been developed because the images were so gruesome.[179]

Capt. Wesley D. "Spike" Harris, 307th AEB, received orders from Colonel Tucker at 0600 hours to prepare for a river crossing at 1400 hours that same day about 600 yards west of the Nijmegen Railroad Bridge over the Waal River. The 26 British boats were initially to be collected near Bridge Number 7, but none could be found. Harris therefore assembled his officers and briefed them. He sent 2nd Lt. Michael G. Sabia after the boats on a captured German motorcycle and assigned the company executive officer, 1st Lt. John Bigler, to select and instruct boat crews. The company was made ready to move under command of Lieutenant Bigler on instructions from Captain Harris.

Captain Harris, his platoon leaders and their platoon sergeants arrived at the riverbank around 1200 hours. D Company, still clearing the south bank of enemy snipers and stragglers, had already picked up some 55 prisoners. Harris sent 1st Lt. Patrick J. Mulloy, 3rd Platoon leader, back to guide the company to the power station. As 2nd Platoon leader Lieutenant Holabird reports: "I had no idea why we were going. I don't think Spike knew much more. We met with Colonel Tucker, Major Cook and other field-grade officers. I was sure something big was going on because ordinarily we wouldn't have been party to all those upper ranks of officers. We walked upstairs in the empty power station—as I recall, very clean and modern."[180]

Much later, Lieutenant Mulloy's impressions were still vivid: "I had my first real look at the stretch of water we would have to cross. My recollection is I somehow saw it from the ground, although I believe some of the others went into a nearby factory [power station]. All I remember thinking about that stretch of water was that it looked formidable. I didn't, and I don't think anyone else did, take it as a picnic. Only a damn fool would be cocky at that moment."[181]

Inside the power station, standing near the large windows on the ninth floor, Captain Harris and his engineer officers looked out over the broad Waal River. Second Lieutenant Thomas McLeod, Mulloy's assistant platoon leader, warned the captain that "our assembly area offered pretty good cover, but it was a long walk across pretty open territory to get to the launching site."[182]

Lieutenant Holabird, struck by the sight of the broad river, finally "began to understand what was up—we were going to cross it—and the engineers in the US Army were the customary boatmen. Ergo, we were there to plot a night crossing. 'Where are the boats?' we asked. 'Coming,' they replied. 'What kind of boats?' 'Press-out, British canvas assault boats.' 'How soon?' 'Afternoon.'

"And then I began to understand that they were really serious about a daylight crossing. 'Who's going to protect us? That is one wide river.' 'We'll lay-in British armor to hit the other side and to lay down a smoke barrage so no one will be able to see.'

"It began to dawn on me that this was one rash, dare-devil idea—and we engineers were going to be a big part of it. I guess Spike and the rest of us went back to the company and we moved up in enfilade to the east of the power station on the down side of the levee or embankment. Spike said I was to take a squad of my platoon over first. Do what I could about miners and support infantry, etc."[183]

Lieutenant Mulloy was "also apprehensive about the crossing," and especially crossing the river in broad daylight: "It was a long way across. Most of us had had some training for assault crossings, using pontoons, and I suppose I drew a certain amount of confidence from that. But the fact remains we were supposed to row across a wide-open stretch of water looking right down the barrels of German guns.

"We were first briefed to push off from a small inlet, almost a basin, really, but for some reason that was changed and we were told to leave right from shore. As I visualize it today, we were back in a partly wooded area with the boats deployed in a line. When the word was given, we were to pick up the boats and go. The 3rd Battalion or a couple of companies from the battalion were assigned boat numbers, and on command were to head for the water double-timing or half double-timing."[184]

Mulloy was sent back to bring the engineers up to the power station. The request for pontoons had meanwhile been forwarded to Col. Charles P. Jones, who commanded the Royal Engineer units within the Guards Armoured Division. Jones alerted two of his engineer units, Maj. John N. Thomas's 14 Squadron, RE, and Maj. Alan R. Neale's 615 Squadron, RE. The latter unit had spent the night north of Grave. According to Sapper Roy W. Tuck: "Our troop was ordered forward to take part in what, we were forewarned, could turn out to be a traumatic assault crossing of the River Waal. We entered the outskirts of Nijmegen in early afternoon, clinging precariously to the top of a pontoon carried by a transporter provided by our specialized 14 Squadron. We arrived in the middle of a battle. Several houses in the close vicinity were already burning furiously. Hurriedly dismounting, I experienced the familiar sudden inner clutch of fear as we learnt that the approaches to the river were under direct enemy fire.

"There was a frightening crackle from small arms as we left the shelter of buildings and raced for the nearest cover. We found ourselves surrounded by the sound of fighting, but at that moment saw no American paratroopers. By the time I had finished crawling the length of a long, dry, shallow ditch, negotiating my way past numerous tree roots and the lifeless body of an American paratrooper, my confidence was virtually non-existent.

"There, at the critical point where I had to leave what little protection there was and make a headlong dash to the river, all further progress was held up. I pushed past the stubborn figure, clambered out of the ditch and sprinted to catch up with the leading members of the section. As we reached the huge road embankment running parallel to the river, we came across two American paratroopers standing at the doorway of a small brick hut. In an obvious state of high tension and excitement, they blurted out that their battalion had just been cut to pieces while carrying out a suicidal crossing of the river. Such startling news, coupled with the ever-increasing sounds of conflict about us, did nothing for my morale. Fighting to suppress my fear, I struggled up the steep grassy gradient.

"As we neared the top, Ron shouted, 'Jerry has the road under fire! You'll be silhouetted against the sky as you cross—run like hell!' In one big final effort, I sprinted up and over the road and down the reverse slope, to gain the relative security of a small creek dwarfed by the vast bulk of an electricity power plant. There, for the time being, shielded from the worst consequences of the surrounding battle, I collapsed on a bank beside my companions, every breath an agony.

"While struggling to recuperate, we could only watch helplessly as an empty long-range fuel tank, released by one of our supporting aircraft, bounced mere yards away. We were for a time strangely cut off from the surrounding battle, while enclosed by the massive and reassuring presence of the power station and the high banked road nearby. Once sufficiently recovered, we set about the rapid building of a Class 9 raft."[185]

Nineteen-year-old Sgt. Roy C. Hamlyn drove one of the Bedford trucks that contained the canvas boats. Hamlyn's unit, 282 Company RASC, was still in Belgium, close to the Belgian-Dutch border, when word was received to drive to a forward depot, where 32 canvas assault boats were loaded onto their trucks. The drivers were told it was of utmost importance to deliver the boats at Nijmegen.

After a long and hazardous drive over "Hell's Highway," they arrived in the outskirts of the city at about 1300 hours. "There was still fighting going on in Nijmegen," Sergeant Hamlyn recalled.[186] One truck was hit, reducing the number of canvas boats to 26. They were trying to figure out which way to go to reach the Waal River, when Lieutenant Sabia appeared on a captured German motorcycle. "Are you the guys bringing the boats?" he shouted. Upon receiving an affirmative reply, Sabia led the way to the power station.[187]

While the engineers unloaded the assault boats, Captain Kappel quickly prepared a battle plan: "H Company was to clean out the trenches in their assignments, all three platoons and Company Headquarters abreast, continue the advance to the cover of the first dike, reorganize, and attack due northeast of the fort to the Arnhem-Nijmegen highway. Second and 3rd Platoons abreast, 3rd Platoon on the right, 1st Platoon following the 3rd, and the 2nd Platoon was to keep visual contact with I Company on the left. Wire communications were to be left behind with the rear CP. Each man was to carry the basic combat load, dropping one bandoleer immediately upon crossing the river."[188]

An assistant squad leader in 3rd Platoon, Cpl. Ralph N. Tison, Jr. was far from happy when he learned of I Company's assignment: "We then got word that the outfit that was supposed to take the bridge at Nijmegen had failed. Some damn fool decided we would go and take it. It was approximately 12 miles away. Our transportation was our feet."[189] His assistant, Pvt. Valentino M. Cortez, carried their machine-gun and ammunition boxes during the heavy walk.

The young Dutch student Ben Bouman also walked to the bank of the river that day. Two days after meeting Lieutenant Smith, he donned an incomplete KNIL [Koninklijk Nederlands Indisch Leger] uniform, left over from his father's combat in the Dutch East Indies, and cycled toward Malden. Discovering B Company lined up along the road to Nijmegen awaiting further orders, Bouman asked Lieutenant Smith, "Can I help you?" Smith answered in the affirmative. In exchange for his bicycle, which was given to Corporal Cleary, Bouman received an American jacket, helmet, M-1, and ammunition. He would soon see more action that he ever could have desired.

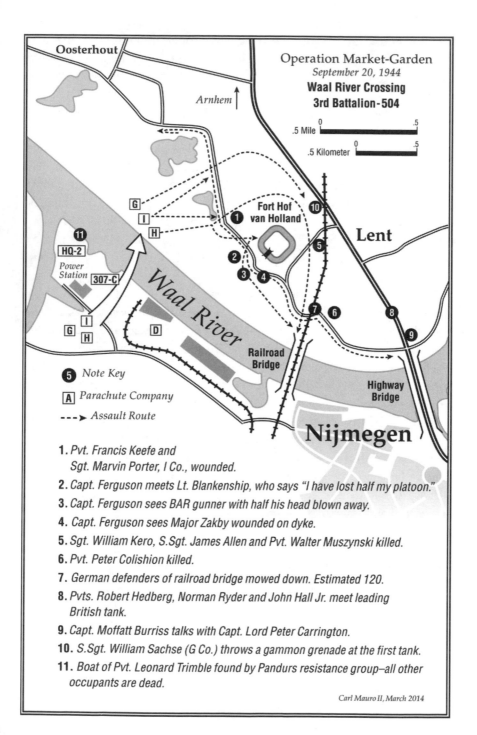

Oosterhout

Arnhem ↑

Operation Market-Garden
September 20, 1944
Waal River Crossing
3rd Battalion-504

0   .5
.5 Mile ▬▬▬▬▬▬

0   .5
.5 Kilometer ▬▬▬▬▬▬

G
I
H

⑪
HQ-2
*Power
Station* 307-C

Waal River

Fort Hof
van Holland ❶

⑩

Lent

❷

❸ ❹

❺

G
I
H
D

❼ ❻

❽

❾

**Railroad
Bridge**

**Highway
Bridge**

Nijmegen

❺ *Note Key*

Ⓐ *Parachute Company*

---▸ *Assault Route*

1. *Pvt. Francis Keefe and
   Sgt. Marvin Porter, I Co., wounded.*

2. *Capt. Ferguson meets Lt. Blankenship, who says "I have lost half my platoon."*

3. *Capt. Ferguson sees BAR gunner with half his head blown away.*

4. *Capt. Ferguson sees Major Zakby wounded on dyke.*

5. *Sgt. William Kero, S.Sgt. James Allen and Pvt. Walter Muszynski killed.*

6. *Pvt. Peter Colishion killed.*

7. *German defenders of railroad bridge mowed down. Estimated 120.*

8. *Pvts. Robert Hedberg, Norman Ryder and John Hall Jr. meet leading
   British tank.*

9. *Capt. Moffatt Burriss talks with Capt. Lord Peter Carrington.*

10. *S.Sgt. William Sachse (G Co.) throws a gammon grenade at the first tank.*

11. *Boat of Pvt. Leonard Trimble found by Pandurs resistance group—all other
    occupants are dead.*

Carl Mauro II, March 2014

CHAPTER 9

"ALL HELL BROKE LOOSE"
NIJMEGEN, SEPTEMBER 20, 1944

The first fatal casualty in the 3rd Battalion that day fell before the river crossing started. Only minutes before the crossing took place, a sniper killed Cpl. Curtiss A. Williams, an assistant rifle-squad leader in the 3rd Platoon, H Company, as he returned to his squad after announcing to Pvt. Hugh D. Wallis that his fiancée had had a baby boy and he was going to get married. "He said the company commander had told him he would be sent in for rotation to the United States after this campaign was over."[190]

T/5 Herbert C. Lucas, a veteran of all the previous campaigns, "was supposed to go over with Major Cook. I was his runner at that time, but my place switched with PFC Bonnie Roberts at the last moment. I had had a run-in with Major Cook on a maneuver in England, so even though I had been assigned to cross in his boat, I was replaced. By the time I got over, there was just occasional fire.

"There was a tremendous barrage that got everyone excited and nervous. Waiting for the first boats to come back, we were laying behind the dike. Colonel Tucker appeared and said, 'If George Washington can cross the Delaware River, then I can cross the Waal.' He tried to boost our morale. In a sense it was true: we too had to face enemy fire."[191]

Twenty-six-year-old Pvt. Paul J. Katonik from Braddock, Pennsylvania, had joined the army in December 1943, and this was his baptism of fire. Married with a one-year-old daughter, Katonik was determined to survive the crossing no matter what. He asked S.Sgt. Robert M. Tallon, the 3rd Battalion operations sergeant, for advice: "A replacement—I didn't even know his name—struck up a conversation as we were waiting to load onto the boats.

He was so very concerned about whether he would know how to use the items in his first-aid kit if he were wounded. He kept repeating his questions about when to use the tablets, the powders, the ointments."[192]

Pvt. Francis X. Keefe, 1st Platoon, I Company, can still "vividly remember the hazy, warm, sunny September day" as he waited "a few hundred yards from the dike road on the south side of the river. In the distance, we could see General Gavin with two or three other soldiers speaking to the line of troopers in front of us. As he was making his way back, he must have been saying the same thing to us as he passed by: 'Not to worry. We have plenty of artillery and tank firepower to support us.'

"When we got to the embankment we just sat behind the road, which was high enough to give us natural cover. The other side of the road went down to the river's edge. There was very little conversation; everyone just looked at one another. It was the same as when we were told about the river crossing in the wooded area the day before. I was confident about myself, as I had been through attacks before, but I was concerned about the others as we waited for the boats to arrive. Everyone wondered what they would look like. I knew we would have C Company engineers with us. They were like part of the regiment. I had a buddy in that company who I tented with in Oujda in North Africa.

"I didn't realize that the tank fire support would come right down the road where we were. The road was wide and there were quite a few tanks. They turned and faced north, then backed up as far as they could to leave room for the trucks to come down with the boats. First Lieutenant Busby started telling different squad leaders who was to go in which boats. I spoke up to Lieutenant Busby, saying that I wanted to go into the same boat as [Leo] Muri since we were always together in this kind of situation. We got into a heated argument. I would go into the boat I was assigned. Right after that the trucks arrived."[193]

Keefe didn't know that First Lieutenant Busby, the 31-year-old executive officer of I Company, had a premonition that he wasn't going to make it. Busby, who joined the 504th in November 1943, had survived the previous campaigns but had lost friends like Lt. Willis Ferrill, killed at Anzio, and Lt. Thomas Murphy, captured in Normandy. He took one of his Camel cigarettes, lit it with his valued Zippo, and threw the lighter and his pack of cigarettes away. "I have no chance of getting across," he told Chaplain Kuehl, one of the men who looked on in disbelief. Some of his friends tried in vain to talk the premonition he would "get it today" out of his head.

As three o'clock neared, Lieutenant Carmichael, Major Cook and Captain Keep discussed "what we were going to do in crossing the river. Each of us emphatically stated we were going to let the men paddle, and Cook said that he was going to imitate George Washington in the well-known picture of his crossing the Delaware. He was going to stand erect in the boat and with clenched right fist pushed forward overhead, he was going to shout, 'Onward men! Onward!'"[194]

Captain Keep tried to persuade Major Cook not to cross in the first wave, but Cook brushed his worries aside: "Henry was a good worry wort. […] We all agreed that we would try to cheer each other up and the men. […] We knew we had to do it. There was no way out. Captain Kappel said, 'Well, can't we wait till tonight?' I said, 'No, that has been argued and we can't do it.' So we made the best of it and kind of joked about things a bit."[195]

Cook recalled that "the battalion was late in getting up to the river crossing site so I moved closer to hurry them up. In fact, I picked the exact spot for them to enter the area and stood on a couple of strands to make the barbed wire stay down so they could hurry up and get lined up for the crossing. I tried to have a word for each man and practically the entire battalion filed by me."[196]

Lieutenant Carmichael "stood in this gap and directed the men with the boats to come first one from the right and then one from the left, and to proceed through the hole in the fence and down the long sloping dike to the river. The men were holding the boats in one hand by the gunwales and carrying their weapons and ammunition in the other."[197]

The War Diary of the 2nd Irish Guards reads: "The Tanks moved up to Hees (6862) and Squadron Leaders began their reconnaissance. The areas allotted were: No. 3 left along a line of gardens behind a wall near a large Power Station (6864), No. 2 right in waste land and rubble heaps stretching from No. 3 as far as another factory 1000 yds to the east. No. 2 had much the better field of fire, but were exposed to the far bank.

"Colonel Tucker's plan was to assault with two battalions from the area of the Power Station under cover of smoke and artillery concentrations, swing east on the far bank and capture the old fort 7064 and north end of the bridges. When his troops were in position, the Grenadier Guards were to assault with tanks from the South end and join up with the Americans. His Command Post was on the ninth floor of the Power Station, whether the Commanding Officer would accompany him to watch the assault and control the fire of the tanks.

"1400hrs: The tanks moved into position.

"1500hrs: The smoke screen went down.

"1515hrs: The smoke screen ended, and the Americans began their assault, which they carried out with great courage and energy. The enemy replied with fairly heavy shell fire on the riverbanks and the tanks did some counterbattery work directed by the Commanding Officer in the Command Post.

"Both Squadrons, especially No. 2, had a great afternoon's shooting, and gave most valuable support to the infantry, being able, so long as they could see them, to shoot them right in to the objective. The old green fort, which was holding up the advance, got particular attention—even AP [armor-piercing] shot to keep the defenders' heads down."[198]

British fire support also importantly included the 55th Field Regiment, Royal Artillery. A forward observer, Captain Philip O. Riddell, who relayed fire missions from his tank on the south bank of the Waal River, was awarded the Distinguished Service Cross "for extraordinary heroism in connection with military operations against an armed enemy in action against enemy forces on 20 and 21 September 1944. As forward observation officer for the 55th Field Regiment in support of the 504th United States Parachute Regiment during crossing of the Waal west of Nijmegen Bridge, Captain Riddell established his tank as a relay station on the south bank. Constantly subjected to heavy enemy fire, he maintained his position and passed back vital fire data which resulted in excellent support for the forward units."[199]

The smoke shells and artillery rounds that preceded the actual river crossing drew deadly fire from German machine-gunners and artillery crews. Lieutenant Carmichael recalled that "as our men emerged through the gap in the fence, the Krauts realized what was happening and guns started firing everywhere. A heavy hail of fire converged on us as we walked down the sloping dike toward the water. Fire came from across the river and from our right on our side of the river, and from all along the railroad bridge and the old Fort Hof van Holland. It was about 100 yards from the top of the dike to the escarpment, which was about three-and-a-half feet high.

"Cook, Keep and I took boats about the center of the column. I had not intended to carry a boat or help carry a boat to the water. As I moved out from behind the fence there was a continuous hail of bullets with small geysers of earth popping up everywhere. There would have been no need to have dodged one way or the other. I walked along beside our men, and I am sure that I must have been talking, but as each boat reached this small escarpment, the men were unable to walk and carry the boats past it. The men in the front of each boat would lay the boat down and then jump off the bank and after that, each boat was almost automatically put on the shoulders of the men and they literally ran to the water's edge with it.

"When my boat reached the escarpment, I took a part of it on my shoulder. Out of one corner of my eye, I saw that both Keep and Cook had done the same and we were all running toward the water's edge. We put our boats into the water and notwithstanding our former protestations, we each grabbed a paddle, and I can tell you that I paddled as fast as I could."[200]

At exactly 1500 hours the first assault wave of 26 flimsy canvas boats containing H and I Companies and the battalion staff departed from the south bank of the river. Major Cook had originally "planned to be like Washington crossing the Delaware (à la painting), but with men being knocked off and feeling the lead around me, I soon grabbed an oar. Being a catholic I began right to pray, 'Hail Mary' (one stroke), 'full of grace' (second stroke), but since 'the Lord is with thee' is too long, I kept repeating 'Hail Mary' (one stroke), 'full of grace' on the next stroke. My S-3, Capt. Henry B. Keep, tried to remember his days at Princeton and his boating experience, so he was going to count 1, 2, 3, 4; 1, 2, 3, 4. He remembered counting 76, 77, 78, 79.

"I also remember the little machine-gunner [Private Jedlicka] from H Company, 3rd Battalion. As our boats got close to the other shore everyone began to jump overboard, as the flanking fire from the Nijmegen Bridge was intense. I was just getting ready to get out of my boat when I saw a bubble of air come up out of the water. I hesitated a moment, and saw a 'bulge' in the water [moving] to the shore. My sensation was one of confusion. [...] Rapidly the 'bulge' emerged from the water—all ashen gray, just the color of the disturbed water. It was the machine-gunner, a little fellow who, seeing the others leave the boat, took his two boxes of ammunition, one in each hand, and simply jumped into the water and started walking, even though the water was a foot or more over his head. The ammo boxes weighed him down, but he walked out with them. Later he told me he knew we needed that ammunition."[201]

Cook's runner, Bonnie Roberts, was in the same boat as his battalion commander: "Major Cook was in the front. Cook said all through the crossing, 'Hail Mary, full of grace. Hail Mary, full of grace.' I think he was just praying that he wouldn't get hit. Captain Kuehl was in the back, rowing too. I wasn't rowing, I was just sitting down. [...] Poor engineers: first to take us across, and then to come back for another load. I tried not to remember much as it scared the heck out of me."[202]

Lieutenant Carmichael recalled "bullets were flying everywhere. Our boat started going around in circles. When I was young I had paddled a canoe quite a bit on the Tennessee River, and knew how it was supposed to be done. So I slipped over to the left rear of the craft, took a paddle from one of the men, and kept the boat steered straight for the other shore.

"One of my men, Pvt. Paul Katonik, had just joined us in England before the Holland jump. He was kneeling next to me when he was hit by what appeared to be a 20mm bullet. Gasping, 'Give me my [sulfa] pills,' Katonik fell over. That's the way it went—we lived or died by a distance of a few inches."[203]

S.Sgt. Tallon, sitting on the left side of his boat, was paddling frantically as Private Katonik, to the right, did the same. "All of a sudden the kid on my right groaned and slumped over in my lap. I looked down at him and knew he had been hit in the chest. It had gone in the front and come out the back. There was no question about it—he was dead, very dead. The bullet had come out almost exactly between his shoulder blades. To our left, a mortar scored a direct hit on a boat. There was a geyser of water and I could see men being blown out and up in the air. The boat just vanished."[204]

The Protestant chaplain, Captain Kuehl, crossed the river with the first wave: "I happened to be with the 3rd Battalion when I heard officers talking about a plan just down from higher headquarters to cross the river downstream and attack the bridges from the rear. I wondered what kind of boats would be used—certainly something with armored protection. And I assumed we would be crossing under the cover of darkness.

"As I listened, I couldn't believe what I heard: we would be using canvas folding boats provided by British engineers and canoe paddles would be our means of locomotion. I was even more stunned to learn that we would be making a daylight crossing. All this against machine-gun positions, mortar and artillery.

"As I recall, H Company under Captain Kappel and I Company under Captain Burriss were to spearhead the attack. As Regimental Chaplain, I would not ordinarily be going on such an operation; but I thought if my men would ever need me, it would be now. As we waited behind the riverbank for the boats to arrive, I doubt if there was one man who didn't consider this a suicide mission. But I heard not a word from any trooper that they weren't ready to go.

"When the boats arrived, we couldn't believe how flimsy they were. [...] I was in the same boat as Major Cook. When the order was given, we hoisted the boat over our heads and ran for the river. We soon were slowed by thick mud on the river's edge. And when we climbed into the boat, it sank from the weight and stuck in the mud of the shallow water.

"Finally, we were afloat. All who had paddles and some with rifle butts stroked furiously to get across. Soon tremendous fire came from the opposite riverbank, the railroad bridge, and the larger German guns."[205]

"Enemy fire was so intense that it reminded me of rain hitting the water. Major Cook was praying in a loud voice, 'Hail Mary, full of grace. Hail Mary, full of grace.' He told me later that he had been trying to say the rosary, but those words were all that came out. I heard a thud and saw that the trooper sitting shoulder to shoulder with me had evidently been hit by a 20mm shell, because the top of his head had been sheared off and you could see inside his skull."[206]

Chaplain Kuehl picked up the paddle the man had been using and started paddling, repeating again and again, "Lord, Thy will be done. Lord, Thy will be done." Kuehl recalled: "There were dead and wounded in every boat. Only 11 or 12 boats out of the 26 made it—the others had been sunk or the engineers killed and the craft drifted aimlessly downstream laden with their human cargo of dead and wounded troopers. One boat reaching the bank had four dead troopers draped across each other. I carried an aid kit, so immediately began working on the wounded, as did Captain [Hyman D.] Shapiro, our [assistant] battalion doctor, and carrying them to the boats to be taken back.

"While leaning over one trooper, who had three bullet holes in his abdomen, a mortar shell exploded behind me, and a piece of shrapnel hit me in the back, knocking me prostrate over the man I was helping. Despite being so seriously wounded, he called out, 'Chaplain, did they get you too?'

"My wound did not prevent me from continuing to treat the wounded and help with their evacuation. All the while we were receiving small-arms fire. Later, when Colonel Tucker came across with Harrison's second wave, he saw me and barked: "Chaplain Kuehl, what in the hell are *you* doing over here?"[207]

Captain Bruns, the 1st Battalion surgeon, made the crossing with Chaplain Kuehl: "A German 88 tore the back out of a soldier standing next to me while we were waiting to load into 16-man British canvas boats. I carried one half of a machine gun while the Protestant chaplain carried the other half. We went through a hail of flak, cannon, machine guns, and exploding shells while whole boats full of men were blown into the Waal. Guys just slumped, some paddled with their hands or rifles or helmets for the opposite bank. When they did get there they were faced with more homicidal fire. They bayoneted the enemy in foxholes and knocked out machine guns with grenades. Running up that open beach all I could hear were bullets zinging past me."[208]

Maj. Ivan J. Roggen, the regimental surgeon, "was at the jump-off point where the 504th crossed the Waal. We had established an aid station in a building near the river, and I was with Colonel Tucker, Major Cook and Chaplain Kuehl. While getting ready to load the boats I recall a fair amount of small-arms fire from the opposite shore, and specifically remember Lieutenant Wisniewski, who was wounded. In short time we were medically overwhelmed with about 25 casualties. I remember Colonel Tucker visited the aid station and was very concerned about the casualties.

"The casualties subsided once the boats departed for the other side of the river. Chaplain Kuehl insisted on going in one of the boats against advice. (When he returned he showed me where bullets had torn up his uniform in several places—he was shaken up quite a bit.) Once our troops reached the far shore, I believe they secured the bridge very quickly. Some casualties were sustained and they were brought back to the aid station via boat."[209]

First Lieutenant William D. Mandle's 3rd Battalion section of the Regimental Demolition Platoon also paddled across in the first assault wave. PFC Darrell G. Harris remembered that "as often happens in war, things did not work out exactly as planned. The enemy was determined not to let us cross, and some of the boats never made it because of the heavy mortar and small-arms fire. We did not all have oars, but we all paddled anyway, some of us using our rifle butts."[210]

In the power station Tucker observed the river crossing with his binoculars: "In less time than it takes to tell, all hell broke loose. Enfilade Kraut machine-gun fire from under the short abutment of the railroad bridge, 88mm fire and small-arms fire. The boats got hit, some sank, but the others drove on to the far side. On the other side, those who were able got out of the boats, formed a line of skirmishers and moved up to shoot or bayonet the Krauts in their positions along the dike. At this time General 'Boy' Browning said, 'What magnificent troops to move forward like that. Any nation should be proud of them.'

"During the first wave crossing, 15 assault boats were sunk or damaged so that only 11 remained for the first return pick-up. By this time Colonel Vandeleur had laid down smoke over some Kraut gun positions and fired his tanks at numerous targets. I would tell him what I wanted and he relayed it to his tanks. His fire was most effective, and although I had been promised considerable artillery support, little if any ever materialized, so the tank fire was our support."[211]

Captain Keep rendered one of the most vivid accounts of the crossing in a letter to his mother: "The battalion was given 26 canvas boats—flimsy, flat-bottomed little things if ever I've seen any—smaller than daddy's tin ducking boat and, as I have said, made of canvas. There were to be 13 men per boat and there were 8 paddles. In such contraptions were we to cross the Waal River under withering automatic-weapons and small-arms fire from the formidable defense line [...], so that we would attack two miles to seize the two largest bridges in Holland—our battalion. (I am afraid I am getting over-dramatic, but I have kept this story so long to myself and I am trying so hard to make you realize what this was like, that I fear I err too much in that direction. Please forgive me.)

"A few dive-bombers were to come over and try to put the forts out of commission five minutes prior to H-Hour; this proved to be ineffective. A smoke screen was to be laid down as we came up over the banks; this was completely ineffective. Besides the supporting fires of our 2nd Battalion on our side of the bank (what a superb job these men did), their role was to lie there, take it, and continue to pour the lead over our heads back at the Kraut. They took it, but certainly dished out a hell of a lot in return.

"Besides these supporting fires, ten tanks on top of the bank continually pounded away at all emplacements causing us trouble. They also deserve tremendous credit. They sat there in those exposed positions constantly. One that I know of was knocked out.

"The trucks with the 26 flat-bottomed canvas boats arrived at ten minutes before 1500. There was a rush to get them unloaded, and then we all stood around the boats to which we were assigned. The tanks were in position, the dive-bombers came and went, the ineffective smoke screen was laid, we waited by our boats. Suddenly, a whistle was blown. It was H-Hour. Each boatload hoisted their boat onto their shoulders and staggered across the flat top of the bank. Our job had begun.

"As we came out into the open, the weight of our boat seemed imponderable; our feet sank deep into the mud. We must have caught the Krauts by surprise, because for the first 100 yards there wasn't a round fired from the enemy side of the river. Then suddenly all hell broke loose. We had run halfway across the flat-topped plateau prior to reaching the drop, when Jerry opened up with everything he had—LMGs, mortars, 20mm guns, artillery and rifles. As if in a rage at our trying anything so dangerous, he was throwing everything he owned at us. And behind us, our 2nd Battalion and the ten tanks were blasting away for all they were worth. I don't think I have ever been prouder of our men. Not one of them faltered. In spite of the withering, murderous fire, they lumbered forward, sinking ankle deep in the soft sand under their cumbersome boats. Here and there men would fall, but their places would only be taken by others. I felt as naked as the day I was born on that exposed spot.

"At last we neared the drop. We let the boats slide down to the beach, and we ourselves slid alongside them. We pulled our boat quickly across the short beach, and everyone piled in. By this time, the automatic and flat-trajectory fire had increased, and the artillery was deadly. Men were falling to the right and left of me. Our ears were filled with the constant roar of bursting artillery shells, the dull *wharm* of a 20mm round, or the disconcerting *ping* of rifle bullets.

"After a false start when we got stuck on a mud bar and several of us had perforce to get out and go through the extremely uncomfortable process of pushing off again, we found ourselves actually floating out in the wrong direction. The current was taking us down toward the bridge. Everyone grabbed a paddle and frantically started to work. Most of the men had never paddled before, and had it not been for the gruesomeness of the situation, the sight might have been rather ludicrous. With all our strength we would lunge forward only to miss the water completely. Gradually we got our boat moving in the right direction, but even though we all paddled with all our might, we were not synchronizing our movements. We lunged forward at different times. Suddenly I had a rather incongruous vision of our coxswain at Princeton on Lake Carnegie pounding rhythmically on the sides of the flimsy sides of the shell and of our rowing in unison, pulling to the time of his beats. And so I started to count 1, 2, 3, 4, and then repeat. All at once for no apparent reason I found myself yelling in a stentorian voice. Feeling rather silly I stopped; anyway, I was out of breath.

"Every movement in excess of the essential paddling was extremely dangerous since the bullets were flying so thick and fast that they gave a reasonable facsimile of a steel curtain. Occasionally I lifted my head to give directions to our engineer steerer and to cast a cursory glance at the other 25 boats. By now the broad surface of the Waal was covered with our small canvas craft, all crammed with frantically paddling men. It was a horrible picture, this river crossing. Set to the deafening roar of omnipresent firing, this scene of defenseless, frail canvas boats jammed to overflowing with humanity all striving so desperately to cross the Waal as quickly as possible to get to a place where at least they could fight was fiendish and dreadful. We looked like a bunch of animals void of everything pertaining to dignity and normality in our frantic effort to get across the river.

"Large numbers of men were being hit in all boats, and the bottoms of these craft were littered with the wounded and the dead. Here and there on the surface of the water a paddle floated, dropped by some poor casualty before the man taking his place could retrieve it from the lifeless fingers.

"The water all around the boats was churned up by the hail of bullets, and we were soaked to the skin. Out of the corner of my eye, I saw a boat to my right hit in the middle by a 20mm shell and sink. Somewhere to my left, I glimpsed a figure topple overboard, only to be grabbed and pulled back into the boat by some hardy soul.

"I turned around as I heard a grunt behind me. I found someone taking the place of a man who had just received a 20mm shell, which went in one shoulder and out the other. 1, 2, 3, 4, 5, 6, 7, 8, 9. We were soaked, grasping for breath, dead tired, and constantly expecting to feel that searing sensation, a bullet tearing through you. I wanted to vomit. Many did. Somehow or other we were three-fourths of the way across. Everyone was yelling to keep it up, but there was little strength left in anyone. It seemed as though the only thing we could do was hang limply over the gunwale and drop the paddle into the water, letting it drift to the rear. But at last we reached the other side.

"We climbed over the wounded and the dead in the bottom of the boat and—up to our knees in water—waded to shore, where behind a small embankment, we flopped down, gasping for breath, safe for the moment from the incessant firing. All along the beach, what was left of our flimsy boats were reaching shore and the men, more dead than alive, were stumbling up the beach to get momentary protection behind the unexpected but welcome embankment, before pushing across the broad, flat plain before us.

"Out of 26 boats that made the initial crossing, I heard later that only 11 got back to pick up the second wave. The original plan had been for the engineers to paddle the boats back after disgorging us on the far shore. This they did with the 11 remaining boats. The rest had been sunk in the crossing, or the engineers had been killed, leaving the now-deserted craft to sink or float downstream, laden with their cargo of human dead and wounded. That, in some respects, was the most horrible aspect of all.

"For about 30 seconds I lay behind the embankment just beyond the small beach getting my breath, and up we (the men with me and myself) got and moved out across the open field into the fire. In many ways this was the most remarkable scene of the whole operation. You have seen in movies pictures of infantry troops attacking across open terrain, employing fire and movement. Well, this made any Hollywood version pale into insignificance. The Infantry School would have reveled in it. All along the shore line now our troops were appearing deployed as skirmishers. They were running into murderous fire from the embankment 800 yards away; but they continued to move forward across the plain in a lone single file many hundreds of yards wide. They cursed and yelled at each other as they advanced, noncoms and officers giving directions, the men firing from the hip their BARs, machine guns, and rifles as steadily they moved forward.

"All this time the 2nd Battalion and the tanks on the other side of the river were giving us marvelous support. Their constant overhead fire into the embankment where the Germans were ensconced was heavy and effective, and somehow it gave you a feeling of security and warmth and pride in your buddies who were helping you out. Because of it you didn't mind the dirt constantly being kicked up around you from Kraut bullets, or the continual whistle of rounds whizzing by you, or the men who grunted and dropped in their tracks on either side.

"Many times I have seen troops who are driven to a fever pitch—troops who for a brief interval of combat are lifted out of themselves—fanatics rendered crazy by rage and the lust for killing—men who forget temporarily the meaning of fear. It is then that the great military feats of history occur which are commemorated so gloriously in our text books. It is an awe-inspiring sight, but not a pretty one. However, I had never witnessed this human metamorphosis so acutely displayed as on this day. The men were beside themselves. They continued to plow across the field in spite of all the Kraut could do, cursing savagely, their guns spitting fire.

"Gradually the German resistance lessened as we approached the big embankment until it had almost completely deteriorated from that particular spot. The Krauts had pulled back to the next defensive line between us and the bridges; and of these defensive positions there were plenty—orchards, houses, embankments, a formidable and impregnable-looking Dutch fort, to say nothing of the bridges themselves. But for the present we were relatively safe. The river had been crossed, the beachhead had been established. The first phase was over.

"For a moment everyone lay on the rear slope of the bank drawing deep, full breaths. A few of us stuck our heads up above the top to see what came next. A [BAR] man had his head blown off. On the other side was another field with an orchard at the end. There was little organization at this point. How could there be? Officers found themselves with heterogeneous groups from all platoons and companies. They mustered whatever men were near them—it made little difference who was who—and prepared to go over the top once more, toward the next objective."[212]

Drawing by I Company veteran Bill Leonard of
the Waal River Crossing. *Courtesy: Bill Leonard*

CHAPTER 10

I COMPANY CROSSING
NIJMEGEN, SEPTEMBER 20, 1944

First Lieutenant Lauren W. Ramsey and his observers from the 81mm Mortar Platoon, 2nd Battalion, watched from the fourth floor of the power plant: "Sgt. Bennie Weeks and I [...] saw the whole crossing taking place. My smoke screen wasn't much good because the wind blew it away. Why they ever decided to go in the afternoon I don't know, but it was a big mistake."[213] S.Sgt. Kenneth S. Nicoll, forward observer for the 81mm Platoon along with Sgt. Charles L. Warren, recalled: "Ramsey told me to get on top of the power house and start firing my mortars at the Germans. When I got up there, the German artillery spotted me and my buddy and started throwing 88mm shells at us. But we stayed behind the smoke-stack and really pounded the mortars on those positions they were preparing for our assault across the river.

"The first boat got ashore and one of the boys [PFC Leo P. Muri, 1st Platoon, I Company] threw a Gammon grenade at a German machine-gun nest, and one of the Germans jumped up and tried to throw it back. He didn't know it was point-detonating. That cleared a path for them to get up the steep bank."[214]

D Company's 2nd Lt. Hanz K. Druener observed German firing tactics from the south bank of the river: "The British tanks were supposed to be up there but arrived late. I do recall smoke but I didn't see who was putting it down. We were in an open area there. They were probably located among the buildings of the factory so I didn't notice that. But I did notice that the smoke screen in some instances had dissipated before the men even got in the boats to make the river crossing.

"From my location I could look downriver and see the whole crossing. If

I had had a camera, I would have had some of the best war pictures you have ever seen. I looked east and personally witnessed the Germans using the overhead fire technique. The shell would burst over the river and I saw boats and people hit."[215]

Another D Company platoon leader, 1st Lt. Earnest H. Brown, recalled that "every weapon on both sides of the river seemed to be firing, including a 20mm German gun firing from upriver. In spite of heavy losses, the 3rd Battalion cleared an area of German soldiers and managed to establish a defensive line."[216]

"At 1500 the assault boats for the 3rd Battalion were finally readied and started across," wrote Lieutenant Garrison in the 2nd Battalion Journal. "D Company opened up with a great volume of small arms, machine-guns and Lieutenant Ramsey's mortars; also the 376th [Parachute] Field Artillery let go under the direction of Lieutenant Stueland, attached to the 2nd Battalion. Lined up bumper to bumper in D Company area, 2nd Irish Guard tanks kept up a hammering of flat-projectile and machine-gun fire. Smoke was laid with some success.

"The bombing missions scheduled for 1330 and 1500 never were accomplished. The enemy, firmly entrenched on the opposite shore, returned fire with everything available. The flak guns were particularly devastating when lowered to rake the river, often killing or wounding practically all occupants of single boats. Several boats overturned or were sunk. Men were finally landed and ran up the shore in the face of continuous fire, often killing the Germans in their positions. Due to the heavy barrage, some of the Germans had begun a retreat when the boats were half across. Their casualties were considerably greater than ours. Had they remained in position, their chances of successfully annihilating the attack would have been good."[217]

Although he expected to die during the crossing, Lieutenant Busby took a place in the bow of the canvas boat, rather than in the back. PFC Matthew W. Kantala, Jr. got in an argument with him while climbing aboard: "He was right in front of me. We had an argument about the seat. He wanted to sit in the front and I wanted the seat. He took the seat and got killed. I was hit in the face and hands."[218]

The 1st Platoon leader in Company I, 1st Lieutenant Blankenship, crossed the Waal River in the first boat of the assault wave and earned a Silver Star for his actions. "As follow-up boats were preparing to land, an enemy machine gun on the left flank opened up, wounding several men and pinning the larger landing force down. First Lieutenant Blankenship unhesitatingly, by crawling and moving by leaps and bounds, moved across 100 yards of open terrain until within 50 yards of the machine gun, whereupon he killed the four-man crew with rifle fire.

"First Lieutenant Blankenship suddenly observed a concealed enemy sniper only five yards from his position firing on his scout. Since he had no time to reload his rifle, he then knocked him out with his fists. First Lieutenant Blankenship then led two of his men within 15 yards of a flak wagon which they proceeded to neutralize with hand grenades. The courage, outstanding leadership, and unselfish actions displayed by First Lieutenant Blankenship throughout the entire action reflect great credit on himself and the army he serves."[219]

PFC Leo P. Muri, one of Blankenship's riflemen, described the scene as I Company set out from the riverbank: "Jerry had several machine guns and anti-aircraft guns which were firing just over the top of the water. So you can just imagine how we felt then, but we couldn't turn back, and in spite of the odds we launched our boat and took off. Bullets were falling around the boat and not all missed. I was in front with my machine gun resting on the bow and shot like hell. Everyone was yelling at each other to row faster as the canvas was ripping. Men who were hit rolled to the center to give more room to those still able to paddle.

"It was nothing less than a miracle that saved my life and we reached the other side just in time. The boat went down when we hit shallow water, and the wounded crawled out and lay on the beach. The rest of us had to advance and keep shooting, and didn't dare to stop too long to help the wounded. We had to make way for other boats to come over to get them. We racked up several machine-gun nests . . ."[220]

Corporal Tison was probably "the only one in our boat who had ever paddled another boat in his life. We were going around in circles. I finally got to the rear of the boat, chased the engineer off and at the top of my lungs told the other men how to paddle. When I told them to stroke, everyone stroked together. I took my paddle to the rear of the boat and used it as a rudder. I could see men being shot out of their boats. (When I was a kid, my father would ask if I wanted to go fishing. He didn't mean for me to fish—he wanted me to paddle while he fished.)"[221]

Pvt. William Leonard, an assistant machine-gunner in another rifle squad, recalled that Sgt. [Lloyd V.] Engebretzen, "lying to us as usual, stated the water was so low we could walk across it, except we might just drop something, and loose it. […] Then we were ordered to go over and help unload our boat from the truck. We struggled to get it down, and after carrying it 70 yards gave it a look. To our amazement, the craft was a canvas assault boat constructed of six pieces of wood, each two 2 inches wide by 12 inches long (to hold the sides up) and a piece of wood that looked like it was for a shower floor." Then the men heard the yell, 'Grab your craft by your hand and get down the embankment.' It was a drop-off of 15 feet. As it was somewhat steep, everybody was holding on for safety's sake, and in no time we were by or already in the water. There was too much talking and misunderstanding as to who was to be where, and with whom."[222]

Private Leonard ended up in the same boat as PFC Robert Hedberg and Pvts. Donald Emmett, Albert Essig and Sgt. George Ham. "After Emmett and Ham dropped in with six cans of machine-gun ammo, everybody else tried to follow. We were already in shoulder-high water! Packs and rolls were thrown on board along with rifles, to be followed by our bodies. With only four hand paddles, the rest of us had to resort to using rifles. Bullets were hitting all around us. Some who weren't looking didn't realize we were being shot at or believe we were under fire.

"Up front, in the first 50 yards […] the fact we were the dead center of their target became apparent. […] As water spouts jumped higher than a foot above the river, we could hear the guys next to us getting hit, and [our own wounded] were calling out. We went backwards downstream. Some were hit badly and had to be helped back after falling out. [Private Albert R.] Essig was on my right, hurting badly. I grabbed him by the shoulder strap and pulled him out of the water into the boat. I tried my darnedest to not let him fall back into the water.

"The 20mm shells were very low over our heads and many men were hit. After going with the current we straightened ourselves and finally headed for the far shore, running straight into the Germans' fire. Steadily spouts of water jumped directly towards us. Just on my left front was Emmett, really low. The noise made everything hard to realize what was happening to us and to those around the boats. Emmett lowered again. His helmet was knocked off and a piece of his right ear was shot off too. More bullets tore fast down his back, cutting his jacket almost in two.

"Within seconds, bullets tore through the machine-gun boxes, also tearing through my horseshoe roll, my two belts of M-1 ammo, my first-aid kit, and the left lower pocket of my jacket, ending up in my left thigh. It felt like someone had hit me with a sledge hammer! It just took my breath away.

Everyone was bleeding something awful. We were receiving direct fire from the German 88s. They made huge water spouts.

"With these and the 20mm tracer shells going by, you had better duck. We felt them whipping past and all of us slumped down as far as possible. With only two wooden paddles remaining, we tried to use our hands and rifle butts. If we braved to look back, the rest of the company was a horrible sight to see. Many craft were taking terrible beatings.

"After we hit the sandy bottom, we tried to get everybody out and on the shore. Some boats were almost half sunk, but only three quarters of the way across. Some were gone. Others were shot all to hell and drifted down-river with the current. With the help of Ham and Emmett, our craft was emptied in a hurry. The craft next to ours was in bad shape. Like ours, it was hard to tell which was more—blood or water—filling the bottoms.

"I was able to fall out of the boat. I stood up on my right foot and felt down in my pants and found nothing but blood, lots of it. Not wanting to go home a girl (there were three sisters already), I called out, 'Kill me, you damn bastards!' A few came ashore so nauseous they vomited. Ham gave me a push down and said, 'Crawl a bit,' which I did for some 25 feet. There I took my helmet and liner apart and started to dig with it. Too many guys were drawing mortar fire, ending up shot or blown over by local blasts. It seemed many troopers were disembarking at the same place as we did.

"Andy's scalp was cut open. The medics grabbed a bunch of 4/4 pads and a handful of gauze. 'Lie still,' they said. They finished him and continued to help others moaning in pain. About 30 minutes later a medic asked if he might help me. I tore my trousers down and showed the still bleeding wound. He made quick work with 4/4's and tape. 'Take care, I'll be seeing you all!'

"[PFC John] 'Jerry' Boggs from California walked past and informed us he lost his BAR, ammo and rifle in the river. I told him he could use my Thompson submachine-gun. Only minutes later he was wounded. [223] Then [Prv.] Dante Sansiveri and several more were hit by the same gun before someone was able to flank and destroy both the German nest and the machine gun. Ham and Emmett took off past me. They opened up and drove the enemy back down their holes. Emmett had his helmet on, while Ham carried the machine gun and shot it. I only had time to dig deep and large enough for my ass, before everybody coming by fell wounded on top of me or further on. Soon they were taking the worst wounded men back across the river.

"Lying there, I could see a group of troopers approximately 400 feet behind me, down on the ground by the bank. Germans were on the other side of the road firing this way. It was later confirmed that George Ham removed a British Gammon grenade with his hand knife out of the bottom of another trooper's leg pocket. The grenade had a plastic screw-cap. It had come off, and the ribbon that would set off the grenade had started to unwind. He very carefully took it down along the leg, set it on the ground, and then rewound it. Minutes later it was thrown over to the other side of the road in hopes of blasting the Germans. It was a very dangerous with the screw-cap off, leaving only the white ribbon and the safety-pin. With any little movement the grenade could have gone off, killing or wounding many all around.[224]

"Minutes later the groups had wiped out the defenders on the opposite side of the road. Later they headed to the fort, a quarter of a mile away on their left. Other German positions were silenced by tank fire. Five pill-boxes and several machine-gun emplacements were taken. Since the smoke screen was ineffective, the ten tanks behind us shot over our assault craft towards emplacements that were giving us harm. One was knocked out by 88mm fire.

"Still, there were deadly automatic and flat trajectories increasing in distance, and our ears were filled with the constant roar of the bursting artillery and the dull *wham* of nearby 20mm shells passing and hitting objects. They were flying so thick and fast they looked like a steel curtain. As the water all around the craft churned up in the hail of bullets, men more dead than alive were stumbling up the beach to get protection from the embankment.

"Suddenly to our right there was Chaplain Kuehl, only a dozen feet from us. With him were six or seven German prisoners who had given up. Lying there, we knew they had run out of ammunition. They looked at us with half-smiles on their faces. I was not the only one who wanted to kill them. There and then the chaplain jumped out in front of them, calling out that they were POWs and he was seeing them back to safety."[225]

S.Sgt. Tallon, resting a short while below the dike near Fort Hof van Holland, remembers machine-gun fire coming from his right, "probably from around the railroad bridge. The bullets were just skimming the top of the dike road; some even were hitting it. Next to me was another young replacement [Pvt. Frederick L. Zentgraf], a kid probably no more than 18 or 19. He kept wondering where the firing was coming from; […] our artillery was supposed to have neutralized it before we got there. I told the kid to forget it; we could do nothing about it, and besides, there was a squad flanking to the right which would take care of it.

"Finally, the kid said, 'I'm going to have a look,' and started crawling up the dike. I shouted, 'No!' But it was too late. He peeped over the top and instantly fell back, with a nice, neat, black hole square in the middle of his forehead."[226]

By the time 1st Lt. Thomas F. Pitt got over to the other side and out of his boat, the Germans were more worried about the troopers who had made it to their side than about the Engineers recrossing the river to pick up the second wave of the assault. "We were coming across another beach-like area [200 to 800 yards wide] before the final dike. They were dug-in, some on the beach and then back in the dike. We were practically running by them and they were just shooting. The only thing to do was to head for the dike because there wasn't a [...] bit of cover anywhere else. We finally got about halfway back to the dike and this kid who is peeling off this wire says, 'I ran out of wire. Should I set the phone up here?' I said, 'Hell with it, kid. Just take it easy now and get to the dike. We'll talk to them some other day.'

"So we finally got over to the dike. It must have been maybe ten yards wide at the top and the Krauts were on the back side. We spent a little time tossing grenades from one side or the other. That was fun and games. They were there with their potato-mashers and we had fragmentation grenades."[227]

T/5 Jack L. Bommer, a wireman with Headquarters and Headquarters Company, had been attached to the 3rd Battalion, and may have been the wireman Lieutenant Pitt saw peeling off wire halfway to the dike. Bommer's group "killed boys not over 15 and men of 65 in their foxholes. Everything went so fast and so hectic—it's hard to explain. Surrenders I saw few of—there wasn't any time. I did see old German men grab our M-1's and beg for mercy—they were shot point-blank."[228]

Private Keefe, I Company, recalled a harrowing crossing. When "20mm or 40mm guns opened up from the north side of the bridge, it was like a continuous streak of lightning, which we knew from Italy. [...] I never looked back at any time to see what was happening, but despite all the noise I could still hear the chants of the troopers in the back boats on the right-hand side of us saying, 'Heave, ho!' We rode right underneath the lightning, which I figured I could have touched with my hand if I stood up. That's how continuous it was. If the elevation of the gun had been any lower, it would have cut us right in half. [...]

"About 40 yards from the shore, I could see a steady stream of machine-gun bullets popping out of the water and coming at us. In only a matter of seconds they were about 20 feet in front of the boat on my side. I stopped rowing because there just was no place to go. Then the firing stopped. (I think the Germans' machine-gun belt ran out and by the time they put in another, we were almost to shore.)"

Private Keefe's boat was the second to reach shore, landing at a place "with approximately three feet of cover. [...] I immediately climbed up to observe what was in front of us. All I could see was the dike road a distance in front and a wooded area to the left of the dike road. The road seemed to curve down toward the bridge. The ground between the river and the dike road was on a slope.

"The firing and lightning continued all around me. [...] Some of the troopers were lying down, exhausted or perhaps wounded. I said, 'If we stay here, we'll all die. Let's move out!' I made a move and a kid from Brooklyn (I didn't know his name as he had just come into the outfit two weeks prior) moved with me. There was a hesitation behind me so I turned around and yelled, 'Move out or you'll die!' I took off and everyone, including me, let out this unmerciful cry. I know my personality had changed. God help anyone in front of us; they would pay.

"After about 40 yards, we ran into a six-foot-high trench that I hadn't seen from the beach. It ran parallel with the beach and the river. I looked sideways and saw Lieutenant Blankenship in the trench with us. The trench curved, so we couldn't see past 25 yards. I told Blankenship that I was going to check around the curve, but it curved some more. I told him I hadn't seen anyone. 'Let's take a rest,' I said, but he said, 'No, let's keep going.' We stepped on our rifles to get out of the ditch. It looked like everyone had their second wind by this time. Sgt. [Marvin C.] Porter and a few others were already at the slope of the dike road, which was pretty steep.

"I figured the best thing was to go over to the other side, make a flanking attack towards the bridge and clean out anything on that side of the dike. I had seen this done successfully at Mussolini's canal at Anzio. I took a Gammon grenade, which is an anti-tank grenade made of a putty substance which I believe is Composition C. The night before we left England, I had put some British slugs in the putty to make it an anti-personnel grenade. I threw it on the other side of the road. It sounded like a bomb going off! Two of the other troopers did the same thing. Immediately we went over the other side of the road."[229]

The "kid from Brooklyn," Private First Class Hughes, later wrote that "one of my movies and stories in school was the *Charge of the Light Brigade*. I've compared it to the Waal River Crossing so many times in my mind, and still do. On first sight, the Waal looked like portions of the Hudson. It had a fairly swift-running current and was wide enough to keep it from being a quick crossing.

"It was scary to me. But seeing the boats unloaded from the trucks really started my heart beating fast. As a seaman I knew boats, and these things didn't look like they belonged in a duck pond, let alone a wide river like the Waal. I started weighing what to discard if we got in the middle of the river and the damn thing sunk. I thought of maybe unlacing my boots so I could kick them off. I certainly wasn't going to swim too far with jump boots on.

"As these thoughts were going through my mind, I never gave a thought to the Germans and how it would be like a shooting gallery. My fear was not the enemy, it was surviving the crossing. There would be time enough to worry about the Krauts when and if we got close to them. The crossing is a blur to me, there was so much noise, screaming, yelling, shooting, so many explosions. I stumbled out on the other side and followed others running toward the shooting and what looked like a dike or embankment."[230]

Captain Burriss, I Company commander, crossed "sitting on the stern of our boat next to the engineer [PFC Willard Jenkins]. Suddenly, I noticed his wrist turn red. 'Captain,' he said, 'take the rudder. I've been hit.' Just as I reached for the rudder, he leaned forward and caught a 20mm HE [high explosive] shell through the head, a round that was meant for me. As the shell exploded, I felt a stinging sensation in my side. I had caught some of the shrapnel, though I felt no real pain. I grabbed the rudder and tried to steer. At that moment, the upper part of the engineer's body fell overboard; when the current hit his head and torso, the drag swung the boat upstream. 'Straighten out! Straighten out!' the men at the front of the boat shouted.

"I couldn't. His feet were caught under the seat, and his body was acting as a second rudder. I was finally able to reach down, disengage his feet, and push him overboard. As I watched his body float downstream, I could see the red blood streaming from what was left of his head. We resumed our frantic paddling toward the opposite shore.

"As we approached the north bank, I looked across the 900-yard plain between us and the dike. The grass was bristling with machine guns, and the only way to reach our objective was to charge straight into them. Not a happy prospect, but we had no other choice. We landed and piled ashore, sheltered for the moment by an embankment. With the river still spouting water [from shells and bullets], three more boats arrived.

"As I gathered my men, I was suddenly hit with a wave of nausea. I bent over and vomited. By the time I straightened up, I felt fine again. 'OK, men,'

I shouted. 'Let's go! Straight ahead to the dike!' Without hesitation, every single man, including several wounded, jumped from the embankment and started running forward, firing furiously at the machine guns on the back side of the dike. At that point, the machine-gunners shifted their fire from the boats to the charging ground troops—us. Men began to drop on both sides of me, some grabbing their legs or shoulders and others falling like sacks of sand. But those who were miraculously unhit continued firing and running toward the dike."[231]

One trooper whose drifting, unmanned craft had received a direct hit miraculously survived the crossing. The explosion had slammed Pvt. Leonard G. Trimble into the plywood bottom of his boat, wounded in the face, right arm, shoulder and left leg. As the boat swung around in circles and then drifted slowly back to the south bank of the river, Trimble felt like he was dying. After what seemed like an eternity, he was lifted out of the boat, discovered by the Pandurs. The young partisans carried Trimble, the sole survivor of his boat, to the first-aid station that Major Roggen had set up in the large hall of the power station. Among the dead, PFC Raymond H. Grummer and Pvts. Anthony Bei, Dale E. Campbell and Jack M. Seitzinger had possibly been in the same boat with Private Trimble. Another I Company trooper, PFC Cainie J. Clemons, drowned during the crossing.

For 1st Lt. Allen F. McClain, the crossing presented especially formidable challenges because "we had all our gear and weapons, radios and ammunition." McClain was to cross "in one of the first 13 boats" in the first wave of the assault. But how was his 81mm Mortar Platoon "to get enough ammunition across the river to be able to neutralize any target or give adequate support wherever necessary? [...]

"As we carried the boat over the bank, I saw two boats receive direct hits from 40mm shells. We reached the water's edge and while the men were putting the boat in the water, I held an 81mm mortar base plate and other assorted equipment. The additional weight caused me to sink hip-deep in the silt-like mud, 400 yards from the other side. But for the super strength of Victor Rosca, a staff sergeant, I might have been left to settle in that slimy mud. The remainder of the regiment, the 1st and 2nd Battalions, came over by barge." McClain saw several wounded lying in the open on the northern shore and instructed his men to make a dash for the dike. There was no time for reorganization or a well-planned orientation. He figured they should be helping to take a bridge, so they headed towards the railroad bridge. Running into fire along the way, they were forced to dig in.[232]

Lieutenant Holabird, C Company, 307th AEB, was one of the few men on the crossing who had had "lots of experience with canoes and row boats." He and others in his craft also benefited from his time on a freshman rowing crew at Harvard. "I took the stern and shouted, 'Stroke! Stroke! Stroke!' as we wallowed across the Waal. I think we were 11 engineers and all had paddles, five to a side, and across we went. There was a whistling of bullets all around us, but for some reason no one was injured. We hit the other bank and took off like cowboys and Indians up the bank. Three of our guys were left to ferry the boat back to pick up another load. I think they had the toughest job of all!

"When we hit the shore we were elated! Intoxicated! We [...] took off gradually east where we knew the highway bridge to be. We didn't find any mines—we just ran and ran. We were eight young men, 19- to 23-years-old, who had just won a new life, and we dashed like a cavalry squadron. Nothing could stop us now! We didn't wait for the 504th. Forward we ran. There was a pillbox in front of us. Who knows if there were any defenders? We tossed in grenades and shot ahead. There were two houses, I think uninhabited, but we tossed grenades there too and romped on."[233]

First Lieutenant Patrick J. Mulloy, 3rd Platoon, had been last to get in his boat, and "stayed in the back." A veteran engineer, he compared the intensity of the fire on the crossing "to the worst we took at Anzio. I felt like a sitting duck; they seemed to be blazing away with heavy machine guns and mortars." Mulloy wore a .45 in a holster strapped on his right side and had a carbine slung over his shoulder. A few yards before they reached the bank, "something smacked into [his] side" and tore his holster off: "At first I thought I had caught one, but the impact was greater than the wound. I had been grazed and a few hours later discovered I had a pretty good-sized bruise across my stomach and hip." Sitting at the front of the boat, one of his men, "Cpl. Lou Gentile, a real nice quiet kid from the east, was not so lucky. Just seconds after Mulloy was grazed, Cpl. Gentile was hit by 20mm shrapnel and slumped over in front of the boat."

The boat hit the north bank of the river, still under enemy fire. "Gentile was in a real bad way. He was pretty well torn up from a shell or mortar. He was conscious, but only just briefly. [...] I got Gentile out and laid him down behind some rocks. He was only concerned that everybody else would be all right. There were a lot of other wounded lying on the bank. [...] I felt terrible about Gentile, but I was glad we were across."[234]

Pvt. Meldon F. Hurlbert, an engineer in the 2nd Platoon, recalled "the man in front of me [Pvt. James F. Woods] got hit, killed by a large-caliber shell which knocked him back. He landed all bloodied in my lap. […] Our boat was sunk about three-fourths of the way across. Luckily at this point the water was up to my chin, so I walked to the other side. There I was hit in the rear end with shrapnel. The situation was chaotic. I remember seeing a railroad track nearby. There was so much going on, with everyone shooting at each other with all kinds of weapons. I also remember seeing Allied fighter planes supporting us."[235]

While the second wave of the assault paddled across, Lieutenant Blankenship's 1st Platoon cleared a patch of woods some 300 yards west of the Fort Hof van Holland. The lieutenant, Sgt. Marvin C. Porter and Pvt. Leo P. Muri charged a flak wagon and a machine gun. Porter knocked the flak wagon out with rifle grenades, firing at about a 75-yard distance. The platoon proceeded to the farmhouse just north of the dike. Private Keefe recalls: "There was a house about 50 yards from the dike road and to the right front of us. I hadn't seen it because of the embankment on the other side. A machine gun fired out of the upper window as our troopers came up from the river. I saw six Germans come along a hedge and run inside the back door. Sergeant Porter then let out a yell; he got shot in the leg. A couple seconds later, the man next to Porter was also hit in the leg. Both were only four feet away from me. Lieutenant Blankenship, Muri, the kid from Brooklyn and someone else were to the right front of them. I was about a few feet in front of Porter when a German seemed to rise right out of the ground about seven feet in front of me. I was stunned that he was so close. Porter must have seen him because he killed him with a burst from his Thompson submachine gun.

"I put a rifle grenade in my rifle and put in the blank cartridge. Blankenship moved to Porter and the other trooper to see if he could assist them. This put him pretty close to me on the right-hand side. I got hit in the left wrist just as I had my rifle in position to fire at the window. My rifle dropped right down next to Blankenship; he was lucky that the grenade didn't go off. I said, 'Lieutenant, they shot off my hand.' A bullet hit the bracelet I was wearing and did a lot of damage. It was one Emmett had made when we were at the airport in Naples. Some of us wore them; they were of a light substance.

"The kid from Brooklyn came over to help me. I told him that there was a first-aid kit in my back pocket. He went into the wrong pocket and pulled out my wallet. 'What will I do with this?' he said. I told him to throw the wallet away and get the first-aid packet. He did. I held my hand and arm across my stomach as my hand hung off if I moved my left arm. Just then I got hit in the upper right arm.

"Then something hit me in the mouth and broke off my front tooth. Muri came over and helped the kid bandage my hand and arm. As Muri gave me a shot of morphine, somebody asked, 'What do we do now?' 'Keep firing at the building,' I said. Blankenship, who knew we were in a bad position, went over to the other side of the road. Meanwhile, the kid from Brooklyn, who never seemed bothered by anything, asked for my .45 and I told him to take it. I couldn't have cared less."[236] (PFC Hughes, the kid from Brooklyn, would put the .45 "to good use later on the stairs of the Waal Bridge.")[237]

Pvt. Lawrence 'Red' Allen grabbed Keefe around the waist and "practically carried" him over to the other side of the road. "When I looked down the road, it appeared that G and H Companies were firing at the building a lot. My flanking attack didn't go too well. Captain Burriss, 1st Sergeant Odom and about 12 troopers from I Company were there. Odom took out his canteen and gave me a drink. It was as if the war had stopped. Everyone was staring at me. Someone said, 'Give him a shot of morphine.' Muri said, 'I gave him one on the other side.' 'Give him another, it won't hurt him.' Someone wanted to look at my wound but I wouldn't let him.

"Captain Burriss then told Sgt. [Alexander L.] Barker, 2nd Platoon, to take two men, cross the river and bring back more ammunition. He detailed two other men to help Porter and the other troopers down to the river. I sat there staring at the other troopers, especially Muri. I was concerned about him, as we had been together two months in Anzio. Neither one of us got a scratch physically. They used to say he was too small and I was too skinny. I guess tears came to my eyes when I realized that I couldn't be of anymore help and would never be back. It was then that Captain Burriss said, 'I'll give you somebody to help you get back.' I said, 'No, you need everyone you have here. I'll get back by myself.' Then he said, 'Get yourself taken care of and we'll see you when you get back.' 'You won't see me again,' I replied, and he said, 'Well, I will never forget you.' That was nice of him to say. To the rest of the troopers he said, 'Let's go!' and they took off along the side of the dike road toward the bridge. I watched them go and then started down towards the river.

"I could see in the distance on the right by the water's edge a congregation of men coming up from the river. Six bodies were strung out about half of the way there. As I got closer, I could see [PFC Robert E.] Dority, the medic, attending to one of the men lying there. The dirt was popping up;

someone was taking pot shots all around him. As I got closer, they started popping around me. I believe the shots were coming from the wooded area on the other side of the dike road. Dority yelled to me to get down and then ran over to me. He said, 'You better stay down or you'll get killed.' I asked him about the condition of the troopers lying there. 'Not good,' he said. He asked if there was anything he could do for me. 'No,' I said. He told me that he had to get back to the other wounded and to stay low.

"As I got closer to the group, I saw some German prisoners, Chaplain Delbert Kuehl with some wounded and Sergeant Barker just getting into a boat to start back across the river. [...] I asked the chaplain why the wounded men lying up above couldn't get some help and he told me they would be all right. He was concerned about the German prisoners. I had to get away from there. I walked back to where we had landed and looked up. There were no dead or wounded lying where we had attacked. We were lucky.

"Someone with a head wound was coming toward me. I recognized him as 'Blacky.' I don't know if he was from H or G Company. We went over to the chaplain and prisoners and Blacky got into a discussion with the chaplain about the prisoners. He came back to me and wanted to know if I had a gun. He said, 'Let's see if we can find one.'

"I walked about 40 yards along the shore towards the bridge. It ran into a little inlet 20 feet in from the water, 15 feet wide and about four or five feet deep. There I saw Lieutenant Busby's body. His legs were still lying in the water. I thought about the argument we had earlier and felt bad. I wished I could pull him out, but it was impossible with my wounds. I called Blacky over but he couldn't get down there by himself. I went back and asked the chaplain for some help. The chaplain told me not to worry about it; Busby would be all right. He spoke to me in a nice way. I must say he was very courageous for making the crossing under such conditions when he didn't have to. I looked at the prisoners again and knew I had to get away from them. Another boat came over; the prisoners and some other troopers got in and started across. I waited for the next boat, got in and started across the river.

"When I got to the other side, I ran into another buddy of mine, [Pvt. Louis P.] 'Lefty' Rigo, from 2nd Battalion Headquarters. We had been together in the 513th PIR and tented together in Kairouan, North Africa. He went bananas when he saw me. He grabbed his gun and looked like he wanted to run across on the water. A couple of other guys grabbed hold of him. I told him I was just fine. As I walked up past the power house, different troopers wanted to know if they could give me a hand. I said, 'No, I'm fine.'

I guess I wanted to be proud of my last walk. A jeep of medics came along and drove me to the aid station. I started to relax when I saw Capt. [William W.] Kitchin."[238]

While Private Keefe walked back to the northern shore, Burriss dispatched 1st Lt. Calvin A. Campbell with ten men and Sgt. Grady L. Robbins from the Machine Gun Platoon to the area of a small lake called Lake Groote Wiel. Campbell had caught a 20mm shell fragment in his right leg, and had earlier knocked out a German machine-gun nest with his men. They were now to defend the west point of the bridgehead to prevent the Germans from retaking the dike road and cutting off the remainder of the 3rd Battalion.

Burriss headed for the road bridge with about 30 officers and men, following the German side of the dike road to the east. Bypassing Fort Hof van Holland, they saw several H Company troopers and ran on to the north side of the railroad bridge. Corporal Tison recalled that the combined group was briefly involved in a "snowball fight" with Germans: "We were on one side of the railroad tracks, the Jerries on the other. First Lieutenant Rivers [La Riviere] tossed a hand grenade over on their side, one Kraut caught it and threw it back. Luckily, no one was hit. Then the lieutenant dug a Gammon grenade out and tossed it over. The German reached out to catch it when—*boom*! It blew him and several other Krauts to wherever they go when they die. The Gammon grenade is a sock that holds three pounds of TNT with a cloth-like belt placed into the detonator. While the grenade is in the air, the belt pulls loose, and it explodes on impact. Three pounds of that stuff blows up a good-sized hole, wherever it lands."[239]

Lieutenant Riviere told Burriss that the railroad bridge guards had been overrun and the situation would be fine. It would be wiser to move on to the road bridge. La Riviere and three of his men joined Burriss's group and ran under the bridge and along the north side of the river dike. About this time, 1st Lt. Edward W. Kennedy and ten members of the 3rd Platoon left the column and moved alongside the railway dike in an attempt to capture the underpass where the railroad and road intersect.

PFC Robert A. Hedberg, 3rd Platoon, who remained with Captain Burriss, recalled that the group received heavy enemy fire between the railroad and road bridges, which split the group into two sections. Tison set up his machine gun and returned fire, while further to the front, Burriss and a couple others searched the houses north of the river dike. At one house Burriss and Sgt. Harold R. Johnson found several sleeping Germans, some of whom were awakened when the Americans opened the door. Sergeant Johnson quickly grabbed a Gammon grenade and threw it into the room and closed the door. A loud explosion followed. None of the Germans inside survived.[240]

Pvt. Peter L. Colishion lay near Hedberg, who shouted for a medic, thinking Colishion had been severely wounded. Pvt. Stanley Christofferson, the platoon medic, showed up, examined Colishion, then turned to Hedberg and said, "He doesn't need me anymore. He needs an undertaker." Christofferson took off immediately to render first aid to another man.[241]

The quick reaction of the troopers in the forward section frightened the Germans away. One German was captured in a house, and the gun crew abandoned a nearby 88mm flak gun pointed at the road bridge. Burriss, who now had about half of his group, noticed some barges along the northern riverbank and sent Pvts. Gerald E. Melton and Robert L. Tope of I Company and Cpl. Eldon F. Young of H Company to check them for snipers. On their way, the three troopers found another 88mm gun pointed at the road bridge. Private Melton threw a Gammon grenade that killed five gunners and the remaining gunner surrendered on the spot. At 1845 hours Captain Burriss sent two runners, Pvts. Elvie W. Bartow and Robert J. Yannuzzi, back to lead the other section across the dike road. Fifteen minutes later the two sections joined forces, and Captain Burriss dashed on towards the road bridge with 20 men.

—————————

CHAPTER 11

FORT HOF VAN HOLLAND AND THE FIGHT AT THE LENT VIADUCT
NIJMEGEN, SEPTEMBER 20, 1944

The members of the 3rd Battalion were only confronted with the enormity of the crossing at the point they started across the Waal River. According to Captain Kappel, H Company, it was impossible to see "the routes leading to the water," and nothing had been reconnoitered "because as we went over the dike, a large, chain-link fence with a couple of strands of barbed wire on top blocked our way.

"I was up front in the lead boat. When we hit the fence and were blocked I was mad as hell. I took a Gammon out and threw it against one of the pipe supports and [2nd] Lt. James Megellas did the same on the next support. Our combined weight against the fence pushed it down and we were able to go on down toward the river.

"We had lined up, intending to go over the dike laterally separated, but we ended up being more or less funnelled down to the river by the fence and the terrain. I was delayed getting to the water because of knocking down the fence. When I finally got there, it was a scene of mass confusion. Some boats had been hit already and men were getting in others. I don't know what caused my boat to sink, but it had.

"I believe one of the privates by the name of Legacie had been in my boat. He was in the water and starting to go down, not too far off shore. I am a pretty strong swimmer. I rarely wore my helmet in combat, and didn't have it on that day. Our weapons were on our suspenders, so it was a simple matter of shucking mine off and going into the water.

"I was worn out by the time I got him back, huffing and puffing like an old man. I touched ground and pulled him back, but I was so tired I couldn't

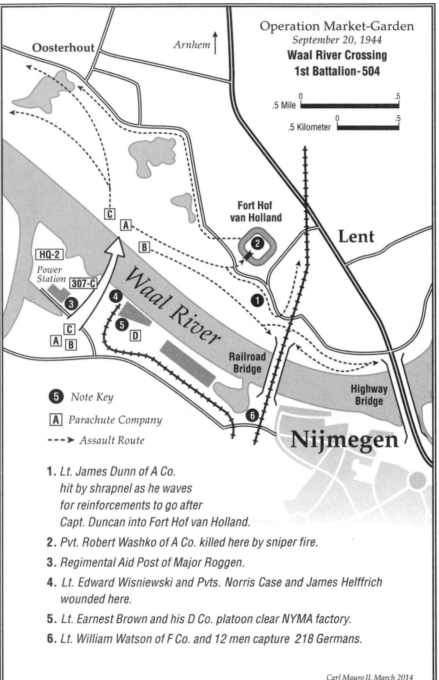

Operation Market-Garden
September 20, 1944
Waal River Crossing
1st Battalion-504

Oosterhout

Arnhem

Fort Hof van Holland

Lent

HQ-2

Power Station

307-C

Waal River

Railroad Bridge

Highway Bridge

Nijmegen

5 *Note Key*

A *Parachute Company*

- - -► *Assault Route*

1. *Lt. James Dunn of A Co. hit by shrapnel as he waves for reinforcements to go after Capt. Duncan into Fort Hof van Holland.*

2. *Pvt. Robert Washko of A Co. killed here by sniper fire.*

3. *Regimental Aid Post of Major Roggen.*

4. *Lt. Edward Wisniewski and Pvts. Norris Case and James Helffrich wounded here.*

5. *Lt. Earnest Brown and his D Co. platoon clear NYMA factory.*

6. *Lt. William Watson of F Co. and 12 men capture 218 Germans.*

Carl Mauro II, March 2014

get him out of the water, so I left him half in and half out. I don't know whether he was hit or not; if he was, I don't think it was too bad."[242]

Legacie, an assistant .30-caliber machine-gunner in the 1st Platoon, escaped wounding and later teamed up again with his close friend, Pvt. Lawrence H. Dunlop. Captain Kappel meanwhile found another boat and crawled in. It carried three airborne engineers, T/5 Flox; S.Sgt. James Allen, Jr., the 2nd Platoon Sergeant; and 1st Lieutenant Russell of the 376th PFAB.

As Kappel relates the crossing, "the engineer on the tiller was knocked off the back. I heaved myself up, grabbed a paddle and used it as a steering oar until we were practically across the water. We were heavily fired upon, mostly from the right flank, and were paddling fast. There was a great deal of overhead fire from the tanks on our side of the river. The smoke that had been laid down was practically gone; there were big, huge gaping holes in it. The British tanks, standing almost track-to-track on the dike, were doing a great job."[243]

For the last 30 yards, only three men were still paddling: Allen, Flox and Kappel, who rowed from his place near the tiller: "A few yards from the shore I dropped off the back of the boat and gave a big shove, which drove us into shore. There were three of us moving. The boat was half-filled with water. Most of it was blood."[244] T/5 Seymour Flox remembers: "The Waal River is only about 200 yards wide, but it seemed we would never get to the other side. [...] Making that crossing was the worst hell I have ever been through. There have been a few tough spots where I thought I would meet my maker, but then I could almost see him reaching out for me. I guess our prayers were heard and that is why I am able to write about it now.

"When we started across, the bullets were coming so close that those that didn't hit you splashed water on your face. We were all paddling like mad, but just couldn't paddle in time with each other and that doubled the job. When we finally did get across, we were all tired-out, but there was no resting then. We stormed the opposite riverbank and fought our way to a railroad bridge about 400 yards away, making several dashes across open fields under machine-gun fire."[245]

Captain Kappel picked up a Tommy gun and some ammo clips in the boat, since he had left his own on the southern shore when he jumped in to save Private Legacie from drowning. He then headed for the dike. "The three of us started running for the first thing to get down behind, a trench or a ditch, I believe, at least 600 yards from the shore. I still hadn't recovered from my swim and I developed a hell of a pain in my side. Flox, Allen and I made the trench and got down. I was in terrible pain; they thought at first I had been hit, but I hadn't.

"We laughed about it and it was at this point that [Staff] Sergeant Allen turned to me and said, 'Our luck is still holding out.' We had a breather and got up and started up the dike. I remember you had to cross a hardtop road on the top."[246]

Pvt. Hugh Wallis and his close friend, Pvt. Cletus J. Shelton, formed the bazooka team for 2nd Lieutenant Megellas's 3rd Platoon: "I had my bazooka in the boat. If my memory serves me right, I was boat number two from the railroad bridge. We were told there would be an artillery barrage on the north bank and that fighter planes would strafe up the north bank and airplanes would lay a smoke screen across over the river. I never heard one British shell explode, nor did I ever see one plane. […] I was on my knees paddling. A shell or bullet came through the canvas boat and made left a hole in the bottom between my legs. I put my knee in the hole to prevent us from sinking. The next thing I knew, I was in the water and had been hit in my right arm. I had bazooka rounds around my neck as well as M-1 ammo.

"As I went to the bottom of the river, I started peeling everything off. I was up and down two or three times. Just as I thought I was going down, someone reached out a boat paddle to me and I was pulled into a boat. I think Pvt. Joseph Jedlicka was in my boat. Cletus Shelton was also wounded. He got some grenade shrapnel in his head, but nothing penetrated deep, so it was not too serious. They shaved his head and extracted the grenade bits. Shelton told me later that he swam to shore."[247]

Pvt. Robert T. Koelle, the 3rd Platoon medic, was in Shelton and Wallis's boat. He was killed by small-arms fire just before Wallis was wounded. His last letter home expressed the desire to be home for Christmas, "but in case I can't make it this year, cigarettes and candy will do nicely."[248] In the same boat, 2nd Lt. Ernest P. Murphy, Pvt. Joe L. Jedlicka and Sgt. Leroy M. Richmond, Wallis's squad leader, were luckier. "We were the lead boat nearing the north bank when suddenly an enemy 20mm shell tore through the canvas sides, opening two gaping holes," Murphy recalled. "The boat started taking on water and we had to swim. On shore I took count of my men. Then I noticed a helmet pop out of water and the missing man, Pvt. Joseph Jedlicka, walked out. Jedlicka, who could not swim, had sunk in about eight feet of water. He was still carrying his BAR and two boxes of ammo when he emerged. Drenched and shaken by his ordeal, he rejoined my platoon thankful to be alive."[249]

Private Wallis was meanwhile helped ashore along with a number of other wounded, whose names he cannot remember: "We were lying with two or three on the west side of a short dam in the river, trying to find some cover. I was taken back to the tents of a field hospital [in Dekkerswald]. I stayed one night in Brussels and then on to Paris and across the English Channel. I still have shrapnel in my right arm."[250]

Wallis's platoon leader, 2nd Lt. James Megellas, lost half of his men, two engineers and 13 paratroopers on the crossing when the boat next to his capsized and sank. He vividly describes the action once his boat reached shore: "I headed for the embankment, with several men from my platoon in close pursuit. Machine guns opened up on us and small-arms fire crackled all around us. It was utter chaos. There were so many bullets in the air that it was difficult to tell who was firing at you and from what direction. Instinctively we attacked in the direction from which most of the fire appeared to be coming, the 15-foot-high embankment in front of us.

"Trying to find cover from the hail of bullets was impossible, and retreating back to the river would have been insane. It was kill or be killed. Men driven by rage were cursing the Germans as they charged forward, running low and firing their weapons as they advanced. In the midst of the confusion, I noticed a small indentation in the flat area about 50 yards to my left. A shallow channel ran from the embankment to the river, undoubtedly used to drain the area of runoff water. Running low, I charged up that ditch toward the enemy, firing my Tommy gun in their direction as a bullet whistled close to my head."[251]

Cpl. John M. Fowler, an assistant squad leader, led a charge directly toward the railroad bridge. For his bravery he was later awarded the Silver Star. Fowler's group probably joined forces at this time with men from 1st Platoon, H Company, led by Lieutenant Sims: "Our first objective was the north end of the railroad bridge. The plan included support from artillery and smoke screen, neither of which helped. We did get good supporting overhead fire from our own 2nd Battalion and a few British tanks that had arrived early from positions along the south bank. [...]

"It seemed like an eternity before my boat landed on the north bank, but it was only about ten minutes. My group had landed some distance west of the railroad bridge and disembarked rapidly into a skirmish line. Another boat landed nearby with many casualties, so I ordered those who had not been wounded to join my group and then led this combined group (18 men) in a frontal assault on the dike that was several hundred yards further north.

I carried an M-1 rifle and directed the assault forward by bounds with rapid fire from all, including myself. Enemy fire from the dike was heavy, but the men with me did not falter. Their courage and determination was obvious and admirable. Because of these few men, the dike was seized within a short time and those German defenders still alive were routed or taken prisoner. I learned later that there were numerous enemy dead on the part of the dike taken by my group."[252]

The 2nd Platoon men in Sgt. Daun Z. Rice's squad used their rifle butts to paddle, while Cpl. Jimmy S. Shields, assistant squad leader, plied the butt of his BAR. Rice's platoon leader put him in for a Silver Star for his heroics that day, but it was later downgraded to a posthumous Bronze Star: "Upon gaining the north bank of the river, Sergeant Rice speedily organized his own squad together with members of other units and led them across a 600-yard stretch of open terrain toward his company's objective, which was the north end of the bridge.

"In spite of the fact that he and his squad were subject to a withering hail of enemy small-arms, machine-gun, and mortar fire, Sergeant Rice by his own exemplary conduct and exhortations led his men to the high ground overlooking their objective. There the unit was pinned down by fierce enemy machine-gun fire coming from the bridge 200 yards to their front. Sergeant Rice, realizing the desperate plight of his unit, unhesitatingly and voluntarily seized a BAR from one of his men and, exposing himself deliberately to the enemy fire, worked his way around to a position on their flank from which he was able to deliver effective fire. This flanking fire forced the enemy to withdraw and enabled the remainder of his men to overrun and hold their objective."[253]

Sergeant Tarbell, a radio operator in Company Headquarters, later recorded the harrowing crossing. Amidst the chaos, single images stand out as if in a dream. The boat to his right took a direct hit, spinning it around. "To this day I can still see the look on Pvt. Louis Holt's face as our eyes met. The boat went down and out of sight. We finally did make the other side—after having lost all but 11 of the 26 boats we started out with. As I was making my way up the road, I met [PFC John] Rigapoulos [2nd Platoon]. He showed me the nub of his left thumb, which had been shot off. 'Well,' he said, 'Here's another Purple Heart.' John and I came from jump school to join the battalion in Anzio as replacements. He was also one of the volunteers for the Pathfinders for Normandy. He was killed that afternoon, shortly after we spoke."[254]

That night, Sergeant Rice of H Company noted in his diary the names of those who had paid the ultimate price, seizing the moment to record deeds fresh to memory, lest the courage and bravery of his men be lost to posterity: "Crossed river at 1600 under heavy fire of all kinds. Only protection after crossing—small ditches—a dike 800 yards ahead. Later learned T/5 [Wilford N.] Dixon killed in boat on crossing. [Sergeant] Tague wounded—others I can't remember, Rigapoulos and S.Sgt. Allen killed. Fighting here was close and terrible. Saw Daun for the first time at railroad bridge. He and I and six or seven (Haas) others there first. Killed and captured approximately 25 Germans there. British tanks started across highway bridge and relieved the pressure—we then moved off to the right for rest. There were many incidents of great individual bravery that will be lost forever here. Someday I'll try and put this in detail."[255]

After Lieutenant Megellas moved out to seize a nearby fort, Lieutenant Sims took his 18-man group "and went for the north end of the railroad bridge. Lieutenant La Riviere, with a few men, moved east to flush out a sniper who had shot and killed one of his men [PFC John Rigapoulos]. Resistance was light and it soon fell into our hands. I then ordered a few men to look for explosives and to cut all wires; then I set up a defense around our end of the bridge. During a hasty search of the supporting abutments, a hold-out shot one of my sergeants, but fast medical treatment was credited for his eventual recovery."[256]

Captain Kappel was joined by Lieutenant Sims at about the point that Staff Sergeant Allen "got it in the thigh. [...] I remember chuckling and telling him he had a good one," Kappel recalled, "meaning it was bad enough to get him out of action for a while, but not a serious or fatal wound. We patched him up and left him bandaged and he was in good spirits. He was dead the same day."[257]

According to Kappel, the 3rd Platoon, commanded by Megellas, cleared part of the fort, but again received fire from within its walls as they were leaving. "The fort remained a definite problem all afternoon, as it consisted of many layers, until it was completely cleared by the 1st Battalion later in the day and occupied as the Regimental CP. The 1st Battalion took some 30 prisoners, plus inflicting numerous casualties before the fort was (written off as) captured.[258]

"Later the 1st Battalion went in and got the bulk of the Germans out. One of the 1st Battalion company commanders [Captain Duncan] told me after the fighting they had taken far more prisoners than we did. I answered, 'You captured yours. We shot ours.' I don't know how I know this, because I didn't get in the fort, but there were two guns on top of it—a 20mm and a 14mm."[259]

In a letter home, Capt. Henry B. Keep, 3rd Battalion S-3, wrote a vivid and detailed account, which he himself called "garbled and confused," due to the requirements on the ground. "The ensuing action was highly disorganized and of necessity the feats of small individual groups. The sector between us and the bridge had to be cleared of all enemy resistance. It was comprised of many isolated strong points widely separated. To complete this successfully, many groups would be required to operate in a divergent area. So off the men pushed—this time in small bunches, each in a slightly different direction—each with a separate mission. But in the back of everyone's mind was the one thought, namely to keep going towards the bridges which must be taken at all costs.

"I was with a group consisting of our battalion commander, Major Cook, a company commander, and about 30 men. By squad we rushed across fields, worked our way through orchards and down ditches; from one house to the next we jumped. I am sure one could write a book on the advance of each group. In our own particular bunch I witnessed countless acts of heroism, all of which deserve decorations, but which, of course, will remain unknown.

"I will recount only one incident in our attack towards the bridges, which is not void of humor. In one particular hot rush across an open field, the bullets were whizzing around us so persistently that yours truly was forced to dive into a nearby hole until things quieted down a bit. Just as I made a lunge for it, two forms slid underneath me and I found myself the third layer of humanity in a foxhole for one. My rear was sticking up what seemed yards above the top of the hole. On the bottom was some poor GI who was practically smothered and kept working to get up, an act which wild horses couldn't have forced me to do. Next came the major and then I. The major and I couldn't help but laugh at the situation. When the bullets stopped whizzing past my fanny with such regularity, I deemed it safe to continue our interrupted rush. I passed the word down to the depths of our Black Hole of Calcutta and the major, the GI and myself squeezed ourselves out of this tight fit and continued on our way. Needless to say, the situation was repeated several times before our immediate objective was reached.

"All this while the sounds of fierce skirmishes were heard coming from all over the area, as our men fought their way towards the bridges. The account of the seizure of the fort is a story in itself, but that will have to wait until a later date."[260]

Lieutenant Megellas and a mixed group of his 3rd Platoon and one squad from the 1st Platoon led by Sgt. Theodore H. Finkbeiner tried to capture Fort Hof van Holland and neutralize its 20mm gun emplacements. "Although the fort had been one of H Company's objectives, we had no idea of its layout or structure," Megellas wrote. "It was ancient and moat-encircled with a drawbridge on the north side. It resembled an inverted bowl, with sides sloping at about a 45-degree incline from the edge of the moat to the top of the fort, a distance of about 50 feet. The sloping sides were earthen and sodded. There was a parapet ringing the top from where the Germans had been firing at us.

"I saw an opportunity to silence the 20mm antiaircraft guns and machine guns that had rained so much havoc on us when we were sitting ducks. I directed all the fire we could mass at those targets, forcing the Germans to seek cover. When the enemy fire ceased, we charged forward and reached the moat. At the time we were not aware of the drawbridge over the moat on the opposite side."[261]

Sgt. Leroy M. Richmond, one of Megellas's squad leaders, took off his helmet and web belt, got into the moat without much noise and swam under water to the base of the fort. Climbing the grassy side, he saw that one 20mm gun emplacement was out of order. He ducked down as a German fired on him. "The bullet grazed the side of his neck but did not seriously wound him," continues Megellas. "He started back down the incline, swam the moat and rejoined us. From our position on the edge of the moat, we lobbed hand grenades over the parapet and inside the fort. That kept the Germans in the bunkers while we circled around the back to the drawbridge."[262]

Megellas and his 11 men ran in defilade around the fort to the six-foot-wide causeway. Megellas sent PFC Robert E. Hawn and another man across the causeway under covering fire. Hawn and the other scout threw Gammon grenades onto the fort, neutralizing part of the enemy fire. The remainder of the group dashed across the causeway and climbed the grassy side of the fort, where PFCs Everett S. Trefethern and James H. Rosser knocked out gun emplacements with Gammon grenades. Rising up to call on the Germans to surrender, Sgt. Robert N. Seymour was wounded by sniper fire, possibly from the railroad bridge. Artillery and increasing small-arms fire started to rain down on the fort, endangering the paratroopers lying on top of the parapet. Megellas sent assistant machine-gunner Pvt. Sylvester J. Larkin to contact G Company, believing they were delivering friendly fire. Several minutes later Larkin returned to report he had delivered the message. As artillery fire was still coming down, it seemed safer to pull back to the north end of the railroad bridge.

As they neared, they encountered a culvert in the railway dike covered with a wooden plate. Cpl. John J. Foley, Jr., believed he heard civilians inside and was shocked when one of the enlisted men in his squad pulled the plate back and tossed a grenade inside. The explosion wounded several people and probably killed some as well. Foley pushed the soldier aside and with the help of Sergeant Richmond and others dragged the wounded out of the culvert and to a nearby Dutch home. There was little time to aid civilians, since 2nd Platoon leader, 1st Lt. Richard G. La Riviere, upset about the loss of PFC John Rigapoulos at the railway dike, showed up with his remaining men. Having left five of them to guard the west side of the culvert, he continued with the remaining five to the north end of the railroad bridge, where he set up a BAR team to cover the north approach.

At this point Megellas's group also split up. Sergeant Finkbeiner and his 1st Platoon rifle squad followed S.Sgt. James Allen (earlier wounded at the dike), in the attempt to capture the underpass in the railway dike where the highway from the bridge intersected the railway line. Sergeant Finkbeiner climbed the embankment and looked right into the muzzle of a German MG-42. He ducked, but the blast blew the wool liner cap off his head. A hand-grenade battle ensued, and "several Germans charged" Finkbeiner's men. "We repulsed the charge, killing a couple and wounding another. I had to restrain the engineer who had stayed with us [Cpl. William E. Kero] from going to the aid of the wounded German.

"One of our men [Staff Sergeant Allen] received a shot that must have severed a femoral artery in his hip, and lived only a few minutes. One of the enemy on the other side behind the machine gun started waving a white flag. The same engineer who wanted to aid the wounded enemy stood up to go capture prisoners, and was immediately shot and killed. We were yelling at him to stay down. The white flag was an obvious ruse."[263]

Corporal Kero of the 307th AEB was an experienced paratrooper of several campaigns. He was posthumously promoted to sergeant and decorated with the Distinguished Service Cross. His citation reads as follows: "Sergeant Kero, squad leader, crossed the river in the leading boat as a member of a squad to remove mines and facilitate the acquisition of a bridgehead by the infantry. He advanced with the forward assault elements to their bridge objective and became separated from the unit with seven others. Sergeant Kero shot two Germans from the bridge trestle. Two 20mm SP guns fired point blank at the group.

"On his own initiative, Sergeant Kero attacked the house sheltering the Germans while a companion [Private First Class Muszynski] set up a light machine gun. Six Germans were killed in the house and three others when they tried to escape. Sergeant Kero took three men on to the embankment to cover the light machine gun and observed nine Germans trying to outflank him 200 yards distant. He opened fire, threw grenades and adjusted direction from a fully exposed location for the light machine gun until most of the enemy detail was killed and the others in retreat. Sergeant Kero was killed as a result of this action. Throughout three hours of fighting Sergeant Kero displayed exemplary courage of the highest order, was constantly in the van of each attack and was a source of inspiration to all who fought with him. The superior leadership, personal bravery and courage of Sergeant Kero made a vital contribution to the successful capture of the important bridges."[264]

Meanwhile 1st Lt. Edward W. Kennedy, S.Sgt. Louis E. Orvin, Jr., Sgt. George Leoleis and eight enlisted men from 3rd Platoon, I Company, had approached the viaduct in a skirmish line. One of their group, PFC Walter J. Muszynski, was killed and posthumously received the Distinguished Service Cross for his extraordinary bravery: "For extraordinary heroism in connection with military operations against an armed enemy on September 20, about one mile north of Nijmegen, Holland. As a light machine-gunner, Private First Class Muszynski crossed the Waal River in one of the lead boats of the initial assault element during the Waal bridgehead operation. As heavy machine gun and 20mm flak fire greeted the forward elements, Private First Class Muszynski quickly mounted his machine gun in the bow of his boat and directed heavy fire on the enemy dug-in on the riverbank. Although fully exposed to enemy fire, which wounded two of his comrades, Private First Class Muszynski disregarded all possibilities of danger and remained at his precarious post.

"Upon reaching the opposite bank, Private First Class Muszynski maintained a continuous cover of protective fire for the movement of his squad to the main dike and from the dike to the railroad embankment, accounting for at least 20 enemy dead and wounded. At times he fired his machine gun from the hip, while moving forward as to keep pace with his squad. At the railroad embankment, heavy opposition from self-propelled flak guns was encountered, and one of the nearby flanking guns knocked Private First Class Muszynski's machine gun from his arms, destroying it.

"Unhesitatingly, and without orders from anyone, Private First Class Muszynski crept to within 15 yards of the gun position directing devastating flanking fire on his platoon, and knocked it out with hand grenades, killing four of the enemy. During this phase of action, Private First Class Muszynski fell mortally wounded from enemy rifle fire. By his brave determination and valorous execution of his duties at the sacrifice of his own life, Private First Class Muszynski set an inspiring example for all his comrades and contributed directly to the successful establishment of the vital Waal bridgehead."[265]

Many engineers had been hit on the first crossing, so 1st Lt. John M. Bigler, the executive officer who supervised loading on the southern bank, took the place of a wounded engineer. More unexpected help arrived from troopers in 2nd Platoon, D Company: "Only half of the boats came back, and with a lot of the engineers either killed or wounded, some of my people just volunteered," stated Lt. Hanz K. Druener. They "got in and helped row these things back and forth."[266]

Capt. Fred Thomas, G Company, recalled "much organized confusion close to the levee" as his men rushed down to the river's edge while British tanks on the top of the levee covered them with machine guns and fired "at point blank range" with their 75s. As they neared the river, however, "everything ran smoothly except for the fact that each time, fewer and fewer boats returned for more men. Consequently, scattered boatloads gathered in small groups and promptly hit the ground, remaining there for a short time only until an empty boat hit the shore. Despite heavy enemy artillery-, mortar- and small-arms fire from the bridges up the river, not one of the boats turned back until it reached the other side and discharged the troops it had carried, and then returned to the other side to pick up more men.

"After beaching our boats in the deep mud on the enemy bank, we ran forward to the small rise that constituted the levee. Retaining our breath, we moved forward across open, level fields for approximately 450 yards. We began assembling our company by platoons next to a raised road. Most of the battalion assembled there with the exception of two companies who were leading the attack."[267]

The company executive officer, 1st Lt. Roy M. Hanna, watched in disbelief as the first wave paddled across, then jumped up and ran to a boat that crossed in the second assault. "I think there were about eight or nine of us in it. I just wanted to get the thing across. I kneeled in about the center of the boat, on the right-hand side, and just started paddling. It took me only 455 strokes to get across, I was paddling so damned fast. I can't remember who was in the boat with me, but I know I felt like I was the only one."[268]

On the other side, Lieutenant Hanna ran to the dike, crossing "a flat, sandy beach, just like the seashore, with sand dunes and brown grass." He took cover below the dike, but seeing others moving across it, he felt somewhat ashamed. He got up and followed them over the dike and out of the sight of the enemy on the south bank.

Captain Ferguson led his boatload of men to the river's edge to pick up a boat that came back, but it drifted downstream below the NYMA factory. A shell hit nearby, blowing him onto his back. He jumped up unharmed and took his men behind the factory where they would be safe from enemy fire. Running around the rear of the building, they passed a British tank and followed a beaten path, coming across several wounded men who had been hit by a sniper located in the factory water tower.

Spotting the canvas boat anew, they sprinted for the river's edge and paddled across, under abated enemy fire. On the other side, 1st Lt. Thomas F. Pitt, Battalion S-1, shouted, 'Come on! Let's go!' and led the group across the dike. His job was to clear the beach area and dike to the left of the railroad bridge.

Colonel Tucker crossed with the third wave with a skeleton detachment of his regimental staff and Milloy's C Company. Staff Sergeant Frank L. Dietrich, a 23-year-old from Michigan, was the C Company platoon sergeant: "As I recall, we had an engineer or two with us. I gathered somewhere between 25 and 28 men together and we started down toward the river. For some reason or another, we didn't take the same route the others had and I found myself in a *Schuh*-minefield. Fortunately, I discovered where we were, backed out and found a different route.

"People were moving about and getting into boats amid a lot of shouting and cursing. [...] There were people already across on the other side and I could see them moving back, toward a steep embankment. There was a piece of long, flat terrain and that embankment or dike was the only prominent thing. Later, I saw the Krauts had four or five 20mm guns set up on it firing at us. [...] I kept wondering what we were going to do when we hit the far side. I couldn't see any cover except for that dike, which must have been at least 600 yards from shore. [...] I don't think the fact that the boats were canvas bothered me. It's funny, though, I remember the water; it looked solid. We were going so damn slow, crazy as it sounds, the water looked heavier than normal water; it almost seemed to want to hold us back. When we got to the opposite bank, there were a few wounded men and several bodies. Medics were moving around them.

"As we touched, everybody got out and made for the dike [...] I spotted several groups moving up in bounds. We ran nearly halfway before we dropped. When we reached it, some advance elements were firing on the old fort where the heavy fire was coming from. I heard later that Sergeant Carter and another fellow by the name of Nix and someone else went up with an advance outfit [A Company] and on into the fort."[269]

Around 1600 hours, Captain Ferguson on the north shore ran into an exhausted 1st Lt. Robert Blankenship of I Company. "We went up over the dike and I lost half my platoon," Blankenship reported. Ferguson told him to sit quiet for a while, but Blankenship stopped only briefly and then ran in the direction of the railroad bridge, following Captain Burriss. As Ferguson also moved further east along the south side of the dike, he suddenly was caught in open ground under a hail of German artillery shells, and dove into the first foxhole he found. It was already occupied by Lieutenant McClain of the Mortar Platoon. "Got room for me?" asked Ferguson. "Go find your own hole, Fergie!" came the reply. He climbed out and found himself an empty hole.

Captain Ferguson was soon joined by a soaking wet Colonel Tucker. Contacting Cook on Ferguson's radio, they learned he was already at the railway dike. Tucker went after him, instructing Ferguson to move to the road bridge. "It was necessary for us to crawl along indentations in the ground, but shortly we managed to get into Fort Lent [Fort Hof van Holland]," Tucker recalled. "The 3rd Battalion continued to arch around and the 1st Battalion was moving over by the boats."[270]

Sergeant Tarbell was meanwhile still looking for his company commander: "After fighting with different groups from H Company, I finally met him at the railroad bridge. We also had quite a fight there. At one point, we were passing Gammon grenades to Captain Kappel, who was throwing them at the Germans through an opening in the north bridge tower entrance. Needless to say, we neither offered nor gave any quarter to the Germans on the railroad bridge."[271]

Lieutenant Sims recalled that "Lieutenant La Riviere and a few men with him joined us, and not a moment too soon. German troops, in mass, were coming across the bridge toward our position. We let them come within range, then opened fire and continued to fire until all enemy movement stopped. After we ceased, we allowed those still alive to either withdraw or surrender. The advantage here was ours, because the Germans on the bridge had nowhere to deploy. As a consequence, they suffered a large number of casualties. (After several weeks, I learned that the bodies of 267 German soldiers were removed from the railroad bridge.) The number that jumped or fell from the bridge into the river will never be determined.

"At the time of this action, my men and I were tense and angry because of the strenuous fighting and the loss of many of our own men during the crossing. […] We had little concern about destroying the large enemy force opposing us. I often relive this particular action in my mind, and always conclude that this terrible slaughter of humans is not something to be proud of or to brag about. It continues to bother me that I had to make the hasty decision that led to the death of so many young men, our own and those opposing us. When will nations stop wasting their young?

"I remained at the railroad bridge while the rest of Company H moved out to help seize the road bridge along with Company I. After a brief fire-fight, the north end of the road bridge was taken, but the Germans continued to hold positions at the center of the bridge that took some time to eliminate. Lieutenant La Riviere and his men did their share in eliminating these hold-outs. Later, during darkness, I joined my company at the road bridge, and with the few men we had left occupied a defensive position east of the road leading to Arnhem. Earlier, a British tank unit had come across the bridge and lined up their tanks on the side of the road facing north. There they remained until the following day when they moved north. By then, the British Red Devils at Arnhem had many more dead and wounded. I will never understand why the British did not immediately push north in order to take advantage of the turmoil we had just created among the German defenders in this area.

"During this operation, Company H had seven men killed in action and 20 wounded. In my opinion, this specific operation was poorly planned and lacked adequate support. It was accomplished only because of the courage and determination of the junior officers and the fine men they led. For my part in this action I was awarded my first Silver Star."[272]

Sims's platoon sergeant, S.Sgt. David Rosenkrantz, recalled that the few dozen paratroopers were outnumbered more than ten-to-one as the German infantry started marching to the railroad bridge, three abreast. The Americans shouted at them to surrender, but the Germans responded with hand grenades, and sent a prisoner forward to negotiate a ceasefire. Other Germans abruptly shot him down.

With no other option left, the American paratroopers opened up with the available machine gun, augmented by three captured German machine guns. "It was typical of what went on during the battle of Nijmegen Bridge," said Staff Sergeant Rosenkrantz, who positioned one of the machine-gun teams and gave the order to fire as the Germans came across the bridge: "Nijmegen did not last as long as Sicily, Salerno and Anzio, but it was tougher and bloodier while it lasted."[273]

As Sgt. Donald Zimmerman, a rifle-squad leader in the 1st Platoon, recalled: "we had crossed the river at Nijmegen and when we got done chasing the Germans, we started walking to the railway bridge. There were Cook and three officers standing on the railroad tracks. We decided to take some K-rations and sat down. There were maybe 12 soldiers near the bridge and Cook was still standing there. It was about dusk and we suddenly heard the loudest noise: there were some 150 Germans charging, row after row, screaming and hollering! We leveled them. We put down about 11 or 12 rows, and at that point Major Cook called, 'Cease fire! Cease fire!' It was an amazing thing. Then came the part where we had to disarm them, and they threw their own weapons—rifles and Lugers—into the river. After they had removed their wounded and dead and sat down, I noticed that there was only one other guy from H Company there. Major Cook had disappeared with the officers."[274]

T/5 Seymour Flox: "When we got to the bridge, someone said Jerries were coming across it, so the captain took three men and me up to the top. I stuck my head over the top and saw two Germans coming, and the captain told me to hold my fire because he wanted them prisoners. I stuck my head up again and saw two columns, one on each side of the track, and then the fun started. They refused to surrender, so we opened up on them. They got about seven feet away and we started throwing hand grenades at them and only got one in return. But it was only a concussion grenade and did no harm except to knock us off our feet.

"We captured one of them, and a fellow who could speak German told him to go back and tell the rest to surrender or else. They refused to give up and we really lowered the boom and poured the lead into them. You have to give those monkeys credit; they fought to the last man. When the fight was over, they counted over 270 dead. We also captured three anti-tank guns, which enabled our tanks to cross the main bridge. When we got them for support, the rest of it was a mop-up. So you can tell [my brother] Bud I did what he asked me and got a couple for him.

"We then marched down to the main bridge to meet the rest of our buddies, who had taken the bridge, and the Limey tanks that had crossed over. The main purpose of taking the bridge was to let the Limey tanks push through to Arnhem to relieve the British paratroops, but you know the English. They just weren't ready. You read what happened to the English boys up there. If those tanks had gone up there like they were supposed to, those boys could have been saved and the war might have been shortened."[275]

First Lieutenant McClain was also present with part of his platoon: "After crossing the Waal, I was at the north end of the railroad bridge when the Germans being pushed to the river by the encircling troops tried to cross over. I estimate better than 500 started across. We had two machine-gun crews and two BARs set up at the end of the bridge. When the Germans were a little better than halfway across, the automatic weapons opened up. Before it was over, they were leaping into the swift current of the river below. Some wounded fell through between the ties. Hardened by over two years of combat and the loss of many of my own men, I still felt sick at this inhumanity to man."[276]

After securing the northern end of the railroad bridge, Captain Kappel's group was strengthened by the arrival of Major Cook, Captain Keep and a radio operator: "I physically had the bridge and we were trying desperately to get to the highway bridge," recalled Kappel. "I had the area and was running the show. Cook had a radio with him and I recommended that he contact [British I] Airborne Corps and have them send the British tanks across the railway bridge. Keep and I both wanted them to cross. With their support, we could fight our way through to the highway bridge. There was a German gun guarding the railroad bridge, just north of it. It was neutralized; in other words, they couldn't get to it, but neither could we. It was probably an 88mm or a 75mm, but heavy caliber, at any rate. Cook relayed the request and Tucker came on and said, 'They are going to act on the bridge.' With the tanks, we could have easily combined with infantry and got the highway bridge."[277]

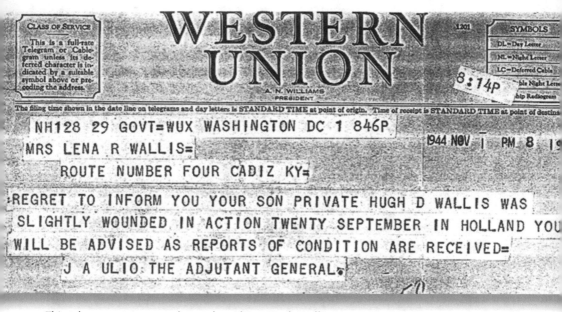

8:14P

The filing time shown in the date line on telegrams and day letters is STANDARD TIME at point of origin. Time of receipt is STANDARD TIME at point of destina

NH128 29 GOVT=WUX WASHINGTON DC 1 846P

1944 NOV 1 PM 8 19

MRS LENA R WALLIS=

ROUTE NUMBER FOUR CADIZ KY=

REGRET TO INFORM YOU YOUR SON PRIVATE HUGH D WALLIS WAS
SLIGHTLY WOUNDED IN ACTION TWENTY SEPTEMBER IN HOLLAND YOU
WILL BE ADVISED AS REPORTS OF CONDITION ARE RECEIVED=

J A ULIO THE ADJUTANT GENERAL.

This telegram was sent to the mother of Pvt. Hugh Wallis
of H Company, informing her of the fact that he had been
wounded in Holland. *Courtesy: Hugh Wallis*

CHAPTER 12

ENLARGING THE BRIDGEHEAD
NIJMEGEN, SEPTEMBER 20, 1944

While most of the engineers were paddling frantically back and forth across the Waal, Lieutenant Holabird remained on the north bank with his squad, which soon became separated in the confusion of battle. "At some point I wrote a brief note to Captain 'Spike' [Harris] and sent it back by one of my engineers. We spread out—from here on I get hazy. I was down to six men, and we were hopping and hollering all over the place. We sounded to ourselves as if we were single-handedly trying to save the bridge.

"Like a bad officer, I got ahead of the group. I remember running through a large pasture, surprised by the whistling of bullets going by and by seeing dead cows up-ended. I wondered if someone was really trying to shoot me. Me! The victorious crosser of the Waal! Finally, after an hour and a half, my euphoria began to wane. I found a little 6 x 6 house, probably storage for farm implements, took off my helmet and looked around. It must have been 1700 or 1730 hours by this time. Bullets were still whistling around, but presumably not at me (I hoped). I wondered what in the world I should be doing. No men, no mission: I was not really an infantryman conqueror. Two of my men arrived. We took council, wondering whether to proceed or go back to the beachhead.

"At this point we discovered Major Cook and elements of the 3rd Battalion coming towards us in a ditch. I reported in, told him everything was OK thus far and that, since I had only two of my squad, I probably should see what I could do at the landing. We three crawled over the top of 20-some 504th men and gradually returned to the beach. It was empty but for some battered boats and six dead troopers—not a very brilliant ending to our crossing. Two of my squad and I remained at the beachhead overnight and made our way across the Waal when a boat came from the other side."[278]

By this time, along with the remaining canvas boats, some wooden row and fishing boats were in use, having been gathered by the engineers along the Maas-Waal Canal. A Company formed the fourth wave that was sent across the swiftly streaming Waal River at 1600 hours that afternoon. The executive officer, 1st Lt. James E. Dunn, quickly scribbled in his diary: "We have only about three boats left, but we'll make it—got to!"[279] There were too few boats now to send the entire company across at one time: Lieutenant Breard's "1st Platoon crossed first about 1600 hours followed by the rest of the company and the battalion. [...] When we got across the river we went straight for the levee. There weren't all that many boats anymore. The 1st Platoon went across in the first boats available to us.

"We were so intermingled with the 3rd Battalion. There were wounded lying around and I remember the chaplain and the medics were helping people. But we couldn't stop, we had to take off and run. I went to all the way to the levee first and then turned to the right and headed down. They [the 3rd Battalion] were strung out. Somebody told me, 'Take the fort.' I was way up front and we were spread out 50 or 60 yards. Part of my platoon was ahead of me too. They went all up the railroad."[280]

Suddenly, at the corner of a road leading down to the fort, Breard and his men came to a house with an 88mm gun next to it: "We knocked the gun out and the rest of the platoon went to Fort Lent [Hof van Holland]. That's where [Private] Waskho got killed. They had got all the way through and he got up on the north side and was shooting his BAR from the hip, and a sniper shot him quick. He was on top of the fort. I didn't see it happen but somebody [Sergeant Rech] reported to me that [Pvt. Robert] Washko got killed. My platoon also had men at the north end of the railroad bridge. Later, after dark, 1st Battalion moved west toward Oosterhout. A Company took up a position just east of the village."[281]

Sergeant Clark, a mortar squad leader in A Company, recalled "we didn't know where we would be dispatched to, until after we crossed. [...] We were using the butts of our rifles, in my case my Tommy gun. [...] Once we got to the far levee, where the monument now is, we gathered waiting for our mission instructions."[282] PFC John B. Isom of Sergeant Clark's mortar squad also remembers that most boats did not contain paddles: "I think we were six or eight men in a boat. [...] When it was my turn we used rifle butts to row across, as there were no paddles." When they reached the far shore, they headed for the embankment to get to cover. A German MG-42 was firing just over the top of it: "I hesitated below the embankment. Suddenly the machine gun stopped and I crawled over. We assembled at a moat bridge."[283]

Pvt. Daren R. Broadhead, in a different squad of the same platoon, mistakenly recalled his wood-bottomed canvas boat as a wooden boat.[284] He did not remember anyone else crossing with them, which is correct since A Company went across in separate waves. According to Pvt. Fred R. Lilley, Company Headquarters, "we used our rifle butts to paddle and a lot of people had never paddled before, causing us to go in circles, till they got the hang of it. About the middle of the crossing the wind blew the smoke screen off the river, and all hell broke loose. Men were screaming, praying, and dying, and all we could think of was getting to shore. Those of us that made it were hell-bent on getting payback for those that didn't."[285]

Captain Duncan led the majority of A Company in a direct assault on Fort Hof van Holland while Lieutenant Dunn waved on reinforcements. Among those who encountered Dunn were Sergeant Carter and Private Nix of C Company, who had become separated from their platoon. As he waved them along towards the fort with troopers from A Company, Dunn was hit in his chest: "I was wounded by shrapnel from a shell which landed about eight yards away. [Lieutenant Earl] Morin was also hit in his head and arm. They moved us to a ditch where we stayed until dark. Doc said he didn't think it was deep enough to hit a lung. We were moved by stretcher to the fort we captured. I had to lie on my stomach and not move, eat or drink all night."[286]

After the fort was taken, Sgt. Mitchell E. Rech's 1st Squad, 1st Platoon took position on one of the high earthen walls in front of the moat: "We were stretched out on the top edge [...] pinned down by small-arms fire. [...] I looked to my left and saw Private Washko face down with his arm on his BAR. There was a perfectly round hole in his temple with a trickle of blood coming from it. He was close enough for me to touch him. It hit me that I was within inches of this being me. I went into the dry heaves, there being nothing on my stomach to vomit. I cried out for a medic even though I knew it was useless. He was gone."[287]

By this time the boat crews no longer entirely existed of engineers. Lieutenant Druener, D Company, explains: "After the first crossing, some of our people helped row these things back and forth. Our mission was to provide the supporting fire. What occurred though was that only half of the boats came back, and with a lot of the engineers either wounded or killed, some of my people just volunteered. […] I went across in one of the boats. The firing was not heavy when I crossed because the 3rd Battalion was already over there. There was sporadic firing and a lot of 88mm fire. The Germans were shooting into the area on both banks for a considerable amount of time."[288]

Before 1st Battalion Headquarters crossed around 1700 hours in the fifth wave, one of their radio operators was killed by German artillery fire. Private Nicholas W. Mansolillo, 1st Battalion Mortar Platoon, saw his close friend T/4 John T. Mullen lying in pool of blood: "We were under a heavy artillery barrage from across the river, and most of us were running for cover. That's when I came across John. I'd run right by him, seeking cover by a wall, when I heard someone say that it was John. I ran over to him, but he was a goner. It looked like shrapnel got him in the neck, and he bled to death. I could see the steam rising from the warm blood. There was nothing anyone could do to save him. We had been together since our days at Fort Bragg.

"John told me just before the mission that he had a strong premonition his number was up. A lot of guys say a lot of things—in most cases it's just talk. But in John's case, the way he talked made you believe it. There was a certain feeling about the way he said it. Nothing I could say could change his way of thinking, for down deep inside me I believed with him."[289]

By the time Pvt. George T. Cutting crossed the Waal with the Communications Platoon, there were "a few 88mm shells landing near us but no hits." Moving toward the railroad bridge, "we encountered a great deal of sniper fire, and some of those bullets were snapping right over my head. We spent time catching our breath in shell holes from previous US bombing. Our company withdrew after the highway and railroad bridges were secure and occupied Fort Hof van Holland."[290]

At 1710 hours Cook sent a runner with a telegram to Tucker at Fort Hof van Holland, which was recorded at 1740 hours in the Regimental S-3 Journal: "Have guns and dike, request tanks to move across the bridge to help them out." Five minutes later, the reply from Colonel Williams was short and clear: "Your request is being carried out. Willliams." About the same time, a direct telephone line was established across the river for contact with the 1st Battalion. Major Zakby was wounded shortly before the wire was hooked up. He had acted as beach master, but late that afternoon as the 1st and 3rd Battalions (excepting B Company) rowed across, his task became obsolete; he was more needed on the northern shore to organize communications with Regiment and establish the 1st Battalion CP.

After crossing in the fifth wave, Zakby's men "proceeded to lay wire about

1730 hours from our temporary CP to Regiment. I went out with the two wire-men to show them exactly where to lay the wire. It was then, halfway through the job, that one of the NCOs was shot dead. I received a burst in my left leg and the palm of my right hand. The other wireman was not hit, so he helped me back to the CP. By then I had bled quite a bit and developed chills.

"At 2300 hours during black-out, the medics carried me and five other men on litters in a jeep to the 82nd Airborne Hospital at Nijmegen. Al-though it was not far, only by miracle did we arrive at 0001 hours. The receiving room was full of men whose wounds were much more terrible than mine. I was carried up to the operating table. A young doctor, whom I had not seen since 1941, but had known well at Fort Dix, New Jersey, operated on me. What a coincidence. He could not tell me whether I would ever jump again or not. As luck would have it, the bone was not shattered—just seared. But all the flesh and ligaments in the middle of my left thigh were burned. He put 17 drains around the leg. At 0700 hours on the 21st, General Gavin came to the hospital and wished me speedy recovery."[291]

Still in his foxhole, Captain Ferguson witnessed Major Zakby on top of the dike with the wiremen. 'Come on, men!' Zakby shouted to his compan-ions. Ferguson at once understood the risk that Zakby was taking, for he was a perfect target for German snipers and machine-gunners. Too late, he shouted a warning for Zakby to get down as machine-gun fire cut loose.

Capt. William A. B. Addison narrowly escaped death at sundown when "an 88mm dud hit three feet from me."[292] He had originally intended to take a load of about 12 tons of ammunition across the Waal by boat, but Colonel Tucker called him on the radio to say such risk was unnecessary, and he should drive across the road bridge instead. Major Cook remembered: "We had called for ammunition and Addison as Regimental S-4 had gotten a large trailer truck loaded with ammo. Hearing that the bridge was taken, he headed for it to deliver the ammo. The report was incorrect and he had a hell of a time, nearly getting shot-up, but he did come over with the truck and ammo as soon as he could."[293]

In the sixth and last wave of the assault, Helgeson's B Company crossed shortly after 1800 hours. A rifleman in the 1st Platoon, PFC Mike Holm-stock, remembered being shelled as they rowed across. As darkness fell, Holmstock was one of the first platoon members to reach the railroad bridge. "We saw people walking on the bridge towards us and figured they were American troops, but as they came close we saw they were Germans. We had quite a firefight."[294]

Dutch volunteer Ben Bouman was still with 2nd Lt. Richard A. Smith and 1st Platoon, B Company: "We advanced and stopped near the large PGEM power station. Because the boats had not yet arrived at 1300 hours, the operation was postponed until 1400 hours. However, the lorries with 26 boats—one lorry had been lost en route—did not arrive until about 1430 hours, so the first group did not leave the bank of the river until just before 1500 hours. It came as an extremely unpleasant surprise to the Americans that they should have to dare cross the river so lightly equipped.

"My boat reached the other side in one piece. Seeking cover against the intense attack from behind the dike, I lay with my feet in the water. The men in my boat had been ordered to press on to the dike 300 or 400 metres away. Nauseous and exhausted though they were by the crossing and the losses suffered, those brave men battled on. Every time I started to get up, bullets whizzed past my ears, so I stayed low.

"When I did manage to get up without being shot at, I headed for the railway bridge. Under the railway bridge in the dike, I happened to join several commanders discussing how they could force the Germans off the railway bridge. The Nijmegen side was still in German hands. The military solution will come of little surprise: fire! I suggested waiting until the shooting died down, then shouting to the enemy in their own language to cease fire. This suggestion met with approval. So once the shooting stopped, I climbed up onto the railway bridge and called to them in German to surrender. Imagine my surprise when some 15 men came towards us with their hands up!"[295]

Colonel Tucker, expecting the Germans on the railroad bridge to surrender once the south side was blocked as well, called Major Wellems and ordered him to have the 2nd Battalion fire on the bridge. "When the fire abated," recalled Tucker, "I radioed back to fire on the Krauts caught on the railroad bridge. I was at the intersection of the railroad bridge and the road from Nijmegen Bridge to Arnhem. No British tanks had come across, but three of them came across before dark and remained in the vicinity of the 504th Advanced CP.

"I walked down to the main bridge and went part way across it toward Nijmegen, but the girders of the bridge were covered with Krauts who engaged in sporadic firing. Many were shot while others were rounded up as PWs [Prisoners of War].

"By dark the 1st and 3rd Battalions were joined up in position. The 2nd Battalion was firing on the Krauts on the railroad bridge and actually collected about 200 PWs. I remained at a small farmhouse at the intersection of the railroad and main road that night and although the British tank commander kept screaming most of the night for close-in security, we had two battalions well out in front of him and our small group could take care of any group attempting to get at his tanks.

"The next day I wanted to move out toward Arnhem but was ordered to remain right where I was and a British Dorset regiment would escort the British tanks to Arnhem. Unfortunately the British tried one road, were blocked by the fire from two 88s, and tried another road with the same results, whereas if they had sent elements up all roads at the same time, they probably could have broken through. That's the way our people would have done it, particularly General Patton."[296]

Arrival of Lieutenant Busdicker's platoon of B Battery, 80th Airborne
Anti-Aircraft Battalion at the Arnoud van Gelderweg in Grave,
September 18, 1944. *Courtesy: Graafs Museum/Jan Timmermans*

CHAPTER 13

MISSION ACCOMPLISHED
Nijmegen, September 20, 1944

"Late in the afternoon the north end of the railroad bridge was in our hands," recalled the 3rd Battalion S-3 officer, Capt. Henry B. Keep. "We organized its defense knowing that there would be a counterattack to get it back. There were reports from everywhere that tanks were coming from one direction, infantry from another. Constantly creeping from the middle of the great bridge towards our end were fanatics who would come as close as possible and then throw potato-mashers. It was absolute suicide, but this type of individual is more than ever prevalent among the present-day representatives of the Herrenvolk.

"And then at dusk a strange thing happened. Out of the growing darkness there loomed a tremendous mass of German soldiers walking from about the middle of the bridge and approaching our end. There must have been 200 or 300 of them. We all thought our goose was cooked and were prepared to open up with what little we had when one of the Krauts called in German that they wanted to surrender. Fortunately we had a man among us who spoke German. He told them to go to the other end and surrender—the Nijmegen end, where by now the rest of the division must be approaching after having cleared Nijmegen. Fortunately they understood and complied. Had they realized what a paltry group we were, I fear all thoughts of surrender would have vanished and a far more bellicose attitude have appeared.

"Just about this time we learned that another group from the battalion had seized the north end of the large highway bridge a little farther on from where we were. There had been a particularly bloody fight but the job had been done and our men had established a thin close-in defense of the bridge.

"The railroad bridge was taken over by the 1st Battalion, and we moved on to reinforce the protection of the all-important highway bridge—the life-line to Arnhem. It was dark now and in the eerie light of the flames from burning buildings set afire by artillery everything seemed grotesque and un-real. As we moved quickly in the shadows of the trees and houses toward our men at the highway bridge (for no one knew what remained to be mopped up), I thought of the day that just had ended. The 3rd Battalion, 504th had accomplished the impossible. We had crossed the Waal, we had attacked across two miles [sic: one mile] of heavily defended open terrain, we had seized the two vital Nijmegen bridges, we had opened up the life-line to Arn-hem. And it had cost the Krauts plenty.

"I have seen a lot of gruesome sights since this war began, but I have never witnessed such absolute carnage as I did that day. Everywhere the bod-ies of the Krauts were sprawled grotesquely; in places they were piled high. For censorship reasons I can say nothing of our losses. Nijmegen had been taken and both ends of both bridges were in the hands of the division."[297]

Captain Bruns recalled that "after the bridgehead had been established and the vital Nijmegen bridges had been flanked, the medieval Fort Hof van Holland was assaulted and captured. I used this as a temporary first-aid sta-tion. The feeling of security this old fort provided with its ten-foot-thick walls was almost like crawling back in the womb; however, we moved out quickly to make contact with the Germans as they retreated north towards Arnhem.

"I established an aid station in a beautiful home the Krauts had hurriedly abandoned while their stew was still cooking. I am happy to say I plundered a beautiful set of ivory chessmen, which I eventually brought back to the States (and somebody lifted!)."[298]

On the south shore, in the small harbour behind the power station, the engineers of the 615th Squadron, Royal Engineers, had finished the two Class-9 rafts they had built to ferry the two attached 57mm anti-tank guns of 1st Lt. Russell G. Busdicker across the Waal River. Sapper Roy Tuck saw an American engineer officer, "all too aware of the horrific ordeal his battalion had just suffered, preparing to take command. It was obvious from his com-ments that he was undergoing an understandable crisis of confidence; anxious not only about tackling an extremely dangerous crossing of the river, but also as to where, if at all, it might be possible to attempt a landing on the other side. Very much sharing his doubts and concerns, it came as a great relief to me when, instead of ordering us to load the (infantry support) artillery piece onto the raft, he decided to wait for further developments.

"Respite, however, was short-lived. A tall, helmeted American lieutenant colonel wearing sun glasses, Edwin A. Bedell of the 307th AEB, strode belligerently down the bank to commence an exchange of words, which are forever etched on my memory. 'Why is this gun still here and not over the river?' he demanded angrily. The young officer started to explain his dilemma, 'Lieutenant,' the colonel interrupted furiously, 'our boys are hurting over there and need that gun; under threat of court-martial I am ordering you take it across!'

"'OK boys, let it roll,'" was the laconic response from the lieutenant. I was totally dismayed—the whole idea seemed completely insane! Every instinct was urging me to seek cover and stay there. Yet instead, loaded with a considerable amount of explosive material, we were about to attempt the crossing of a huge expanse of open water under enemy fire and all this on the slowest of unwieldy craft.

"Hastily loading the gun and cases of shells on board, we flattened ourselves on the deck. In a high state of nervous tension, I checked to make sure that there was a round in the breech of my rifle. Alas, because of high stress I inadvertently put pressure on the trigger before applying the safety catch. Even allowing for all the extraneous noise about us, the single shot, which buried itself into a wall, echoed loudly under the close lee of the power station, startling everyone. All eyes turned in my direction, and I felt distinctly embarrassed.

"Shortly afterwards, the two diagonal outboard engines burst into life and we inched our way out of the creek onto the vastness of the River Waal. Immediately, our cumbersome raft, caught in the grip of the fast flowing current, turned full circle. Tense moments passed before the straining engines finally overcame the racing tide. The response from the enemy was both immediate and aggressive; a salvo of mortars sending up fountains of water as they exploded uncomfortably closeby. There could be little doubt; we had embarked on a perilous enterprise.

"Between our under-powered craft and the distant bank stretched a daunting 400- to 500-yard mass of powerfully surging water. Upstream, towards Nijmegen, the mighty river curved towards the huge rail and road bridges, its surface gleaming in the late afternoon sunshine. Much of the town seemed to be on fire. Flames reflected in the river and glowed on the underside of a vast billowing column of smoke as it towered an enormous height into the sky before drifting away over the flat countryside.

"Against the background chatter of automatic weapons and the crump of shells, we headed, alarmingly exposed and all too slowly, towards the opposite bank. In mid-stream, a rowing boat, constantly turning in the swiftly flowing water, approached us rapidly from the town. Someone, suspecting it might contain fleeing Germans, opened fire as it swept by, but there was no discernible reaction.

"It did not escape me entirely that, with the bridges still held by the enemy, we would be the very first land troops of the British Second Army to be crossing the river. Consequently, with this in mind, as the raft finally reached the shallows, inspired by a youthful enthusiasm to be one of the first ashore, I grabbed a rope and, with a totally unexpected and momentary sense of personal drama, plunged into the water to help pull the ungainly craft into the bank.

"Our arrival immediately attracted mortar fire. After hurriedly helping to disembark the gun, I frantically sought cover by diving into one of the shallow foxholes recently vacated by American paratroopers, who, by this time, had moved away towards the bridges. The shelling eventually ceased. Twilight gave way to darkness, and an uneasy calm settled over the scene of recent conflict. High overhead a full moon sailed serenely in the clearest of skies, while nearby the silent river was dark and impassive, with thin mists beginning to form upon its surface and threading the long grass upon its banks. For a time, guns crackled and tracers weaved their intricate patterns as our tanks finally stormed the distant road bridge—then all was still. The surrounding flat marshy ground, bathed in a cool light, appeared strangely peaceful, yet we knew only too well that, not far away, an unseen enemy would be watching and waiting, and that careless noise or reckless movement could spell disaster.

"As we waited, alone and vulnerable, we received orders to recover an American officer, a captain, reported to be lying badly wounded against a distant fence. Four of us, accompanied by our corporal, set out to find him. Moving as silently as possible, dragging a stretcher and keeping very low, we crawled, with no little apprehension on my part, towards the reported position of the stricken man. Eventually we discovered him face down in the wet grass, and clearly in dreadful pain from a serious back injury.

"Before we carefully eased him on to the stretcher, Ron gave him a shot of morphine to help ease his agony. 'Be as gentle as possible and keep him off the ground,' he whispered. Such urging was not needed, the man's low pitiful moans providing all the necessary motivation for providing as smooth a progress as possible.

"However, I soon found lifting and moving while struggling to keep a heavily laden stretcher just inches above the grass required a technique entirely outside my experience. The totally unaccustomed repetitive move-ment—my right arm lifted and moved the surprisingly heavy stretcher for-ward before I used my left to lever my body in the same direction—resulted in a most unnatural contortionist twisting crawl.

"Now came the tricky bit—a return to the other side. Thankfully, within minutes, a thick fog, quite miraculously, blanketed the whole area, muffling the sound of the engines and cutting visibility to a few feet. Once we had re-crossed the river without incident, we hurried the wounded man up the em-bankment to where a temporary casualty station had been set up in the power plant. By the time we lowered him onto the bare concrete floor, dimly lit by its one hanging naked electric light bulb, he had lapsed into unconsciousness. I turned away, feeling far from confident about his chances of survival."[299]

Although Sapper Tuck could not be certain after more than 65 years, both he and the author believe the wounded captain was Wesley D. Harris. Captain Harris was awarded the Distinguished Service Cross "for extraor-dinary heroism in connection with military operations against an armed enemy while serving as Commanding Officer, Company C, 307th AEB, 82nd Airborne Division, in action against enemy forces on September 20, 1944, in Holland. Captain Harris, while under heavy enemy fire, personally directed the loading and movement of assault boats which enabled the 504th PIR to successfully cross the Waal River and establish the vital Nijmegen bridgehead. Crossing the river in the face of heavy enemy machine-gun, 20mm, and artillery fire in one of the first assault boats of the initial assault wave, Captain Harris was painfully wounded in the back and arm but con-tinued to supervise the movement and unloading of the boats. After returning to the south bank of the river he refused medical evacuation, but effected rapid and thorough reorganization of the remaining boats and engineer per-sonnel for the crossing of the second wave.

"While [he was] leading the second wave, a pontoon near his boat was hit by enemy fire and capsized, but Captain Harris plunged into the river and despite his wounded condition assisted three men to other boats. Captain Harris then returned to the south bank and while supervising loading of the third wave, fainted for the loss of blood. Captain Harris's intrepid direction, heroic leadership, and superior professional ability contributed directly to the success of the bridgehead operation and were in keeping with the highest traditions and standards of the United States Army."[300]

After reaching the dike on the north bank, Lieutenant Hanna, G Com-pany executive officer, assembled the balance of the 1st and 2nd Platoons and set off for the railway dike. With him were 1st Lt. Steve Seyebe (2nd Platoon leader) and 2nd Lt. James R. Pursell (assistant platoon leader, 1st Platoon). Their mission "was to go straight forward and clear the area where the main highway to Arnhem crossed under the north-bound railroad tracks. Pursell and I were leading this group. [...] I don't know where Captain Thomas was at the time. Thomas may have been leading part of G Company in attacking the Fort [Hof van Holland] located on the knoll to our left that Pursell and I bypassed.

"At the overpass we suddenly started receiving heavy small-arms fire from the railroad track area, elevated at this point as it went over the highway. Our entire group ended up pinned down in the wide and fairly deep ditch to the south side of the highway that ran parallel to the tracks.

"We were in a precarious position and generally pinned down from enemy fire. All of a sudden we heard tanks approaching from the direction of the bridge with their machine guns blasting at full speed. I, for one, thought they were German. Suddenly, two tanks came racing under the railroad overpass and started up the road in front of our position. We, not realizing they were British, knocked the lead tank's track off with a Gammon grenade. This stopped the two tanks. The commander of the lead tank raised the tank lid and yelled, 'Yanks! Hold your fire!' This ended that little battle. Once the shooting from the railroad tracks had stopped, we ran up the side of the tracks to clear the other side and found many dead German soldiers; those that might have survived the British tank fire were gone."[301]

Captain Thomas's G Company After-Action Report on the Waal River Crossing reads: "Retaining our breath, we moved forward across open, level fields for approximately 450 yards. We began assembling our company by platoons next to a raised road. Most of the battalion had assembled there with the exception of two companies that were leading the attack. Company G then moved across the road by running one at a time because the road was under enemy machine-gun fire and the house at the far side of the road had been set on fire by an artillery shell.

"After crossing the road, the company moved forward again through small ditches that ran all around, diagonal to the main road from the Nijmegen Bridge. Upon reaching the road, the company was stopped by the enemy who were just on the other side of the large railroad embankment. A hand-grenade battle began, with both sides tossing grenades up over the top of the railroad embankment. About 75 or 100 feet to the right down the road was a railroad underpass. The Jerries were in the underpass in strong force.

"It was at this point that the platoon leader of the 2nd Platoon [Lieutenant Seyebe] was killed while rushing the embankment. At this time we received information over the battalion radio that the railroad bridge had been taken. A short time later word was received that the British tanks had started across the bridge. All of this time the company was surrounded on three sides, with night beginning to fall and ammo running real low. All at once we heard much heavy firing and a tank broke through the underpass coming in our direction. At first we thought it was a British tank that had crossed the bridge, but when the tank […] kept up its machine-gun fire and fired its 75mm into the orchard on our right, we thought it was German.

"The platoon sergeant of the 2nd Platoon [S.Sgt. William D. Sachse] threw a Gammon grenade under the tank and it exploded directly underneath. The tank stopped and the top opened and a typical British voice announced that it was a British tank. It was truly a story-book finish, as our situation was becoming more and more critical with the darkness falling around us. The tanks stopped there, one of them having been knocked out. The men from the company were on the road talking to the British tank men when Colonel Tucker and Captain Shelley drove up in a jeep. The British commander and Colonel Tucker had a conference, and the various company commanders who were in the area, including Captain Thomas, were called into it for information.

"Later the company was assembled, moved under the underpass and marched up the road leading to the Nijmegen Bridge. We had already received information that the British infantry were crossing the bridge and were coming over to relieve us. About 200 yards from the railroad underpass, a large house was in flames, lighting up the whole area. We passed by this and also passed a British tank that had been knocked out along the road. We arched up to the approach to the bridge where we were halted, and prisoners captured during the battle were marched across the bridge into the burning town of Nijmegen. This was a very eerie sight, the prisoners marching past as fires from the town lit up their faces as they passed us. The company was then marched back down the road to the town of Lent, where we had just come from. We set up our defenses and posted guards, the rest of the men lying down to get some well-deserved sleep."[302]

Unknown to Hanna and other paratroopers at the Lent Viaduct, British tanks had also almost fired on the leading I Company troopers at the north end of the Waal Bridge. A mixed H and I Company group under Captain Burriss had made it to the objective first, and split up into two small groups.

PFC Hedberg and Pvts. John W. Hall, Jr., and Norman J. Ryder of I Company ran up the left concrete steps that led to the northern bridge ramp, followed by Pvt. Leo P. Muri and others who were cutting wires. They were the first paratroopers on the road bridge: "When the tanks came rolling over the bridge," recalled Hedberg, "I was alone with Privates Hall and Ryder. They stopped in front of us and a man in the tank opened the tank hatch and said, 'He is a German spy.' I started to yell I was friendly, but he demandingly asked, 'Where is your commander?' In that kind of tone. I said, 'I don't really know.' Then he said, 'He is a spy—shoot him!' I was scared then but they didn't shoot—luckily, they just drove on and left us standing there in all the excitement. Shortly afterwards Captain Burriss arrived."[303]

Meanwhile Burriss moved with "about 17 men underneath the bridge. The Germans were taken by surprise. We used the column of the bridge as a prison for them. I took the right concrete steps up onto the bridge and was first officer on the bridge. The Germans in the girders were still firing and the first British tanks came up."[304]

The four Sherman tanks that crossed the bridge were part of the 1st Squadron of the 2nd Battalion Grenadier Guards under the command of a 25-year-old captain, Lord Peter Carrington, second in command of the 1st Squadron. Sgt. Peter Robinson reports that Carrington was "sitting with my squadron on a mound fairly close to the bridge," when he received his orders: he was to cross with his Sherman directly behind the four tanks in Robinson's No. 1 Troop, which would lead the advance across the bridge. "We don't know what to expect when you cross, but the bridge has to be taken. Don't stop for anything," Robinson's squadron commander, Maj. John Trotter, told him. Robinson's lead tank was hit as it drove onto the south bridge ramp, but all seemed operational except for the radio. He climbed out and ran to the second tank, commanded by Sgt. Jack Billingham. "Get out of that tank damned quick and follow along in mine," Robinson shouted to Billingham. Robinson then jumped into Billingham's tank and ordered the others to follow.[305] Meanwhile, the third Sherman tank, commanded by Sgt. Cyril Pacey, had bypassed them and rolled onto the bridge, followed by Robinson's tank, Billingham's tank and that of Sgt. "Rocky" Knight. As they rolled across the bridge, Carrington remained "in contact with them all the time."[306]

Sergeant Pacey's tank stopped near the concrete blocks on the northern bridge ramp, and fired at all possible targets while Sergeant Robinson took the lead and rolled onto the Lent Viaduct in the railway line, then stopped on the other side. On the way, Sergeant Billingham's tank was knocked out by a German 88mm gun, and Sergeant Knight, in the rear, was also fired upon. Knight played dead, but his crew members climbed out and scattered, only to be captured by the Germans. Later that evening Knight made it to the viaduct, after managing to start his tank with the help of two American paratroopers. Sergeant Pacey's tank had meanwhile rattled forward and linked up with Robinson at the viaduct.

"When I arrived at the north end," Captain Carrington later wrote, "there were Germans in the girders of the bridge and Germans with the equivalent of bazookas quite close to the north end. I stayed at the north end until further tanks arrived and then moved to where Sergeant Robinson was with the Americans. By this time it was dark and Captain Burriss cannot conceivably have known what Germans there were between Nijmegen and Arnhem. He records that he crossed the river under a hail of fire, but does not say where the Germans went. Much of what he says is exaggerated. My orders from my battalion were to stay there until reinforcements arrived."[307]

The Military Cross Citation Captain Carrington received reads as follows: "On September 20, 1944, this officer was ordered to guide a troop of tanks down to Nijmegen Bridge and then to push them across with a view to capturing the bridge intact. The troop duly attacked, captured the bridge, and then pushed the main road on the far side for some distance to consolidate their gain. Hearing that the enemy had infiltrated between the troop and the bridge, this officer, on his own initiative, crossed the bridge in his tank and engaged the enemy, driving them off, and remained holding the far side of the bridge until relieved by another tank. He then proceeded up the road and joined the troop holding the centre line. By his devotion to duty and initiative, this officer was undoubtedly instrumental in control being retained of the northern approaches to the bridge at a very vital time."[308]

According to Captain Burriss, the fifth Sherman tank that came across stopped after it had maneuvered through the concrete blocks the Germans had placed there as a precaution for a possible Allied armored advance across the Waal. The tank commander was Lord Carrington. He opened the hatch of the turret and started a conversation. "Why are you stopping?" enquired Burriss. Carrington explained that he had spotted an 88mm gun ahead that could knock out all his tanks. Burriss offered to accompany the tanks with several of his paratroopers and Lieutenants Blankenship, La Riviere and Rogers. Carrington crisply answered, "I can't go without orders," and finally closed the hatch after both La Riviere and Burriss threatened with drawn .45 pistols to shoot him if he didn't move.[309]

Minutes became hours and still no movement was undertaken. A sad in-cident took place when Private Hall beckoned an SS-officer to climb down from a girder on the bridge. As PFC James Musa, H Company, remembers it, "We deployed on both sides of the bridge. The Germans were firing at us from the girders and there were more on the bridge. Some Germans tried to escape the advance of the Allied forces on the south and ran towards us. We held our fire until they were within close range and then opened fire. Some turned around and started back towards the south end, trying to surrender. Other Germans were still holding out in the girders. We called for them to come down and surrender. One of our men [Private Hall] was climbing a girder when an SS-officer shot him in the chest. We retaliated with a hail of bullets, knocking him out of the girder and into the river below. About 40 Germans surrendered to us. Lieutenant Rivers told Private Young and me to take them back to the north side and look for H Company. We met Captain Kappel, who said they would take control of the prisoners."[310]

Captain Burriss had meanwhile divided his force into two groups: Lieu-tenant Rogers and eight men set up a roadblock 150 yards north of the bridge on the highway to Arnhem. Lieutenant Blankenship and another eight I Company troopers dismantled a 20mm position 200 yards east of the bridge and set up a roadblock there. "We moved towards the [road] bridge—the Ger-mans guarding it took off like a bird," recalled Cpl. Tison. "Guess they got tired of the whole thing and decided to skip out. We had all the Germans out, except for one, a lieutenant up in the rafters who wouldn't come down. We had a kid [Private Hall] who had just joined us in England. He was going up the rafters to throw the lieutenant off into the river. When he got close, the lieutenant shot and killed him. We lost more new men than we did the old, even if there weren't but five of us left that went overseas together. You didn't have a chance to meet some of the new ones. They were dead before they could get into a hole. Anyhow, the lieutenant was shot and fell into the river.

"There was a dugout next to the bridge. That was where I set up my ma-chine gun. On the other side of the river, Nijmegen was on fire. During the night, I spotted a German patrol on our side. The burning city made excellent targets of the patrol. As I was adjusting the machine gun, Lieutenant Blankenship said he wanted to look at the weapon, and then began to fire the thing. Several men ran up to us with a white flag to surrender. The rest lay where they fell."[311]

Several Germans who had escaped the machine-gun fire ran to the shore of the Waal, but there was no place for them to go, because the burning city lighted the area. "After we had captured the main highway bridge," recalled 1st Lt. Virgil F. Carmichael, the 3rd Battalion S-2 officer, "we could look back and see the fires in Nijmegen reflected in the waters of the river, and this lighted up the river bottom on the north shore. I was along the dike on the north side of the river with Private [Fred] Toensjost of my unit who spoke German. [...] We could see great groups of Germans milling about in the bottom lands near the river, and I had Toensjost call to them to surrender. He finally talked one man into coming up to where we were, and we prevailed upon him to go back and encourage the others to surrender.

"This German went back, then reneared us and yelled that he was unable to get the others to come with him. In the meantime we had rounded up a small (60mm) mortar barrel with two or three rounds of ammunition. Practically all of our troops were out of ammunition at that time. Using this mortar tube without either a base or a bipod, I had Toensjost yell at the Germans that we would blow them to kingdom come if they did not surrender.

"When they did not come within a short time, we hand-sighted the mortar tube and dropped a shell into it. It landed in the river bottom, but by expending a couple of wildly aimed shells and by Toensjost yelling at the men, we finally got about 115 of them to come up onto the road. This seemed to be all of them, though we did not check. I could tell by their camouflage uniforms that they were paratroopers, and I knew that their officers did not wear insignia on the outside of their uniforms.

"I asked the group if there was an officer among them, and even though I am sure there was more than one officer there, none announced himself. I then asked for the top-ranking noncom, and a first sergeant stepped forth. I told this sergeant to have the men line up and fall in. In the best Prussian manner, this sergeant had the men to snap to attention.

"All of this time, I had the bolt drawn back on my .45-caliber submachine gun, which I had gotten from the Air Corps crew chief. However, immediately after the men fell in under the supervision of their noncom, I felt safer about having so many unsearched men, and felt they were under control, relatively speaking. I tripped the catch on my submachine gun and let the bolt fall home. I had not realized that I had gotten sand into the cartridge magazine. Grit had kept the spring depressed and had allowed a live cartridge to fall out of the magazine clip and into the chamber.

"When the bolt slid home this bullet fired from my gun and struck the first sergeant in the leather part of the heel of his boot. It surprised me. The sergeant evidently was shocked, and feeling that I was disappointed in the manner in which he had called the men to attention, immediately called his men to attention again and they really snapped to that time. Then we marched the men to the large concrete support on the north end of the Nijmegen Highway Bridge, which was hollow. With a flashlight I could tell it was about six or seven feet from an opening down to ground level inside this concrete pier. I had the men jump into it one at a time; of course, the first men in helped the others down, and I put a man on guard. There was only one small opening.

"Later they were turned over to the British [3rd] Irish Guards Battalion and our battalion took a receipt for the delivery of the prisoners. This receipt came in handy when the British tried to claim that they had taken the men, but Cook and Colonel Tucker, our regimental commander, proved otherwise to their superiors."[312]

More and more members of the 3rd Battalion arrived at the bridge site, including Major Cook and Captains Keep and Kappel. The latter started a search for demolition charges: "There were some wires there but they were communications wires. I did not find any explosives on the north side. There was a bunker there and I entered it, but my recollection is some of our own men were there already."[313]

First Lieutenant Mandle and his 3rd Battalion demolition squad joined in the search, but as PFC Darrell Harris recalls, they were spared the task of disabling the charges once they were found: "When we saw the massive size and extent of those charges, it was apparent that it would be beyond the capability of a single demolition squad to do this job in a reasonable period of time. We disconnected some of the wiring and detonators, but removal of the explosives was left to an engineering battalion."[314]

British tanks had linked up with the 3rd Battalion, but were not moving on to Arnhem. For Captain Keep, "there was one more thing causing us trouble. Countless Krauts who had been trapped in the middle of the bridge when both ends had been secured had sought temporary refuge high up in the steel girders. From these vantage points they continued to fire at us and also at the vehicles as they passed beneath them. In spite of the darkness we constantly sprayed them with our automatic fire. As dawn broke a gruesome sight greeted the eyes of the men guarding the bridge. Intertwined grotesquely throughout the massive steel girders were the bodies of some 200 dead Krauts, looking for all the world like a group of gargoyles leering hideously at the passersby hundreds of feet below.

"Now that we had taken the bridge, we had hoped that someone else would push on and secure the bridgehead more advantageously; but it was not to be. The British took over the close-in defense of the bridge itself and we attacked 1,000 yards to the north to establish an outer defense ring. And so at 2100 that night our dead-tired men moved out, knowing damn well what they would run into—stiff, bitter opposition on the part of fanatical crack Nazi troops who were furious at the loss of the vital bridge. Our greatly depleted companies met determined resistance as they pushed forward in the darkness; the fighting was bitter, but by 0200 in the morning we were in position, holding the line assigned to us."[315]

At 2300 hours I Company moved out along the dike road towards Fort Lent, east of the road bridge. Moving in columns of two preceded by two scouts, they were taken under fire by 20mm guns and machine guns. The 2nd Platoon lead scout, 21-year-old T/5 Winfred K. Smith, was killed outright by machine-gun fire. He was the last 504th trooper to give his life that day. Burriss withdrew his company a few dozen yards and they dug in.

As 2nd Battalion S-1, 1st Lt. Chester Garrison reported in the battalion journal: "except for occasional sniping, the bridge was under Allied control by 2000." Having turned over some 25 prisoners and been relieved by the British, F Company reached the battalion at 1730 after a long march from Grave involving a sniper fight. "E Company had never been relieved of its area as scheduled." As the battalion was again preparing to cross the river, "an F Company patrol under Lieutenant Watson, sent [...] to help clear snipers off the south approach to the bridge, returned with 218 prisoners, including two officers. Thus, F Company was needed to guard the POWs throughout the night. As T/3 Joseph J. Hotter processed the prisoners, the battalion secured its position against attack from the north, and D Company crossed the river to maintain the beachhead. Among 2nd Battalion casualties (D Company) was Lieutenant Wisniewski (later died)."[316]

Pvt. Philip H. Nadler, F Company, 2nd Platoon, who thought Captain Richardson had gotten lost in the western outskirts of Nijmegen, recalled their encounter with the sniper as they made their way to the 2nd Battalion area. As the German's bullets snapped across the street, the platoon crossed the road and moved into the church. "Hey, why are we supposed to be here?" Nadler asked his platoon leader. "What do you want to do? Go outside and get shot at?" was the reply. They rushed up to the belfry and captured the sniper.[317]

Lieutenant Watson, whose 3rd Platoon, F Company patrol captured the many German prisoners Garrison records, has also detailed how his patrol, consisting of a rifle squad and light machine-gun crew, discovered "a large number of German soldiers standing on the railroad tracks of the bridge." Noting the group included "only two or three German officers," Watson set up the machine gun, and "yelled to them to surrender or else we would shoot them. One of the officers yelled back 'Yes,' and that was all I needed. He understood my English. I told them, 'Form your men in a column of four.' They assembled in formation and we marched them back down the riverbank to the Regimental CP [… and] handed the 218 prisoners over to Regiment. It took all night to interrogate them. We meanwhile tried to get some sleep there."[318]

Shortly before the river crossing began, General Gavin had left the power station to view the situation at the towns of Beek and Mook, where the Germans launched a counterattack. Around 2100 hours, Gavin showed up with his radioman at the house along the north side of the road bridge to discuss the situation with Tucker, Cook and a senior British officer.

"A British staff car came along and out got the British commander," recalled Lieutenant Pitt, 3rd Battalion S-1. "He was, I guess, the corps commander. […] Gavin said, 'We'll put some men up on the tanks and in front of the tanks, and let's head for Arnhem.' I think it was 20-some miles or so, it wasn't far. This British commander said, 'We don't move our tanks at night.' Gavin said, 'You don't move them at night? Well if we wait 'till daylight then they [the Germans] will move stuff in.' The Brit said, 'Well, we can't move tanks at night.' Gavin said, 'If they were *my* men in Arnhem, we would move tanks at night. We would move *anything* at night to get there.' This guy said, 'We are not. We will move them in the morning.'"[319]

For decades since the end of the war, veterans of the Guards Armoured Division have maintained that the area between the Rhine and Waal Rivers was unsuitable for tanks; that enemy opposition was considerable between Arnhem and Nijmegen; and that their 1st Grenadier Guards infantry was still involved in heavy fighting for Hunner Park and the Valkhof Citadel against Kampfgruppe Euling. Earlier that September, the advance of the British 11th Armoured Division from the Seine in France to the Belgian port Antwerp had been swift, almost around the clock. But the evening and night of September 20, this was not the case for the Guards Armoured Division. That evening, the tanks of the 2nd Irish Guards were pulled out of position at the power station and directed to a bivouac area near Malden, close to the Maas-Waal Canal.

At the end of each day, Guards Armoured Division Headquarters compiled an intelligence summary of daily activities and the following day's objectives. The reports were to be subsequently destroyed to prevent them from falling into enemy hands. Fortunately, those pertaining to the Waal Crossing survived, and were supplied to the author. Here published for the first time, the reports cast new light on the thoughts of Maj. Gen. Alan Adair and officers of his staff, and further clarify the situation of enemy troops on September 20.

"The road bridge at Nijmegen was captured intact this evening after an attack through the town which started yesterday by our own troops and an assault crossing further west by the Americans who worked their way round to the north end of the bridge. Over 100 PWs had been captured and reports say that 200 more are on their way in. It has not yet been possible to identify all these PWs, but from a preliminary interrogation of two of them, who were from 5th and 7th Companies 9th SS-Panzer Grenadier Regiment (9th SS-Panzer Division only has one Panzer Grenadier Regiment now), it appears that a high proportion of the troops defending the Nijmegen Bridge were SS, but from many odd units.

"There were also a large percentage of odds and sods. These particular PWs had been brought over from Arnhem the day before, where they had been defending the bridge there. They described the fighting as extremely tough, and said their unit had had heavy casualties. However, they said that fighting at Nijmegen was more unpleasant still owing to our artillery and mortars, which they described as 'almost unendurable.' One of them said that in his section of 12 men, eight were killed by artillery fire. Their susceptibility to artillery fire was increased by the hard ground in the town into which it was impossible to dig.

"They also said that our attack yesterday evening was very nearly successful, and that a large number of the garrison, in fact, rushed across the bridge in an attempt to get away, only to be met [on] the other side by an SS-Captain with a revolver who ordered them back, saying that 300 SS were being sent up as reinforcements the next day. 150 did, in fact, arrive from Arnhem.

"The situation at Arnhem itself is not clear. The road bridge is intact and a report received this evening states it is held, with difficulty, by our airborne troops, although it is understood this was not the case earlier in the day. The rest of our parachutists are believed to be concentrated in approximate area 6978 where they are being heavily counterattacked, the enemy having brought up some tanks. The pontoon bridge [...] has had the centre pontoon removed and moored to the north bank.

"A large proportion of the enemy in Arnhem are reported to be SS, although the exact number is not known. No doubt they consist of a mixed collection from various SS units like those at Nijmegen. They are reported to have received reinforcements in tanks, the numbers and types of which are not known. It is not thought that the enemy garrison in Arnhem are very numerous, nor particularly highly organised, comprising the usual heterogeneous collection of men from all types of units. However, it does include some tanks, and it is thought to have been primarily these [which] have caused trouble to our airborne troops already there. The question therefore arises as to what extent the enemy is prepared to reinforce this sector. [...]

"However, when the enemy realises that he no longer holds Nijmegen he may switch part of this force to go farther north, to be directed to Arnhem. It is obvious that Nijmegen and Arnhem are nodal points of the greatest importance to the enemy and that he will attempt to recapture them when they are in our hands is a certainty, and he may even send some tanks to help in this. But with German transport as it is, it is doubtful if the enemy can reinforce these places at once to any extent, except with such troops as are available locally, e.g., 4267.

"Therefore, the main direction of the enemy's attack must be expected from the Forest Reichswald, which offers an excellent forming-up place. Mook and Beek, at both of which places the enemy have been reported in at least battalion strength with some tanks, are likely to see still more and fiercer fighting. 8th Company 1051th Grenadier Regiment and 3rd and 4th Companies 1052nd Grenadier Regiment have been identified in this area. At the same time the enemy will certainly try and reinforce Arnhem and fighting is likely to continue there for some time, even after we have captured the place."[320]

The battle report of the Waal Crossing by *Hauptmann* Sieger of Landesschützen Battailon II/6 is also here published for the first time in its entirety: "In the early morning the company received orders to defend the narrow bridgehead at the railroad causeway immediately adjacent to the bridge. The causeway was fired upon. Losses were not yet sustained, since we obtained sufficient cover by digging-in. The hauled ammunition cart was placed under the cover of the causeway. In the forenoon about half of the company, which was still 91 men in the morning, was used to secure the streets and build barricades in the area between the railroad and road bridges on the order of Major Melitz.

"In the early afternoon we observed from the bridge that the enemy had started to cross the Waal in row boats about two kilometers to the west, with the purpose of overrunning the bridgehead from the rear. All available weapons on the bridge were fired at the crossing site. The preceding air and ground bombardment had almost entirely knocked out our artillery guns. Firing from the bridge on moving targets affected our accuracy, so that the enemy succeeded in crossing. Shortly after, T-mines we had set in the underpass leading to the railway bridge prevented an armored attack.

"In the late afternoon we learned that the road bridge had fallen into enemy hands. Given the circumstances, Major Melitz came to the bridge house at the railroad bridge to discuss the position with *Hauptmann* Runge, *Hauptmann* Zyrus, *Hauptmann* Sieger and *Leutnant* Königsmann, and decided to subtract about 150 men from the defense to form a bridgehead north of the railway bridge. The oldest men of units Sieger and Zyrus were chosen for the front line. *Hauptmann* Zyrus, whose force consisted of approximately 50 men, held the center of the new bridgehead. *Hauptmann* Sieger held the left flank and *Leutnant* Königsmann the right flank, each also having about 50 men. Except for one wounded, the bridge crossing went without incident. Some men, however, independently separated themselves from the group. Our establishment of a new bridgehead met with many difficulties, partly because enemy forces who had crossed were attacking the bridge in strength, and also because we had just discovered the night before that Einheit Wesel [a hastily formed 'battalion' of officers and men on leave from various units that had been raised in Wesel on September 17] had already occupied positions toward the north—a fact unknown at our former discussion of the situation. The company placed itself under command of the unit and extended its defenses on the right flank. However, the enemy had already arrived on the opposite side of the embankment and fire was exchanged. Einheit Wesel's counterattack at the north exit of the bridge failed under heavy losses. The enemy managed to take the bridge guards by surprise and set the bridge on fire, blocking the way out for cut off-troops in Nijmegen.

"All officers were ordered to the Einheit Wesel command post. As darkness rapidly descended, their command post and position at the railway dike were attacked by an armored car that had managed to cross the road bridge."

The Germans suffered significant losses and their position at the Lent Viaduct became untenable. The battalion was squeezed between Roy Hanna's G Company men, to the left of the viaduct, and tanks and an armored car to the right (east), most probably commanded by a British Engineer, Lt. Anthony Jones. Strong enemy fire prevented *Hauptmann* Sieger and *Leutnant*

Königsmann from quickly returning to their former position to collect the remnants of the company, which moved northeast under cover of darkness, where SS units employed it for night security. Sieger and Königsmann arrived at their new headquarters at Lent-Bemmel Street, where formerly scattered elements were also assembled. Given the impossibility of locating their company in the dark in unknown terrain, they checked to see if any of their men were among those present, then proceeded to *Oberst* Hartung's headquarters in Bemmel. Here they were ordered to assemble all men gathered and push through to Einheit Wesel at first light.

Hauptmann Sieger recounts: "At dawn, only two officers and two enlisted men could be found, so Einheit Wesel released us. On our way back to Bemmel, about 40 men showed up after the SS released them from their position facing Bemmel. It was necessary to rest up since the company had been in continuous battle since September 17. After *Oberst* Hartung announced he could not use the men, we marched to Doornenburg, where General of the Waffen *SS-Brigadeführer* Harmel (10th SS-Panzer Division) stopped the company. After inquiring about our circumstances, he assigned the company to the division staff, to give the men time to rest and recuperate while carrying out road security, guarding prisoners, etc. The company moved into quarters in Pannerden and encountered the transport group during the displacement."[321]

Twenty-five-year-old *Hauptsturmführer* (SS-Captain) Karl-Heinz Euling, commander of the battalion of SS-Panzer Grenadier Regiment 21 at the Valkhof citadel just southwest of the road bridge, was also responsible for the defense of the bridge itself. From Tuesday, September 19 on, *Kampfgruppe* Euling had tenaciously defended the citadel surrounding Hunner Park, and the traffic circle in front of the south bridge ramp. Realizing around 2230 hours on September 20 that his situation had become hopeless, Euling and a mixed group of 60 officers and men—including a few survivors of his own battalion, Fallschirmjägers led by Major Bodo Ahlborn and some Herman Göring Division soldiers of *Hauptmann* Runge—found some rowboats on the south bank of the Waal River and paddled east unseen under the road bridge. *Hauptsturmführer* Euling later received the Knight's Cross of the Iron Cross for his leadership in the battle: "When due to strong enemy attacks the evacuation of the bridgehead was ordered, I held the bridge as long as possible until the evacuation had been completed. Although we were surrounded and the citadel was on fire, I broke out with the remnants of my *Kampfgruppe* and all their weapons. In a tactical move, we marched west along on the riverbank [in order not to arouse suspicions], then east under the bridge, escaping capture and secretly reaching our own lines."[322]

Hauptsturmführer Euling had served in Normandy and several battles on the Eastern Front before he took part in the fight for the road bridge in Nijmegen. Asked which enemy forces forced him to pull out, Euling stated: "The American paratroopers [the 505th] and British troops in Nijmegen were not the ones who forced us to give up our position. It was because the other American paratroopers [the 504th] had successfully crossed the river that I knew the situation had become untenable."[323] But the price had been high: eight engineers killed and 27 wounded or exhausted; 22 3rd Battalion men lost or killed the same day, and 78 wounded. The 1st Battalion had two killed and a number of wounded, including several A Company men. In total, the final casualty rate for the Waal River Crossing was 48 paratroopers.

Cpl. Fred Baldino of A Company, who was
wounded in an artillery barrage on October 2,
1944. *Courtesy Fred Baldino*

CHAPTER 14

THE ISLAND

LENT, OOSTERHOUT AND NIJMEGEN, SEPTEMBER 21–23, 1944

During the night of September 20–21, Major Cook ordered G and I Companies to push north and northeast to widen the bridgehead. Major Harrison's 1st Battalion would simultaneously make similar attempts west of the railroad dike, pushing to the north and northwest. The attack was to jump off at 0900 hours. At 0855 hours Burriss radioed Cook to request artillery fire preceding the battalion's new attack. Cook did not have much artillery available, but alerted the 81mm the 3rd Battalion Mortar Platoon. Shortly after 0900 hours, as 1st Lt. McClain followed the advance route I Company had taken the previous night, his platoon was ambushed. "Lieutenant McClain took us down the wrong road," recalled PFC John J. Horvatis. "I Company had run into an ambush there a few hours earlier. A mortar shell came down and we all took cover. Nicholas Esposito was lying in a culvert. His pants were shot-up and his backside was all jelly. I knew he wouldn't survive. He was still awake when we dragged him out. He died of his wounds in the aid station. I think another man was wounded at that time."[324]

The other man, PFC Myron A. Bundrock, was wounded but survived. At 0910 hours I Company again pushed forward toward Fort Lent, supported by a few tanks. First Lieutenant Calvin A. Campbell, who had already caught a 20mm shell fragment in his right leg during the crossing the day before, was hit by a machine-gun bullet that lodged in his neck after passing through the head of Sgt. Grady L. Robbins of the attached machine-gun squad. Campbell's assistant platoon leader, 2nd Lieutenant Joseph D. Shirk, deployed machine guns and bazookas to counteract the enemy fire. While the enemy machine gun was knocked out, the 20mm flak gun continued to fire, hitting a bazooka man—possibly Pvt. Warren R. Johnston, Headquarters Company, 3rd Battalion, who was killed—and wounded Lieutenant Shirk. Captain Burriss withdrew the company and tried to flank enemy fire by moving Lieutenant Blankenship's 1st Platoon to the left.

Major Cook moved forward to I Company to find out what had happened. He located Captain Burriss and the 1st Platoon just as heavy machine-gun and 20mm fire pinned them down. Cook asked Burriss to sum up the situation. "Does that give you the answer as to what the situation is?" replied Burriss, pointing towards the enemy fire.

"Our work was finished for a while," remembered T/5 Seymour Flox, H Company, "so we set up a CP in an old brewery and reorganized. While the rest of the company arrived in ones and twos, we drank beer and ate. We found some preserves and made a meal of them. We even found some German cigars, which most of us smoked. Give me a good old American rope anytime. We were lucky: our casualties were light this time, only about 50-percent."[325]

Sergeant Tarbell sat in the H Company CP as dawn broke: "We had set up our command post northeast of the Nijmegen Bridge, in the cellar of a building. I was directly above with my SCR-300 radio set. The company clerk, PFC Harold K. Shelden, was sitting next to me; PFCs Douglas Reich and James Rosser and Sgt. Donald Zimmerman were standing at the far end of the room, opposite the window. Shelden and I were making a list of our casualties. I was contacting the different platoons, and Shelden was writing down the names as I was receiving them. We started getting artillery or mortar fire, every round hitting closer to our CP. First Sergeant Kogut yelled for me to get down to the cellar with the radio. He said it looked like they were zeroing in on us.

"The radio was sitting on the floor between Shelden and me. To my left was a large window looking out onto a courtyard. As I leaned over to pick up the radio, Shelden bent down to help, his head next to mine. Another shell whistled down and landed in the courtyard behind us. The shrapnel blew in from the window, catching Shelden in the head and nicking Reich, Rosser and Zimmerman. Shelden died instantly, but the other men were only slightly wounded. I was nearest the opening where the shrapnel came through, but I wasn't hit at all. The worst part of the incident was adding Shelden's name to the casualty list he had been transcribing only seconds before the shell hit. How I ever made it through that day I'll never know.

When I went down to the cellar, the captain had the medic give me some kind of shot. I went to sleep under the stairway."[326]

At the break of dawn, Sergeant Zimmerman was still searching for the Company CP, in hopes of locating his platoon: "I found the H Company CP the next morning [...] established in a house. Tarbell was there, and I asked if he had something to eat. He said, 'We have cans of German bread.' It was bread with raisins and tasted real good. This can saved my life when a mortar shell came in. I was behind Shelden as he was killed outright working on the casualty list, and shrapnel hit me in the hip. They told me where the aid station was and I reported to the medics.

The same barrage wounded 1st Sgt. Curtis Odom of I Company. "We were patched up and went outside again at daybreak. We looked in the houses on the bank of the river between the north ends of both bridges. They were all vacant, and in one garage I found a 1937 Ford Marmon-Harrington half-track in mint condition. We first checked it for booby-traps, then turned the ignition on. We used it for nearly a week."[327]

One of the wounded evacuated by Odom and Zimmerman was Lieutenant Dunn, A Company: "I was evacuated back across the bridge to a civilian hospital in Nijmegen, where I was held for three or four days because the corridor to Belgium and France was cut. I got great care in the hospital, and still have a hand-painted Dutch boy plywood cut-out given to me by the nurses!"[328]

When Captain Thomas rose at about 0700 hours, most of G Company was looking over the previous night's battle ground or searching for something to eat other than the usual rations. "A large number of dead Germans were lying on the railroad tracks and in nearby fields and yards. One German was on a mattress in one of the houses, seriously wounded, and our battalion surgeon, Captain Shapiro, went to see what he could do to help. The soldier had not had any previous first aid, and had lain there all night suffering with a serious belly wound. Captain Shapiro told the Jerry he would have to wait for an ambulance to evacuate him, but he privately told one of the fellows with him [Shapiro] that the man was going to die.

"About an hour later the Jerries began shelling, and most of the company in the area retired to their foxholes. At 1130 the company was alerted they were to attack at 1300. The attack was divided into three phase lines, the first two of which we passed with no opposition. Company I was on our right flank. The Company CP was finally established in a house at about 1600 hours. A message was sent back to the Battalion CP requesting a platoon of men from Company H to fill in a gap between the 1st and 2nd Platoon. A carrying party from the battalion, including the battalion adjutant, arrived at the Company CP bringing ammunition, and another arrived with rations at about 1700 hours.

"As dusk fell, a gap of about 150 yards between Company G's right flank and Company I's left flank was discovered. The 2nd Platoon sergeant took charge of the platoon, and the platoon leader, 1st Lt. Donald E. Graeber, placed all available mortar and company headquarters men in position along this gap about 20 yards from the enemy positions. Periodical enemy hand grenades ensued. Late that night, word was received from battalion that at 0700 hours the next morning the company was to withdraw back to its first phase line. For most of the night, a carrying party ferried back all the rations and ammunition that had been brought up earlier in the afternoon. The wounded men and, alas, the dead, were carried back during the night."[329]

One of the dead was 2nd Platoon squad leader, Sgt. Jack D. Howard. "The thing that touched me the most," commented Major Cook, "was that for the next couple of days many of the NCOs simply came up and shook my hand, and with traces of tears in their eyes saluted and took off. This action confused me until one of the officers got it out of the men—it was their way of taking back their dirty remarks about me not sticking with them up front in combat. From that day, I never had any disciplinary problems with my battalion. For nearly eight weeks of combat, I had only one court-martial case (and that was against a relatively new man), no AWOLs and the fewest incident reports of the 504th PIR."[330]

Shortly before dawn, Lieutenant Breard's 1st Platoon, A Company, moved out toward Oosterhout along a gravelled road north of the dike with deep ditches on either side. Covered from German observation by thick fog, they made good progress. When the fog lifted, "we found we were in an orchard with Germans on our left and right," recalled Breard. "It was a 20mm flak unit. We jumped in the ditches and started firing. They were surprised. We killed some and captured some and burned the guns. Soon after, British tanks came up the highway. They fired on everything, so we stayed in the ditches. We dug in at this point and were relieved late that night by the British 43rd Division."[331]

Sergeant Clark, 2nd Platoon, remembered that everybody was upset when 3rd Platoon leader 1st Lt. Robert S. Currier was killed: "We moved up to the little village of Oosterhout, where a German unit with at least one tank held us up. We were in a ditch towards the highway, and we dug in. The report I got was that Lieutenant Currier was sitting in his foxhole and a machine gun just about cut him in half. He wasn't in my platoon. Currier was a helluva nice young fellow and everybody liked him. We were all upset when Currier got killed. Waiting for something to happen, we could see the German tank moving. We did not have any artillery—only a couple of bazookas, and then the [bazooka] team with us was called to report to the Company CP."[332]

Also near the southern outskirts of Oosterhout, Pvt. John R. Towle, a bazooka man in C Company, posthumously won the Congressional Medal of Honor when the enemy counterattacked his company with infantry and tank. Towle left his foxhole, crossing open ground under heavy fire and beat off tanks with rocket fire. He killed nine Germans with one round and was attacking a half-track when he was killed by a mortar shell. His citation reads: "For conspicuous gallantry and intrepidity at the risk of life above and beyond the call of duty on September 21, 1944, near Oosterhout, Holland. The rifle company in which Private Towle served as rocket-launcher gunner was occupying a defensive position in the west sector of the recently established Nijmegen bridgehead when a strong enemy force of approximately 100 infantry supported by two tanks and a half-track formed for a counterattack.

"With full knowledge of the disastrous consequences resulting not only to his company but to the entire bridgehead by an enemy breakthrough, Private Towle immediately and without orders left his foxhole and moved 200 yards in the face of intense small-arms fire to a position on an exposed dike roadbed. From this precarious position Private Towle fired his rocket launcher and hit both tanks to his immediate front. Armored skirting on both tanks prevented penetration by the projectiles, but both vehicles withdrew slightly damaged.

"Still under intense fire and fully exposed to the enemy, Private Towle then engaged a nearby house which nine Germans had entered and were using as a strongpoint, and with one round killed all nine. Hurriedly replenishing his supply of ammunition, Private Towle, motivated only by his high conception of duty which called for the destruction of the enemy at any cost, then rushed approximately 125 yards through grazing enemy fire to an exposed position from which he could engage the enemy half-track with his rocket launcher.

"While in a kneeling position preparatory to firing on the enemy vehicle, Private Towle was mortally wounded by a mortar shell. By his heroic tenacity, at the price of his life, Private Towle saved the lives of many of his comrades and was directly instrumental in breaking up the enemy counterattack."[333]

Pvt. Elbert E. Winningham, a machine-gunner in company headquarters, witnessed the death of Private Towle: "My buddy and I had a .30-caliber machine gun in a ditch along the dike road. [Pvt.] James Killimayer [Towle's assistant] came back from the road out of his head. We set him down and tied his hands behind his back to calm him down. He started to eat dirt and almost bit my finger off when I tried to stop him.

"There were two Tiger tanks up there, and we could see them once in a while. Towle calmly came back for his bazooka and knocked them out, one by one. Then he came by me and asked, 'Do you have a cigarette?' I gave him one and a light, and when he was about 30 feet away from me a mortar shell came down close and a piece struck him in his throat. He was about half on his back when he died."[334]

Cpl. William J. "Bill" Rothweiler of A Company then moved forward with his BAR and killed the German half-track crew one by one, covered by Pvt. Angus M. Giles, Jr. Both received a Bronze Star for this action. Colonel Tucker became concerned about the tanks when another report came in at 0720 hours on September 21 that Dutch civilians had spotted 21 tanks at Elst, heading toward Lent. At 0755 hours this report was updated to three Tiger tanks moving in the direction of Lent.

Shortly after 1100 hours Tucker visited the 1st Battalion CP to discuss the situation with Major Harrison. Expressing his concern about the presence of German tanks north of Lent, he ordered Harrison to send out a patrol to find the exact location of the German tanks. Tucker left the 1st Battalion at 1121 hours.

At 1200 hours Major Harrison called Captain Duncan, whose A Company was holding the 1st Battalion's most forward position. Harrison told Duncan that German tanks were somewhere between Arnhem and Nijmegen in the vicinity of Elst. Responding to the imperative to find them, Duncan sent out three of his more experienced 3rd Platoon troopers. Armed with a bazooka, PFC Ervin E. Shaffer led the patrol, accompanied by his assistant gunner, Pvt. Arthur W. Bates, Jr.: "I was told to take two men and go up the main road. I guess it goes to Arnhem. I had a bazooka and we were looking for tanks, scout cars or anything. We got up to the crossroads and after about 20 minutes received a message that we were to return to company headquarters and that the British were coming out of the woods on the edge of Nijmegen. They were about to make a tank attack. We got back to our men, and the British came out and moved in about 200 yards from where we had been. One of the tanks hit a mine or a shell and stopped the whole tank drive.

"When the shooting started they told us to keep our heads down. Now, we had a patch, a piece of orange cloth, on our uniforms so American or British airplanes would know we were Allied troops. Some of the men put those orange cloths on sticks and raised them above their heads and waved them back and forth. The British tanks started shooting at us. Somebody yelled out, 'What do we do? Do we return fire? Do we shoot back?' The officers answered, 'Hold your fire!' After about three minutes the British stopped shooting at us."[335]

Pvt. Louis C. Marino, 2nd Platoon, remembered that the small pieces of orange cloth were attached to the lapels on their uniforms. Several troopers used them to signal to the British tanks of the 2nd Irish Guards that they were Americans. Marino and PFC Clarence L. Fuhrman manned a .30-caliber machine gun on the far side of A Company's defensive position along the road from Arnhem to Nijmegen. He knew that the British tanks were heading for trouble as they rolled by at full speed toward Arnhem: "I was on a machine gun right at that corner when three Germans came and planted a land mine. I froze on the damn machine gun and it wouldn't fire. I told my assistant gunner to tell Captain Duncan that three Germans had a teller mine planted up there in the turn of the road. Captain Duncan told my assistant gunner, 'That major, he thinks he knows it all. So we just let him go find that mine himself.' Well, that was poor judgement on the captain's part. The British tanks coming down the road were firing on us. That poor tank leading the British there got blown up. I don't know the exact number, but one or two more got blown up by the mines."[336]

Dutchman Ben Bouman was still acting as interpreter for 2nd Lt. Richard Smith, 1st Platoon, B Company: "We halted near the woods in Oosterhout and immediately dug a slit trench, as indeed you should. While we were sitting shoulder-to-shoulder on the excavated soil, a German grenade suddenly hit a tree branch about 15 feet above the ground, to my right. We both dived into the slit trench, Smith first and I on top of him.

"When the shooting stopped, it appeared that Smith had been severely injured by shell splinters. I got away with a relatively minor splinter wound in my right knee. We were both transported to a British transit hospital. Smith was transferred to England, and two days later I was moved to the address where I was hiding, and was back on my feet within a few weeks."[337]

PFC Emilio J. Papale of B Company, mortally wounded in the same barrage by a treeburst, died the next day of his wounds. According to Major

Roggen, the regimental surgeon: "Once the bridge was secure, we [the Regimental Medical Detachment] did not have any further contact with the enemy, with the exception of a small amount of strafing from enemy aircraft. I recall one incident where an elderly Dutchman was shot during a strafing incident and had his right leg severed at the hip.

"One reason I recall this is because there was absolutely no bleeding. We administered morphine and bandaged the leg; I believe he was evacuated by ambulance to a Dutch hospital. There is no way to predict how an individual will react to a specific injury, and this was an example of blood vessels contracting following a severe traumatic injury. It was essential to get him to a medical facility before the bleeding started. We never found out what happened to this man. In fact, we rarely found out what happened to troopers once they were evacuated to the rear, and this was often frustrating."[338]

A platoon leader in D Company, 2nd Lt. Hanz K. Druener, recalled that the Germans "were still shelling the Nijmegen Bridge periodically. The whole company had to go back across that bridge, and the only way we could get back was by timing the artillery shells. The Germans were very precise: they would shoot a round at the bridge, and then about two minutes later shoot another round. We would have to move between the rounds. I remember that specifically because I was acting as a sort of traffic cop getting my people across the bridge."[339]

In the early hours of September 22, the regiment was gradually relieved by the British 231st Infantry Brigade. I Company repulsed a German counterattack during the morning. "With the aid of a couple British SPs [self-propelled guns] and British artillery," recalled Captain Keep, "we pushed forward another 1,000 yards. Every inch of this advance was hotly contested. The Krauts had all the advantages. They controlled the orchards, ditches, farmhouses, and other strategic positions; and it was necessary to wrest every square foot from them. But by late afternoon, we had once again reached our prescribed line, and here we held on with determination, fighting off numerous counterattacks. We continually ran out of ammo and had to replenish it every hour or so.

"About 2200 that night, the regimental commander called Major Cook over to his command post. I went with him, and we were told we would be relieved at 0600 the next morning. *Relieved* is a strange term to use in conjunction with this operation. We were to pull out of our present positions, and no one was to take them over. It had been decided that a close-in defense of the bridge was sufficient and that we were no longer needed.

"It was going to be a ticklish situation. We were to withdraw from our present position with the Nazis hot on our tails as soon as they realized what was going on. Could our companies get back to the security of the bridge without being cut off by the Krauts? We were to receive no assistance or cover from anyone.

"That night, our company commanders started to move their wounded back, as well as other non-combatants; and at dawn the rest of the men started to infiltrate to the rear. It was a skillfully directed maneuver. One platoon would cover the withdrawal of the other, and then the unit that had just pulled back would stop and perform the same service for its former covering forces.

"Just what we expected occurred. As soon as the Nazis realized what was taking place, they were breathing hard down our backs. To make a long story short, our troops eventually reached the security of the British close-in defense of the bridge; and we moved across this huge structure, still littered with the dead we had killed what seemed like aeons ago (in reality, barely two days). We turned the bridge completely over to the British. We had captured it. Now our job was finished. We were needed for other things."[340]

The relief of the 3rd Battalion was completed by 0720 hours. The battalion marched across the road bridge into Nijmegen, where British amphibious DUKW vehicles (also known as *Ducks*) transported them to the division assembly area in Dekkerswald, a wooded area where they would get a short rest. Captain Thomas recorded that G Company "began withdrawing from their positions under a heavy fog at 0700. The company withdrew to the 1st phase line of yesterday's attack. It may be noted that the fog saved the company from many casualties. There the company assembled and then moved back to Lent, where yesterday's attack had started from. At 1130 the company marched across the Nijmegen Bridge. All across the bridge lay the bodies of German soldiers who had died there the day before. The company was loaded on English trucks and moved to a rest area about five miles southwest of Nijmegen, where the company bivouacked for rest. The company went out late that afternoon and dug reserve positions behind the 508th Parachute Infantry positions."[341] Corporal Baldino remembered passing a particular dead German soldier on the Nijmegen side as A Company was withdrawn across the bridge: "his arm was up in the air and seemed to be pointing across the bridge [to Arnhem]."[342]

In the afternoon German rations obtained from a captured supply dump at Oss were issued to the troops. Up until then, most food had consisted of cold K-rations and whatever was offered by Dutch civilians or the men could pick from orchards. Pvt. Harvey W. Schultz of Headquarters Company died that day of wounds earlier sustained. "The company stayed in the rest area all day," wrote Captain Thomas the next day. "Battalion called all first sergeants to a meeting in order to straighten out morning reports—records which had been sadly lacking since the river crossing. At 1400 Colonel Tucker spoke to the battalion and commended them upon their excellent performance of the river crossing."[343]

The Guards Armoured Division intelligence summary for that day reads: "After our seizure of the bridge last night it was only to be expected that the enemy would react quickly and as fiercely as possible, and today has shown this was to be so. The night was fairly quiet both north and south of the river, the town was systematically cleared up and most of the snipers left behind disposed of. (Some of the most annoying of these were men left in the girders of the bridge itself, who fired down on soft vehicles going across.)

"During the day, however, the enemy was much more active. A strong counterattack was put in against the northern bridgehead this morning but successfully held, and from the southeast the enemy attempted all day to break through our lines and cut our route to the bridge. But at Mook 7252 and Wyler 7858, he was halted with considerable losses.

"At about midday our armour broke out of the bridgehead but found very quickly that the going was most unfavourable for tanks. Raised dike roads and ground allowing no deployment meant that enemy anti-tank guns, though few in number, had only to be well-sited in order to cause damage and delay entirely out of proportion to their strength.

"Therefore, a firm line was consolidated before nightfall, and tomorrow will see other elements pushing on until the way has been cleared and armour once more can go through. The position of the airborne troops in Arnhem has been *GREATLY IMPROVED* today by the landing of supplies, but the situation is still far from perfect and a link with the south is most eminently to be desired."[344]

The reality at the Rhine Bridge in Arnhem was totally different than implied in the battle report for British paratroopers. On the morning of September 21, they were forced to surrender and the Germans took control. Five days later the battered remnants of the 1st British Airborne Division north of the Rhine River were withdrawn. Their mission might well have concluded successfully if the British tanks had advanced to Arnhem the evening of the Waal Crossing.[345]

CHAPTER 15

NO "WALK IN THE PARK"
HOLLAND AND GERMANY,
SEPTEMBER 24–27, 1944

Colonel Tucker held a meeting in his Regimental CP at 1055 hours on September 24 to instruct his battalion commanders on the task that now lay ahead. General Gavin had ordered the relief of the 505th and 508th PIRs by the recently arrived 325th GIR and the 504th PIR. Capt. William Pratt's 80th AA–C Battery would come under Tucker's orders at 1130 hours, supplying the 504th with eight 57mm anti-tank guns. These were meant to relieve Col. Roy E. Lindquist's 508th PIR, which was holding a seven-mile defensive line extending from the brickyard in Erlekom on the Waal east of Nijmegen to a point on the Wylerbaan, a large road about one mile northeast of Groesbeek—quite a stretch to defend with one RCT. Information received from the 508th PIR was scanty, requiring strong patrols to the front.

At 1600 hours that afternoon the 3/504 was the first unit into the lines to relieve the 2/508. The battalion defended a stretch of less than two miles along the Wylerbaan, aggressively patrolling the Vossendaal, Groenendaal, Den Heuvel and Heuvelhof farms on the east side of the road. H Company would maintain contact using joint patrols with the 325th GIR at Groesbeek. Major Wellems's 2/504 would relieve the 3/508 between Erlekom and Beek, supported by Sherwood Forest Yeomanry tanks. Major Harrison's 1/504 received the central position, relieving the 3/508 at Beek and tying in to the right flank of the 3/504 not too far from the Vossendaal farm. Major Roggen would set up the Regimental Aid Station in Beek, with Regimental Head-quarters in nearby Berg en Dal.

Enroute to a church service that morning, PFC Gerald P. Hereford, Jr.,

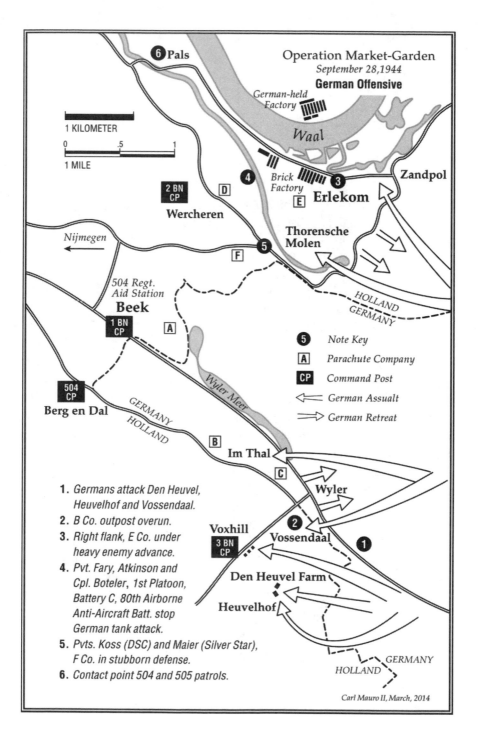

Operation Market-Garden
September 28, 1944
German Offensive

Carl Mauro II, March, 2014

1. Germans attack Den Heuvel, Heuvelhof and Vossendaal.
2. B Co. outpost overrun.
3. Right flank, E Co. under heavy enemy advance.
4. Pvt. Fary, Atkinson and Cpl. Boteler, 1st Platoon, Battery C, 80th Airborne Anti-Aircraft Batt. stop German tank attack.
5. Pvts. Koss (DSC) and Maier (Silver Star), F Co. in stubborn defense.
6. Contact point 504 and 505 patrols.

D Company, was killed by artillery fire.[346] Back in a field hospital east of Nijmegen, Lieutenant Dunn, A Company, wrote in his diary: "Moved last night into a room with a bed. [Lt. Earl] Morin with me, [Lt. George] Presnell from 505 on left. Feel OK—just have ache in left chest. Reason for no evacuation is road to rear cut by Krauts."[347]

At 1220 hours Colonel Williams issued the order to use 60mm mortar ammunition whenever possible. The 81mm Mortar Platoon support of the 3rd and 1st Battalions in the Waal crossing had caused a shortage of ammunition. C and D Batteries, 80th AA, were attached to the 1/504 and 2/504 to cover against air raids or tank attacks. Capt. Thomas reported that G Company "moved out about 1600 and relieved Company A of the 508th Parachute Infantry. The company took over the same positions that Company A had used. Also sent out patrols during the night."[348]

"When it became apparent that the Arnhem mission had failed, we were ordered into defensive positions," recalled Capt. Frank D. Boyd, chief liaison officer of the 376th Parachute Field Artillery Battalion (PFAB). The 504th unit to which Boyd had been assigned "established a line on the high ground east of Wyler Meer. Our headquarters was in Berg en Dal for about seven weeks. The regimental headquarters was in a well-constructed house on the east side of a north-south street [… with] a steel observation tower in the back yard. It probably was 50 feet (16 meters) tall and had a platform on top large enough for several men to stand on. We lived entirely in the large concrete basement. It could be identified by a small room with a ceiling made of steel H-beams or railroad rails, evidently a bomb shelter."[349]

Around 2300 hours on September 24, F Company was the first in its battalion to relieve a company of the 2/508 on the front line. Major Wellems recalled that "nothing happened in the relieving, and from September 25–28 there was nothing much but patrols, creating roadblocks and setting up a new outpost line. The 14 British tanks with the 508th remained with the battalion on the 25th. [...] Generally the tanks pull back at night, but the 508th persuaded them to remain in positions on the flanks at the road junctions. [...] They didn't have to fire during the night. They had four 57mm guns along, anti-tank guns attached by division from the 80th Airborne Anti-Aircraft Battalion."[350]

Lt. Carl Mauro, E Company, recalled "the 508th had left four dead men in what was now the F Company area, and 14 German dead were scattered about the area occupied by E Company. Capt. Wade H. McIntyre, a friend of mine from North Africa and England, was the regimental officer responsible for evacuating the dead bodies, ours and theirs, but he was not available. No seemed to know where he was—a common occurrence. […]

"E Company moved its CP forward to the extreme front of the brickyard, which consisted of many huge kilns where the bricks were made. Some civilians found it safer to sleep in the kilns than to remain in the basements of their own bombed houses. We were forward of this area on the 2nd Battalion left flank up to the dike, the high bank of the Waal River. The Battalion CP was in a large farmhouse in an apple orchard several hundred yards behind E Company and most of its personnel worked in a large barn."[351]

The night of 24 to 25 September had seen sniper activity to the front of H Company positions. A couple patrols were therefore sent to farmhouses east of the Wylerbaan road. One large complex, the Den Heuvel farm belonging to the Damen family, was especially interesting because its farmhouses and barns lay on slightly higher ground, dominating surrounding fields and farms. Second Lieutenant Donald E. Graeber and two of his 2nd Platoon rifle squads, 17 paratroopers in all, were to capture the farm. The G Company Journal for September 25 reads: "Company still in the 508th holding position but moved the Company CP over to the corner of a clump of woods about 200 yards from the road. During the day periodical artillery and mortar fire was thrown at the company positions. One mobile 88mm gun was knocked out after several rounds had landed on our 1st Platoon. Many Jerry aircraft were in the skies during the afternoon and strafed our positions.

"During the later part of the afternoon several small 50mm mortar shells landed near our mortarmen, wounding several. Captain Thomas came back from a meeting at Battalion Headquarters with the word that the 2nd Platoon would move forward and attack the Den Heuvel woods, about 800 yards to the front of the Company CP at 2100 hours. No flares had been seen from that area at midnight to signify that the attack had reached its objective."[352]

The Luftwaffe strafed regimental positions and carried out a hit-and-run bomb mission, hitting the southwest corner of the road bridge at Nijmegen. Major Harrison sent three patrols from A, B and C Companies to the front that evening. First Lieutenant William A. Meerman took 20 3rd Platoon men to the Vossendaal farm, where they reported at 0251 that they had seen no Germans and were setting up their outpost. One lieutenant and three enlisted men from A Company went to the outskirts of Wyler. At 0250 hours they reported that the town was clear of German vehicles, but they had spotted German infantry digging in. Two officers and 20 men from C Company set up an outpost on a ridge.

That same night a German patrol hit one of the buildings occupied by H Company. A grenade thrown through a window killed Sgt. Daun Z. Rice, an original member of the company. Daun Rice had an older brother, Sgt. William V. Rice, in the 2nd Platoon. Pvt. John A. Beyer, in the same outpost as Rice, remained unscathed.

Meanwhile, Lieutenant Graeber and his patrol got lost and returned to the G Company CP at 0230 hours. Captain Thomas reoriented him on the map and sent him back off, along with a three-man .30-caliber machine-gun team and two additional riflemen. At the woods just north of the Den Heuvel farm, five men were sent ahead to reconnoiter. When no opposition was reported, Lieutenant Graeber positioned most of his men in pairs at the edge of the woods, the .30-caliber machine gun at the far-east corner, and four men at the Platoon CP. When nothing transpired, he fired a green flare at 0430 hours to indicate they had taken their objective.

The 3rd Battalion S-2, 1st Lt. Carmichael, in charge of interrogating prisoners, was informed that Lieutenant Graeber had taken his objective against little opposition. Another H Company patrol, led by 2nd Lt. Ernest Murphy, reported nothing particular, but a 1st Platoon, H Company patrol led by Sgt. Theodore Finkbeiner captured a German officer. Finkbeiner crossed some railroad tracks and entered a farmhouse "from the rear through a sort of livestock or garage addition. Evidently we made some noise, because a German officer opened the door issuing orders, I assumed to us."[353]

Lieutenant Carmichael recounts: "at 0530 the H Company patrol returned to our lines and reported that they had captured a German captain as he stepped outside the house he occupied to answer a call of nature. They took him quietly in the dark and carried him back to our lines without his comrades ever knowing what happened. I arrived on the scene just after the patrol had returned, and the H Company men and officers had learned that this very captain had sent the patrol from his company that killed our sergeant [Daun Rice]."[354]

The rumors around Rice's death led to harsh treatment of the German prisoner. Not only was it said that the captain had ordered the patrol; according to Finkbeiner, "the German officer had an 82nd Airborne patch in his pocket."[355] Only with great difficulty did Lieutenant Carmichael manage to calm the agitated H Company troopers and save the life of the German officer: "Our men had part of a nylon camouflage parachute around this captain's neck and they were twisting it as tightly as they could, slapping him on the face and beating him, and I verily believe that had it not been for my intervention, that they would have beat the poor man to death right there. I prevailed upon them to turn him over to me, since he was a very valuable prisoner and we might in that way avoid patrols for a day or two."[356]

Lieutenant Carmichael escorted the German officer to the 3rd Battalion CP, where Major Cook personally intervened in the interrogation. "Lieutenant Forestal wouldn't let the men kill the prisoner," Cook recalled, "because I knew of his capture. [...] The prisoner would not talk. Knowing he understood English, I told him I would give him two minutes to start talking, or else I would kill him as he was of no use to me. Regiment and Division were yelling for him, but we told them the prisoner was difficult, etc.

"When the two minutes were up, I dramatically pulled out my .45 and the S-3, Captain Keep, and the S-2, Lieutenant Carmichael, who were on either side of the prisoner, stepped away. For once I saw real fear in a man's eyes, and he started answering questions and turned out to be of good intelligence value to us.

"He explained he knew from the way the men talked that he was going to be killed anyway, so why talk. But somehow he got my message, which is why he became so willing to talk. They always claimed we didn't know how to handle prisoners!"[357] The officer informed Cook that he belonged to the 58th Infanterie Bataillon, and gave the major the dispositions of his unit. Satisfied with the answers, Cook called to regimental headquarters shortly after 0600 hours to report that the officer would be sent up.[358]

Before daybreak it appeared that the Germans had infiltrated Lieutenant Graeber's 2nd Platoon at Den Heuvel. A German soldier approached Sgt. Henry C. Hoffman and demanded his surrender. Hoffman pulled out his .45 and shot him, giving away the platoon's position. By daybreak, about 11 Germans had worked their way in. A firefight broke out and Lieutenant Graeber was seriously wounded by a bullet in one eye. Sergeant Hoffman gave him a shot of morphine.

The platoon had no radio contact with G Company headquarters, and the situation became chaotic. The Germans' presence was made known through yells and shouts. In addition to Lieutenant Graeber, two enlisted men were wounded, and Sergeant Hoffman assumed command. The infiltrators were all shot down, but the situation remained precarious, as Captain Thomas, the company commander, describes: "The platoon had attacked right through the German positions in the dark but at dawn they had a fierce firefight and were sorely pressed. Their weapons were all wet and muddy and several of them would not even fire. The platoon leader was seriously wounded and brought out of the house up the road to a British tank which had been put down there to help."[359]

Major Cook received four medium tanks and alerted 2nd Lt. Bernard E. Karnap, who had recently assumed command of the 2nd Platoon, I Company. Karnap's 17 men were deployed in column on either side of the road running from the Wylerbaan to the Den Heuvel farm until the tanks showed up at 1015 hours. Although the road was only a third of a mile long, the advance was slow, stopping twice due to apprehension about German tanks.

Meanwhile, the Germans had occupied the three buildings on the Den Heuvel farm. Karnap's platoon split in two: he led two tanks and one squad to the north, while S.Sgt. Leon E. Baldwin took the other squad along the southeastern road circling the houses. Seeking to knock the Germans out, a tank fired 12 HE shells at the houses, one of which caused a treeburst that killed Pvt. Einar Flack, the 2nd Platoon medic in G Company. Riddled with shells, the farmhouse still stood firm. The German defenders moved to the rear of the building while the tanks fired their last shells and pulled out, taking their three wounded. At 1200 hours, Lieutenant Karnap led back his platoon, all those from Lieutenant Graeber's platoon whom he could locate, and seven prisoners.

It had been impossible to relieve all the G Company troopers; firing could still be heard, and Karnap's mixed group was sent back. At 1230 hours, they moved up to the intersection of the Den Heuvel farm road and the Wylerbaan. S.Sgt. William D. Sachse, 2nd Platoon, G Company, deployed 18 men on the left of the road and Sgt. Alexander L. Barker's rifle squad from Lieutenant Karnap's platoon on the right. Both units cleared the immediate area, but Sergeant Barker hesitated to move east, as this meant crossing an open field. At 1300, Lieutenant Karnap took Staff Sergeant Baldwin and five men from Barker's squad and rushed up to the Den Heuvel farm where he lobbed a Gammon grenade through a window and knocked out an enemy machine-gun nest, taking the wall along.

While Staff Sergeant Baldwin and two men trained their weapons at one side of the farmhouse, Karnap and three men circled the house and moved between the two barns. Spotting six Germans at a machine gun about to fire on Sachse, they killed them all with a single volley. Karnap directed PFC Solon W. Whitmire, Jr., to set up his BAR. He gunned down four Germans on the road circling north of the farm as they attempted to reach the machine gun. Placing his other two men at the rear of the farmhouse, Karnap ran over to Sachse, whose men had captured 19 Germans. He crossed the road, picked up four more men from Sergeant Barker's squad, and placed them between the G Company men and the farmhouse.

Clearing the Den Heuvel woods was no "walk in the park." Major Cook made his way to the Den Heuvel farm at 1400 hours with Captain Keep to ascertain the situation. Learning from Lieutenant Karnap that the opposition was far stronger than expected, they radioed Captain Thomas to send 2nd Lt. Pursell, seven 1st Platoon, G Company men, and three British tanks to Den Heuvel. When Pursell's force arrived at 1445 hours, he saw Lieutenant Karnap and 11 men escorting 28 German prisoners from a big orchard just north of the farm to the 2nd Platoon CP, which was under German shell fire. Pursell found seven G Company troopers in the orchard, whom he positioned with a machine gun to silence German small-arms fire from the northeast.

Having drawn up near the woods, the British tanks were suddenly fired on by an 88mm gun that knocked out the rear tank. Lieutenant Karnap repositioned the foremost tank so it could shell one of the farm buildings and a wooded area to the left of the house. The tank-gunner machine-gunned a whole hedgerow until a shell struck in the breech and he was forced to cease fire. The remaining tank was brought forward and parked next to the first. It fired another 20 rounds of HE shells on the house and woods and sprayed them with some 1000 rounds of .50-caliber machine-gun fire before the tanks withdrew at 1555 hours.

As Lieutenant Karnap organized the defense around the farmhouses, Lieutenant Pursell sent Staff Sergeant Sachse and nine men to outpost the north side of the orchard. Meanwhile, Cook and Keep reported to the 3rd Battalion CP, informing Colonel Tucker that the situation was grave. A German battalion command post had been overrun, and the remaining force clearly had some heavy artillery guns at its disposal. German losses were estimated at 150 men. In addition to Private Flack, killed by friendly fire, two of Lieutenant Graeber's platoon, PFCs Charlie B. Powell and Harold T. Williams, were killed, and several men had been wounded.

At 1630 hours a soldier reported to Lieutenant Pursell that Staff Sergeant Sachse and seven other troopers had been wounded by an artillery shell. Pursell and his platoon medic, PFC Roger E. Chapin, found the wounded men, but Chapin was almost immediately hit by machine-gun fire, making a total of eight wounded. Pursell arranged their evacuation and pulled his outpost in the orchard back to the edge of the woods.

When Thomas requested more reinforcements, Cook sent two squads out with 2nd Lt. Robert E. Rogers, 1st Platoon, I Company, to reinforce Lieutenants Karnap and Pursell. Sims's eight-man squad was added to Lieutenant Pursell's platoon, and Sgt. George E. Ham's nine-man squad was attached to Lieutenant Karnap's. Thomas ordered Pursell to send a runner to the G Company CP, where Lieutenant Hanna received the order to assume command at the Den Heuvel farm, and Pvt. David B. Cassetti arrived to guide him to the location at about 2300 hours: "Just me and the runner [Private Cassetti] went back to the position first. As we got there an artillery shell burst. We hit the ground and a chunk of shrapnel [...] took the whole damn top of his head off. I got up and said, 'Come on, let's go,' and then I realized he was dead. That is one of my close episodes."[360]

Harassing sniper and artillery fire continued to fall around Den Heuvel. At 2400 hours Lieutenant Hanna called for artillery fire on a spot where he thought a large number of enemy troops were concentrating in preparation for an attack. At 0130 hours, as he returned from inspecting H Company positions, 1st Lt. William H. Preston was killed by friendly fire. According to a good friend of Preston's, 1st Lt. Virgil F. Carmichael, Preston was "a little hard of hearing."[361] He recalled an incident between Preston and an inexperienced replacement who had joined H Company in England. The replacement, on guard duty, challenged Preston as he went into his own command post. He "vigorously swore to us that he challenged Preston three times [... but] we always doubted that the man said much more than 'Halt!' Anyway, he emptied a clip of submachine-gun ammunition into Preston. Nothing was ever done about the incident other than the fact that he was sent on patrol for several straight nights. He developed into an excellent soldier and performed good service throughout the rest of the campaign."[362]

Captain Kappel appointed Sims to succeed Lieutenant Preston as executive officer. A veteran of all the 504th campaigns, Sims had twice been acting company commander. The task of leading the 1st Platoon now fell to 2nd Lt. Joseph F. Forestal, Jr., formerly Sims's assistant platoon leader. In the 2nd Platoon, 1st Lt. Richard G. La Riviere remained in command. Only the 3rd Platoon of H Company still retained two officers, 2nd Lieutenants Megellas and Murphy.

At 0600 hours G Company captured a German deserter, who was sent back to battalion headquarters. Five troopers dispatched to Vossendaal at 0745 hours to check the woods returned without spotting any Germans. At 0925 hours Lieutenant Carmichael informed Captain Gorham, the Regimental S-2, that the G Company prisoner, who had walked down from Cleve, had seen six Mark IV tanks in the village of Kranenburg, beyond the border town of Wyler, and spotted heavy guns north of the church tower.

Following an artillery barrage on the east side of Den Heuvel, G Company made a limited attack, taking three prisoners. Messages came in from Dutch civilians reporting the presence of 50 tanks in the German town of Zyfflich. Major Cook reorganized the force, ordering Captain Burriss to move the remainder of I Company into the line and relieve G Company at Den Heuvel. The withdrawal of G Company troops enabled Captain Thomas to send 1st Lt. Lory G. McCullough's entire 1st Platoon to outpost three farmhouses north of Den Heuvel and place anti-tank mines on the road, preventing a German flanking attack from the north. These movements were completed at 1100 hours.

Burriss had a total of 85 men at his disposal, including an attachment of 15 machine-gunners from Headquarters Company. Entering the woods "carefully and quietly," they nevertheless immediately "heard the boom of the artillery and the whistle of shells. The treetops burst into flames all around us and the ground shook like an earthquake. From midnight until 0500, the Germans poured in the damnedest artillery barrage I had ever witnessed. An artillery barrage in the woods is deadly. As the shells hit the treetops and burst, they scatter a shower of shrapnel in every direction."[363]

Early that evening artillery also rained down on the 1st Battalion sector. Sergeant Clark of A Company was hit by numerous shrapnel pieces, putting an end to his fighting days: "Headquarters Company, 1st Battalion, had a heavy machine-gun section stationed with us. We had fired on a German mortar about 2,000 yards from our location, but it was out of our range, and we were unable to get artillery fire on it. Sgt. Vernon R. Sult, who was in charge of the machine guns, and I were checking our positions for the night when that mortar threw a barrage in on us. Sult and I were talking when the first round came, and after it hit I said something to him and got no answer. He was just behind my right shoulder and when I turned, he was not there. The last round of about ten rounds got me.

"When I heard it coming I hit the ground face down, with my arms stretched out in front of me. I saw the shell come through the trees and hit about 25 or 30 feet away. After it exploded I saw debris go flying through the air and thought, 'here is the end of me.' When it started falling I could feel it hitting me; I looked around and thought, 'I don't feel dead.' Then something hit my left arm that felt like someone had hit me with a sledgehammer.

"Then it hit me that I was still feeling things! I figured I was still alive, so

I crawled into a foxhole on top of two of my men. They asked what was wrong, and I replied, 'The bastard got me.' One piece of shrapnel had gone straight through my left arm. I've still got a little piece in my right arm and that one bled more than the left. When I started to crawl out, I put my weight on my left arm and got a face full of sand because there wasn't anything here. The arm was broken between the shoulder and the elbow. I got back to the foxhole and John Isom and Andy Starling cut my sleeve off and bandaged my arm.

"That was the end of my fighting days. When I walked back to the Company CP, probably half a mile, I found Captain Duncan on the phone with Starling. It was completely dark by then so I said there was no use trying to fire on the position, even though they knew where it was, because they couldn't tell where the shells were landing. The captain then got on the phone with Regiment and told them what had happened.

"When he finished, he said, 'I'm sorry you had to get it, but they have promised me air strikes on the position tomorrow.' Then the company called for something to pick me up and they sent a jeep out from Regiment. There were two trails between us and the Battalion CP and I decided to walk. I don't remember who was with me, but we took one trail and the jeep came up the other, and just as we got to the battalion area the jeep came in behind us. I walked about a mile or better with my left hand tucked into my belt, and at almost every step I could feel those broken bones rub together. I don't know how far we walked that night, but it seemed like a couple of miles.

"When I entered headquarters, the first person I met was Sgt. Milton Knight, who was a very good friend. I asked the whereabouts of Captain [Charles] Zirkle, the battalion surgeon, and a voice said, 'Right here.' So I went around the corner with a big grin on my face and said, 'Well Doc, I feel real goldbricken this time.' He removed my sleeve and put a bandage on my arm. He looked at me and shook his head. He knew I was through, too. [...] It was about 1900 hours when I was hit, and by 2300 hours I was lying on an operating table in a Dutch hospital which our people used a part of. I can still see those stainless steel overhead lighting fixtures.

"As I was going out, I asked what time it was. A nurse answered, '0120' and I wondered what an American nurse was doing 63 miles behind established front lines. I woke up the next morning on a litter in the hall of the hospital. I was in a cast from waist to neck, and my left arm was across my chest with just my fingertips sticking out of the cast. The plaster had dried that night and my arm felt just like ice.

"Those of us that had come in the day before [... were] loaded in ambulances and headed out to the south. The road was cut by artillery fire and we were held up […] four or five times. We did make it to Brussels late that afternoon and spent the night in a British hospital. The treatment was very good for what little they did, but every half hour like clockwork, someone came around and wanted my life history, so I got very little sleep. The next day I was loaded in a Canadian C-47 with quite a few other litter cases and flown back to England. By five o'clock I was in the hospital in Burford, about 50 miles from Oxford. I was wounded on September 27 and I […] was in the first bunch evacuated. I was in traction for 27 days, as my arm was broken on an angle."[364]

Capt. Wade McIntyre, the Regimental Special Services officer, was also wounded by artillery shell fragments. Recuperating in the 97th General Hospital in England, he wrote a letter describing the seizure of Berg en Dal: "I climbed a little hill right on the border to spot the German guns. I had a good view of Nazi territory, but they also had a good view of me. The shell landed very close and knocked me back into Holland. When I realized what had happened, I got up and staggered back about 200 yards to a small shell hole for cover. My aide [1st Lt. Fred W. Vance] had been knocked into the air and thrown back about 35 feet, but didn't receive any shrapnel wounds. I called to him and he came over. Later, medics took me to the aid station, where I was operated on. I was taken to hospitals in Brussels and later flown by plane to England."[365] Lieutenant Vance assumed Captain McIntyre's duties as Regimental Services Officer. In one week of combat, Tucker had lost several junior officers. Little could he know that this number would double over the next week.

CHAPTER 16

BATTLE ALONG THE WYLERBAAN
HOLLAND AND GERMANY,
SEPTEMBER 28–OCTOBER 2, 1944

On September 21, Ultra, the British signals intelligence service, intercepted and decrypted a vital German radio message at Bletchley Park: Adolf Hitler had personally ordered the transfer of the XII SS-Korps Headquarters from the Eastern Front to Army Group B on September 20. *Generalfeldmarschall* Walther Model transferred command of the 180th and 190th Infantry Divisions, brought up from other locations in Germany, to the new headquarters.[366]

Five days later another message indicated reorganization within Army Group B. All German units west of the Allied corridor from the Dutch-Belgian border to the Island were placed under the command of the Fifteenth Army; to the east, the II SS-Panzer Korps, II Fallschirmjäger Korps, LXXXVI Korps, Korps Feldt and XII SS-Korps were subject to the First Fallschirmjäger Army of *Oberstgeneral* Kurt Student.[367] Plans were laid for quick action to restore German superiority in Holland. Student and Model envisaged a simultaneous attack on Nijmegen from three points—Wageningen, Arnhem and Cleve—to drive the Allies back south of the Maas River at Grave. The Germans believed the recapture of the Island and Nijmegen was the key to halting the advance of Allied operations toward Arnhem. Set to begin in the early hours of September 28, the operation received no name as a precaution against leaks to Allied intelligence.

Due to transport problems, German bombing and a strike by Dutch railway workers, the 363rd Volksgrenadier Division that had been allotted to XII SS-Korps in Wageningen arrived from Denmark a day late. Likewise, the rail transfer of the 9th and 116th Panzer Divisions from the Aachen front

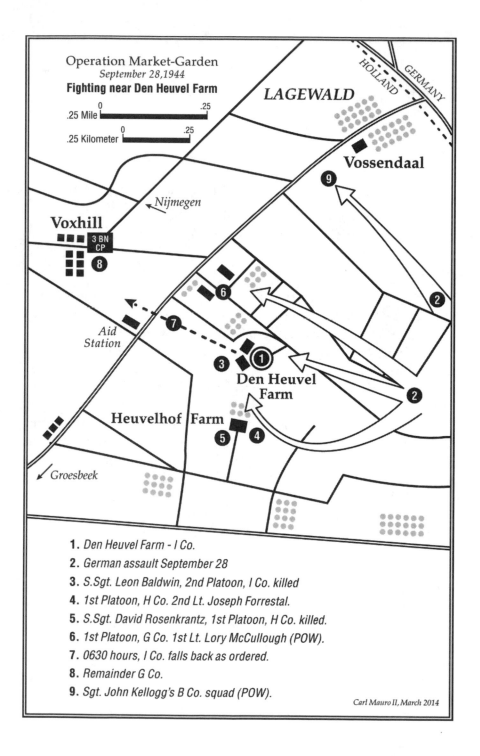

Operation Market-Garden
September 28, 1944
Fighting near Den Heuvel Farm

.25 Mile
0   .25

.25 Kilometer
0   .25

HOLLAND

GERMANY

LAGEWALD

Vossendaal

←Nijmegen

Voxhill

3 BN CP

Aid Station

Den Heuvel Farm

Heuvelhof Farm

↙ Groesbeek

1. *Den Heuvel Farm - I Co.*
2. *German assault September 28*
3. *S.Sgt. Leon Baldwin, 2nd Platoon, I Co. killed*
4. *1st Platoon, H Co. 2nd Lt. Joseph Forrestal.*
5. *S.Sgt. David Rosenkrantz, 1st Platoon, H Co. killed.*
6. *1st Platoon, G Co. 1st Lt. Lory McCullough (POW).*
7. *0630 hours, I Co. falls back as ordered.*
8. *Remainder G Co.*
9. *Sgt. John Kellogg's B Co. squad (POW).*

Carl Mauro II, March 2014

to Arnhem took much longer than anticipated. Thus the attack of II SS-Panzer Korps from Arnhem was also set back to October 1. This made the II Fallschirmjäger Korps the only army component ready to attack on September 28. At the time, this comprised the 180th and 190th Infantry Divisions; Panzer Brigade 108; Panzerjäger Abteilung 741, equipped with 45 Jagdpanzer tanks and 38 tank destroyers; Fallschirm Artillerie Regiment 4; a battle group from the 1st SS-Panzer Division; and various smaller artillery and guards battalions.

Previously unaware of German plans, Tucker's troopers were alerted on the night of September 27–28. At 0445 hours the enemy launched a terrific artillery barrage from the Den Heuvel farm that soon extended to the entire Wylerbaan. This preceded an attack on the 504th between Erlekom in the north and Groesbeek on the far right flank of the regimental sector. Cpl. David S. Stanford and Pvt. Darrell D. Grooms of I Company received a direct hit by a large-caliber shell. "I was in a foxhole next to Corporal Stanford when our position was overrun," remembered Pvt. James J. Wallace. "He was in the foxhole with Private Grooms. When I withdrew I saw Corporal Stanford slumped forward, and could not tell if he was wounded, dead or alive."[368] Pvt. William Hahn and T/Sgt. Lewis Spalding spotted Stanford running over to Grooms as the barrage started, and observed the direct hit on the foxhole. Both occupants were covered in blood and obviously dead. Stanford's body was never recovered.

"During the barrage," recalled Captain Burriss, "Sgt. Robert [G.] Dew, who was in the trench with me, received a shrapnel wound to the chest, and Lieutenant Blankenship suffered a concussion. Dew, a huge, quiet man, lay gasping beside me. He was in a bad way. Two medics, one carrying a stretcher, came running toward us. 'Put the sergeant on your stretcher and get him out of here!' I yelled, knowing he couldn't last much longer without medical care. They nodded, slid into the trench, and expertly rolled him onto the stretcher. Just as they lifted him out and started to move between the trees, a burst of 20mm fire from one of the tanks ripped through the middle of the stretcher and killed Sergeant Dew instantly."[369]

Supported by at least three tanks, German infantry overran I Company's outpost line at the Den Heuvel farm. PFC Robert Hedberg was captured and made to carry badly wounded PFC David L. Gautney under the trained weapon of a German guard. As they were crossing a field, the German suddenly pointed at Gautney. *Kaputt! Kaputt!* he shouted, meaning Gautney was dead. Forced to leave him behind in the field, Hedberg was taken to a village, where "quite a few others were gathered," including Corporal Tison.[370]

According to his burial file, Private First Class Gautney died that day in the nearby hospital of Bedburg-Hau. Cpl. Ralph Tison recalled the scene at dawn on September 28: "The Krauts had moved in with many tanks and large artillery. You can say they pounded the hell out of us. When the shells hit the top of the trees they exploded and the chunks of lead came straight down, so our holes were not much protection. The corner of the house was about 50 yards from my hole. The German troops kept trying to come around the corner. We were doing all right with that. Some of them got around, but didn't get back.

"Then they decided to fire artillery into the top of the trees. When the shells hit in the top, it threw the shrapnel straight up, sideways and down. The down did us in. One piece hit the machine gun and the concussion knocked my assistant [Pvt. Valentino M. Cortez] and me out. Coming to and looking up, I saw several kids in uniform who looked as though they were twelve- or thirteen-years-old. I guess I should have said 'Hello, comrades.' There was no place to go.

"As I was climbing out of the nest, I saw Staff Sergeant Baldwin firing from behind a tree with an M-1 rifle. He would then fall back to another tree to unload and reload his gun. This happened several times. I do not know how many Krauts went down, as I wasn't counting. Soon a tank came up and got him with its machine gun. I remember talking with the sergeant a few days before. He had received word that a brother of his had been killed in combat. From the accounts I've read, I think the sergeant should get the highest citation, but I guess under the circumstances I was the only one alive who witnessed his actions.

"We were then taken to a barn-like building that may have been a mile away from the farmhouse. After questions and answers for an hour the German interpreter told me I was stupid and didn't know anything. I knew there was no such thing as a corporal or private who wasn't stupid. If they had any intelligence at all, they would have stayed home and let the officers and top enlisted grades fight the stupid war!

"After this we were trucked further back, possibly a five-hour ride. Then we went into a building, I suppose to wait for the next day's train ride, and spent the night on a concrete floor. In the darkness I saw a figure easing his way toward me. It turned out to be Private Cortez, a Mexican-American who had joined us in England. He had a guitar and every break we had he was plucking on that thing. He told me he did not like the Krauts or the place we were in, and I wasn't overenthused either. He wanted us to escape, but I told him I had looked, and with all the guards and dogs out there we wouldn't stand a chance. It was all I could do to hold him back, as I was still woozy from the blast I'd received before we were captured."[371]

Captured in the same attack were Pvt. Stanley E. Christofferson, the 3rd Platoon medic; PFCs Albert R. Essig and Emil J. Mierzwa; and Pvts. Robert C. Colman, William P. Mink, Charles W. Pearce and George C. Roberson. Also captured were attached personnel from Headquarters Company, 3rd Battalion: Cpls. Charles Brown and Clifford E. Dennis, PFC Vance E. Garwood and Pvt. Talbot P. Shelby.

At one point Captain Burriss saw PFC Norman Heiden fire his bazooka at a Tiger tank "and watched the shell bounce off the armor like a tennis ball. The tank continued forward and ran over him."[372] He contacted Major Cook around 0630 hours and received permission to withdraw to the Wylerbaan. Cook recalled two decades later that "my figures for crossing the Waal River were 132 or 134 casualties (killed, wounded or missing). Therefore my Battalion was [the] smallest of the three battalions in the 504th. Ridgway would not send replacements in hopes of getting us relieved and back under his control. The British felt replacements were an American problem. If we wanted to fight at reduced strength there, that was our problem but a battalion was a battalion and it would be given battalion missions. Gavin ordered the Den Heuvel woods reconnoitered and wanted it manned by OPLR [Outpost Line of Resistance]."

Major Cook continues in telegraphic style: "The woods were deceiving—we started out with a platoon and wound up with my reserve company trying to occupy—really needed a battalion. Tucker had bet there weren't seven men in [those] woods: I still have the $5.00. Ordered first prisoners (19) marched into [the] Regimental CP. One G Company platoon was captured while asleep.[373] Gavin and Tucker's effort to take [the] woods authorized me to commit [my] reserve company but I had to keep getting permission to commit troops. I personally was against this affair but I also disliked the piecemeal method of handling it.

"On the night of [the] 27th I was so worn-out that when Tucker visited me I acted so stupidly (so he says) he turned on his heel and walked out. I sat down in a chair and woke up the next morning on a mattress. I don't remember them laying me out or anything. I woke up to the barrage on the morning of the 28th and soon authorized the withdrawal.

"Two Air Corps base ammo officers who had been in England since

1942 [...] just couldn't believe all these bombs were being dumped [...] so they got a three-day pass or something and hitched a ride on a C-47. They wanted to see action so they were directed to Holland to the 82nd Airborne Division. The supply people there suggested the 504th. The 504th suggested the 3rd Battalion. [...]

"I sent them into the woods with I Company and one got wounded slightly and they both came out with I Company. They stopped to thank me and assured me they were heading directly back to the US. They had seen enough. [...] Little did they realize that they had been enduring one of the hardest poundings [...] the 504th had ever been subjected to. Naturally we didn't want to discourage them in their admiration for our hardiness, so we didn't bother to enlighten them. They did assure us that although they had enjoyed the experience, their desires for adventure were fully satisfied, and if it was left up to them they would cheerfully sit out the rest of the war in England.

"We never knew whether or not the wounded one got a Purple Heart, but we often felt sorry for those two fellows trying to tell their stories to the boys back at their United Kingdom base. I'll bet they were the 'unchallenged champion liars' for simply telling the truth. Who in hell would believe them?"[374]

Captain Burriss bumped into these two air corps officers as he was moving to the Wylerbaan, the main line of resistance. "The lieutenant had caught a piece of shrapnel during the night, and the glassy-eyed captain was helping him hobble along. I stopped them a few yards from one of our 57mm anti-tank guns. As I was about to say something, the gun boomed, sending several rounds at a Tiger tank coming out of the Den Heuvel woods. The shells missed. The Tiger tank spouted flame, and it didn't miss. The 57mm gun was turned into a steel pretzel, and the three-man crew was killed instantly. [...]

"As we approached the aid station, a mortar shell went through the roof and exploded. I rushed inside and found Lt. Charles ('Charlie') Snyder, one of my [former] platoon leaders, lying unconscious on the floor. I knelt down, lifted his head into my lap, and said, 'You're going to be OK, Charlie.' He let out a groan and that was his last breath. He was killed not by shrapnel but by the concussion. That was a hard one for me to take. Charlie was one of my best friends."[375]

Staff Sergeant Baldwin was posthumously awarded the Silver Star: "At dawn an estimated battalion of enemy infantry supported by tanks and under the protective cover of a heavy artillery barrage made a determined attack upon the company position. Staff Sergeant Baldwin saw an enemy infantry-man kill one of his machine-gunners about 20 yards to his left flank and crawl into the foxhole behind the gun. Without hesitation and completely unmindful of his own safety, Staff Sergeant Baldwin leaped from his own foxhole, charged across the open ground in full view of the advancing enemy, and bayoneted the German. He then threw the dead German aside and turned the gun on the enemy. Remaining exposed to the full concentration of enemy fire, he caused innumerable casualties in the enemy ranks by his fearless and skillful operation of the gun.

"Seeing the untenable situation the company was in, the company commander gave the order to move to the main line of resistance. Staff Sergeant Baldwin took charge of 45 enemy prisoners and started to evacuate them. Suddenly, an enemy tank bore down on them and drove between Staff Sergeant Baldwin and his prisoners, thus cutting him off from all possibility of withdrawing. As a result of this action Staff Sergeant Baldwin has been missing in action. The cool courage of Staff Sergeant Baldwin, exhibited in the face of great personal danger, and his unselfish willingness to sacrifice himself in the aid of his comrades will long inspire the remainder of his company who witnessed his actions. His unswerving devotion to duty reflects the highest credit upon his military training."[376]

The War Department did not always reveal the complete circumstances of a soldier's death to his relatives. First Lieutenant William D. Mandle, the Regimental Demolition Platoon leader, repeatedly received questions concerning conflicting reports about the death of Cpl. Leonard W. Beaty of I Company: "He was with a group trapped in the Den Heuvel woods—I know because I was there. When the rest of us were forced out, a few had to be left. He was one of those, and his chances of being taken prisoner were good; we definitely know that some of that group was taken."[377]

Also killed or mortally wounded were Sgt. Alexander L. Barker; PFCs Garland E. Cooper, Norman H. Heiden and Solon W. Whitmire, Jr.; and Pvts. Dennis Collins, Harold R. Jacoby, Andrew T. Swift and Victor J. Willson, Jr. From the attached Headquarters Company, Pvts. Cornelius E. Curry and Gerald W. Kight, a machine-gunner, were also killed. Total casualties for the fighting around the Den Heuvel farm on September 28 totaled 14 captured and one officer and 16 other ranks KIA or DOW. Private First Class Gautney is counted twice in these numbers. Strangely, the date for all the above casualties is erroneously recorded as September 27.[378]

"My platoon was dug-in behind an embankment just to the right of I

Company when the attack started," recalled Lieutenant Megellas. "The enemy opened with a heavy artillery barrage; then German infantry, supported by tanks, came charging out of a wooded area heading straight for us. [...] When they came within range, we opened fire while their artillery was still pounding our positions and shells were impacting all around us. Occasionally a shell would hit a tree and burst, sending shrapnel down on men in the foxholes."[379]

One of Megellas's men, PFC James Musa, received shrapnel wounds in his right leg, which started to bleed profusely. As there was no medic nearby, Megellas decided to take Musa to the aid station himself, leaving 2nd Lt. Ernest P. Murphy as acting platoon leader. Megellas delivered Musa, then made a beeline back to his platoon, his parka covered in blood. Captain Kappel recommended him for the Bronze Star, but it was turned down by Colonel Williams, who handled most such requests. Williams agreed the action had been heroic, but thought Lieutenant Megellas's place was with his platoon, not at the aid station.[380]

To the east, south of the Den Heuvel farm, Lt. Joseph Forestal's 1st Platoon became surrounded as the German attack progressed towards the Wylerbaan. The platoon was dug-in around the farmhouse, where Lieutenant Forestal had set up his CP. S.Sgt. David Rosenkrantz, his platoon sergeant, effectively executed command because Forestal had just been transferred-in the previous day, and hardly knew his men. Having suffered casualties during the flight and Waal River Crossing, the platoon was understrength, functioning with about 20 enlisted men and a very few non-commissioned officers.

A German tank hit the barn behind machine-gunner Pvt. Lawrence Dunlop, setting it on fire: "The lieutenant was frantically cranking on the field phone, but I was certain lines were cut or blown up. By now artillery was firing at the Germans and driving them back, along with troopers from G and I Company. I remember Finkbeiner saying, 'We'll try to get back to our own lines when it gets dark.'

"Just around four o'clock, I decided to try and get back to our lines. I crouched down low and started out [on] the path that we had originally come from the night before. I hadn't gone 100 yards and there staring at me 50 feet in front of me were two big Germans. I turned around and was gone in a flash before the two Germans could move. I made it back to the house and took cover, looking in the direction of the Germans."[381]

Suddenly Staff Sergeant Rosenkrantz ran past Dunlop. Rosenkrantz crouched behind a tree about 15 yards from one of his squad leaders, Sergeant

Finkbeiner. Unaware that they were already surrounded, Rosenkrantz stood up to shoot at Germans some distance east of him. Finkbeiner shouted a warning: "Rosy! Rosy! Get down!" Almost simultaneously, Dunlop cried out a similar warning, but Rosenkrantz seemed not to hear him. "I heard the burp of a German Schmeisser machine pistol that got Rosie 50 feet in front of me. I could see him when he went down and I was pretty sure he was killed. If I tried to get anywhere near him I would be a goner too."[382] Staff Sergeant Rosenkrantz was killed near a tree in front of the house, but apart from his dog tags no remains were ever recovered. Pvt. John J. Baldassar was also killed. Sergeant Finkbeiner, now in command as platoon sergeant, led the remnants of the platoon back to the H Company area after dark.

The 1st Platoon of G Company, positioned in front of three houses north of Den Heuvel facing the Germans, was not so fortunate. Sgt. Clarence A. Heatwole, the 23-year-old 1st Squad leader, saw the enemy crossing the fields towards his position in front of a farmhouse. Heatwole, from Oklahoma, had been an EGB 448 replacement to G Company. His platoon sergeant, S.Sgt. (Charles) Reese Dickerson, and his platoon leader, Lieutenant McCullough, were close by. Twenty-four-year-old McCullough had been in command of the 1st Platoon since he had joined the company at Anzio as a replacement officer. To Heatwole's knowledge they had no radio, although they were way out in front of G Company.[383]

Platoon headquarters, Heatwole's squad and the mortar squad of Sgt. Stephen A. Douglass were overrun by the German assault and all captured. Lieutenant McCullough tried to hide in the house, but the Germans threw in a grenade, burning the farmwife's face.[384] Not wanting to put civilians at risk, McCullough gave himself up. Captured with him were Douglass, Heatwole, and Dickerson; Cpls. Charles L. Gallagher and Charles R. Mercer; PFCs Jack K. Kincaid, John T. McKay, Ernesto M. Puntorno, Carl N. Ramberg and Fred L. Schilling; and Pvts. Orlan H. Manning, Vincent R. Marrone and Michael Wagner.

The prisoners were loaded on trucks and driven to Düsseldorf where they were interrogated before they were split up. Lieutenant McCullough was taken to Oflag 64, where he met many other wounded 504th officers. "All the non-commissioned officers were sent to Stalag IIIC at Kustrin on the Oder River," recalled Heatwole. "We were liberated when the Russians arrived in January 1945. A long march started back to the Russian rear. Eventually we made it to Odessa where we boarded a ship to Port Said. From there we went home."[385]

Positioned just a few hundred yards north of the G Company platoon was a ten-man rifle squad from 2nd Platoon, B Company, led by Sgt. John W. Kellogg. Kellogg was busy making coffee in a barn next to a farmhouse, where he and his men had gathered not far from the field where they were dug-in, when he suddenly heard Germans shouting outside. Ordered to check what was happening, PFC Henry Horn, who spoke German, went outside and discovered the Germans had surrounded them and were demanding their surrender.

Horn reported to Kellogg that the Germans wanted them to come out and surrender. "First we have this cup of coffee," Kellogg replied. The words were barely out of his mouth before a panzerfaust fired at the barn, blowing a big hole in one of the walls. Kellogg and his men came out of the smoke-filled barn and were captured.[386] Besides Kellogg and Horn, the group included T/5 Gerald P. Ground, PFCs James E. McManus and Scott R. Rienschild and Pvts. Eugene W. Dickson, Michael Dziezgowski, Charles B. Morris and Joseph A. Sims. PFC Hubert A. Wolfe and Pvt. Francis B. Fallon, the only two men from the squad who were not in the barn, found it a strange to be the only ones left. PFC Ronald P. Ellis of Headquarters Company, 1st Battalion, was also captured making, in all, one officer and 38 other ranks captured in the counterattack. The 2nd Platoon, B Company rifle squad was rebuilt with replacements over the following weeks.

To the rear of Lieutenant McCullough's unfortunate platoon, the remainder of G Company became involved in the fighting. Paratroopers fell back to their lines and automatic weapons and artillery blasted off. Captain Thomas, McCullough's company commander, recalled that "the Jerries began a very heavy artillery and mortar fire" at 0500 hours, which further increased about 0630, when "they began an attack reinforced by tanks. They pushed through Company I and drove them back. Two British tanks came down to the road opposite our Company CP and shelled the woods directly to their front."

When 88mm shells began dropping in the CP area, the CP was moved about 100 yards to the right. Around 2000 hours, Company G received word that it was would be relieved by Company E, 508 PIR. "At 2130 hours the company was relieved and marched back to a bivouac area where the cooks from the rear-echelon seaborne group served coffee. The men pitched pup tents and slept."[387]

Up through September 27, Luftwaffe attacks on the railroad and road bridges across the Waal had been unsuccessful. After reconnaissance by two frogmen, it was decided that *Oberleutnant* Richard Prinzhorn's Marine Einsatz Kommando 65 would undertake a mission at 0400 hours on September 29. Bearing torpedo mines, Prinzhorn and his 11-man team swam to the road bridge, where they split up. Four men swam on and successfully blew up the middle section of the railroad bridge, but the other eight were able to detonate only half of their explosives under the road bridge, blowing a gap of about 80 feet in the deck. Ten frogmen, including *Oberleutnant* Prinzhorn, were captured later that night.

While the British troops in and around Nijmegen were well supplied, the 504th RCT constantly lacked for food, gasoline and other items. Two 3rd Battalion members, 1st Sgt. Curtis Odom of I Company and Sgt. Donald Zimmerman of H Company, went scrounging for supplies with a "liberated" car they had discovered in a garage in Lent. "We used it for nearly a week," Zimmerman recalled. "Odom would haul supplies, transport wounded on makeshift stretchers to the hospital in Nijmegen and deliver prisoners to the stockade area. He would talk to the British drivers to draw away their attention as I stole their jerry cans of gasoline, and that kept us supplied."[388]

On September 28 the two men heard the explosion at the railroad bridge and learned their battalion had been counterattacked. Feeling they were needed by their own, and that they had sufficiently recuperated from their shrapnel wounds, they returned to their respective units in the 3rd Battalion bivouac area located in the Dekkerswald Forest, just behind the Division CP. Zimmerman was dealt a blow when he learned of Staff Sergeant Rosenkrantz's death, and that Baldassar had been killed and Moecia was missing.

On September 29, G Company "did not wake up until about 0900 hours and then had breakfast prepared for them by the cooks. Our duffel bags were brought to us and we were able to acquire clean clothes and then we were shuttled into Nijmegen to get hot showers. Upon return, the men dug in and lay around resting the rest of the day. That night the company sent out contact patrols."[389]

That morning the remnants of Lieutenant McCullough's missing 1st Platoon of showed up, led by 2nd Lt. James Pursell. Sixteen troopers were all that remained of the platoon. Later that day 2nd Lieutenant Forestal got in trouble for joy-riding in Gavin's jeep. In Lieutenant Mandle's version of the story, the men discovered an unattended jeep, which was against the general's orders. "So we took it and cruised into Nijmegen. Along the way everyone was madly saluting us. After a jaunt in Nijmegen, we noticed the front end of the jeep had two stars on it. We had the general's jeep! Very carefully we drove out of the city, back to the regiment and 'lost' the jeep in the front lines. It took the general about three minutes to discover who had taken it. Because he had ordered no one to leave their jeep unattended, we were 'free' to go. But every patrol thereafter Joe took. I was in demolition and over the next week, behind enemy lines, we set 2,200 booby traps! Which proves it doesn't pay to goof off in the wartime army!"[390]

Sergeant Zimmerman told a different version of the story: "Lieutenant Forestal and I had each filled a clean gasoline can with wine in Nijmegen and carried it back. At the time, we were billeted in pup tents behind division headquarters. On the way back Lieutenant Forestal said, 'I'm tired.' 'So am I,' I replied. When we saw a couple of jeeps, Forestal said, 'Get in,' so we dumped our cans in and drove away. When we pulled into our quarters, there stood Captain Kappel with an angry look on his face. 'What the hell have you done?' he asked. 'We didn't do anything wrong,' Lieutenant Forestal answered. Kappel said, 'Do you know whose jeep that is?' We just shrugged our shoulders so he said, 'Turn around and look at the front.' There were two white stars. I drove it back and parked it and then walked back to camp."[391]

On the evening of September 30, Lieutenant Megellas received the unpleasant task of taking out a combat patrol to catch prisoners and find out what the Germans were up to. This came close to a suicide mission, as the Germans had massed a large number of troops in the area. Late that evening, Megellas led his 24-man platoon across the footbridge over the Wyler Meer, a small lake northeast of the Vossendaal farm where the squad from B Company had been captured. The patrol captured six Germans. One of the paratroopers, Sgt. John M. Fowler III, was wounded and later awarded the Silver Star, and Megellas received the Distinguished Service Cross "for extraordinary heroism in connection with military operations against an armed enemy as a Platoon Leader, Company H, 504th PIR, on September 30, 1944, in Holland. First Lieutenant Megellas led his platoon on a combat patrol to secure information and prisoners. Arriving at the enemy observation post, he crawled forward alone and killed two outpost guards and the crew of a machine-gun nest. He brought forward his patrol, attacked the main enemy defenses and single-handedly secured three prisoners and killed two more. Two blockhouses were then attacked and destroyed. The aggressiveness of this patrol action thoroughly demoralized the enemy in the sector.

"His mission completed, First Lieutenant Megellas withdrew his platoon through the enemy lines and under mortar fire. He personally carried a wounded man while firing his Thompson submachine gun with one hand.

Right: Maas Waal Canal near Bridge Number 7 at Heumen, September 1945. *Courtesy: Mandle family*

Below: Pvt. William Lanseadel of D Company (killed during the Battle of the Bulge) with children of the Langewouters family at Arnoud van Gelderweg 41 in Grave, September 18, 1944. Backrow: Gerrie, Mies, Els, Pvt. Lanseadel and Janneke. Front row: Frans and Loeki. *Courtesy: Graafs Museum/Jan Timmersmans*

Aerial view of the small harbor, PGEM power station and a part of the
opposite shoreline. To the top left is the area where Pvt. Leonard Trimble
was rescued by the Pandurs resistance group. *Courtesy: Arjen Kuiken*

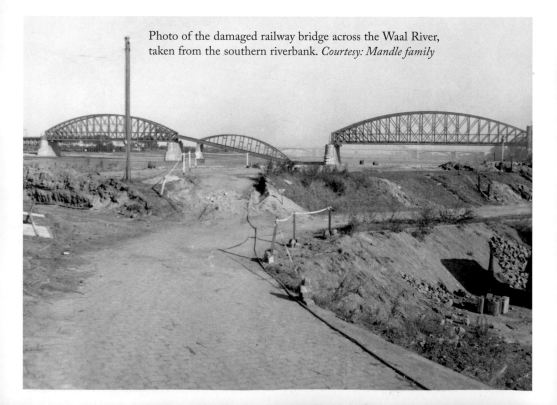

Photo of the damaged railway bridge across the Waal River,
taken from the southern riverbank. *Courtesy: Mandle family*

Highway Bridge at Nijmegen, September 1945. *Courtesy: Mandle family*

Knocked-out British tank in the Nijmegen area, September 1945. *Courtesy: Mandle family*

Lt. John Thompson of E Company captured the south end of the Maas Bridge at Grave on the first day of Operation Market Garden. He was known as the most handsome officer in the regiment. *Courtesy: Jeanne Thompson*

Pvt. Fay Steger of A Company befriended the orphan Jan van Deelen at Bridge Number 10 across the Maas Waal Canal. *Courtesy: Sue Krukonis and Mary Beth Wood*

Maj. Julian Cook smiling during a break on maneuvers in England. Cook earned respect from his entire battalion for his performance during the Waal River Crossing. *Courtesy: Roy Karnap*

Lt. Carl Mauro of E Company saved his platoon leader on the first day in Holland. He was severely wounded on October 3 as a German shell hit the E Company CP. *Courtesy: Carl Mauro II*

Lt. John Holabird of C Company, 307th Airborne Engineer Company, was the only officer who crossed with the first assault wave over the Waal River to aid in the removal of demolition charges on the bridges. *Courtesy: Carl Mauro II*

Lt. William Mandle of the Regimental Demolition Platoon accompanied the first assault wave across the Waal River. He later wrote the Regimental History in 1945 with PFC David Whittier. *Courtesy: Mandle family*

Col. Reuben H. Tucker III, regimental commander of the 504th Parachute Infantry Regiment from December 1942 to May 1946, photographed as a recently graduated West Point officer in 1935. *Courtesy: Tucker family*

Pvt. Robert Koelle, platoon medic in Lt. James Megellas' H Company platoon, was killed during the Waal River Crossing. *Courtesy Peggy Shelly*

Pvt. Walter Muszynksi of I Company earned a posthumously awarded Distinguished Service Cross for his action at the Lent viaduct on September 20, 1944. *Courtesy: Kathleen Muszynski*

Lt. Joseph Forrestal of H Company standing in front of the Heuvelhof Farm barn, September 27, 1944. *Courtesy: Ben Overhand*

Pvt. Stanley Christofferson served as a medic in I Company and tried to save the life of Pvt. Peter Colishion. *Courtesy: William Christofferson*

Right: Lt. William Preston of H Company was accidently shot by one of his own men while returning at night to the Company CP. *Courtesy: Ben Overhand*

Below: PFC Ted Bachenheimer photographed in jump school, summer 1942. Bachenheimer was a legendary scout who was captured and killed behind enemy lines while aiding the Dutch resistance. *Courtesy: Ethel Betry*

Above: Lt. Russell Busdicker of B Battery, 80th Airborne Anti-Aircraft Battalion, and his two 57mm gun crews were attached to the 2nd Battalion on September 18, 1944 and crossed the Waal River on British rafts. *Courtesy: Gregory Busdicker*

SS-Hauptsturmführer Karl-Heinz Euling of the 21st SS-Panzergrenadier Regiment was responsible for the defense of the south end of the Waal Bridge. According to him, the Waal River Crossing forced him to abandon his position. *Courtesy: Karl-Heinz Euling*

Captain Lord Peter Carrington (center) and his tank crew of the 2nd Grenadier Guards. *Courtesy: Lord Peter Carrington*

PFC Gerald Page Hereford, Jr. and his father just before Page shipped out to North Africa. He was killed while on his way to a church service on September 24, 1944. *Courtesy: Hereford family*

Medic Richard Bertolette, Capt. Edwin Kozak (Catholic chaplain), Capt. Robert Halloran (dentist) and TSgt. Eddie Migues in Beek, late September 1944. *Courtesy Ivan Roggen*

PFC John Isom and Sgt. Albert Clark of the Mortar Squad, 2nd Platoon, A Company, photographed in their Class A uniforms. Isom would be promoted to sergeant after Clark was wounded on September 27. *Courtesy: Kathleen Clark*

Maj. Gen. James Gavin (left) decorating the 504th Regimental Surgeon Maj. Ivan Roggen in July 1945. *Courtesy Ivan Roggen*

A wounded paratrooper of the 504th is loaded into an ambulance
for transport to a field hospital. *Courtesy: Mandle family*

Regimental Aid Post of the 504th Parachute Infantry Regiment,
September 1944. *Courtesy: Mandle family*

The Heuvelhof farmhouse where SSgt. David Rosenkrantz and
Pvt. John Baldassar of H Company were killed. *Courtesy: Mandle family*

View from Regimental Outpost at Berg en Dal overlooking the
area to the northeast, September 1944. *Courtesy: Mandle family*

Col. Reuben Tucker (left) visiting the Division Cemetery at Molenhoek, September 1945. *Courtesy: Mandle family*

Lt. Reneau Breard of A Company leading the 504th PIR Honor Guard across the Graaf Lodewijk Plein to the Waal Bridge during the first commemoration of the liberation of Nijmegen, September 1945. *Courtesy: Mandle family*

Maj. Gen. James Gavin presenting a plaque to mayor Charles Hustinx
of Nijmegen, September 1945. *Courtesy: Mandle family*

Capt. Delbert Kuehl (Protestant Chaplain) shaking hands with the departing
Lt. Roy Hanna of G Company, June 1945. *Courtesy: Moffatt Burriss*

K-house at Imthal. The position, used as an outpost, often switched sides between Germans and Americans. *Courtesy: Mandle family*

Pat Schilling in April 2013, on the place where his father, PFC Fred Schilling of G Company, was captured on September 28, 1944. *Courtesy: Author's Collection*

The extraordinary heroism and brilliant leadership displayed by First Lieutenant Megellas enabled his patrol to inflict disproportionate casualties on the enemy, secure vital information and force the Germans to abandon their planned offensive in the area."[392]

That evening behind the lines, Sergeant Zimmerman again ran into trouble: "I was walking with my rifle squad—only six of them were left—when we spotted a huge house with a round tower like a castle and the lights on the top floor all lit up. A tower like that would be visible to the enemy, so we hollered, 'Put the lights out!' No one paid attention, so I gave the order to fire and the seven of us shot the lights and windows out.

"When we got back to the H Company area, Captain Kappel said, 'I have a place for you guys for a while.' We were then posted to an outpost. It appeared that we had fired on the I Company CP. We didn't know it was a CP since no jeeps or anything indicated it as such. I was busted to private for ordering to shoot the lights out.

"We were in a sandbagged position overlooking a small valley. One night we saw a V-2 rocket go up, looking like it had been fired about 20 miles away. At night it was easy to see its trail. We reported this to company headquarters, and they connected us through to battalion headquarters, then through regimental and division headquarters all the way up to the British Second Army Headquarters. They asked us the distance and direction of the V-2 launch site. It kept us up all night pin-pointing the exact position with a map and our compasses. I finally got to sleep at 0300 or 0400 hours. The next morning we were woken up by hundreds of planes. They bombed the area we had pin-pointed. The sky was almost black with planes. It made us feel great: here we were, doughboys on an outpost, and we'd arranged a bombardment.

"Some three days later General Gavin and three officers carrying .45s on their hips came down from the woods. Gavin jumped into our enclosure and started looking through his field glasses out on the valley. I was right beside him, and pointed to where we had radioed in the bombardment. The Germans must have spotted him because all of a sudden they mortared us with some five or six shells. He dove in my foxhole and I dove on top of him. After a certain time, Gavin asked me, 'Are you ever going to get up?' 'As soon as it stops,' I answered. After the barrage he and the three other men took off again. It was quite a thrill to be first punished for shooting the lights out and then be up with the all the officers a few days later."[393]

This bombardment took place on the morning of October 2, when the Royal Air Force bombed Cleve, where not only a V-2 launch site, but also the headquarters of II Fallschirmjäger Korps were situated. Crossing flat, open terrain on his way from Erlekom to the Regimental CP at Berg en Dal, Capt. Adam A. Komosa witnessed British bombers flying "overhead to bomb the small town of Cleve in Germany. […] The bomber train extended as far as one could see, blackening the sky. As usual the planes were flying in no formation—just like gnats. It was an awe-inspiring sight. This was the first time that the British bombers came out into the open in broad daylight. In the past they had done their bombing solely at night.

"As I was looking up towards the approaching bombers, a German artillery shell swooshed by and exploded into orange smoke. I expected the British to release their bombs, thinking this was their target being marked by orange smoke. But thanks to the clear identity of their objective, Cleve, they continued without falling for the German trick.

"When the British released their tons of bombs upon hapless little Cleve, I noted a strange phenomenon. The tremendous explosions created such an atmospheric disturbance that I was able to see horizontal waves of air passing through the sky. I don't see how anyone could have survived that bombing. This was definitely a case of overkill."[394]

Pvt. Eldridge L. Hensley of H Company, who had disappeared on October 1, reported back to the 3rd Battalion CP the evening of October 11, stating he had been a German prisoner for ten days. That same day, 1st Lt. Charles Drew, 3rd Platoon, G Company, received the order to lead another combat patrol. The vicinity of Wyler Meer was again the area to be combed. Lieutenant Drew had a premonition that he was going to be killed, a prediction that almost came true. At 2115 hours his patrol was pinned down by machine-gun fire and five men were wounded. In addition to other wounds, Drew was hit in the head by a bullet that creased his skull and took off part of an ear. The seriousness of his wounds caused him to spend months in the hospital, but he never fully regained his original strength and stature.

At 0040 hours on October 2 approximately 12 German artillery rounds landed near the 3rd Battalion CP. A shell explosion killed PFC Alphonse L. Konietzko, who had served in Headquarters Company with Bonnie Roberts: "Alphonse Konietzko wasn't in my section, but he was a real good friend of one of my buddies in the section. That's how I got to know him. In the army you become a close-knit group. You get used to the people you work with all time."[395] During the night the 3rd Battalion sector was further struck by German artillery: by 0635 hours, a situation report revealed 20 casualties: four men were killed, including Cpl. John A. Zito and Pvt. James H. Walters, and T/4 Stanley S. Stencel was mortally wounded.

A few days after the German attack, PFC Dominic Moecia, inadvertently left behind at the Heuvelhof farm, managed to slip back to American lines: "I had dug a foxhole out in front of the farmhouse and was not aware of the order to pull back in the morning. I just didn't get the word. I looked up out of our foxhole and I didn't see anyone, they were all gone. Shortly after, the Germans retook the farmhouse. Several were next to my foxhole, and I could hear them talking, so I lay motionless in my hole with a piece of camouflage cloth over my head. They must have thought I was dead.

"I stayed in my foxhole all day, too frightened to move until dark when the Germans moved out. Several hours after darkness fell, I decided to try and make it back to our lines. I must have walked about a mile when I was stopped and challenged in English. I didn't know the countersign for the new password, so I responded with the one from the previous day, then shouted out, 'Don't shoot! I'm lost!' I was taken back to the unit's CP. I don't know what outfit it was, but it wasn't H Company. I stayed with them for several days before I could find the H Company CP."[396]

Capt. Walter Van Poyck (photographed here in 1947) and his
E Company dropped at Velp, southwest of the Maas Bridge.
Van Poyck lost a leg on October 3 when a German shell hit
the E Company CP at Erlekom. *Courtesy: Jan Timmermans*

CHAPTER 17

BATTLE AT ERLEKOM
HOLLAND AND GERMANY,
SEPTEMBER 28–OCTOBER 4, 1944

I n the town of Erlekom to the north, E Company was also rudely awakened by German artillery fire. Lt. Carl Mauro, 1st Platoon, recounts: "On Thursday morning, September 28, our lines were pounded by artillery and mortars about 0500. Such bombardment usually was followed by an enemy attack. E Company received artillery fire from self-propelled guns across the Waal River. A heavy barrage knocked out our telephone wires, as happened in most enemy barrages, and our linemen had to scurry out unprotected to patch the old or lay new lines; radios and walkie-talkies were always available for back-up."[397]

To the 1st Battalion's rear, Major Wellems in the 2nd Battalion CP was notified early of the German counterattack. "About 0500 on September 28, a lot of heavy artillery and mortar fire was received—mostly 88s. At 0600, the attached tanks reported having knocked out either an SP gun or a Mark IV on the right flank. At 0610 two tanks and infantry forced our roadblock at 788627. At 0615 the tanks were reported knocked out, one by one of our tanks, the other by a 57mm.

"At 0658, the tanks reported knocking out four [enemy] tanks, two near Company E on the left flank, and two near Company F in front of our right flank. Captain Van Poyck reported an estimated 200 or 300 infantrymen in front of his position, Company E on the left. Approximately 100 men were on the right flank facing Company F. These included pioneer troops equipped with flame throwers but did not get into action for they could not get close enough.

"The German infantry were pinned down in front of their positions, and it was a matter of pelting them with artillery, mortar and machine-gun fire. About 23 were captured and 200 killed or wounded. We found that we had knocked out eight tanks, four in front of each flank, and one armored car."[398]

On the right flank of the 2nd Platoon and to the left of F Company, the 1st Platoon men noticed the assault on the 3rd Platoon at Erlekom as well. Lieutenant Mauro thought "the enemy infantry advance was particularly heavy on E Company, hitting [1st Lt. John] 'Jocko' Thompson's 3rd Platoon head on. At this time Jocko was on my (the 1st Platoon's) left flank, 2nd Platoon with Lieutenant Sharp and F Company were on my right flank, and Captain Van Poyck's Company CP was right behind Thompson; battalion headquarters and the aid station were further back.

"The enemy action was very heavy, most of it on Jocko's platoon on my left and some thrown at F Company on my right, leaving me and the 1st Platoon with little to do except hold our position protecting the flanks of the troops on either side of us. Foxholes were our main and only shelter. [First Lieutenant Patrick C.] Collins was unobtrusive—I don't remember seeing him at all during this fracas.

"Jocko's undaunted men were very aggressive, quickly crawling forward to occupy their previously dug foxholes, which served as listening posts at night. They were doing what paratroopers believe is the best strategy: attack—if at all possible, from defensive positions.

"I saw the threat of a strong, concentrated enemy breakthrough aimed at the 3rd Platoon, so I went to Van Poyck's CP and asked him if we, 1st Platoon, should try to join what seemed to be a private battle. Jocko was there conferring with our company commander. Nearby Lieutenant Kline and company headquarters men were directing several heavy mortars on the encroaching enemy. Several British tanks assigned to us were sending shells into the attacking German ranks and their several tanks. We may have had some artillery behind us too. Jocko said he didn't need my help at that time—that holding my position was the best thing for his troopers. [...]

"I went to a small barn closeby. The worst of the attack was now over, after more than an hour's fighting—and the 3rd Platoon was doing the job with the support of the mortars and several stationary tanks. I believe four had been assigned to Van Poyck. From my position behind the barn, I could see a small enemy tank to our front, 75 yards away, that seemed bogged down right in the middle of where much of the action had been. [...]

"I went back to the Company CP just as a couple of medics struggled up to us carrying a stretcher, and laid a body on the ground, dead. The young, handsome, brave Cpl. Arthur S. Lewandowski—killed in action! One of Jocko's men. What can you do? You hold back the tears and quickly go on with your business. You can't help but think: will that happen to me? Am I next? Another E Company soldier was killed that day, PFC Kenneth S. Pinney. He lived a short time and died of wounds. [...]

"By late morning things quieted down. Several Germans who had advanced the farthest in the battlefield in front of the 3rd Platoon stood upright, dropped their weapons and raised their hands yelling something in German that I believe meant, 'I surrender.' Then some others behind them did the same thing, waving handkerchiefs as they advanced through our front line.

"Some of them became confused when Jocko kept yelling, 'Bring in your wounded!' and waving them back. Of course they didn't understand English. The Germans further back hadn't surrendered but when they saw their comrades in front of them going up—they ran towards the rear. I yelled. 'God, no! No!' because now they would be running targets for our men, and they did receive a volley or two of fire as they retreated out of sight. How many were killed or wounded by this maneuver we'll never know.

"Now the surrendering Germans were herded to the Company CP. We were surprised how young-looking most of them were. They were frightened, thinking about what we might do. What we did made me think again how stupid war is. We cared for them as we would our own men coming back for a respite. We immediately sought out the medics to treat the wounded. Our boys gave them small things from our rations such as chocolate and American cigarettes and they offered us theirs, and we told them we didn't want the watches and other personal belongings they were trying to give us, thinking this was the correct suppliant behavior."[399]

Captain Van Poyck recalled that some of the wounded German prisoners were suspicious about the morphine syrettes the American medics wanted to use: "Before we could dress their wounds or give them morphine, I had to convince their medical corporal that we weren't attempting to inject them with a poison. When they learned we were American paratroopers, they were convinced we would murder them. I spoke no German of any consequence, and the medical corporal conversed in French."[400]

E Company had fire support in the form of four 57mm anti-tank guns from the 1st Platoon, C Battery, 80th AA, commanded by 1st Lt. Marshall W. Stark. His After-Action Report for September 28 reads: "from 0440 until approximately 0550, a heavy artillery barrage was laid down on the MLR [Main Line of Resistance] of the 2nd Battalion of Cider (504). My platoon was attached to this battalion. Prior to the lifting of the barrage, just at first light, a German infantry attack supported by several armored vehicles, mostly Mark III and Mark IV tanks, was launched."[401]

PFC Raymond E. Fary, a 19-year-old baseball pitcher from Indiana, was in a 57mm anti-tank gun crew in Stark's 1st Platoon, Battery C. His gun and one other were part of the 1st Gun Section on the Kerkdijk, the main road running east from the church in the center of town. The 2nd Gun Section was positioned at the brickyard, close to E Company, 3rd Platoon. "Just before dawn, it was my turn to be on guard. As dawn broke, a German 88mm was fired into our immediate area. I jumped into my foxhole as a steady shelling continued, mostly mortar fire, for about 30 minutes."[402]

When the mortar fire lessened, a paratrooper appeared with the message that a German tank was moving out from the edge of the forest, heading east straight for the village. Spying it slowly moving along the dike, he "ran to the nearest foxholes to get help, those of Cpl. Roland Boteler and PFC Robert Atkinson. We ran to our 57mm gun, which was about 25 yards behind our foxholes. While we were running to the gun, a German machine-gunner on the tank was firing along each side of the dike. Why he did not fire in our direction I will never know."[403]

The three gunners quickly removed the camouflage netting and sandbags around their gun; the enemy tank was less than 150 yards away. By the time Fary was loading the gun, the tank was only 70 yards away but, for no apparent reason, it did not concentrate any fire on the American crew: "I threw an AP shell into the chamber and Atkinson and I jumped on the trails." Corporal Boteler fired and the shell hit the Germans' drive sprocket wheel. The tank came to an abrupt stop and the German infantry began retreating, feeling insecure without mobile tank support.

Immediately after Corporal Boteler fired on the tank, his platoon leader, 1st Lieutenant Stark, ran over to the other gun at Kerkdijk. Other crew members were still in their foxholes, leaderless after their staff sergeant had been killed the previous day. Lieutenant Stark loaded the unmanned gun, sighted it, fired on the tank, then reloaded and fired again. The German crew decided they had had enough and abandoned the tank, providing excellent targets for the .50-caliber machine guns that 80th AA–D Battery had deployed nearby. The Germans were all killed or wounded.

Meanwhile, Lieutenant Stark spotted another German tank firing behind some nearby hedgerows several hundred yards to his front. "I studied the hedgerow through field glasses but could see nothing. Estimating where the tank should be from seeing the smoke from the gun, I fired three rounds (AP) at the spot. The tank gun did not fire after that and I could see men jumping down [behind the bush]. I then fired one HE round at the same spot."[404]

Late that morning, after the enemy had been subdued, Lieutenant Stark toured the area. Behind the hedgerow he "saw three Mark IVs knocked out. Two of them were behind the hedgerow at the spot I had fired on that morning." Lieutenant Thompson told Stark that "whoever had fired had done a good job of knocking out those tanks."[405]

The 80th AA brass took seriously the sudden appearance of numerous German tanks, and dispatched an officer to fetch A and F Batteries north of the Waal River in order to bolster 505th defensive positions in east Nijmegen. Capt. Norman Nelson, A Battery commander, was also notified of the possible loss of two guns in C Battery, to which he was ordered to dispatch two 57mm guns with crews. One of the two C Battery guns reported out of service was found abandoned near the brickyard, following an earlier order by Lieutenant Thompson.[406] The gun was repositioned some 100 yards to the west. Stark's platoon had suffered three men wounded during the German counterattack. E Company's losses were two dead and six men wounded.

In addition to British tanks and the 57mm guns, E Company was backed-up by machine-gun teams from 1st Lt. Edmund H. Kline's Headquarters Company, 2nd Battalion LMG Platoon. Joseph J. Jusek, a corporal from Cleveland who led one of these teams, was honored with the Distinguished Service Cross: "Corporal Jusek was in charge of a light machine gun when the right flank of Company E was fiercely attacked by approximately two companies of infantry supported by artillery, mortars, and five tanks. Despite heavy artillery and mortar fire falling near his position, Corporal Jusek, disregarding his own safety, continued to expose himself so as to direct effective fire on the oncoming infantry.

"Presently, tanks appeared on the scene to support the forward movement of the enemy foot troops, and one enemy tank moved within 200 yards of Corporal Jusek's position. The first volley of fire from the tank scored a near hit on his position, disabling the other three members of his gun crew and causing Corporal Jusek to suffer painful lacerations about the face and shoulder.

"Despite the acute pain of his wounds, Corporal Jusek refused to evacuate his position and continued to deliver effective fire on the enemy. He remained in position for approximately two hours, during which time he continually laid down fire against the foe. By his unselfish conduct, unstinting devotion to duty, and indomitable courage, Corporal Jusek set an inspiring example for all those who witnessed his heroic actions, which reflect the highest traditions of the armed services."[407]

Four other F Company .30-caliber machine-gunners also earned medals that day. PFCs Joseph M. Koss and Robert D. Maier were raking the oncoming German infantry with their machine gun when a German tank fired its main gun on them from some 100 yards away, wounding both. Maier's Silver Star Citation details the action: "During the initial moments of a strong enemy counterattack, Private First Class Maier, machine-gunner, and his assistant squad leader moved their LMG from a covered position to a spot that afforded no cover or concealment but more effective fire on the onrushing enemy. From this position Private First Class Maier, operating the gun alone, delivered fire on the advancing Germans, temporarily pinning them to the ground.

"When a tank, about 100 yards to the front, began shelling the LMG position with point-blank fire, he continued to fire on the enemy. One shell wounded Private First Class Maier and his assistant squad leader and temporarily damaged the gun. Private First Class Maier field-stripped his LMG and restored it to action. Ignoring the pain of his shoulder and leg wounds and refusing medical aid, he maintained his effective fire on the attacking Germans. Another shell burst killed his companion, but Private First Class Maier stood his ground and fired his machine gun until anti-tank fire knocked out the enemy tank. His courageous devotion to duty and cool determination were greatly responsible for his company's success in repelling the enemy thrust aimed at reaching the vital Nijmegen Bridge."[408]

Private First Class Koss, who died during this action, was posthumously awarded the Distinguished Service Cross. Private First Class Henry Covello recalled that "Koss was hit by a treeburst. Together with three other men I carried him back to the Battalion CP."[409] His citation reads: "For extraordinary heroism in connection with military operations against an armed enemy on September 28, 1944 in the vicinity of Wercheren, Holland. During a fierce enemy attack supported by tanks against his company's defensive positions, Private First Class Koss, acting as an assistant rifle-squad leader, directed the movement of his squad's light machine gun from its position of cover to an exposed position affording a better field of fire against the onrushing infantry.

"After an approximate belt-and-a-half of ammunition had been fired with effective results, an enemy tank not less than 100 yards distant shelled the position with point-blank fire, and with the third round wounded both Private First Class Koss and his gunner and put the gun temporarily out of action. Although painfully wounded, Private First Class Koss fired upon the enemy with his Thompson submachine gun with telling effects while his gunner corrected the stoppage.

"Despite the continued point-blank fire from the tank, Private First Class Koss continued to fire for at least 15 minutes after being wounded until he fell mortally wounded from one of the tank shells. His utter fearlessness and unselfish conduct in the face of overwhelming odds and certain death so inspired all his comrades that a superior enemy force was driven from the battlefield with heavy losses. His extraordinary heroism and tenacity at the cost of his life were in keeping with the highest traditions of the United States Army. Entered military service from McKeesport, Pennsylvania."[410]

PFC Duane V. Sydow received a Silver Star for preventing German engineers from removing an anti-tank minefield: "Private First Class Sydow, machine-gunner, was occupying a forward position covering an anti-tank minefield when a strong enemy attack of approximately company strength supported by tanks and self-propelled artillery was launched against his company's defenses. Private First Class Sydow immediately began engaging the infantry moving with a tank towards the minefield for the ostensible purpose of clearing a path for the tank. His burst of machine-gun fire was met by direct fire from the tank's cannon, and Private First Class Sydow suffered multiple wounds in the arm, shoulder and neck. Mindful of the importance of his responsibility, Private First Class Sydow refused medical treatment and despite his painful wounds continued to engage the oncoming enemy.

"A second cannon burst completely put his gun out of action, but Private First Class Sydow, instead of withdrawing from his position, continued to engage the mine-clearing detail with his rifle. His outstanding courage and unselfish devotion to duty accounted for heavy enemy casualties and in no small measure enabled his company to successfully repel the enemy thrust. Only after it was quite apparent that the enemy assault had failed did Private First Class Sydow evacuate his position and retire for medical aid."[411]

The fourth decorated F Company machine-gunner, Private First Class Oscar E. Ladner, was also awarded a Silver Star: "Ladner [...] was in his company's forward line of resistance when it was suddenly and fiercely attacked by a number of tanks and self-propelled artillery supported by infantry. Private First Class Ladner quickly engaged this superior force and exposed himself continually while bringing his fire to bear on the enemy.

At the outset of this action, he received a painful bullet burn across the cheek which temporarily blinded him. Despite the acute pain, Private First Class Ladner tenaciously continued to operate his gun, causing an undetermined amount of damage to the enemy.

"During the most critical moments of the attack, Private First Class Ladner was again wounded by shell fragments. Refusing medical aid for the second time, he kept his gun in action, unmindful of both the wounds he had suffered and the danger of his exposed position. Not only was the firepower he was able to deliver by the continued operation of his gun highly instrumental in successfully repelling the determined enemy attack, but his unsurpassed courage and devotion to duty inspired all who witnessed his actions to exert their utmost efforts in holding their positions."[412]

First Lieutenant Chester A. Garrison, 2nd Battalion adjutant, described the attack in his unit's journal: "A general attack preceded by a pounding of our lines by artillery, self-propelled arty [artillery guns], mortar, etc. fire began at 0500. E Company received SP fire from across the river. Later artillery fire from there laid down a barrage. All wires were knocked out; so we had to resort to radio. One small enemy tank almost reached F Company before it was spotted and knocked out by English tanks. A second tank was knocked out in the same sector—one of these by a 57mm gun.

"The infantry advance was particularly heavy on E Company, which had to maintain a prolonged and intensified small-arms fire. Estimated 130 casualties to the enemy—many dead. Our 81mm mortar fire was particularly effective. All companies' ammo supply became very low. Things quieted down by late morning.

"A civilian taken in E Company area, suspected of trying to go through lines to the Germans, forwarded to Regiment. Four of the Battalion killed (one from each company), and about 25 were wounded, including Lieutenants [Richard] Swenson and [Stuart] McCash (F Company). Twenty-four Germans surrendered to E Company. They were disgusted with the war. Our opposing forces consist of a conglomeration of varied third-grade replacements, who are untrained or unfit for front-line duty.

"Enemy planes dropped phosphorous markers in the area; the planes are after the bridge again. Lieutenant [John C.] Barrows and the demolition section booby-trapped our mines to our front. A German plane crashed directly into D Company line—no Americans injured."[413]

The German plane was shot down by a 1st Platoon, D Company machine gun. According to rifleman Private Widger, for several days, a German plane had been passing over the brickyard where the platoon was located, and shelling would ensue shortly thereafter. The pilot flew so low they could clearly see him laughing at them. This daily insult and shelling prompted 1st Platoon to plan a little surprise party. They somehow managed to mount a .30-caliber machine gun on a paratrooper's back, and everyone else readied their individual weapons. The next time the German paid them a visit, they all opened up. The last they saw of him, he was trailing smoke and losing altitude. That was the last time a German plane circled their position.[414]

In the early morning darkness of that same morning, September 28, Pfc. Edward F. Baker, Jr., was instantly killed by a direct hit on his foxhole. His platoon leader, 1st Lt. Earnest H. Brown, also had a close call: "Our area was fairly level with a bank about six feet high. I had started one foxhole a few feet below the small ridge, but very quickly abandoned that start for a foxhole with a better view across the front. My communications man [Baker] had been delayed. When he appeared, he asked if he could finish the hole I had started. Of course I said OK. That night the artillery scored a direct hit on that hole, and of course my communications man was killed."[415] PFC Raymond E. Myers, Headquarters Company, 2nd Battalion, was also killed the same day.

Leutnant Heinz Bliss, the 1st Battery, Fallschirm-Artillerie-Abteilung 4 Adjutant, recalled that Kampfgruppe Jenkel received orders on the evening of September 27 "to attack the next morning at 0700 hours between the Querdamm and Thornse Molen in the direction of the Erlekom brickyard. At that exact time—and while the previous artillery fire was still continuing—we were ready with two assault groups. As we crossed through a muddy meadow at a narrow spot between two dikes, we were quickly identified and received heavy enemy fire from all weapons. The muddy ground had reduced the effect of preceding enemy shells of all calibers. Our own artillery and mortars, like our tanks, which attacked to the right from us on the Leuth-Erlekom road, took the enemy's positions under direct fire. This allowed us to advance a little. Taking casualties, we reached the edge of the Erlekom brickyard, which American paratroopers [under Lieutenant Thompson] were fanatically defending. Our tanks alone somewhat relieved our situation. We managed to take the brickyard in close combat and hold it.

"While we were fighting for the brickyard, our tanks and supporting infantry moved into Erlekom and broke through to the western edge of town. We also suffered heavy losses: some of our tanks broke down. Things brightened when our planes, which we had not seen for some time, appeared. They supported us well, untiringly bombing and strafing the enemy. It especially got our attention when that afternoon a ceasefire was suddenly announced so both sides could see to their dead and wounded. This actually happened. From our position, we observed American medics carrying away their dead, attending to their wounded and evacuating them by armored ambulance. There was not only battle and dying, but also humanity and consideration. Later that evening we were relieved and marched back to Wyler, where we rested in a cellar in the western part of the village."[416]

Private Philip Nadler, who used a Garand rifle, had a particular good word for one of the medics who was active that day. "If you load a Garand right-handed and are careless, it can smash your thumb, but left-handed, your left thumb is at its mercy. I lost some skin from my thumb with every clip I loaded in a firefight. There was no time to be careful. Just shove in another clip and keep that lead flying. Because of my thumb, I often needed medical aid after a fight, and became good friends with our platoon medic, Fred Schiele from Paterson, New Jersey. He played guitar and sang 'Cool Water.' He said we would get together after the war—we lived just seven or eight miles from each other. [...]

"When a man is hit, he or his buddies scream for a medic. Schiele never hesitated, regardless of conditions, to respond to that call. When men are being hit it's no time to be running around, it's time to keep down low. That's when Schiele had to leave the safety of his foxhole and go to someone's aid. Someone should tell the army to teach its men not to call the medic if the wound is slight. Many wounds he risked his life to reach were so minor that the man never left the front lines. Small cuts, tiny pinholes, near-misses when a man believed he'd been hit. Oh, I know as well as anyone the tension of waiting to be killed and then being wounded. Screaming 'Medic!' relieves the tension and gives comfort in the shock that follows hurt. Still, I wish a man would check and see if he needs immediate aid before screaming. I walked to an aid station for both my wounds without calling 'Medic.'

"I'll always remember Schiele bringing up the rear of the platoon, carrying his medical bag and often a folded stretcher. He presented a grim sight, but he was a light-hearted man and good for my moral. We never got together after the war. He became, I think, the E Company medic and was fatally wounded a few days after his transfer. That was during the Battle of the Bulge."[417]

On September 28, when a strong German force attacked C Company's 2nd Platoon outpost about half a mile from Im Thal, Sgt. William Reed earned a Bronze Star for heroic conduct: "Sergeant Reed, rifle-squad leader, and his squad were pinned down by intense fire from four enemy machine guns plus small-arms fire and hand grenades during a close-in firefight. Without regard for his personal safety, Sergeant Reed led his squad boldly through the enemy fire so as to deliver flanking fire on the enemy force. Under his superb leadership the squad silenced one of the machine guns, during which action several of his men were wounded.

"As attempts to evacuate the wounded were being made, a group of seven enemy counterattacked, whereupon Sergeant Reed and another man engaged the Germans for 30 minutes until completely out of ammunition. As a result of his heroic conduct, four of the enemy were killed or wounded, thereby enabling all of the wounded to be carried safely to their own lines. Sergeant Reed's heroic and unselfish conduct enabled the platoon to accomplish its mission with a minimum of casualties and was a source of inspiration and encouragement to all the men of his unit."[418]

On September 29, Pvt. George F. Mosebach, D Company, was killed in a barn by German artillery fire. The next day E Company's makeshift 3rd Platoon was hit by a mortar shell and fragments struck Lieutenant Thompson in the leg. He was patched up and placed in the basement of the E Company CP to recuperate, while Lieutenant Mauro assumed command of the platoon. That same day Pvt. Jack J. Beste, F Company, died of sustained wounds.

PFC Ted Bachenheimer "was recommended for a battlefield commission," most likely that same day, but ended up with a lot of bad luck instead. Colonel Williams recalled that Bachenheimer was "directed to report to Division for an interview by a board of officers. When he left the 504th CP, he picked up a steel helmet with a first lieutenant bar on it instead of his own helmet. When he reported to Division wearing this helmet, he was sent back to Regiment for consideration. Before this matter could be resolved, he was captured by the Germans. Had it not been for inadvertently grabbing the wrong helmet, he would have undoubtedly been a lieutenant rather than an enlisted man when he was captured."[419]

On the night of October 1–2, the Germans opened up a large barrage on A Company positions that continued throughout the next morning. Lieutenant Breard, 1st Platoon, was in the Company CP "in the cellar of a house behind the highest point overlooking the north end of Wyler Meer." He was in the hall talking to the operations sergeant, Norman Tesch, and four others when a 120mm mortar shell hit just outside the door. "The five I was talking with in the hall were all wounded. […] The supply sergeant [Clarence B. Williams] was killed in his foxhole. I was unscathed. I went back to my platoon and from then on while we were in Holland, I never visited the Company CP again. I found it much safer to use the telephone or the radio!"[420]

Positioned close to the Company CP, 2nd Lieutenant Morin's 2nd Platoon was subjected to the barrage as well. In the 2nd Squad, Corporal Baldino and his buddy PFC Danny F. Brisco were both wounded: "One day my good friend Danny Brisco got to go to town. I was in my foxhole and some British artillery observers came up. Pretty soon German mortar shells started to fall nearby and one landed ten or so feet from me.

"I […] had moved back to the cover of some trees when my friend Danny came back from getting cleaned up. He said, 'What's the matter, Freddie? You look as pale as a ghost.' I said, 'A mortar shell just missed me.' Just then one landed real close to the both of us. I said, 'Let's get the hell out of here,' and we took off at a run toward our CP a few hundred yards to the rear. (When shell fire got too heavy we would dash back a hundred yards or so and when it let up, we would return to our foxholes.)

"We only got about 20 feet. I was in the lead by about eight feet, and next thing I know I was knocked cold. When I came to, it felt like I had a hole in my back six inches wide. The mortar had landed between the two of us. I got hit in about nine places in back, and on top of my head (I didn't have my helmet on). I also got it in the left forearm, which cut a nerve. I couldn't open my left hand for about six months until it healed. Danny got hit in the left eye and lost his sight in that eye.

"My buddy [Pvt. Bethel] Goolsby came down to help me, and I remember asking him if there was a big hole in my back. 'No Baldy, it isn't too bad,' he said. They took us to the first-aid station, put some bandages over our wounds, and got us back to Nijmegen in a jeep. We were treated there somewhat and then sent further down the line to a field hospital where they operated to take the shrapnel out. I then lost track of Danny because he got trucked back to Brussels. I got a plane back to England where I stayed until January 17, and then I got the *Queen Elizabeth* back to the States."[421]

Early in the morning of October 3, Lt. Edmund H. Kline, 81mm Mortar Platoon, noticed light, sporadic mortar fire to the front of E Company's position at Erlekom. He sent Lieutenant Mauro from E Company to report to Captain Van Poyck that he was ready to use his two 81mm mortars to retaliate. Mauro spoke briefly to the recuperating 1st Lt. Jocko Thompson before reporting to Van Poyck. "I returned to Kline's gun emplacements about 100 yards to the front of the CP," recalled Mauro. "He was holding his retaliation in abeyance so as not to reveal our positions, and was not yet certain what or exactly where his targets would be. As always [...], we had to conserve our shells for moments of greatest efficacy.

"Kline [...] sought his targets carefully and wisely. [...] We had return fire from the enemy mortars, fortunately all misses. [...] We couldn't see them and I'm certain they couldn't see us. [...] When he was pretty certain where his target or targets were, Kline ordered the gunners to 'fire for effect,' which meant they let loose a small but efficient barrage on the enemy gun emplacements. Then everything became quiet. [...] 'I think we've knocked them out,' he said. 'Let's go tell Van.' Kline and I walked back to the Company CP. [...]

"Just before entering the house, I opened a small, round can of cheese that came with our rations. I [...] took off my helmet and held it by the chin-strap as I began to eat the cheese and opened the door to the kitchen where Captain Van was. I heard a large bang, and for just a fraction of a second saw a light burst through the kitchen ceiling as I felt myself reeling backward, stunned and falling. I remained conscious, but went numb in numerous parts of my body. The area was hazy and smoky, with many splintered pieces of wood all about.

"I couldn't see him from where I was lying, but I heard Van say, in what I thought was his usual, calm voice: 'Carl, can you come here? I need some help.' I told him I was sorry, but I couldn't move. About this time, I noticed I still had the cheese in my hand. I thought, 'Why am I eating this? I'm going to die!' and tossed the cheese to one side. I've never known where Kline was in relation to me at that moment, but I saw him crawling on the floor among all the debris and told him to stop moving because he would exacerbate his injuries. He paid no attention to me; he appeared quite dazed. I said, firmly, 'If you don't stop moving around, I'm going to whack you with my pistol.' He never heard me and kept slowly crawling in a small circle. Later, I learned he had received leg injuries that troubled him the rest of his life. [...]

"I was aware of one hit, but I learned later that two 80mm mortar shells bombed that house. They went through the kitchen roof and into the cellar, where Jocko and five or six others slept. Jocko wasn't there. The Germans had zeroed-in perfectly, or was it luck? They had seen smoke emanating from the stove from the cooking rabbits.

"A minute or two later, help came running to us from all directions. A medic looked after Kline; another one came to me. He took off my pistol belt with the container of morphine and syrette that all paratroopers carried, and gave me the shot of morphine. He saw that my boots were torn in many places [… and] unsuccessfully tried—trembling—to unlace them. I yelled, so he stopped trying. I couldn't see what was going on in the kitchen inches away, and I was unaware of the tragedy in the basement.

"Possibly three or four minutes later, I saw Jocko standing there, trying to give me a reassuring smile and make me feel good. 'You lucky bastard,' he said. 'Tonight you're going to sleep between clean, white sheets.' His exact words. I'll never forget them. Jocko told me that he'd gone to the 3rd Platoon CP to get a cup of coffee about five minutes before the bombing. [...]

"I was told that Lieutenant Nelson had run to the artillery company a half mile away and come back to the house with a jeep and a driver. Someone found a door that had been blown away and put it across the front and back seats of the jeep, [and …] placed Kline on the door in a supine position. I was carried to the backseat of the jeep and placed behind the driver. I had to reach out and hold Kline, who was dazed and nearly unconscious, to keep him and the door from flying off the jeep, especially on the turns.

"The driver took off for the battalion aid station. Most of the trip was […] over rough terrain. I had a very painful, horrible time keeping myself erect, let alone keeping Kline and the sliding, bouncing door from falling off. My bleeding, battered feet kept bouncing on the steel floor of the jeep, each bounce more excruciating than the last. I know men are capable in wartime of suffering super-human feats, often unknowingly.

"At the aid station, probably ten agonizing minutes from the bombed house, I was put on a stretcher on the ground. […] Before I passed out, Major Wellems came over to me [… and said], 'Carl, you seem to know better than anyone what happened. Can you tell me?' I could now hear Van Poyck's voice, but didn't see him again. He seemed to be happily chatting away. I thought Van might have a better understanding of what happened than I at this time. I still didn't know about the multiple deaths in the basement."[422]

Captain Van Poyck "suffered a traumatic amputation of my right leg and a shattered left foot. Corporals [William H.] Gotts and [Harold H.] Roman, flanking me, each ultimately lost a leg. While busy applying belt and bootlace tourniquets, I remember one of them said, 'I've lost my leg,' and my replying, 'I think I've lost both of mine.' My immediate concern was to contact battalion. Lieutenants Mauro, Kline and Nelson, 1st Sergeant Dumas, and T/5 [Romeo J.] Hamel and Sergeant [Amos E.] Overholt were also wounded. Lieutenant Nelson, severely wounded when I was hit, ran for help from our CP, to a platoon position. Later, in the hospital in England, a doctor told me it was physically impossible for him to stand on his shattered feet, let alone run on them.

"We were evacuated in a jeep, involving four trips in broad daylight on the dike road, directly under the German gun positions. We flew a Red Cross flag from a tree limb staff, and they held their fire. I was hospitalized for two years."[423]

Lieutenant Garrison learned that the German shells "came through the tiled roof and exploded on the table, around which a meeting was being held. Everybody in the room became a casualty; Sgt. Elbert Kitchen survived because he had just left the room. Hearing about the catastrophe, I rushed from my CP to the aid station to check on the personnel damage: who and how many were hit and who had to be replaced. The jeeps, first with wounded and then with dead, began to arrive and unload. I discovered my two close friends on stretchers on the ground. Ed Kline was in shock from a severe leg injury; he was hospitalized for a year and had to walk ever afterwards with a cane. Alongside him was Van Poyck. By the configuration of the blanket covering him, I could see that he was missing much of a leg. Even with additional injuries, he was not in shock, which would have killed him. He recognized me and gave me his wrist watch to care for. He was weak but conversant—too bull-headed a Dutch descendant to give in.

"Sergeant Kitchen told me later that after the explosion Van had pulled himself into an upright sitting position against the wall. Seeing his loss of blood, he pulled off his belt and used it as a tourniquet. When Kitchen offered to help, Van refused any and directed Kitchen to assist others in the room. Upon Kitchen's getting back to help Van, he directed Kitchen to use scissors to cut through the thin stretch of skin that kept the leg attached to the thigh. Appalled, Kitchen refused until Van threatened him with a direct order and court-martial."[424]

The total casualties amounted to 12 wounded, including four officers. Cpl. John W. Morris and T/5 Romeo J. Hamel both died that day of their wounds. Another trooper, PFC Kenneth B. Thomson, was killed outright when a mortar scored a direct hit on his jeep. He may have been the jeep driver who evacuated Lieutenant Mauro. This left E Company with three officers: Lieutenants Collins, Sharp and Thompson. Captain Norman, the Battalion S-3, was sent down to E Company to take command and Lieutenant Thompson was moved up to become executive officer. Sadly, 23-year-old Elbert Kitchen was killed the next day. Sgt. Amos Overholt died of his wounds four days later in the 61st General Hospital in England.

On October 4, German artillery fire caused four deaths in F Company, 3rd Platoon. Lieutenant Watson recalled that Pvt. Joseph M. Smith was in a hayloft when a shell came through the roof and fragments fatally struck him in the back. S.Sgt. Esmer O. Partridge was killed in his foxhole when a shell exploded in the tree above him, raining down shrapnel. Pvt. Bernard M. McDermott and Sgt. John M. Duncan, a Native American who led 2nd squad, 2nd Platoon, were also killed. PFC Donald E. Morain, a rifleman, recalled that Sergeant Duncan "had received a letter from his wife, telling him she wanted a divorce. He asked me for advice. But what could I tell him? Two days later he went over to another platoon position, where he'd heard some men were staying in a house. He knew the Germans could easily zero in on them, and told them to get out of there. He was in the house as the shells came down."[425]

Another 2nd Platoon member, Pvt. Albert Musto, was in the house with Sergeant Duncan and Pvts. James F. Lyons and Joseph Smith when a smoke bomb exploded about 50 yards away. "Lyons saw it go off and said, 'We should go outside. They're going to shell us!' We both yelled to Joe Smith and Sergeant Duncan to get out, but Smith shouted back, 'If you're going to get it, you'll get it.'[...] Lyons and I ran to the dugout we had prepared in the back garden. The next shell landed on the building and the whole roof was blown to smithereens. Later that day we had to bring their bodies out to the crossroads where Graves Registration would pick them up."[426]

Although it has not formerly been disclosed, the Mark IV Panther tanks that were knocked out during the attack on the 504th RCT were part of Panzer Brigade 108, commanded by *Oberstleutnant* Friedrich H. Musculus, a veteran of the famous Afrika Korps. Formed in Gräfenwohr on July 24, 1944, Musculus's brigade consisted of the 2108th Panzer Battalion (three companies of Mark V tanks and one tank-destroyer company of Mark IV/L70 tanks, plus flak guns); the 2108th Panzergrenadier Battalion (five heavily armed infantry companies in half-tracks) and several smaller supporting units such as pioneers and artillery. Combat began on September 19 near Manderfeld, Belgium, but the troops were soon pulled out for the September 28 counterattack. After suffering the loss of numerous tanks near Nijmegen, the remaining tanks were lost in the battle for Aachen and the brigade was dissolved on October 30.

The repulse of the counterattack by the 504th RCT and supporting British tanks and artillery halted the concerted efforts of the German II

Fallschirmjäger Korps to recapture Nijmegen from the east. The Allies likewise won the hard, bitter fight that ensued on the Island, although battles there involved many more troops, including the British 43rd and 50th Infantry Divisions, British 8th Armoured Brigade, the 101st Airborne Division and portions of the 82nd Airborne Division. The author's research into numerous British and German sources reveals that the Germans launched a single, concerted counterattack of epic proportions against the 504th RCT and multiple forces on the Island, although these battles have long been regarded as separate and discrete actions. Why the true scope of the enemy action has never before been revealed is a matter of speculation, but news sources at the time were likely silenced to help maintain morale on the home front. In addition, many contemporaneous records and eyewitness accounts, including war diaries by the German high command, have only recently become available.

German fanaticism and the sheer proportion of the German counteroffensive in late September and early October 1944 caused the Allies to abandon all plans for a breakout to the Reichswald east of Nijmegen. The 50th British Infantry Division suffered severe casualties on the Island against the battered II SS-Panzer Korps formations. In order to provide replacements for other British units, the division was stripped of its strongest battalions and sent back to England as a skeleton force to train replacements.

Shocked by the German offensive, General Eisenhower prevailed on Field Marshal Montgomery to prioritize clearing the enemy from the north and east sides of the Scheldt estuary. With extended supply lines from the beaches in Normandy, it was vital to create a safe sea route to British-held Antwerp, where major port facilities were still intact. The Canadian II Corps was given the assignment to clear several Dutch islands along the estuary. It also meant that all efforts to capture Arnhem were indefinitely suspended.

These necessities caused the 504th PIR and other units of the 82nd ABD to be stuck in static combat positions. As the weeks passed by, both sides dug in deeper, laying minefield after minefield and booby trap after booby trap. The Germans abandoned the recapture of Nijmegen and the Allies halted their offensive in Nijmegen, but night patrols, an aspect of combat most troopers dreaded, nevertheless remained essential.

Convalescing 3rd Battalion veterans of the Waal River Crossing photographed in Camp Sissonne (France), November 1944. Pvt. Hugh Wallis of H Company is on the far left in the middle row. Front row, left to right: Pvt. Cletus Shelton (H), newly promoted S.Sgt. Leroy Richmond (H) and Sgt. Horn (I). *Courtesy: Hugh Wallis*

CHAPTER 18

HOLDING THE LINE
HOLLAND AND GERMANY,
OCTOBER 5–NOVEMBER 14, 1944

E arly October 1944 saw an increased need to mount additional patrols. The 504th had taken no prisoners for several days, and Tucker and his battalion commanders were anxious to find out more about German activity and especially if another surprise attack like that at Den Heuvel was in the making. Word was put out that if small patrols did not take any prisoners, then a squad would be sent out the next night. If they, too, failed, a platoon would go out the following night, and so on.

PFC David Whittier, Headquarters and Headquarters, best described the regiment's general situation: "The 504th was holding the heavily wooded high ground in the vicinity of Berg en Dal, Holland-Germany, overlooking the flat, ditch-laced lowlands that run on to Arnhem to the north and Cleve to the east. The rapidly flowing waters of the lower Rhine churned an S-like course along the limit of visibility on our left flank. At the foot of our wooded plateau lay the Wyler Meer, a shallow, elongated body of water, the west shore of which formed the front line of four-fifths of the regimental sector.

"Our only avenue of entry into the German line lay along the one-fifth of our sector that was not fronted by water. Every patrol that left our lines, of necessity, had to pass through this area. With five or six patrols moving out each night, this particular sector of the front became about as busy as Macy's basement in the days before Christmas. Each successive patrol ran into heavier opposition from the enemy, and each had a shorter distance to cover before they tangled with machine guns, machine pistols, minefields and barbed wire.

"In short, the enemy had developed their defenses to such a point that our patrols were getting nowhere. Every night they went out and every night they returned with the same information—enemy contacted, engaged in fire-fight, casualties inflicted, but no prisoners taken. Always it was the same—no prisoners taken, and a prisoner was what we wanted more than anything else. Enemy defenses were sprouting up like mushrooms during the night and we had to find out what it all meant—the sort of thing that a Kraut PW might be able to tell us. Division was becoming most insistent on the subject of PWs. Our capture of an enemy soldier became an A-1 priority. Something had to be devised that would get results or our fondly held reputation as one of the toughest parachute regiments in the army would soon become a hollow phrase."[427]

The evening of October 6, Captain Richardson's F Company mounted a platoon-sized patrol in the woods near the Wylerbaan. Third Platoon's Lieutenant Watson, in the company since Sicily, was a veteran platoon leader; his assistant, 2nd Lt. Robert V. Heneisen, had joined the platoon at Anzio. Cpl. Richard H. Gentzel and Pvt. William L. "Sandy" Sandoval were the lead scouts. "Regiment ordered a platoon attack (F Co.) into woods to front so as to push enemy line back to dike to straighten out regimental front," the 3rd Battalion Unit Journal reports. "G Co. supposed to move in from the right. The platoon was able to get to the location; however it proved advisable to pull it back to the original as the enemy was too firmly entrenched with good troops. There was a considerable exchange of fire. Casualties = 5 evacuated, 4 believed K.I.A., 1 M.I.A., Lts. Watson and Heneisen were wounded."[428]

According to Watson, the platoon was about to "jump off this big levee that came right along those woods when machine-gun fire broke out. I was hit just before that, but remember a huge amount of soldiers lying along the woods before they took me back. I was leading the men when I was hit with artillery shell fragments that tore into my right leg, fracturing my femur. I could see them across the levee, but was not sure if they were Germans. I recall hearing that they had machine-gun nests all over, and they were some elite German force [Fallschirmjägers]. Medics gave me morphine, then I was transported behind the lines and sent to Brussels. From there I was in several hospitals in a body cast for almost two years."[429]

Private Nadler, 2nd Platoon, heard from a close 3rd Platoon friend that Sandy Sandoval "was first wounded, and then bayoneted" in the woods. "We seemed to know for sure that he was dead, but the army listed him as missing for many years. [...] Sandy had become sullen in England. [...] Maybe trouble at home, maybe some girl? He wouldn't talk about it even to us. When we left England I put all my money into his spearhead account. (The army held your money during a battle and gave it back in the rear.) If you were killed it was sent home. I had $120 in Sandy's account. After Holland I was broke, but I was glad it went to Sandy's family. Maybe they needed it. I mean that from my heart."[430]

PFC John C. Atkins assumed control of Gentzel's leaderless rifle squad, "and led them successfully to win their objective," according to his Bronze Star Citation. "When a heavy enemy barrage forced them to displace, Private First Class Atkins, with unfaltering courage, led them one by one across an enemy minefield swept by machine-gun and mortar fire to prepared positions. Disregarding his own safety, he carried two wounded men to safety, reorganizing the remainder of his squad, and he deployed them in positions and directed their fire in such an effective manner as to be instrumental in repelling the enemy's counterattack."[431]

The wounded men were most likely Lieutenant Watson and Pvt. Ray D. Wilbanks. Contrary to Lieutenant Garrison's report, Lieutenant Heneisen was killed and buried in a field grave in the Ooijpolder area near Erlekom along with PFC William K. Pierce. Private Wilbanks died the same night of sustained wounds and was also buried in a field grave, but his remains were later repatriated and buried in his home state of Georgia.

Not until the next day, October 7, did the regimental commander learn the full extent of the casualties. According to the 2nd Battalion Unit Journal, F Company worked on normalizing the situation until about 1630. "In return, it received a heavy pounding of artillery fire all day. The F Company CP [was] fortunately situated in a well-constructed cellar, as the walls of the house were completely knocked down from the encounter. Colonel Tucker was in area during the afternoon. Everyone is concerned over last night's losses."[432]

The evening of October 7, Pvt. William A. Cox's foxhole was found empty: the C Company trooper had been captured by a German patrol. Four days later another trooper was captured, Pvt. Eugene J. Corcoran, also from C Company, who ended up in Stalag IIB Hammerstein. On October 12, an enemy artillery shell hit the 81mm Mortar Platoon. It instantly killed Cpls. Edward P. Collins and William J. Storm and PFC Joseph V. Hamilton, and wounded S.Sgt. William E. Altemus, who died in the aid station the next day. Minutes before they were struck, the men had been exchanging banter with 1st Lt. Allen McClain: "A short distance from my CP, four of my men, including the platoon sergeant, sat around a small fire frying potatoes country style. I chided them about turning into a potato since we were dug-in in a potato field and chow was scarce. From their position there was no possible way for the Germans to see them or even suspect they were there. Yet within the hour all four [sic] were dead from one lone shell that landed amongst them. These were my friends."[433]

The password list for F Company had been lost on the DZ, and had to be assumed to be in enemy hands. Private Nadler recounts how the men astutely "converted this problem to an aid to ourselves. At best, to challenge was a big hazard. Without passwords, we were forced to hug the ground and study the approaching man or men. We all found that we could recognize every man in the company in silhouette. The slouch of one shoulder, a slight limp, his size and gait, a nervous twitch or shrug, two inseparable friends, the wheeze from Charlie's cold. I never made a mistake in identity. This became very important when we became shorthanded.

"We had large openings in our line near the end of the campaign. We had to operate connecting patrols in these gaps. A slow walk halfway to the next position, meet the other guy and a slow walk back to report everything OK. Picture yourself all alone beyond help from anyone, looking for someone in the dark. Several times I ran into an enemy patrol, watched and waited until they returned to their own lines. When it happened often enough we set a trap for them and took good care of them.

"We had one area in which we held a slight rise in the ground (you could call it a hill). From this hill a road ran out to the enemy. There was a crossroads exactly 1500 yards out. At night we manned an outpost out there and one about halfway out. During the day two men stayed in a nice bomb shelter at the halfway outpost. We had sound-power phones for each outpost. I pulled many patrols in that area. We always felt quite at ease till we passed that last outpost at the crossroads. We never got much beyond the crossroads before we got knocked around. We kept trying for a prisoner. […]"[434]

On October 21, a small group of replacement officers arrived from the Parachute School in Ashwell, England: 2nd Lt. Edward M. Scheibelein; 2nd Lt. James R. Allmand, Jr., a graduate of the New Mexico Military Institute; and 1st Lt. Leo D. Van De Voort. Van De Voort, formerly with the 29th Infantry Division, had earned a Distinguished Service Cross as a platoon leader in Company B in Normandy. With his company down to 40 men, he had been the only officer standing at the end of D-Day. Although he had been wounded, Van De Voort, still eager for action, had recently qualified for the paratroops before joining A Company as assistant platoon leader, 2nd

Platoon. Second Lieutenant Scheibelein was assigned as assistant platoon leader, 2nd Platoon, F Company, while Lieutenant Allmand took command of 3rd Platoon, G Company.

The same day, Cpl. Frank L. Heidebrink, an assistant squad leader from Newport, Kentucky, in 1st Platoon, A Company, came to Lieutenant Breard with a plan to capture a few prisoners: "He told me that he had been watching and [...] knew where they were, and that is what started it." Breard "talked to the 81mm mortar platoon leader" and was told the patrol would receive "all kinds of support. [...] We worked out the fire and the time they were supposed to fire. Then we could move off through the minefield and they would hold fire as we passed through Wyler."[435]

Unfortunately, these preparations did not work, wrote PFC David Whittier, "so it was decided to try a daylight patrol that afternoon just before dusk. Previously any movement through the enemy lines during the day had been regarded as suicidal, but in desperation headquarters *would* try it—daylight being selected in order that minefields might be more safely penetrated. Every weapon at our disposal [...] would be brought into play, for this was to be no ordinary raid, but a high-powered, concentrated effort with just one objective—the capture of a prisoner.

"The Nijmegen–Cleve road runs along the friendly bank of the Wyler Meer; as it approaches the southern end of the lake it passes into the German line, where it is shrouded in heavy, tangled underbrush. One hundred and fifty yards from the paratroopers' forward outpost, the enemy had constructed a roadblock, a dozen felled trees buttressed by a wrecked vehicle and surrounded by teller mines. Entrenched enemy covered the roadblock and its approaches with rifles, machine guns and Panzerfausts—a new rocket-type anti-tank weapon.

"It was strongly believed that the raiding party could not hope to achieve success without a preliminary mortar barrage and plenty of direct support from artillery, and so the following mortar-artillery schedule was drawn up to cover the operation: at 1635 one 81mm mortar would drop 40 rounds of HE during a five-minute period on the enemy's most forward positions, then elevate 25 yards and fire another 40 rounds, and so on through the length of the woods. (Only one mortar would be used to ensure precision-firing under conditions requiring the rapid laying and relaying of fire.) The patrol would follow as closely on the heels of the barrage as possible and at 1715 the mortar would lift and fire on Wyler. One 60mm mortar [of the 1st Platoon] would maintain continuous fire on a machine-gun emplacement known to be located in a house off to the right in a position to deliver flanking fire against the paratroopers.

"Two battalions of 75mm airborne howitzers and one battalion of 105mm airborne howitzers, plus two British batteries of 25-pounders and 5.5 inch guns would pummel Zyfflich, Wyler, Lagewald, and all suspected mortar and gun positions in the vicinity from 1710 until 1740. This total of 52 artillery pieces was to interdict the enemy's communications with an allotment of 500 rounds, thereby containing for a period of 30 minutes the scene of the patrol's activities. Two more British field regiments of 25-pounders were to remain on call to make sure that the enemy elements in the woods should remain isolated from their rear.

"Breard increased the firepower of his 27-man platoon by borrowing extra automatic weapons from the company. The patrol left the LD [Line of Departure] with eight Tommy guns, three BARs, and two bazookas; the rest of the men carried M-1 rifles. Wire cutters and engineering tape enabled them to cut through barbed wire entanglements and mark a path through the minefield. One medic accompanied the party.

"Three hours before the scheduled departure, one man [Corporal Heidebrink] slipped out to reconnoiter the area through which they must pass. He found the minefield, which had been previously reported, and ran into three enemy soldiers placing additional mines. After watching long enough to determine the type of mines they were using, the paratrooper shot one man and then retired to his company position to report his information." [436]

Carrying a BAR, Breard and his platoon maneuvered their way through the minefield and into the woods, under the lead of Corporal Heidebrink: "His squad moved out first," Breard recalled. "The other two rifle squads followed. We left the mortar squad behind. They gave us covering fire with a 60mm mortar. The squad could get 36 rounds off in a minute. Several times at night we hit the German over there across the lake [Wyler Meer]. I let them fire 36 rounds fast. […] Everybody jumped in their holes, and all those damn rounds would come down on those Germans across the lake. We would get the biggest kick out of that. That was in the same area where earlier Megellas got prisoners out of [their own] fox holes."

"We had three squads. We were supposed to have three squads of about nine men each and a mortar squad of about six or seven men: a sergeant and a gunner, an assistant gunner, two ammunition carriers and probably a corporal, but only 27 men made that attack. We also had artillery fire put on Zyfflich and Wyler. It kicked them real hard for half an hour before we went out. We left the mortars in front of us, moved when they moved out there and went in fast after we got through that minefield."[437]

On return, Breard and Heidebrink reported to Captain Duncan at the A Company CP. Major Harrison was eager to hear their report as well, and a jeep was sent down from battalion headquarters to collect them. When Harrison asked how many casualties they had taken, Breard smiled and answered, "We didn't have any." All patrol members were cited for their action and an article written by Whittier appeared in *Yank Magazine*.

The Germans, too, were eager to capture prisoners. Thus it was the inspiring story of PFC Ted Bachenheimer of Headquarters Company came to a tragic end on October 22 when he was captured in Echteld, a town beyond the Waal River, during a recon mission with Capt. Peter Baker of intelligence unit IS9. Ted escaped, jumping from a train bound for a POW camp in Germany, but was recaptured the same night. Placed this time on a truck, Bachenheimer jumped again just north of the village of 't Harde, knowing his recapture meant questioning by the Gestapo, who could learn he was a German Jew who had emigrated in the 1930s. Guards fired bullets into the back of his neck and head along the roadside, thus ending the life of the most able German-speaking master scout in the entire regiment.

With Division Headquarters especially interested in the identity of German defenders at the lost Den Heuvel farm, Colonel Tucker sought to take prisoners amongst the enemy facing 2nd Battalion positions. The evening of October 24, this task fell to F Company, now commanded by 1st Lt. William J. Sweet. The patrol also comprised a few Headquarters Company personnel and German-speaking members of Headquarters and Headquarters. "Late in the afternoon we got the charcoal to blacken our faces, checked our weapons, and got a briefing on what we were to do," stated PFC Leo Hart. "It was a simple mission. An outpost was the target, and the surprise was with us."[438] A recent D Company transfer, 2nd Lt. Vance C. Hall, Jr., would lead the way with the 2nd Platoon, since their original leader, 1st Lt. Martin E. Middleton, was now acting as company executive officer.

According to Capt. Adam A. Komosa, Assistant Regimental S-3, this was "the largest combat patrol that we had employed during the whole war. As Regimental Plans and Training Officer, I took it upon myself to move out to the outpost to observe the attack. I took particular interest in this patrol because if this company failed to yield a prisoner tonight, the [entire] 2nd Battalion would have to go out tomorrow night to do the job. And none of us looked forward to this.

"Like a darned fool, I passed through our front lines before jump-off time and walked out across no man's land to the outpost. It was dark and eerie. Skeletons of our gliders lay silhouetted like ghosts all along no man's land. They were stripped of their canvas fabric by the Germans, who in all probability used it for shelter. Along the way to the OPL (Outpost Line) I noted florescent objects along the trail. These were the remains of glidermen who had previously been shot by the Germans. It was a strange and spooky experience.

"Finally, I arrived at the OPL, several hundred yards forward of the MLR and just short of the Den Heuvel woods. Then I was halted by a soft tone of command. Upon identifying myself, I shared the stand-up foxhole [with] the outpost sentry who halted me. As I was waiting for the preparatory artillery fire to come into the woods in advance of the company's jump-off, the young soldier looked at me very closely and asked: 'Sir, aren't you Captain Komosa?' When I replied I was, he said, 'I'm the one you shanghaied down to D Company at the Anzio Beachhead.' There we were—only he and I. Oh! How sweet revenge could have been. […] But it appeared that if this private had any resentment over being shanghaied it soon mellowed. Besides, it was a pretty eerie situation out there alone in a foxhole, and it was comforting to have an ally nearby. We listened and waited."[439]

Following the prearranged artillery barrage, Hall's patrol moved across the flat terrain with absolutely no resistance for about 200 yards while PFC Willard G. Tess, Pvt. Joseph Montbleau and a few others ran out ahead. PFC Leo Hart was about 40 feet behind PFC Marshall J. Cornelius, a bazooka man from Headquarters Company, 2nd Battalion, when a burst of sudden machine-gun fire "cut waist-high from my right to the left. I was knocked off my feet. At first I thought I was hit, but the bullet slammed into my M-1 right at the slide, making it useless." After this first burst, "everything went dead quiet. Then out of the quiet I heard Cornelius, who must have taken the burst right in the middle, cry very softly, 'Mamma . . . Mamma.' He then began reciting, "Now I lay me down to sleep, I pray—" and that was all. I can't express how I felt, but the enemy artillery came barreling in, and cover was of the utmost importance from then out."[440]

Hart soon heard the pleas of his friend Private Montbleau, who lay wounded on the other side of the knoll between his company and the German machine-gun post. Eager to meet his first combat, Montbleau had "rushed well ahead of the patrol, shouting at the top of his voice," and been "immediately wounded." Since there "was no immediate action," Hart handed his rifle to Hall, "climbed over the mound that was our saving factor, and crawled flat on my belly until I got to Montbleau. He got on my back, and we crawled back to our line. We then went into rapid retreat."[441] Montbleau's foot was later amputated and Hart was slightly wounded when a bullet scratched him behind the ear.

From his foxhole at the OPL, Captain Komosa had indeed "observed the British and American artillery lay down its barrage into the Den Heuvel woods" and had "heard much shooting, some screaming and a hell of a lot swearing" during "angry exchanges of machine-gun and small-arms fire." When it was all over and the troopers began to emerge from the woods, it sounded as though they were arguing among themselves. "I heard one say, 'Let me throw my bayonet through that son of a bitch.' One of the noncoms—I believe it was 1st Sgt. [Jack] Bishop—stepped in and barked in his usually commanding manner, 'Look, you stupid ass! If we don't bring this dried-up little bastard back to the CP alive, we'll have to come out here tomorrow night and do this all over again.' From that moment on, and until they returned to the CP, they guarded their prisoner with unusual caution.

"The prisoner was just a little squirt who probably didn't weigh over 90 pounds soaking wet. He looked and shook like a starved chicken that had been abandoned in the slush for some time. But it turned out that he carried very impressive credentials. He was a pilot, a paratrooper, and a graduate of a number of schools of higher learning, including one of the Nazi party schools. Why he was an ordinary soldier, I'll never know.

"F Company suffered heavily, considering the nature of the mission. Among its casualties was a newly assigned platoon leader [Lieutenant Scheibelein]. It was the lieutenant's first and last combat action. As the company emerged from the woods in scattered groups, the company commander assembled his men as though he were on a peacetime garrison parade ground and marched it back in cadence as though it was passing in review. I had the feeling that he wanted to 'jack the company up' in order to take their mind off the casualties they had suffered.

"Soon I found myself out there in the weird darkness all by myself. About that time, the Germans returned to the woods and opened fire with their angry machine guns. The bullets sounded like hundreds of snapping whips overhead. Then the artillery came in. I was pinned down and spread myself in a low depression like a jellyfish. When the firing stopped, I worked myself back to our lines. As I approached one of the machine guns on our MLR, I was halted. When I identified myself, I was permitted to pass through. About that time, I assume, these troopers were wondering what that damned fool was doing out there all by himself. [...]"[442]

Among the awards for heroism that day were troopers who came to the rescue of their comrades. For example, PFC Willis J. Kresge, D Company, received a Bronze Star for voluntarily leaving his position with two companions in order to evacuate wounded men who had been on F Company's combat patrol. "As they approached the disabled patrol, they met an enemy attacking force that was coming in to hit the patrol's right flank. Private First Class Kresge worked his way forward toward the enemy under their fire and when about 20 yards from the enemy, he threw a grenade and immediately assaulted the position by himself, killing two of the enemy and forcing the remainder to retreat. He then rejoined his two comrades, proceeded to the disabled patrol under a heavy enemy mortar barrage, and helped to evacuate all of the wounded to a safer area."[443]

Members of the patrol like Private Nadler also "helped carry wounded back those 1500 yards. Four of us started back with a wounded man in a blanket. We got down to two [carriers] part way back, when we found another wounded man. For the last 200 yards I ended up carrying the first man alone. When I put him down, a doctor told me he was dead. My company commander was there. He said, 'Nadler, the 1st Platoon must have missed the signal flare to return. You know this area well by now. Go out there and tell the platoon leader to return to our lines. Help him make sure all his men get the message and leave as a platoon. No stragglers. You bring up the rear. Hurry! It will be getting light in about an hour.'

"Someone had taken my rifle when I took a corner of that blanket. I had no weapon, [but ...] there was no time to talk of trifles. Even double-timing all the way, I had very little time to prevent a disaster. I started out [...] at a fast trot. I must have been in good condition because I only stopped when I reached the crossroads, which was deserted completely. I remember wishing I had a weapon. I had to turn right in about 300 yards to reach the 1st Platoon. There was no time for caution or a sneak approach. I decided I would trot down that road until someone stopped me or my nerve ran out. [...] It seemed like I was going too far and something was very wrong. I was trying to remember if I could recall extra-heavy action in this sector that could have wiped out the entire platoon [when] I heard someone call my name.

"I found the lieutenant and gave him the message. He had seen the flare but thought we were to wait for a second one. [...] It seemed to me they could have just gotten up and left, yet it took 15 minutes before we started back. There were no wounded with this group. [...] It was light before we reached the shelter of our front lines. The last 100 yards or so we were sprayed by enemy machine-gun fire.

"I had orders to bring up the rear. I had to be the last man back or face the wrath of my company commander. I wouldn't give him that pleasure. I hit the ground and lay there until the last lead-foot crossed our line. Then I got up and ran in. My company commander said he thought I had been hit when I went down. I wonder why he didn't send someone out to help me if he thought that. He was probably looking for [medic Frederick R.] Schiele. I am glad he didn't send anyone, as a guy could get hurt out there at that moment."[444]

Second Lieutenant Hall received a Certificate of Merit for leadership in close action against the strong point in the woods, which killed or wounded some 15 enemy and knocked out two of six German machine guns. In all, three American lives were lost and at least seven men were injured. In addition to Lieutenant Scheibelein and Private First Class Cornelius, F Company trooper Pvt. Kostanty A. Sadoski was also killed by machine-gun fire, and Lieutenant Hall was wounded. This brought the F Company toll to six lieutenants killed or wounded in just four short weeks. Only Captain Richardson and Lieutenants Sweet, Middleton and Harris remained; two of the wounded, McCash and Hall, would later rejoin the unit.

As Captain Komosa summed up: "It was indeed an expensive operation—all for one prisoner. Nevertheless, Division Headquarters obtained the information it wanted: the identification of the German unit to our front. Our patrols were henceforth conducted in a more conventional manner. And almost without exception, these were conducted at night, since the terrain, other than that we occupied, was flat and open."[445]

The position, albeit elevated, nevertheless proved consistently dangerous. The afternoon of October 25, 1st Platoon, A Company was shelled. Pvt. Victor C. Rettell was killed instantly, hit in the head and side by shrapnel. Two days later around noon, the 1st Battalion was finally relieved from its front-line position by the 3rd Battalion. A soldier from 3rd Platoon, A Company, Pvt. Paul G. Stinson, was tragically killed in the woods east of Nijmegen as the 1st Battalion arrived at its new location. "The packs were in a pile when we arrived at our new position," recalled Lieutenant Breard. "Stinson was looking for his when he disturbed a Panzerfaust. It did not explode, but the blast from the pipe disemboweled him. I gave him my morphine and my medic gave him a shot also. He died in our arms but was not in any pain. It was fast."[446]

After a short rest, the "1st Battalion took over a line running from the Berg en Dal-Wyler road to near Voxhil. Every night one platoon would go out to outpost Vossendaal. The Germans would also try to outpost it, so we would fight nearly every night. We always tried to arrive first so we would be protected in the cellars. The SCR-536 radio was used for communication between squads and platoons. I usually used the soundpower phones to communicate with my squad leaders. The SCR-300 radio was operated at the Company CP in a large white hotel at the Nieuwe Holleweg in Beek."[447]

On Monday, October 30, 1944, Captain Burriss received the order to send out another combat patrol to snatch prisoners. He assigned the mission to 1st Lieutenant Kennedy, the most experienced platoon leader in I Company. Kennedy's 3rd Platoon was severely understrength due to losses suffered in the Waal Crossing, the fighting at the Den Heuvel farm and a previous patrol on October 27. The patrol was thus forcibly small in order to maintain over-stretched I Company defensive positions.

S.Sgt. William H. "Whitey" White, 1st Platoon, had just hitchhiked all the way back from England, where he had been hospitalized due to wounds from the Waal Crossing. Although barely healed, he offered to join the 3rd Platoon patrol and even convinced Kennedy that he was best suited to act as lead scout.

White had a map marked by wounded S.Sgt. Louis Orvin that indicated where an I Company patrol had previously been fired upon. Kennedy, White and three other men, including Cpl. Russell J. McDermott from Brooklyn, set out to Imthal to acquire a prisoner. About an hour later, White hit an anti-personnel mine, and almost immediately a second mine detonated. As Corporal McDermott and Lieutenant Kennedy moved forward to drag White back, Kennedy stepped on another mine. He was severely wounded and McDermott was blinded by steel fragments. The other two men carried Kennedy's body back to I Company, guiding McDermott along the way.

The patrol reported in around 2130 hours, but did not at first tell Captain Burriss the fate of Staff Sergeant White. The 1st Battalion S-3, 1st Lieutenant Goethe, spoke with Kennedy, whose his left leg was half gone. Kennedy "said he would take that to get home. [...] I believe the medics gave him too much morphine. I personally stopped a fourth one from giving him a syrette."[448]

Captain Burriss requested permission to retreat the 3rd Platoon from their outpost and replace the now leaderless platoon. Major Cook ordered Lieutenant Hanna to relieve the decimated platoon with 2nd Platoon, G Company. Hanna visited Kennedy before setting out: "Ed had, by this time, stepped on a mine and been brought back to [...] the control CP station for this bit of action [...]. Kennedy was stretched out on a stretcher attended by Captain Kitchin. Colonel Tucker was there and, I believe, Lieutenant Goethe; maybe also Major Cook. [...] Ed was very rational and did not appear to be in much pain. He asked me how badly his foot was injured. I looked up at Kitchin, and he shook his head no. And so I told Ed that it didn't look too serious to me. Actually, the leg and ankle were completely gone with just a bone and flesh showing.

"I took my men with a guide from I Company through the minefield that led to the remains of a house. This was the outpost CP and the men were in foxholes along the edge of a wooded area. My group relieved I Company and remained at this outpost for the night and the next day. We were relieved the next night, maybe two nights later. We received no enemy fire and had no contact with the enemy.

"When I got back, I heard that Kennedy had died in the ambulance on the way to the hospital. At the time I also had the same thought as Jim Goethe—too much morphine. I don't remember ever volunteering for a patrol or to man an outpost. I also don't remember anyone volunteering for these duties; we just took our turns as directed."[449]

The blinded Corporal McDermott, eyes now bandaged, had shared a hospital room in Nijmegen with Lieutenant Kennedy. Kennedy had joked that McDermott would have to do the dancing and he would do the seeing at the next dance party. Kennedy had been operated on, and the two men were being transported to the 24th Evacuation Hospital when Kennedy died of shock on October 31. McDermott recovered his eyesight and returned to I Company a few days later, where he informed Staff Sergeant Orvin about the ill-fated patrol and the conversation with Lieutenant Kennedy.[450]

Sergeant Leoleis volunteered to go out with the two unwounded troopers and another man to retrieve Staff Sergeant White's body. One of the men refused to return and the other was very nervous as they set out. The patrol returned empty-handed. Later that evening, Leoleis took out a larger patrol, again without success.

In the evening of November 1, 2nd Lt. Robert S. Wright, G Company, stepped on a mine while leading a patrol and was killed. Three days later, front-line troops eligible to vote received ballot for the upcoming presidential election. The sentiments of 1st Lt. William D. Mandle, Regimental Demolition Platoon, were typical of many front-line soldiers: "The guys over here don't care who's in power as much as they are concerned about fighting Germany, so she won't be able in 20 years or so to start another one of these things. In other words, they want a president who will back the complete defeat of Germany and then ensure America's participation in some kind of international organization for preserving the peace.

"Whenever we talk to a German now (which isn't often because we have nothing to do with them), their first line is, 'Oh, I didn't like Hitler—he was forced on us.' Then their second line is inevitably, 'Why is America fighting *Der Fuehrer* when we have so much in common?' [...] That is why the 'poor German people' story is having the opposite effect on us over here, and I hope it has the same effect on those at home."[451]

On November 10, PFC Edward J. Kelly, H Company, was severely wounded near the road from Groesbeek to Wyler. Evacuated back all the way to the United States, he remained in hospitals over the next six years, finally dying of his wounds on October 3, 1950. Just two days after Kelly was wounded, the 8th Infantry Brigade, Canadian 3rd Infantry Division, relieved the 504th PIR.

Brigadier J. A. Roberts and his men relieved the 3rd Battalion at 2130 hours, November 14, but the Canadian battalion slated to relieve A Company had not yet arrived. Captain Duncan ordered Lieutenant Breard to take one of the present Canadian platoons to the Vossendaal outpost, which A Company had already vacated. As they approached, the Germans opened up with machine guns. Breard led the platoon to a house back in the woods, where the Canadian lieutenant called his company commander and received orders to withdraw to his company's defensive position. The outpost was abandoned and Breard returned to 1st Battalion headquarters. Learning the happy news that "everyone had been relieved," he caught a ride back to his own battalion, positioned south of the Grave Bridge. "The next morning as we entrucked for Reims, France, it started to snow. After a very cold two-day ride, we arrived at Sissonne, France."[452]

That day, two men from Service Company, 1st Sgt. Frank P. Namayeski and PFC Harvey H. Herbert, were tragically killed on the Wylerbaan, most likely by German artillery. On February 8, Canadian 2nd Infantry Division retook the Vossendaal, Groenendaal, Den Heuvel and Heuvelhof farms in Operation Veritable. An artillery barrage preceded the attack on each—a strong contrast with the support available to Tucker's troopers, whose smaller bands had taken them all without benefit of barrage the previous September.

On September 17, 1945, the 504th PIR and a few dozen other 82nd ABD paratroopers and glidermen arrived by truck in Nijmegen. Officers included Colonel Tucker and 1st Lieutenants Breard, Garrison and Mandle. "Southern hospitality found its equal in the cities of Grave and Nijmegen, Holland, last week when 82nd men, including a 30-man delegation from the 504, returned to the scenes of their airborne conquests of a year ago," wrote Mandle in an article published in *Propblast* on October 6. "Dutch citizens from miles around lined the streets to the Nijmegen Bridge as their liberators marched over the same ground that a year before had been one of the hottest in Europe. [...] Morning ceremonies were staged for the 82nd at the bridge, where Maj. Gen. James M. Gavin presented Dutch Underground leaders with individual awards and the city of Nijmegen with the American flag [that had] flown above the Division CP while the 82nd was in Holland.

"Afternoon ceremonies were held at the Molenhoek 82nd Airborne Cemetery, where Dutch school children decorated each grave with flowers. Wreaths were placed at the base of the Cemetery flagpole by General Gavin, the Burgomaster of Nijmegen, and the Orange Committee of Groesbeek. Perhaps the most spontaneous and whole-hearted welcome of the entire celebration came when the 504 delegation arrived in Grave for festivities given by the citizens of that town for men of the regiment. The first objective captured in the Holland invasion was the Grave Bridge, the longest span bridge in Europe, captured by the 504 two hours after the regiment had jumped. Inhabitants of Grave swarmed over the highway leading into town as 504 trucks arrived."

The 504 PIR and all other regiments and supporting units of the 82nd Airborne Division that fought so valiantly to liberate the Netherlands in WWII remain and always will remain loved and honoured by a grateful Dutch populace. It is only fitting that a history of the 504th PIR in Market-Garden close with one of the myriad stories of abiding friendship, loyalty, and mutual appreciation the Dutch and Americans still tell today.

"One time, after the war," wrote Lieutenant Mandle in 1962, we were invited to jump on Grave, Holland, where we had, just one year previously, jumped in wartime. Our battalion made the flight and jumped. The people were wonderful, some of them even wearing jumpsuits, boots and the like. Particularly, I remember a blonde who was dressed in a jump suit.

"We had the division band there—they had traveled by truck—and ceremonies were held at the graves of the many American soldiers who had died. Incidentally, they were kept in immaculate condition! The blonde joined ranks and stood at attention while the band played and the general spoke. Afterward, she said she had met a sergeant who had proposed to her. She had accepted. She was standing there because one of the graves had her sergeant."[453]

POSTSCRIPT
SEPTEMBER 1945–MARCH 2014

Some 6,000 officers and men served in the 504th PIR in WWII, a number to which we must add the veterans of C Company, 307th Airborne Engineers and the 376th Parachute Field Artillery Battalion. A summary of the post-war careers of even a small fraction of the regiment's former members would exceed the entire length of this book. The below is thus limited to the post-war biographies of senior officers and a few of the more famous junior officers who have now passed away.

As of March 2014 the highest living officers (as reckoned by their ranks in WWII) are Capts. Lewis P. Fern (2nd Battalion S-2) and T. Moffatt Burriss (I Company), both nonagenarians. Of the 23 Distinguished Service Cross recipients of the 504th PIR, only John C. Granados, Roy M. Hanna, Shelby R. Hord, James A. Kiernan and James Megellas are alive today. DSC awards for the Normandy and Holland Campaigns are listed in Appendix A.

The post-war careers varied, although many veterans made the US Army their career. Others studied law or went into politics; several founded construction companies or became building contractors; others taught history, art or English. But all had one thing in common: they did not brag about their accomplishments during the war. On the contrary, many remained silent about their war experience, even—or perhaps especially—to their wives and children. In the course of writing this book, I contact over a hundred veterans between 2002 and 2013 and even then, up to up to 60-odd years after the war, I was the first person to whom numerous veterans had ever spoken about the war.

The characteristic humility of 504th veterans toward their outstanding war record most certainly applies to their "founding father" as well. Col. Theodore L. Dunn, the regiment's first commander, was also the first senior officer of the 504th to die after the war. He passed away in Columbus, Georgia, on December 14, 1950, and was buried at the Fort Benning Post Cemetery, section C1, site 221. Surprisingly, not a single history book on American Airborne Forces in WWII mentions his name. I first found reference to him when I received photocopies of *504th Parachute Battalion. A Historical and Pictorial Review of the Parachute Battalions* (1942).

Colonel Dunn worked as Assistant to the Chief of Army Transportation of the Army Forces Western Pacific for the remainder of the war. Two years after the war, Dunn was made Senior Instructor of the Officer Reserve Corps in Wisconsin in 1947, a position he occupied until he retired due to physical disability in 1949 with the rank of colonel.

Dunn's successor, Col. Reuben H. Tucker III, remained with his beloved regiment until May 10, 1946, the third anniversary of the regiment's arrival in North Africa. Next posted to West Point as commanding officer of the 1st Regiment of Cadets, Department of Tactics, he remained at West Point until August 19, 1948. During that time another two sons were born, making four in all: Glenn (1947) and Scott (1948). A fifth son, Christopher, was born in 1957.

While serving at West Point, Tucker received a letter from Mayor Charles Hustinx of Nijmegen, requesting his recollections of the Waal Crossing and the German failure to detonate the bridge. Tucker ended his detailed report: "I sincerely hope that what I have set down will be of assistance to you and to your historians, and can only add that if I can be of any further help to you, I shall be only too glad to do so."[454]

After his assignment at West Point, Colonel Tucker attended the United States Air Force Air War College at Maxwell Air Force Base and United States Army War College at Carlisle before serving as Eighth Army operations officer under Lieutenant General Ridgway in Korea. He had served in this capacity at a much lower level as Battalion S-3 in the 504th Parachute Battalion, before the formation of the 504th PIR. Ridgway knew that Tucker was a seasoned combat leader and good tactician. This appointment somewhat served to rectify the past, when Ridgway had doubted Tucker's ability to serve as an assistant division commander or senior staff officer back in the summer of 1944.

After several years in Korea, Tucker was reassigned to Fort Dix, New Jersey, as post commander before becoming Professor of Military Science at

The Citadel, Charleston, South Carolina, in 1955. Gen. Mark W. Clark, the former Fifth Army commander, also appointed him Commandant of the Cadets. A year later, now a brigadier general, he was transferred to the 101st Airborne Division as assistant division commander. This he remained until he was given command of the (secret) Military Mission to Laos in 1960.

After a lighting *coup d'état* failed to remove the right-wing government of Gen. Phoumi Nosavan in 1960, the situation in Laos stabilized for a while. Tucker was promoted to major general. Now Chief of Infantry in the Office of Personnel Operations in Washington, he attended the activation ceremony of the 2nd Airborne Battle Group of the 504th Infantry at Fort Bragg in July 1960. The new Battle Group replaced the 2nd Airborne Battle Group of the 503rd Infantry, which was headed to Okinawa; Major General Tucker arranged a visit to Washington for their officers to view their records before they marched in President Kennedy's Inauguration Parade on January 20, 1961. The following year he became G-3 of the US Army Pacific in Fort Shafter, Hawaii. Major General Tucker retired from the US Army in 1963 after 28 years of continuous service, but remained active in the Reserves and returned to The Citadel to become permanent Commandant of Cadets.

On October 1, 1967, tragedy struck the family when General Tucker's oldest son, Maj. David Bruce Tucker, was killed in Vietnam. During the last two years of his life, General Tucker was aware of Cornelius Ryan's work on *A Bridge Too Far*; he contributed material, but did not live to see the publication.

On January 6, 1970, while crossing the campus of The Citadel, General Tucker suffered a heart attack, sat down under a tree, and died. He was only 58 years old. Reuben Henry Tucker III was buried with full military honors on January 9 after a funeral service in the National Cemetery of Beaufort, South Carolina, at plot 20, grave 61. Among attending generals were retired General Clark, Lt. Gen. John J. Tolson III (who had served in the 503rd PIR) and Brig. Gen. John S. Lekson, one of Tucker's former regimental officers. His widow Helen died on February 5, 1998, and rests in the same grave. Their sons Bruce (1939-1967) and Glenn (1947-2010) are buried in the same cemetery.

All of Reuben and Helen Tucker's sons were graduates of The Citadel: Bruce in 1961, Jeff in 1964, Scott in 1970, Glenn in 1973 and Christopher in 1979. Christopher rose to the rank of brigadier general and in September 2009 was made commander of the US Army Security Assistance Command (USASAC) at Redstone Arsenal, Alabama. He retired two years later.

Julian A. Cook, the 3rd Battalion commander, remained in the 504th PIR. In January 1946, he tried in vain to persuade Capts. Robert C. Blankenship and James Megellas to remain in the US Army as well, and although he regretted their departure, he never held it against them. Assigned to the French Army in 1953 as a liaison officer in Vietnam, Cook became ill and spent eight months in various hospitals, which affected his career advancement. After commanding the 77th Special Forces Group from 1957 to 1958, he served on the staff of the Commander-in-Chief, Atlantic Command (CINCLANT) in Norfolk, Virginia, and in the later 1960s served on the staff of the Allied Forces, Southern Europe (AFSOUTH) in Naples. In 1967, he returned to Holland where he visited former battlefields, and he was interviewed extensively by Cornelius Ryan in 1968. He retired not long afterwards with the rank of colonel.

In June 1977, after the publication of *A Bridge Too Far* and Ryan's death, Colonel Cook wrote to Kathryn Ryan to find out more about the film version directed by Richard Attenborough and produced by Joseph Levine: "As of this date," he wrote, "no one associated with the production of the movie has contacted me for any purpose whatsoever except for the publicity mail-outs Joe Levine mailed out in 1975—hardly a personal contact. A few reporters or writers from the news media have called me for possible stories in conjunction with the release of the movie. They were uniformly quite surprised to find out that I knew nothing more than what I have read or heard in the news. Certain questions asked [to] me, implied with articles I have read, lead me to believe that I may have serious reservations about how I am portrayed in the movie."[455] Colonel Cook later contributed to William Breuer's *Geronimo!* and Clay Blair's *Ridgway's Paratroopers* though letters and interviews signed "Aaron Cook," the name he used after the war.

Deactivated in 1957, the 3/504 was shortly reactivated in July 1968, but deactivated again December 15, 1969. Overjoyed to learn in early 1986 that the battalion would be again reactivated, Colonel Cook travelled to Fort Bragg with I Company veterans Sam Clecker, Darrell Edgar, Arthur Flaherty, Francis Keefe, William Leonard and George Leoleis to be present at the activation ceremonies that April. Less than four years later, on June 19, 1990, he died at age 73 in his hometown of Columbia, South Carolina. His beloved 3rd Battalion was deactivated once more on January 15, 2006.

Lt. Col. Warren R. Williams, Jr., saw his two-year-old daughter for the first time when he returned to the United States in January 1946. A career soldier, Williams served in Korea and later became Director of the US Army

Board for Aviation Accident Research at Fort Rucker, Alabama. His department was responsible for investigating aviation accidents and recommending improvements to prevent future accidents. Retiring with the rank of colonel in the late 1960s, Williams contributed to several books, including earlier-mentioned titles by Blair, Breuer and Ryan. He also corresponded extensively with Father Gerard Thuring of the Liberation Museum in Groesbeek, the Netherlands, supplying data for the *Roll of Honor* for the 82nd Airborne Division that the Museum finally published in 1997. One month short of his seventieth birthday, Col. Warren Rand Williams, Jr., passed away on May 11, 1986, and was buried with full military honors at Arlington National Cemetery, plot 65, grave 4121. Although he is rumoured to have earned the Distinguished Service Cross for gallantry in action on the Anzio Beachhead, the author has been unable to discover any conclusive evidence. Williams had the honor of being the only battalion commander to serve with the regiment in every campaign, beginning with the arrival of the 504th in North Africa in April 1943.

Lt. Col. Edward N. Wellems remained in the US Army; promoted to the rank of colonel, he became Deputy Chief of Staff for Personnel and Administration at West Point on March 11, 1955. After slightly more than three years, he left the academy or another assignment, and finally retired in early 1972, after 31 years in the armed forces. In the spring of that year, he and his wife settled in Lakewood, Washington, where he passed away on September 22, 1976 at age 60. He is buried at Holy Cross Cemetery in Fargo, North Dakota. Wellems never shared his war experience with parents or siblings although he did on one occasion speak highly of his regimental commander to his youngest brother, John. First Lieutenant Chester A. Garrison, his former 2nd Battalion adjutant, received an unexpected phone call from Wellems in January 1970, when he tearfully reported that General Tucker had just died. Garrison recalled that his normally strict battalion commander was "stricken by this news because they had been very close. Ed's sentimentality had indeed broken through."[456]

Maj. Ivan J. Roggen, the former regimental surgeon, returned to his native Michigan and settled down in Saginaw. A recipient of the Purple Heart, Legion of Merit and a Bronze Star, Roggen returned to the University of Michigan, completed a three-year residency and fellowship program in pediatrics at the University Hospital. He married Jane A. Moskal in 1947, and the couple raised five children in Saginaw, where Roggen practiced General Pediatrics in from 1950 until his retirement in 1985. Throughout the years he kept in touch with Chaplain Kuehl, his fellow wartime surgeons and several of his medics. He passed away at age 96 on November 28, 2010. His remains were cremated at his own request.

Chaplain Delbert A. Kuehl remained in the army until his retirement at age 55 in 1962, when he entered the Army Reserves, eventually reaching the rank of colonel. His second career was as a missionary in Japan and later as associate director of The Evangelical Alliance Mission (TEAM) in Wheaton, Illinois. He married in 1946 and raised five children with his wife Delores. He kept in close contact with other 504th RCT veterans until his death at age 93 on September 13, 2010. Interviewed countless times (present book included), he also authored a privately published wartime memoir, *Front Line*. Chaplin Kuehl is buried in the Abraham Lincoln National Cemetery in Elwood, Illinois.

Maj. Abdallah K. Zakby served as Deputy G-4 of the Berlin Command after the war and retired as a lieutenant colonel. In the 1960s he began A. K. Zakby & Associates, a company that sold new and rebuilt heavy equipment in the Middle East. Zakby returned the questionnaire he received from Cornelius Ryan in 1968, and requested the addresses of Capts. William Addison and Arthur Ferguson, whom he had remembered well. He passed away on his 88th birthday on March 9, 1997, in Monterey, California. He is buried with his wife Rosalie (died 2006) in the El Encinal Cemetery in Monterey.

Capt. Henry B. Keep returned to Pennsylvania after the war and settled down in the town of Villanova. His detailed account of the Waal River Crossing was translated by the Dutch newspaper *De Gelderlander* on November 7, 1953 and wrongly attributed to his step-father, Charles J. Biddle.[457] Henry Keep became administrative assistant of the Department of Surgery at the University of Pennsylvania School of Medicine in 1960, and assistant to the chairman of the department in 1974. Contacted by Cornelius Ryan in 1968, he contributed a copy of a letter about the Holland Campaign he had written to his mother in November 1944 and donated three wartime photos to Ryan's project. Henry Keep died while undergoing heart surgery at the Hospital of the University of Pennsylvania on July 11, 1983 at age 65. His name lives on in the Henry B. Keep Fund which supports acquisitions by the Philadelphia Museum of Art.

Capt. Carl W. Kappel also remained the US Army, becoming an instructor at the Parachute School in Fort Benning, where he met 1st Lt. Herman Littman in 1946 for the first time since Littman had been captured in Sicily.

A year later Kappel left the Parachute School to attend the Advanced Infantry Officers Course at The Infantry School, where he graduated in class no. 1 in 1948. His 42-page monograph on H Company operations during the first five days of the Holland Campaign is preserved at the Donovan Library, Fort Benning.

Kappel served in Korea and Vietnam and rose to the rank of colonel. His contribution to Cornelius Ryan's research on Operation Market Garden is among the most significant. Retiring around 1970, he moved from Springfield, Virginia, to Hubert, North Carolina, where he died at age 67 on September 19, 1984, exactly one day before the 40th Commemoration of the Waal Crossing. Col. Carl William Kappel was buried with full military honors at Arlington Cemetery, Section 68, grave 1575.

On October 8, 1945, Capt. Robert C. Blankenship was made Knight of the Military William Order (MWO) by Royal Decree of Queen Wilhelmina of the Netherlands. First awarded in 1815 by King William I, this is the oldest and highest military honor of the Kingdom of the Netherlands, comparable to the French Légion d'Honneur but awarded far less often. The same honor was bestowed on Colonel Tucker, Lieutenant Colonel Cook, Capt. Wesley D. Harris, and the posthumously knighted Sgt. William E. Kero, 307th Airborne Engineer Battalion. In January 1946, Blankenship turned down a regular army commission and returned to civilian life, much to the disappointment of Lieutenant Colonel Cook and Colonel Tucker. Entering private business, he settled in Alexandria, Louisiana, where he was named "Citizen of the Year." Blankenship was similarly honored in 1962 by DeRidder, Louisiana, where he served as mayor from 1968 until his death. Contrary to the report of his fellow veteran James Megellas in *All The Way To Berlin* Blankenship died not from old combat wounds in 1973, but of a major heart attack at age 49 on August 13, 1970.

APPENDIX A
DISTINGUISHED SERVICE CROSS RECIPIENTS

(* indicates a posthumous award)

RANK	FIRST NAME	INITIAL	LAST NAME	COMPANY	PLACE OF ACTION
Major	Julian	A	Cook	3rd Bn CO	Nijmegen
Sergeant	Shelton	W	Dustin	B	Heumen
Major	Willard	E	Harrison	Detached	Normandy
Corporal	Joseph	J	Jusek	E	Erlekom
PFC	Joseph	M	Koss*	F	Wercheren
1LT	James	–	Megellas	H	Wylermeer
PFC	Walter	J	Muszynski*	I	Nijmegen
Corporal	Charles	E	Nau	B	Heumen
PFC	Thomas	L	Rodgers*	Detached	Normandy
Colonel	Reuben	H	Tucker	Regt CO	Nijmegen

APPENDIX B
ORDER OF BATTLE FOR OPERATION MARKET GARDEN

REGIMENTAL STAFF

Colonel Reuben H. Tucker III	Regimental commanding officer
Lieutenant Colonel Warren R. Williams, Jr.	Regimental executive officer
1st Lieutenant Louis A. Hauptfleisch	S-1 (Personnel)
Captain Fordyce Gorham	S-2 (Intelligence)
Major Mack C. Shelley	S-3 (Operations)
Captain William A.B. Addison	S-4 (Supply)
Major Ivan J. Roggen	Regimental Surgeon
Captain Delbert A. Kuehl	Protestant Chaplain
Captain Edwin J. Kozak	Catholic Chaplain

1ST BATTALION

Major Willard E. Harrison	Battalion commander
Major Abdallah K. Zakby	Executive battalion commander
Major John T. Berry *(from September 21, 1944)*	
Captain Paul D. Bruns	Battalion Surgeon
Captain Charles W. Duncan	A Company
Captain Thomas C. Helgeson	B Company
Captain Albert E. Milloy	C Company
Captain Roy E. Anderson	HQ Company

2ND BATTALION

Major Edward N. Wellems	Battalion commander
Captain William Colville	Executive battalion commander
Captain William W. Kitchin	Battalion Surgeon
Captain Victor W. Campana	D Company
Captain Walter S. Van Poyck	E Company
Captain Beverly T. Richardson	F Company
Captain Robert J. Cellar	HQ Company

3RD BATTALION

Major Julian A. Cook	Battalion commander
Captain Arthur W. Ferguson	Executive battalion commander
Captain Hyman D. Shapiro	Battalion Surgeon
Captain Fred H. Thomas	G Company
Captain Carl W. Kappel	H Company
Captain T. Moffatt Burriss	I Company
Captain Warren S. Burkholder	HQ Company

LIAISON OFFICER TO THE DIVISION G-3 SECTION

Major John S. Lekson
Liaison Officer to the US Ninth Air Force
1st Lieutenant Elbert F. Smith

NOTES

Author's note: Unpublished sources were sometimes also untitled or unpaginated, or both. These have been documented as fully as possible; sources lacking full bibliographical information are designated by last name only on second reference. All translations from Dutch and German are my own and initialled FVL. I have similarly indicated my own questionnaires and interviews; sources from the Cornelius Ryan Collection are designated CRC.

CHAPTER 1

1 David K. Finney, "My Time with the 504th," Privately printed memoir (San Diago, CA, 2006).

2 Ernest W. Parks, "The War Years (WWII)," Unpublished memoir (2008).

3 Paul D. Bruns, "Flight Surgeon," Unpublished memoir (1987). Courtesy of Charlotte Baldridge, 359th Fighter Group Historian.

4 Ibid.

5 Ibid.

6 Adam A. Komosa, "The Holland Invasion," Questionaire, CRC. (January 12, 1968). Courtesy of Timothy Rose.

7 Edwin M. Clements, Untitled manuscript. http://www.marketgarden.com (accessed August 15, 2006).

8 Walter E. Hughes, "My Remembrances No. 1." Unpublished manuscript. Courtesy of Walter E. Hughes.

9 Ibid.

10 Ibid.

11 Walter E. Hughes, Telephone interview by Frank van Lunteren, January 10, 2010.

12 Hughes, "Remembrances."

13 James M. Gavin, cited in Clay Blair, *Ridgway's Paratroopers* (Annapolis, MD: Naval Institute Press, 2002), 301.

14 Julian A. Cook, Letter to Cornelius Ryan (February 26, 1968), CRC.

15 Hughes, "Remembrances."

CHAPTER 2

16 Chester A. Garrison, *An Ivy-League Paratrooper* (Corvallis, OR: Franklin Press, 2002), 140.
17 Albert A. Tarbell, Questionnaire, CRC.
18 Albert B. Clark, Unpublished manuscript, August 2005, 21. Courtesy of Albert B. Clark.
19 Clements
20 Hanz K. Druener, Questionnaire, CRC.
21 Louis A. Hauptfleisch, Questionnaire, CRC.
22 Arthur W. Ferguson, Questionnaire, CRC.
23 Walter S. Van Poyck, Questionnaire, CRC
24 Carl Mauro, "Memoirs of Captain Carl Mauro," Unpublished memoir, 18-21. Courtesy of Carl Mauro II.
25 John S. Thompson, "After-Action Report on the Capture of the Maas Bridge" (1944). Courtesy of Carl Mauro II. Original in the National Archives.
26 Willard M. Strunk, Questionnaire, CRC.

CHAPTER 3

27 Warren R. Williams, Jr., Questionnaire, CRC.
28 James S. Wells, Letter to his parents, November 1944. Courtesy of Tyson Davis.
29 Nicholas W. Mansolillo, Questionnaire, CRC.
30 Ibid.
31 Fred J. Baldino, Questionnaire, CRC. Originally completed for *A Bridge Too Far*, but not submitted until 2005. Courtesy of Fred Baldino.
32 Fay T. Steger, Questionnaire, CRC. Originally completed for *A Bridge Too Far*, but not submitted until 2005. Courtesy of Fred Baldino.
33 Ibid.
34 Ibid.
35 Clark, 21-22.
36 Steger
37 Clements
38 Bruns
39 David K. Finney, *My Time with the 504th*. Privately published memoir, 2006. n. p.
40 Williams
41 Hauptfleisch
42 George D. Graves, Jr., Letter to his father (October 7, 1944). Courtesy of Mike Bigalke.

CHAPTER 4

43 Carl W. Kappel, 'The Operations of Company H, 504th Parachute Infantry (82nd Airborne Division) in the Invasion of Holland 17–21 September 1944," 1949, 11. Unpublished manuscript. Donovan Research Library, Infantry School, Fort Benning, GA.

44 Ernest P. Murphy, Questionnaire, CRC.

45 Fred E. Thomas, "Holland Mission, G Company 504th Parachute Infantry Regiment" (September 1944), CRC.

46 Seymour Flox, Letter to his mother, November 18, 1944. Courtesy of Margaret Shelly, niece to Robert Koelle.

47 Ferguson

48 Dot Ferenbaugh, "Alumni News," *The Flat Hat* (College of William and Mary, Williamsburg, Virginia), March 8, 1944.

49 Thomas N. Carter, Telephone interview by Frank van Lunteren, April 24, 2010.

50 George Willoughby, Unpublished manuscript. Courtesy of George Willoughby.

51 Walter P. Leginski and Everett R. Ridout, Unpublished manuscript, November 7, 1944. Courtesy of Mike Bigalke.

52 Carter

53 Virgil F. Carmichael, Questionnaire, CRC.

54 Willoughby

55 Leginski and Ridout

56 Carter

57 Willoughby

58 Leginski and Ridout

59 Carmichael, Questionnaire, CRC.

60 Julian A. Cook, Interview by Cornelius Ryan, February, 25, 1968, CRC.

61 Ferguson

62 Thomas, "Holland Mission."

63 Allen F. McClain, Questionnaire, CRC.

64 James H. Legacie, Jr., Telephone interview by Frank van Lunteren, February 13, 2011.

65 Edward J. Sims, "Sicily and Holland with the 504th Parachute Infantry Regiment, 82nd Airborne Divison", 3. Unpublished manuscript. Courtesy of Edward J. Sims.

66 Flox

67 Hugh D. Wallis, Questionnaire, FVL.

68 John J. Foley, Jr., Telephone interview by Frank van Lunteren, February 25, 2012. The unknown trooper who fell to his death may have been Pvt. Max Edmondson, A Company.

69 Carl W. Kappel, Questionnaire, CRC.

70 Albert A. Tarbell, Questionnaire, CRC.

71 William A. B. Addison, Questionnaire, CRC.

72 Delbert A. Kuehl, cited in T. Moffatt Burriss, *Strike and Hold. A Memoir of the 82nd Airborne in World War II* (Washington DC: Brassey's, 2000), 116-117.

73 Henry B. Keep, Letter to his mother, November 20, 1944.

74 Hughes, "Remembrances."

75 Carmichael, Questionnaire, CRC.

76 Kappel, Questionnaire, CRC.

77 Thomas, "Holland Mission."

78 Kappel, "Operations of Company H", 19-20.

79 Silver Star Citation (posthumous) for Staff Sergeant William H. White. 82nd Airborne Division, General Order No. 60, November 30, 1944.

80 Ferguson

CHAPTER 5

81 Some crew chiefs released the bundles first; others released them in the middle of the stick, when the seventh man went out the door. This latter was more dangerous, especially for the seventh jumper, but had the advantage of making the bundles more readily accessible to the entire stick, and ideally equidistant from both ends. See Clements, note 7; Steger, note 32.

82 Mauro, 8-10.

83 Thompson

84 Victor W. Campana, Questionnaire, CRC.

85 Harry W. Rollins, Sr., Interview by his son Harry Jr., 2007. Courtesy of Harry W. Rollins, Jr.

86 Druener

87 John E. Scheaffer, Questionnaire, CRC.

88 Philip H. Nadler, Questionnaire, CRC.

89 Leo M. Hart, Questionnaire, CRC.

90 Curtis C. Morris had a "streamer" during the jump when some of the parachute suspension lines tangled around his canopy. He tried his reserve parachute, but was already too close to the ground. He plummeted through a tree in the yard of farmer Jan van der Hoogen, who called in the local Roman Catholic priest. Morris died later that day of his injuries, one day short of his twenty-seventh birthday. His daughter, Carol Cady, traced in January 2006, received the helmet her father had worn on September 17 from the Van der Hoogens, who wanted to return it to his family.

91 Campana, "Report on the Capture of the Maas Bridge at Grave" (November 1944), CRC.

92 Nadler, Questionnaire, CRC.

93 Bronze Star Citation for Private Raymond S. Thomas. 82nd Airborne Division, General Order No. 6, January 12, 1945.

94 Edward N. Wellems, Combat interview by Maj. Jeremiah O'Sullivan (1944), 4-5, CRC. Courtesy of Carl Mauro II.

95 Nadler, Questionnaire, CRC.

96 Silver Star Citation for 1st Lieutenant John E. Scheaffer. 82nd Airborne Division, General Order No. 129, October 24, 1945.

97 Earnest H. Brown, Untitled manuscript. Courtesy of his son, Terry Brown.

98 Campana, "Report."

99 Garrison, *Paratrooper*, 144.

100 Wellems, Combat interview, 7.

101 Alex Misseres, Combat interview by Maj. Jeremiah O'Sullivan (1944), CRC.

102 Bronze Star Citation for 1st Lieutenant Carl Mauro. 82nd Airborne Division, General Order No. 4, January 4, 1945.

103 Mauro, 31-33.

104 Paul A. Kunde, Telephone interview by Frank van Lunteren, August 1, 2012.

105 Louis E. Napier, Telephone interview by Frank van Lunteren, January 4, 2008.

106 Jeremiah O'Sullivan, "Combat Interviews, Company E, 504th Parachute Regiment, 82nd Airborne Division," (September 1944), 12-13, CRC. Courtesy of Carl Mauro II.

CHAPTER 6

107 Thomas C. Helgeson, Combat interview by Jeremiah O'Sullivan (1944), CRC. Courtesy of Mike Bigalke.

108 Robert D. Stern, Interview by Robert Wolfe (son of Hubert Wolfe, B/504), August 2007. Courtesy of Robert Wolfe.

109 Distinguished Service Cross Citation for Corporal Charles E. Nau. XVIII Airborne Corps, General Order No. 8, November 14, 1944.

110 Helgeson

111 Stern

112 Clements

113 Stern

114 Robert E. Waldon, Untitled manuscript, http://home.comcast.net/~b504pir/waldonmeM-1.html (accessed August 4, 2008).

115 Helgeson

116 Ibid.

117 Distinguished Service Cross for Sergeant Shelton W. Dustin. Headquarters XVIII Airborne Corps, General Order No. 8, November 14, 1944. I am indebted to Flossie Dustin, widow of Sergeant Dustin, and her daughter, Florence Corson, for faithfully retyping and sending me his DSC Citation.

118 Albert E. Milloy, Combat interview by Maj. Jeremiah O'Sullivan (1944), CRC.

119 Silver Star Citation for Sergeant Thomas J. Leccese. 82nd Airborne Division, General Order No. 57, October 29, 1944. Courtesy of John Leccese, son of Thomas Leccese.

120 Reneau G. Breard, Letter to Frank van Lunteren, February 18, 2005.

121 Steger

122 Clark, 22.

123 Clements

124 Ernst Sieger, "Bericht über den Einsatz der Kompanie während der Kampfhandlungen im Raum Nymwegen-Arnheim" (September 22, 1944), 1-2. Translation, FVL.

125 S-3 Journal, Entry for September 18, 1944, CRC.

CHAPTER 7

126 Campana, "Report."

127 Garrison, *Paratrooper*, 144.

128 Wellems, Combat interview, 7-8.

129 Chester A. Garrison, "Unit Journal of the 2nd Battalion, 504th Parachute Infantry Regiment, 82nd Airborne Division." The James M. Gavin Papers, Box 12, Folder "Letters to and from 82nd Vets on Airborne Operations in Holland, September 1944," USAMHI. Courtesy of Robert Wolfe, son of Hubert Wolfe (B/504).

130 Thomas, "Holland Mission."

131 Kappel, "Operations of Company H", 21.

132 Komosa

133 Reuben H. Tucker, "Commendation for Corporal Kokhuis," October 10, 1944. http://www.soldatenvanoranje.nl. The website, about Dutch commandos in WWII, was owned by René Swankhuizen and is now no longer in operation.

134 Albert A. Tarbell, Email to Frank van Lunteren, August 3, 2003.

135 Kappel, "Operations of Company H", 22.

136 Komosa

137 Reneau G. Breard, Letter.

138 Wim van Lunteren was a cousin of the author's grandfather.

139 Jan van Deelen, Letter to Fay T. Steger, July 19, 1946. Courtesy of Mary Beth Wood (Fay Steger's daughter) and her husband, Tim Wood.

140 Fred J. Baldino, Email to Frank van Lunteren, October 17, 2002. This friendly fire incident deeply shocked the men of the 2nd Platoon. Baldino received an email in January 2003 from Edward McGowan, a British veteran then living in Australia, who was looking for the family of "Pvt. John F. Burnett of the 504th Parachute Infantry Regiment." Baldino sent a copy of this email to me and I began corresponding with Bombardier McGowan of the 21st (Self-Propelled) Anti-Tank Regiment of the Guards Armoured Division. McGowan, wounded on September 21, 1944, had received Private Burnett's jacket to use as a blanket while in an aid station in Nijmegen. He had kept it for 59 years, and now wanted to return it to Burnett's family. McGowan died from a heart attack while swimming in the sea a few years later.

141 Sieger, 2-4.

142 Regimental S-3 Journal (September 18, 1944), CRC.

143 Strunk

144 Bronze Lion Citation for PFC Theodore H. Bachenheimer, Royal Decree No. 24, January 7, 1952.

145 Thompson

146 Paul A. Kunde, Interview, FVL; Willis D. Sisson, Telephone interview by Frank van Lunteren, January 2010.

147 Williams

148 Komosa

149 Thomas, "Holland Mission."

CHAPTER 8
150 Cook, Interview, CRC.

151 Reuben H. Tucker, "504th River Crossing, Holland" (Circa 1968), CRC.

152 Virgil F. Carmichael, cited in William Breuer, *Geronimo!* (New York, NY: St. Martin's Press, 1992), 347-348.

153 Cornelius Ryan, *A Bridge Too Far* (New York, NY: Simon and Schuster, 1974), 457.

154 Alexander McKee, *Race to the Rhine Bridges* (New York, NY; 1971), 213.

155 Keep, Letter.

156 Tucker, "River Crossing."

157 Garrison, "Unit Journal."

158 Wellems, Combat interview, 8-9.

159 Brown

160 Jaap van Gent, cited in Hen Bollen, *Corridor naar de Rijn* (Zutphen: Terra Publishing, 1988), 106. Translation, FVL.

161 Pandurs were irregular soldiers who fought as a paramilitary regiment under the command of Baron Franz von der Trenck in the War of the Austrian Succession (1740-1748). Most of the partisans knew each other from De Ruyter, the nautical college in Nijmegen, where they had been pupils; Jacques Brouwer baptized the group after watching the 1942 film *De Held der Pandoeren' (The Hero of the Pandurs)*.

162 Prior to September 1944, the Pandurs's primary activities had been delivering and selling illegal newspapers and fighting with German collaborators. They did rifle training at various locations, some using homemade wooden rifles, as there were not enough of the real thing to go around. A severe setback occurred in January 1943 when the *Sicherheitsdienst* (SD) raided the house of Jaap Visker, where they discovered rifle ammunition. Visker was sent to a concentration camp for the remainder of the war, and the other 11 Pandurs were arrested and sent to a detention center in Arnhem. Brouwer had previously instructed them to insist, if interrogated, that they were a sports club. Despite harsh treatment, all maintained their story and were released in early March 1943 due to lack of evidence. Soon after, the group diminished to nine members, but was reinforced in April 1943 with Theo Rietbergen and Martien Kempen. In spring 1944, Albert van der Sande and Jacques Bouman joined their ranks, bringing the total to 14 members.

163 Jacques G. Brouwer, Letter to the Commissie tot Documentatie van het Verzet in Nijmegen, 1945-1948. Bandung, June 12, 1947. Nijmegen Regional Archives, Archives Commissie tot Documentatie van het Verzet in Nijmegen, 1945-1948, archive inventory number 42. Translation, FVL.

164 Brouwer, Letter. In 1945 Jacques Brouwer joined the Royal Dutch Indian Army and fought in the Dutch East Indies. After the independence of Indonesia in late 1949, he was transferred to the Royal Dutch Army and commissioned as a second lieutenant. He retired as a lieutenant colonel in the Fuseliers and died at age 83 on July 14, 2005, in his hometown of Ospel. Martien Kempen, another Pandurs member, was mortally wounded on the afternoon of September 21 on his way home.

165 Bollen, *Corridor naar de Rijn*, 128.

166 Druener

167 For decades it was incorrectly assumed that Norris Case had been a member of E

Company and was wounded at De Elft. The author's examination of regimental rosters and D Company Morning Reports shows he died of wounds due to the Waal River Crossing and that he served in D, not E, Company. His name will be added to the new war monument to be dedicated in June 2014.

168 Carmichael, Questionnaire, CRC. Edward Wisniewski died of wounds on September 26 in the field hospital. A girlfriend was unaware of this for many months. When her Christmas package was returned as undeliverable in January 1945, she knew something was wrong, but not until the summer of 1945 did she learn he had been killed. She never forgot him. Robert Hoffmann, email, August 24, 2006.

169 Campana, Questionnaire, CRC.

170 T. Moffatt Burriss, *Strike and Hold. A Memoir of the 82nd Airborne in World War II* (Washington DC: Brassey's, 2000), 109-110.

171 Carl W. Kappel, Telephone interview by Frederic Kelly (assistant to Cornelius Ryan), February 27, 1968, CRC.

172 Cook, Interview, CRC.

173 Keep, Letter.

174 Reuben H. Tucker, cited in Burriss, *Strike and Hold*, 111.

175 Keep, Letter.

176 Cook, Interview, CRC.

177 Tucker, "River Crossing."

178 Frank D. Boyd, cited in Jan Bos, "Circle and the Fields of Little America. The History of the 376th Parachute Field Artillery Battalion, 82nd Airborne," DVD Book, 200. Courtesy of Jan Bos.

179 Jan Bos, Email to Frank van Lunteren, July 1, 2009.

180 John J. Holabird, "The Second Omaha Beach. Crossing the Waal", http://www.the-dropzone.org/europe/holland/waal1.htm (accessed August 22, 2010). Manuscript dated 1998; website by Patrick C. O'Donnell.

181 Patrick J. Mulloy, Questionnaire, CRC.

182 Thomas McLeod, Questionnaire CRC.

183 Holabird

184 Mulloy

185 Roy W. Tuck, "One More River to Arnhem," Unpublished manuscript, 2-3. Courtesy of Roy Tuck. A Class 9 raft was a propelled pontoon raft that could carry a jeep or 57mm gun.

186 Roy C. Hamlyn, Interview by Frank van Lunteren, May 7, 2009.

187 Michael G. Sabia, Telephone interview by Frank van Lunteren, November 26, 2006.

188 Kappel, "Operations of Company H", 27.

189 Ralph N. Tison, Jr., "The Way I Remember It," Unpublished memoir (1995), 5. Courtesy of Francis Keefe.

CHAPTER 9

190 Hugh D. Wallis, Telephone interview by Frank van Lunteren, January 8, 2010.

191 Herbert C. Lucas, Telephone interview by Frank van Lunteren, November 21, 2007.

192 Robert M. Tallon, Questionnaire, CRC.

193 Francis X. Keefe, Unpublished manuscript, unpaged. Courtesy of Francis Keefe.

194 Carmichael, Questionnaire, CRC.

195 Cook, Interview, CRC.

196 Cook, Questionnaire, CRC.

197 Carmichael, Questionnaire, CRC.

198 War Diary 2nd Irish Guards, Entries for September 20, 1944, http://ww2talk. com/forums/topic/29427-2nd-armoured-battalion-irish-guards (accessed May 2, 2012).

199 Distinguished Service Cross Citation for Captain Phillip O. Riddell. Headquarters, European Theater of Operations, US Army, General Order No. 264. September 25, 1945.

200 Carmichael, Questionnaire, CRC.

201 Cook, Questionnaire, CRC.

202 Bonnie L. Roberts, Interview by Frank van Lunteren, May 29, 2004.

203 Carmichael, cited in Breuer, 352-353.

204 Tallon

205 Kuehl, cited in Burriss, *Strike and Hold*, 116.

206 Kuehl, cited in Breuer, 353.

207 Ibid., 353–354.

208 Bruns

209 Ivan J. Roggen, Questionnaire, FVL.

210 Darrell G. Harris, *Casablanca to VE Day. A Paratrooper's Memoirs* (Pittsburgh, PA; Dorrance Publishing, 1995), 15.

211 Tucker, "River Crossing."

212 Keep, Letter.

CHAPTER 10

213 Lauren W. Ramsey, Telephone interview by Frank van Lunteren, November 20, 2007.

214 Kenneth S. Nicoll, Questionnaire, CRC.

215 Druener

216 Brown

217 Garrison, "Unit Journal."

218 Matthew W. Kantala, Jr., Questionnaire, CRC.

219 Silver Star Citation for 1st Lieutenant Robert C. Blankenship. Courtesy of Richard F. Blankenship, son of Robert Blankenship. 82nd Airborne Division, General Order No. 66, December 20, 1944.

220 Leo P. Muri, Letter to his sister, May 24, 1945. Courtesy of Francis Keefe.

221 Tison, 6.

222 William R. Leonard, Unpublished manuscript. Courtesy of Bill Leonard.

223 John H. Boggs was not killed in action, but wounded.
224 Pvt. George E. Ham was awarded the Bronze Star for this action on October 29, 1944.
225 Leonard
226 Tallon
227 Thomas F. Pitt, Sr., Interview by his son, Thomas F. Pitt, Jr., 1992. Courtesy of Thomas Pitt, Jr.
228 Jack L. Bommer, Questionnaire CRC.
229 Keefe
230 Hughes, "Remembrances."
231 Burriss, *Strike and Hold*, 113-114.
232 McClain
233 Holabird
234 Mulloy
235 Meldon F. Hurlbert, Unpublished manuscript, 2. Courtesy of Meldon Hurlbert. James F. Woods is buried in Locust Hill Cemetery, Chester, West Virginia.
236 Keefe
237 Walter E. Hughes, Email to FVL.
238 Keefe
239 Tison, 6.
240 Burriss, Questionnaire, CRC.
241 Robert A. Hedberg, Telephone interview by Frank van Lunteren, May 20, 2008.

CHAPTER 11
242 Carl W. Kappel, Interview.
243 Ibid.
244 Ibid.
245 Flox
246 Kappel, Interview.
247 Wallis, Questionnaire, FVL.
248 Robert T. Koelle, Letter to his family (Summer 1944). Courtesy of his niece, Margaret Shelly.
249 Ernest P. Murphy, cited in James Megellas, *All The Way to Berlin* (New York, NY: Random House, 2003), 123-124.
250 Wallis, Interview, FVL.
251 James Megellas, *All The Way to Berlin* (New York, NY: Random House, 2003), 121-123.
252 Sims
253 Bronze Star Citation for Sergeant Daun Z. Rice. 82nd Airborne Division, General Order No. 58, October 29, 1944.
254 Tarbell, Questionnaire, CRC.
255 William V. Rice, Personal diary, Entry for September 20, 1944.
256 Sims

257 Kappel, Interview.

258 Kappel, "Operations of Company H", 31.

259 Kappel, Interview.

260 Keep, Letter.

261 Megellas, 128-129.

262 Ibid.

263 Theodore Finkbeiner, cited in Megellas, 131.

264 Distinguished Service Cross Citation for Sergeant William E. Kero. Headquarters XVIII Airborne Corps, General Order No. 8, November 11, 1944.

265 Distinguished Service Cross for Private First Class Walter J. Muszynski. Headquarters XVIII Airborne Corps, General Order No. 8, November 14, 1944.

266 Druener

267 Fred E. Thomas, G Company Journal, Entry for September 20, 1944.

268 Roy M. Hanna, Telephone interview by Frederick Kelly (assistant to Cornelius Ryan), March 5, 1968, CRC.

269 Frank L. Dietrich, Telephone interview by Frederic Kelly (assistant to Cornelius Ryan), February 29, 1968, CRC.

270 Tucker, "River Crossing."

271 Tarbell, Questionnaire, CRC.

272 Sims. Part of 1st Platoon, A Company, led by 2nd Lt. Reneau Breard, also fought near the railroad bridge.

273 David Rosenkrantz, cited in B.J. McQuaid, "Nazis Died Like Flies in Battle of Nijmegen Bridge," *Los Angeles Times* (October 10, 1944). Courtesy of Phil Rosenkrantz, nephew of David Rosenkrantz.

274 Donald Zimmerman, Telephone interview by Frank van Lunteren, August 13, 2011.

275 Flox

276 McClain

277 Kappel, Interview.

CHAPTER 12

278 Holabird

279 James E. Dunn, Personal diary, Entry for September 20, 1944. Courtesy of Mike Dunn, son of James Dunn.

280 Reneau G. Breard, Letter.

281 Ibid.

282 Clark, 23.

283 John B. Isom, Telephone interview by Frank van Lunteren, February 21, 2005.

284 Both Lieutenant Holabird and Corporal Wickersham, 2nd Platoon, C Company, 307th AEB, confirmed to the author that only canvas boats were used during the crossing.

285 Fred R. Lilley, Questionnaire, FVL.

286 Dunn, Diary, September 20, 1944.

287 Mitchell E. Rech, Email to Frank van Lunteren, December 5, 2005.
288 Druener
289 Mansolillo
290 George T. Cutting, Letter to Frank van Lunteren, September 8, 2002.
291 Zakby, Questionnaire, CRC.
292 Addison
293 Cook, Letter to Cornelius Ryan.
294 Mike Holmstock, Interview by Frank van Lunteren, February 10, 2012.
295 Benjamin Bouman, "Brief Speech to Mark the Unveiling of the Plaque in Nijmegen" (September 20, 2007), 3. Unpublished manuscript. Courtesy of Ben Bouman.
296 Tucker, "River Crossing."

CHAPTER 13
297 Keep, Letter.
298 Bruns
299 Tuck, 4-6.
300 Distinguished Service Cross Citation for Captain Wesley D. Harris. XVIII Airborne Corps, General Order No. 8, November 14, 1944.
301 Roy M. Hanna, Email to Frank van Lunteren, August 21, 2012.
302 Thomas, "Holland Mission", 4-5.
303 Hedberg
304 T. Moffatt Burriss, Telephone interview by Frank van Lunteren, May 20, 2008.
305 Ryan, *Bridge Too Far*, 471-472.
306 Lord Peter Carrington, Letter to Frank van Lunteren, August 1, 2002.
307 Ibid.
308 Military Cross Citation for Capt. Lord Peter Carrington, October 2, 1944. http://www.ww2guards.com/ww2guards/GRENADIER_GUARDS/GRENADIER_GUARDS.html (accessed June 12, 2013).
309 Burriss, *Strike and Hold*, 123.
310 James Musa, cited in Megellas, 134.
311 Tison, 6.
312 Carmichael, Questionnaire, CRC.
313 Kappel, Interview.
314 Harris, 15.
315 Keep, Letter.
316 Garrison, "Unit Journal."
317 Philip H. Nadler, Telephone interview by Frederic Kelly (assistant to Cornelius Ryan), December 7, 1967, CRC.
318 William L. Watson, Telephone interview by Frank van Lunteren, March 17, 2012.
319 Pitt
320 Guards Armoured Division, "Intelligence Summary No.72, up to 2359 Hours, September 20, 1944." Courtesy of Jan van Alphen.

321 Sieger, 4–5.
322 Karl-Heinz Euling, Letter to Frank van Lunteren, May 7, 2007.
323 Euling, Telephone interview by Frank van Lunteren, March 23, 2007.

CHAPTER 14
324 John J. Horvatis, Telephone interview by Frank van Lunteren, April 24, 2008.
325 Flox
326 Tarbell, Questionnaire, CRC.
327 Zimmerman, Interview, August 13, 2011.
328 Dunn, Questionnaire, FVL.
329 Thomas, "Holland Mission", 7.
330 Cook, Questionnaire, CRC.
331 Breard, Letter.
332 Clark, 24.
333 Medal of Honor Citation for Private John R. Towle. First Allied Airborne Army, General Order No. 18, March 15, 1945.
334 Elbert E. Winningham, Telephone interview by Frank van Lunteren, November 20, 2007.
335 Ervin E. Shaffer, Telephone interview by Frank van Lunteren, March 29, 2004.
336 Louis C. Marino, Telephone interview by Frank van Lunteren, November 22, 2005.
337 Bouman, 4.
338 Roggen, Questionnaire, FVL.
339 Druener
340 Henry B. Keep, "Waal River Crossing," *De Gelderlander* (November 7, 1953). Translated Report published in Dutch. Back translation from Dutch to English, FVL.
341 Thomas, "Holland Mission", 7.
342 Baldino, Questionnaire, CRC.
343 Thomas, "Holland Mission", 6.
344 Guards Armoured Division, "Intelligence Summary No. 73, up to 2359 hours, September 21, 1944." Author's collection.
345 As John C. McManus has pointed out, "It was absolutely inexcusable that the British commanders did not at least try" to reach Arnhem immediately after the Waal Bridge was taken. See McManus's excellent *September Hope. The American Side of a Bridge Too Far* (New York, NY: NAL Caliber, 2012), 333.

CHAPTER 15
346 Gerald P. Hereford is listed on the Waal Crossing Memorial, although his death was not related in any way with this heroic crossing.
347 Dunn, Diary, Entry for September 24, 1944.
348 Thomas, "Holland Mission", 6.
349 Boyd, cited in Bos, "Circle and the Fields", 200.
350 Edward N. Wellems, "After-Action Report on Operation Market (1944)," 12-13.
351 Mauro, 51.

352 Thomas, "Holland Mission", 7.

353 Finkbeiner, cited in Megellas, 146.

354 Virgil F. Carmichael, Letter to Cornelius Ryan, October 13, 1967, CRC.

355 Finkbeiner, cited in Megellas, 146.

356 Carmichael, Letter.

357 Cook, Questionnaire, CRC.

358 The officer may have belonged to Infanterie-Ersatz-Bataillon 58 of the 526th Reserve Division, which was deactivated in September 1944 and divided among various other units at the Western Front.

359 Thomas, "Holland Mission", 8.

360 Roy M. Hanna, Telephone interview by Frank van Lunteren, May 3, 2008.

361 Carmichael, Questionnaire, CRC.

362 Carmichael, Questionnaire, CRC. William H. Preston is erroneously buried as an officer of the 508th PIR at the American Cemetery in Margraten, plot F, row 2, grave 16.

363 Burriss, *Strike and Hold*, 148.

364 Clark, 25-26.

365 Captain Wade H. McIntyre, Jr., Letter printed in *The PeeDee Advocate*, early October 1944. Courtesy of his son, Doug McIntyre.

CHAPTER 16

366 F. H. Hinsley (Ed.), *British Intelligence Service in the Second World War. Its Influence on Strategy and Operations. Volume III, Part II* (London, UK: Her Majesty's Stationery Office, 1988), 388-389.

367 Hinsley, 389.

368 James J. Wallace, Statement of Pvt. James J. Wallace, I Company (October 21, 1944). IDPF-file, David Stanford. Courtesy of his nephew, Rob Stanford. Darrell D. Grooms is buried at the Morris Hill Cemetery in Boise, Idaho; David S. Stanford is memorialized on the Wall of the Missing at the American Cemetery in Margraten.

369 Burriss, *Strike and Hold*, 148. Robert G. Dew is memorialized on the Wall of Missing in Margraten.

370 Hedberg

371 Tison, 5.

372 Burriss, *Strike and Hold*, 148.

373 This is incorrect. Only 1st Lt. Lory L. McCullough and 12 non-commissioned officers and enlisted men were captured. Second Lieutenant James R. Pursell and 17 men got back to G Company.

374 Julian A. Cook, "Story behind Den Heuvel" (1968), Addendum to Questionnaire, CRC.

375 Burriss, *Strike and Hold*, 150. Charles Snyder is buried in Virginia.

376 Silver Star Citation for Staff Sergeant Leon E. Baldwin. 82nd Airborne Division, General Order No. 61, November 30, 1944.

377 William D. Mandle, Letter to his parents, January 12, 1945. Family correspondence courtesy of his son, Steve Mandle. Leonard W. Beaty's remains were located and he is buried in Wichita, Kansas.

378 Statistics compiled from Morning Reports, Roll of Honor and interviews with participants.

379 Megellas, 150.

380 Ibid, 152-153.

381 Lawrence H. Dunlop, cited in Megellas, 147.

382 Ibid.

383 Clarence A. Heatwole, Telephone interview by Frank van Lunteren, June 20, 2008.

384 Patricia McCullough Lay (daughter of Lieutenant McCullough), Telephone interview by Frank van Lunteren, May 23, 2009.

385 Heatwole

386 I am indebted to the late Clarence Heatwole, G Company, who heard this story from Henry Horn the day of their capture. The late Joseph Sims confirmed that this was what actually happened.

387 Thomas, "Holland Mission", 7.

388 Zimmerman, Interview, August 13, 2011.

389 Thomas, "Holland Mission", 7.

390 William D. Mandle, Unpublished manuscript (1962). Courtesy of the children of Willliam Mandle.

391 Zimmerman, Telephone interview by Frank van Lunteren, May 5, 2010.

392 Distinguished Service Cross Citation for 2nd Lieutenant James Megellas. XVI Corps, General Order No. 69, August 24, 1945.

393 Zimmerman, Interview, August 13, 2011.

394 Komosa

395 Roberts

396 Dominic R. Moecia, cited in Megellas, 148-149.

CHAPTER 17

397 Mauro, 52.

398 Wellems, "After-Action Report", 13-14.

399 Mauro, 52-54.

400 Van Poyck

401 Marshall W. Stark, cited in Raymond E. Fary and Robert J. Burns, "80th Role in Holland a 'Classic': Operation Market Garden," *The Outpost Vol. 12 (Winter 2005)*, 6. Published by the 80th Airborne AA Battalion Association.

402 Fary, "80th Role", 6.

403 Ibid.

404 Stark, 7.

405 Ibid.

406 Ibid.

407 Distinguished Service Cross Citation for Corporal Joseph J. Jusek. XVIII Airborne

Corps, General Order No. 11, December 9, 1944.

408 Silver Star Citation for Private First Class Robert D. Maier. 82nd Airborne Division, General Order No. 60, November 30, 1944.

409 Henry D. Covello, Telephone interview by Frank van Lunteren, November 26, 2007.

410 Distinguished Service Cross Citation for Private First Class Joseph M. Koss. XVIII Airborne Corps, General Order No. 11, December 9, 1944.

411 Silver Star Citation for Private First Class Duane V. Sydow. 82nd Airborne Division, General Order No. 60, November 30, 1944.

412 Silver Star Citation for Private First Class Oscar E. Ladner. 82nd Airborne Division, General Order No. 60, November 30, 1944.

413 Garrison, "Unit Journal."

414 Virgil W. Widger, Questionnaire, FVL.

415 Brown

416 Heinz Bliss, *Achtung. . . . Einschlag! Fallschirm-Artillerie im Kampf um Paris, Mons, Nymwegen, Graudenz und Weichselmündung* (Witzenhausen, Germany: Feldmann, 1987), 72–73. Translation, FVL.

417 Nadler, Questionnaire, CRC.

418 Bronze Star Citation for Sergeant William L. Reed. 82nd Airborne Division, General Order No. 57, October 29, 1944.

419 Williams

420 Reneau G. Breard, Interview by Frank van Lunteren, May 8, 2005.

421 Baldino, Questionnaire, CRC.

422 Mauro, 58-62.

423 Van Poyck

424 Garrison, *Paratrooper*, 151-152.

425 Donald E. Morain, Telephone interview by Frank van Lunteren, June 16, 2012.

426 Albert Musto, Telephone interview by Frank van Lunteren, June 21, 2012.

CHAPTER 18

427 David Whittier, "Division Wants Prisoners: Patrol Along the Wyler Meer," *Infantry Journal* (April 1945), 23-24.

428 Garrison, "Unit Journal."

429 William L. Watson, Interview by Karen Dugan (niece of Richard Gentzel), December 30, 2008. Courtesy of Karen Dugan.

430 Nadler, Questionnaire, CRC. The bodies of Private Sandoval and Corporal Gentzel were never recovered. Their names are on the Wall of the Missing at the American Cemetery at Margraten, Netherlands.

431 Bronze Star Citation for Private First Class John C. Atkins. 82nd Airborne Division, General Order No. 102, July 2, 1945.

432 Garrison, "Unit Journal."

433 McClain

434 Nadler, Questionnaire, CRC.

435 Breard, Interview, FVL.
436 Whittier, 24-25.
437 Breard, Interview, FVL.
438 Hart, Questionnaire, CRC.
439 Komosa
440 Ibid.
441 Leo M. Hart, Email to Frank van Lunteren, October 25, 2009.
442 Komosa
443 Bronze Star Citation for Private First Class Willis J. Kresge. 82nd Airborne Division, General Order No. 129, October 24, 1945.
444 Nadler, Questionnaire, CRC.
445 Komosa
446 Breard, Letter.
447 Ibid.
448 Goethe, Questionnaire, CRC.
449 Roy M. Hanna, Email to Frank van Lunteren, June 17, 2008.
450 Dora and Louis E. Orvin, Jr., Email to Kathleen Buttke (niece of Walter Muszynski), July 12, 2008. Courtesy of Kathleen Buttke.
451 Mandle, Letter to his parents, November 4, 1944.
452 Breard, Letter.
453 Mandle, Unpublished manuscript.

POSTSCRIPT
454 Reuben H. Tucker III, Letter to Mayor Charles Hustinx (March 15, 1947), CRC.
455 Julian A. Cook, Letter to Kathryn Ryan (June 3, 1977), CRC.
456 Garrison, *Paratrooper*, 135.
457 It is possible that Henry Keep's step-father, Charles Biddle, provided Keep's account and journalists wrongly assumed Biddle to be the author.

LIST OF CONTRIBUTING VETERANS

etween 2002 and 2013, I interviewed and/or corresponded with the following veterans. Ranks given are the highest-held during the war. An asterisk indicates veterans who have since passed away. Without their contributions, this regimental history could never have been written.

REGIMENTAL HEADQUARTERS: *Capt. Delbert Kuehl (Protestant Chaplain), *Maj. Ivan Roggen (Regimental surgeon), *PFC Warren Tidwell (A Co. and jeep driver of Capt. Fordyce Gorham).

HQ & HQ COMPANY: *PFC David Finney (Communications Platoon), PFC Darrell Harris (Demolition Platoon)

1ST BATTALION: *Sgt. James Addis (A Co.), *Cpl. Fred Baldino (A Co.), 1st Lt. Reneau Breard (A Co.), *Sgt. Albert Clark (A Co.), Sgt. George Cutting (HQ/1 Co.), *Sgt. Virgil Danielson (A Co.), *1st Lt. James Dunn (A Co.), Cpl. Glenn Frew (A Co.), PFC Mike Holmstock (B Co.), *Sfc. John Isom (A Co.), S.Sgt. John Kaslikowski (HQ/1 Co.), *Sgt. Fred Lilley (A Co.), PFC Louis Marino (A Co.), *Capt. Albert Milloy (C Co.), *T/Sgt. Mitchell Rech (A Co.), *Sgt. Ervin Shaffer (A Co.), *Pvt. Joseph Sims (B Co.), *Sgt. Dennis Speth (A Co.), *Sgt. Elmer Swartz (C Co.), *Sgt. Robert Waldon (B Co.), *PFC Elbert Winningham (C Co.), PFC Hubert Wolfe (B Co.), *Capt. Charles Zirkle, Jr. (1st Battalion Surgeon).

2ND BATTALION: Pvt. Henry Covello (F Co.), *1st Lt. Leonard Greenblatt

(D Co. and E Co.), *PFC Leo Hart (F Co.), Pvt. Paul Kunde (E Co.), *PFC Maurice McSwain (F Co.), PFC Donald Morain (F Co.), PFC Albert Musto (F Co.), *Cpl. Louis Napier (E Co.), 1st Lt. Lauren Ramsey (HQ/2 Co.), *2nd Lt. Harry Rollins (D Co.), PFC James Sapp (HQ/2 Co.), Sgt. Willis Sisson (E Co.), *Sgt. Roy Tidd (E Co.), 1st Lt. William Watson (F Co.), *Sgt. Bennie Weeks (HQ/2 Co.), *PFC Virgil Widger (D Co.).

3RD BATTALION: Capt. Moffatt Burriss (I Co.), *Sgt. John Foley, Jr. (H Co.), 1st Lt. Roy Hanna (G Co.), *Sgt. Clarence Heatwole (G Co.), PFC Robert Hedberg (I Co.), PFC John Horvatis (HQ/3 Co.), PFC Walter Hughes (I Co.), Pvt. Francis Keefe (I Co.), *Pvt. James Legacie, Jr. (H Co.), *Sgt. George Leoleis (I Co.), T/5 Herbert Lucas (HQ/3 Co.), 1st Lt. James Megellas (H Co.), *PFC Paul Mentzer (HQ/3 Co.), *T/Sgt. Louis Orvin, Jr. (I Co.), PFC Bonnie Roberts (HQ/3 Co.), *PFC John Schultz (H Co.), *1st Lt. Edward Sims (I I Co.), *Cpl. Walter Souza (H Co.), *Sgt. Albert Tarbell (H Co.), Pvt. George Willoughby (H Co.), Sgt. Donald Zimmerman (H Co.).

C COMPANY 307TH AIRBORNE ENGINEER BATTALION: *1st Lt. John Holabird, PFC Alexander Nemeth, *1st Lt. Michael Sabia, Cpl. Obie Wickersham.

VETERANS, OTHER AMERICAN UNITS: 1st Lt. Rufus Broadaway (507th PIR and 82nd ABN Div HQ), *Capt. Paul Donnelly (376th PFA Battalion), PFC Raymond Fary (80th Airborne AA Battalion), *M.Sgt. Leonard Lebenson (82nd ABN DIV HQ), *1st Lt. Harold Roy (376th PFA Battalion).

BRITISH VETERANS: Capt. Lord Peter Carrington (2nd Battalion Grenadier Guards), *Sgt. Roy Hamlyn (283rd Company, Royal Army Service Corps), Spr. Roy Tuck (615th Squadron, Royal Engineers).

GERMAN VETERANS: SS-Hauptsturmführer Karl-Heinz Euling (21st SS-Panzer Grenadier Regiment).

DUTCH VOLUNTEERS: Benjamin Bouman (attached to B Company, 504th PIR), *Gatse "Bob" Tiemstra (attached to 508th PIR).

SELECTED BIBLIOGRAPHY

Interviews and Questionnaires (FVL):

Burriss, T. Moffatt	Kunde, Paul A.	Rollins, Harry W.
Carter, Thomas N.	Legacie, James H.	Roggen, Ivan J.
Dunn, James E.	Lucas, Herbert C.	Sabia, Michael G.
Foley, John J.	Lilley, Fred R.	Sims, Edward J.
Hamlyn, Roy C.	Napier, Louis E.	Sisson, Willis D.
Hedberg, Robert A.	Ramsey, Lauren W.	Wallis, Hugh D.
Hughes, Walter E.	Roberts, Bonnie	Widger, Virgil W.

Archival Sources:

Athens, Ohio: Ohio University Library, the Cornelius Ryan Collection (CRC)

Carlisle Barracks, Pennsylvania: United States Army Military History Institute (USAMHI)

College Park, Maryland: National Archives and Records Administration II, Modern Military Reference Branch

Fort Benning, Georgia: Donovan Research Library

Government Archival sources include After-Action Reports for: 82nd US Airborne Division Headquarters; the 504th, 505th, and 508th Parachute Infantry Regiments; the Guards Armoured Division; German battle reports for September through November 1944. Especially noteworthy are the 2nd and 3rd Battalion Unit Journals and the 504th Regimental S-1, S-2 and S-3 Journals, which provided a timeframe for many eyewitness reports.

Published Works:

Alexander, Mark. J and John Sparry. *Jump Commander: In Combat with the 505th and 508th Parachute Infantry Regiments, 82nd Airborne Division in World War II.* Havertown, PA: Casemate Publishing, 2010.

Anzuoni, Robert P. *I'm the 82nd Airborne Division!* Atglen, PA: Schiffer Publishing, 2005.

Blair, Clay. *Ridgway's Paratroopers: The American Airborne in World War II.* Annapolis, MD: Naval Institute Press, 2002.

Bliss, Heinz. *Achtung.... Einschlag! Fallschirm Artillerie im Kampf um Paris, Mons, Nymwegen, Graudenz und Weichselmündung.* Witzenhausen, Germany: Feldmann, 2005.

Bollen, Hen. *Corridor naar de Rijn.* Zutphen, the Netherlands: Terra Publishing, 1988.

Bos, Jan. "Circle and the Fields of Little America. The History of the 376th Parachute Field Artillery Battalion, 82nd Airborne." DVD book, Privately published, 2007.

Breuer, William B. *Geronimo!* New York, NY: St. Martin's Press, 1989; 1992.

Burriss, T. Moffatt. *Strike and Hold. A Memoir of the 8nd Airborne in World War II.* Washington, DC: Brassey's, 2001.

Carter, Ross S. *Those Devils in Baggypants.* Kingsport, TN: Kingsport Press, 1979.

Dawson, W. Forrest. *Saga of the All American.* Atlanta, GA: Albert Love Enterprises, 1946; 1978.

———. *Stand Up and Hook Up.* Austin, TX: Eakin Press, 1989; 1997.

Fitzgerald, Dennis L. J. *History of the Irish Guards in the Second World War.* Aldershot, UK: Gale & Polden Ltd., 1949.

Garrison, Chester A. *An Ivy-League Paratrooper.* Corvallis, OR: The Franklin Press, 2002.

Gavin, James M. *On to Berlin: Battles of an Airborne Commander 1943-1946.* New York, NY: Viking Press, 1978.

Hinsley, F. H. (Ed.), *British Intelligence Service in the Second World War. Its Influence on Strategy and Operations. Volume III, Part II.* London, UK: Her Majesty's Stationery Office, 1988.

Hoyt, Edwin P. *Airborne: The History of the American Parachute Forces.* New York, NY: Stein and Day, 1978.

Harris, Darrell G. *Casablanca to VE Day. A Paratrooper's Memoirs.* Pittsburgh, PA: Dorrance Publishing, 1995.

Leoleis, George. *Medals.* New York, NY: Carlton, 1990.

Liberation Museum Groesbeek. *Roll of Honour 82nd Airborne Division World War Two.* Nijmegen, the Netherlands: Nijmegen University Press, 1997.

_____. *Market Garden–Waalcrossing: 20 September 1944, Nijmegen, Holland.* Nijmegen, the Netherlands: Nijmegen University Press, 1992.

LoFaro, Guy. *The Sword of St. Michael: The 82nd Airborne Division in World War II.* Cambridge, MA: Da Capo Press, 2011.

Lord, William G. *History of the 508th Parachute Infantry.* Washington DC: Infantry Journal Press, 1948.

Mandle, William D. and David H. Whittier. *Combat Record of the 504th Parachute Infantry Regiment*. Paris, France, 1946; Nashville, TN: The Battery Press, 1976.

McKee, Alexander. *Race to the Rhine Bridges*. New York, NY; Stein and Day, 1971.

McManus, John C. *September Hope. The American Side of a Bridge Too Far*. New York, NY: NAL (Caliber), 2012.

Megellas, James. *All the Way to Berlin*. New York, NY: Random House, 2003.

Mrozek, Steven J. (Ed.). *Propblast. Chronicle of the 504th Parachute Infantry Regiment*. Fort Bragg, NC: 82nd Airborne Division Historical Society, 1986.

Nigl, Alfred J. and Charles A. Nigl. *Silent Wings, Savage Death*. Santa Ana, CA: Nigl & Nigl, 2007.

Nordyke, Phil, *All American All the Way. The Combat History of the 82nd Airborne Division in World War II*. St. Paul, MN: Zenith Press, 2005.

_____. *More than Courage. The Combat History of 504th Parachute Infantry Regiment in World War II*. Minneapolis, MN: Zenith Press, 2008.

Outridge, Peter. *Baggy Pants and Warm Beer!* Bognor Regis, UK: Woodfield Publishing, 2007.

Ryan, Cornelius. *A Bridge Too Far*. New York, NY: Simon and Schuster, 1974.

Tieke, Wilhelm. *Im Feuersturm letzter Kriegsjahre. II. SS-Panzer Korps mit 9. Und 10. SS-Division Hohestaufen und Frundsberg*. Selent, Austria: Pour le Mérite, 2006.

Turnbull, Peter. *I Maintain the Right. The 307th Airborne Engineer Battalion in WWII*. Bloomington, IN: Author House, 2005.

Wurst, Spencer F. and Gayle Wurst. *Descending from the Clouds. A Memoir of Combat with the 505th Parachute Infantry Regiment, 82d Airborne Division*. Havertown, PA: Casemate Publishing, 2004.

UNPUBLISHED SOURCES: MEMOIRS AND HISTORIES

Bruns, Paul D. "Flight Surgeon." Unpublished memoir, 1987.

Finney, David K. "My Time with the 504th." Privately printed memoir. San Diego, 2006.

Lunteren, Frank W. van, "Brothers in Arms: A Company, 504th Parachute Infantry Regiment, 82nd Airborne Division, from North Africa to Berlin." Privately printed company history. Arnhem: the Netherlands, 2007.

Parks, Ernest W. "The War Years (WWII)." Unpublished memoir, 2008.

Tison Jr., Ralph N. "The Way I Remember It." Unpublished memoir, 1995.

Turner, John C. "Sicily as I Remember It." Unpublished memoir, 1999.

UNTITLED WORKS AND SHORTER CONTRIBUTIONS

Bouman, Benjamin (Dutch citizen attached to B Company)

Brown, Earnest H.

Clark, Albert B.
Hughes, Walter H.
Hurlbert, Meldon F.
Kappel, Clark W.
Leginski, Walter P.
Leonard, William R.
Mandle, William D.
Mauro, Carl
Ridout, Everett R.
Sims, Edward T.
Tuck, Roy W.
Tiemstra, Gatse (Dutch citizen attached to the 508th PIR)
Willoughby, George

INDEX